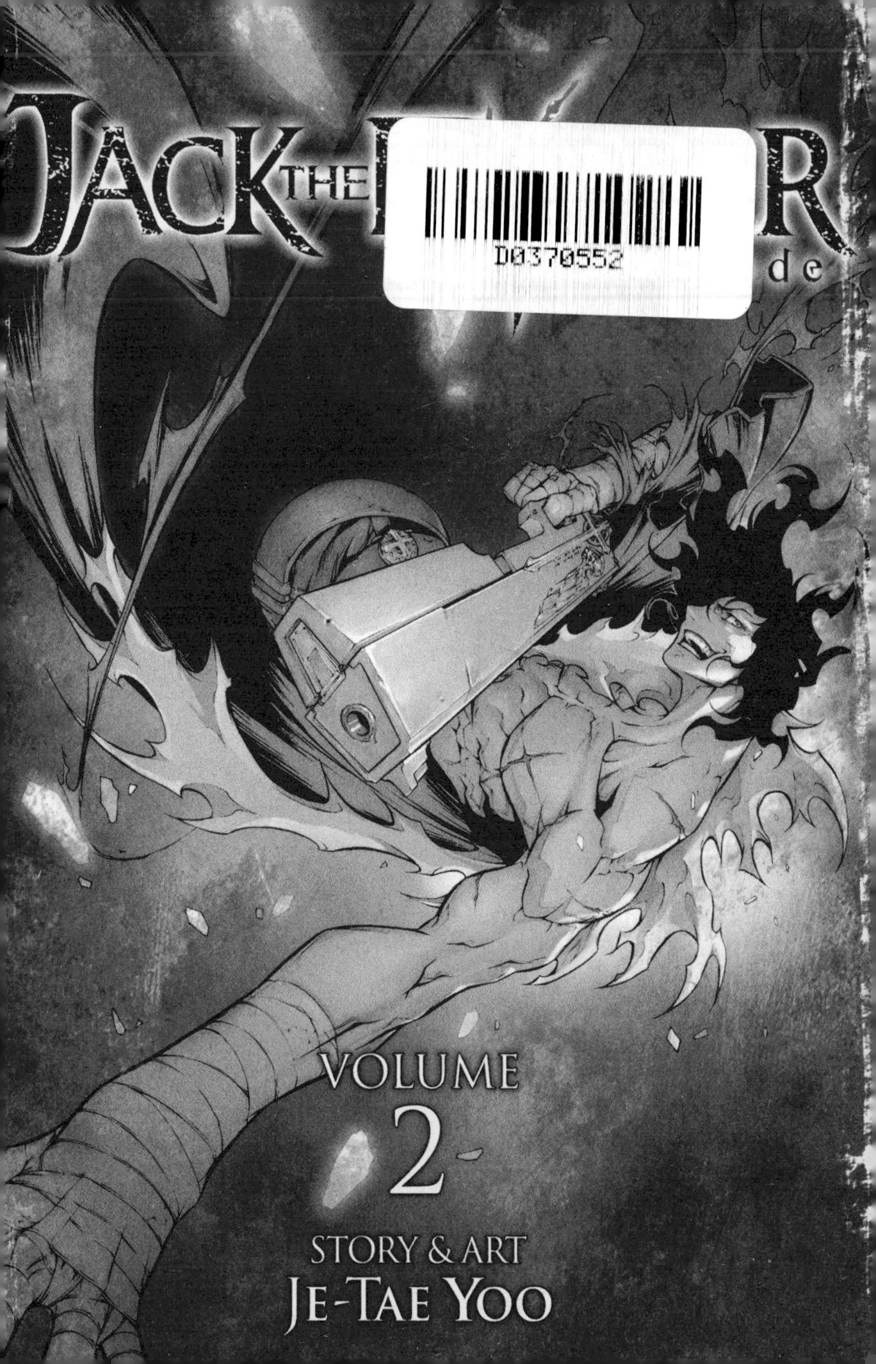
JACK THE
R
de
VOLUME
2
STORY & ART
JE-TAE YOO

JACK THE RIPPER
Hell Blade
VOLUME 2

STORY & ART BY
Je-tae Yoo

STAFF CREDITS

translation **Lauren Na**

adaptation **Janet Houck**

lettering & design **Nicky Lim**

assistant editor **Shanti Whitesides**

editor **Adam Arnold**

publisher **Jason DeAngelis**
Seven Seas Entertainment

JACK THE RIPPER: HELL BLADE VOL. 2
©2010 by YOO Je-tae, Daewon C.I. Inc.
All rights reserved. First published in Korea as HELL BLADE VOL. 2
in 2010 by Daewon C.I. Inc.
English translation rights arranged by Daewon C.I. Inc. through Topaz Agency Inc.

No portion of this book may be reproduced or transmitted in any form
without written permission from the copyright holders.

This is a work of fiction. Names, characters, places, and incidents are the
products of the author's imagination or are used fictitiously. Any resemblance
to actual events, locales, or persons, living or dead, is entirely coincidental.

Seven Seas and the Seven Seas logo are trademarks of
Seven Seas Entertainment, LLC. All rights reserved.

ISBN: 978-1-935934-97-4

Printed in the USA

First printing: October 2012

10 9 8 7 6 5 4 3 2 1

FOLLOW US ONLINE: www.gomanga.com

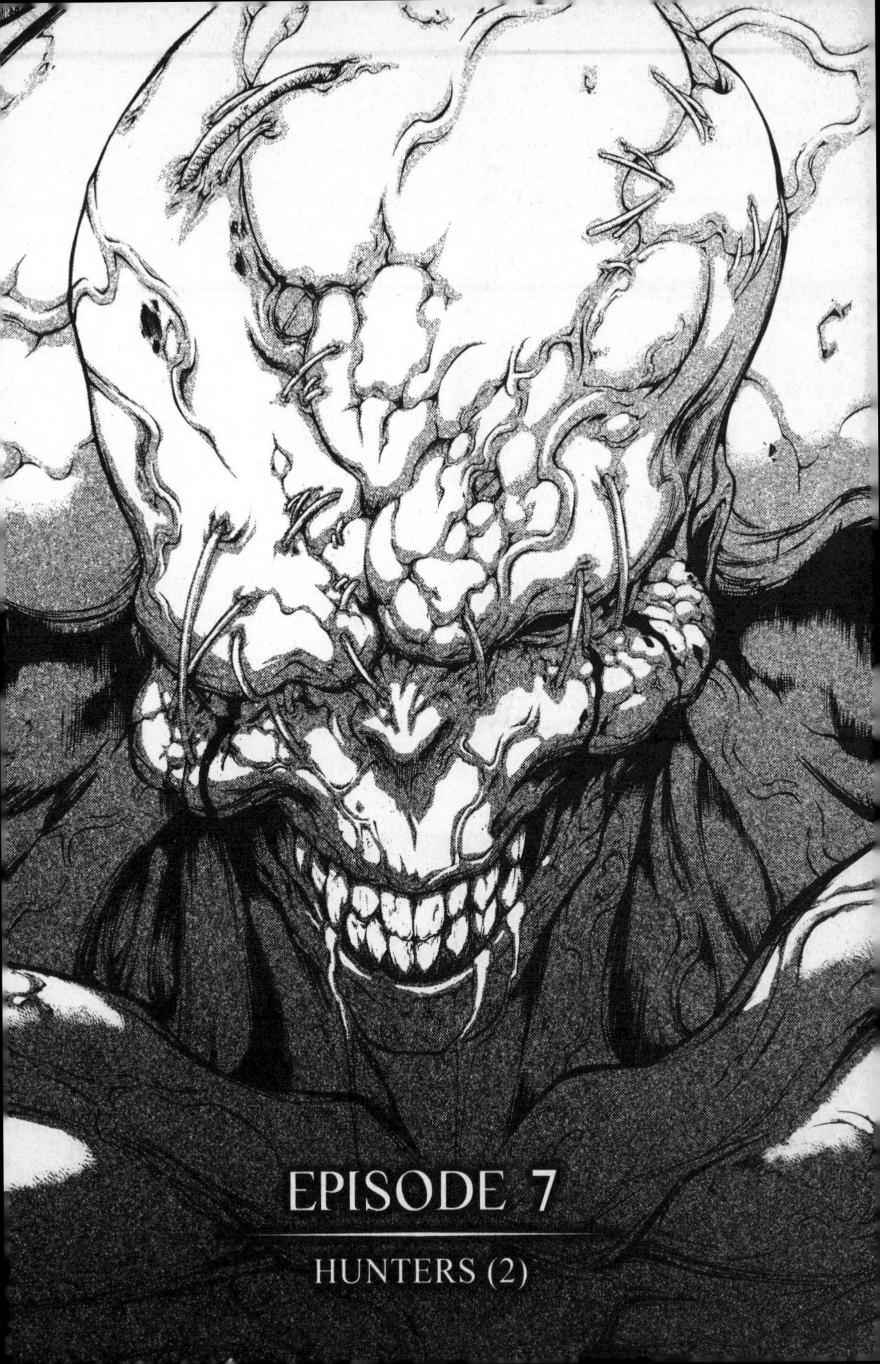

EPISODE 7

HUNTERS (2)

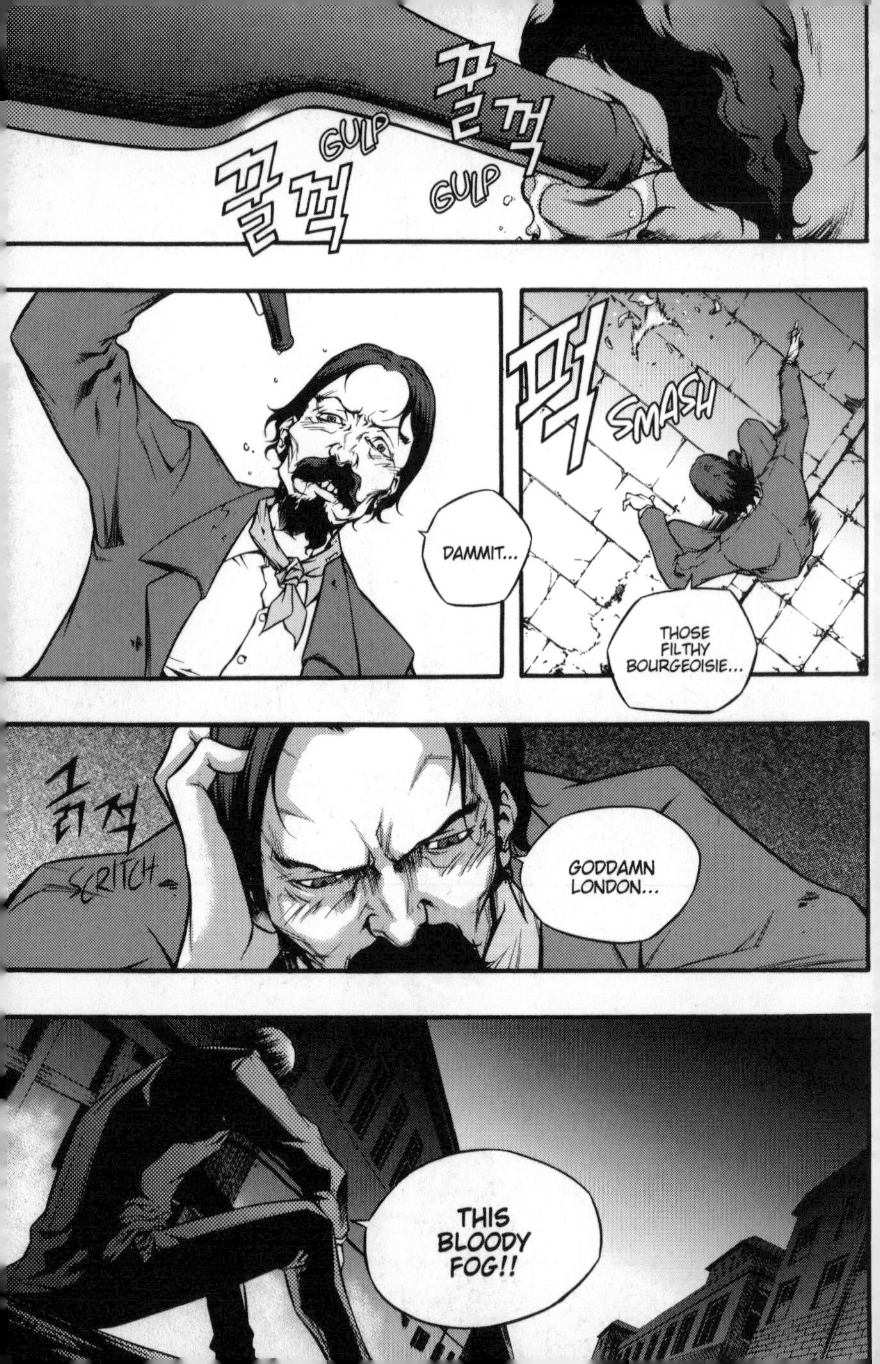
꿀꺽
꿀꺽
GULP
GULP
DAMMIT...
퍽
SMASH
THOSE FILTHY BOURGEOISIE...
긁적
SCRITCH
GODDAMN LONDON...
THIS BLOODY FOG!!

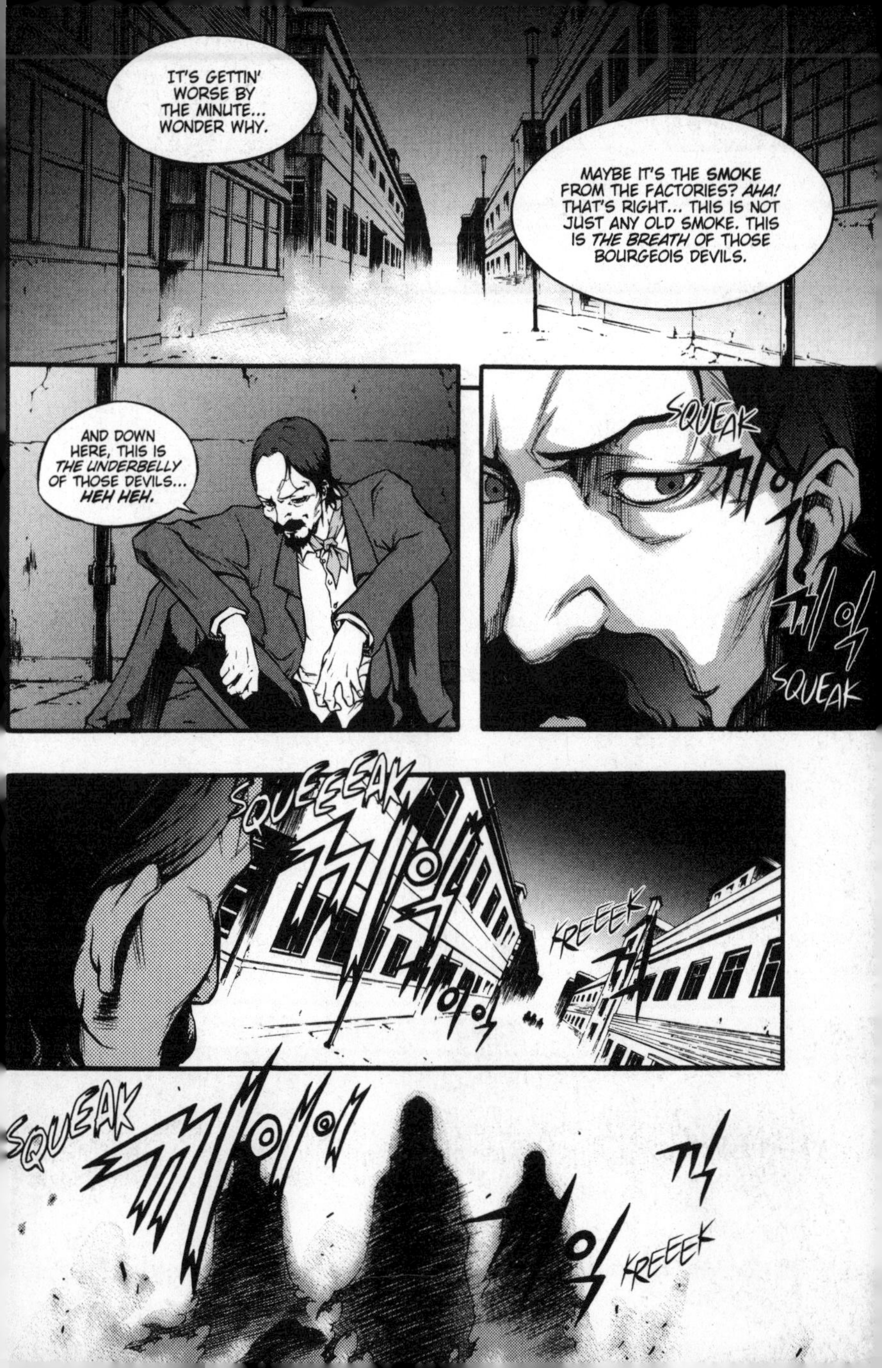
IT'S GETTIN' WORSE BY THE MINUTE... WONDER WHY.
MAYBE IT'S THE SMOKE FROM THE FACTORIES? *AHA!* THAT'S RIGHT... THIS IS NOT JUST ANY OLD SMOKE. THIS IS *THE BREATH* OF THOSE BOURGEOIS DEVILS.
AND DOWN HERE, THIS IS *THE UNDERBELLY* OF THOSE DEVILS... ***HEH HEH.***
SQUEAK
SQUEAK
SQUEEEAK
KREEEK
SQUEAK
KREEEK

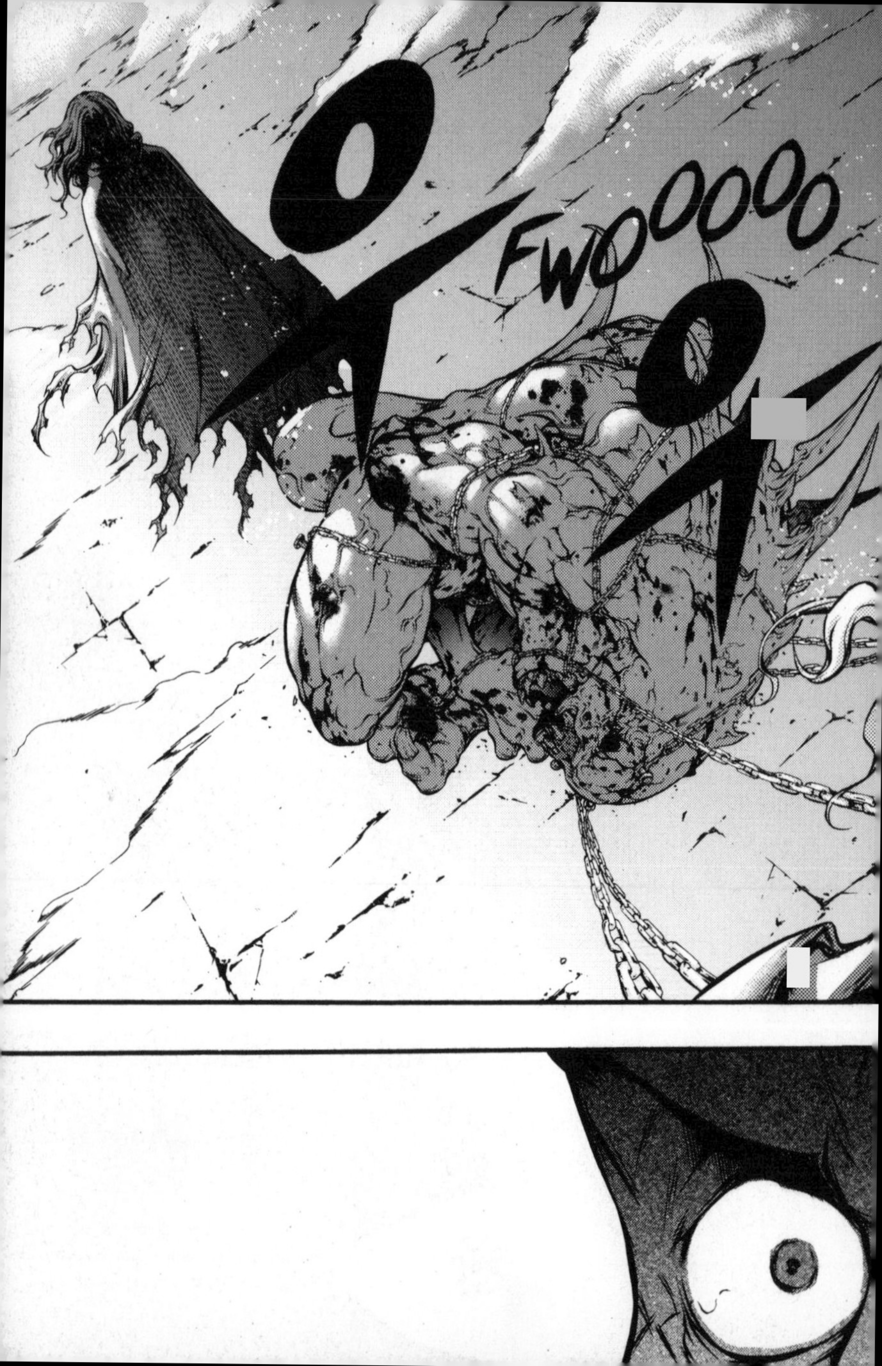
FWOOOOO

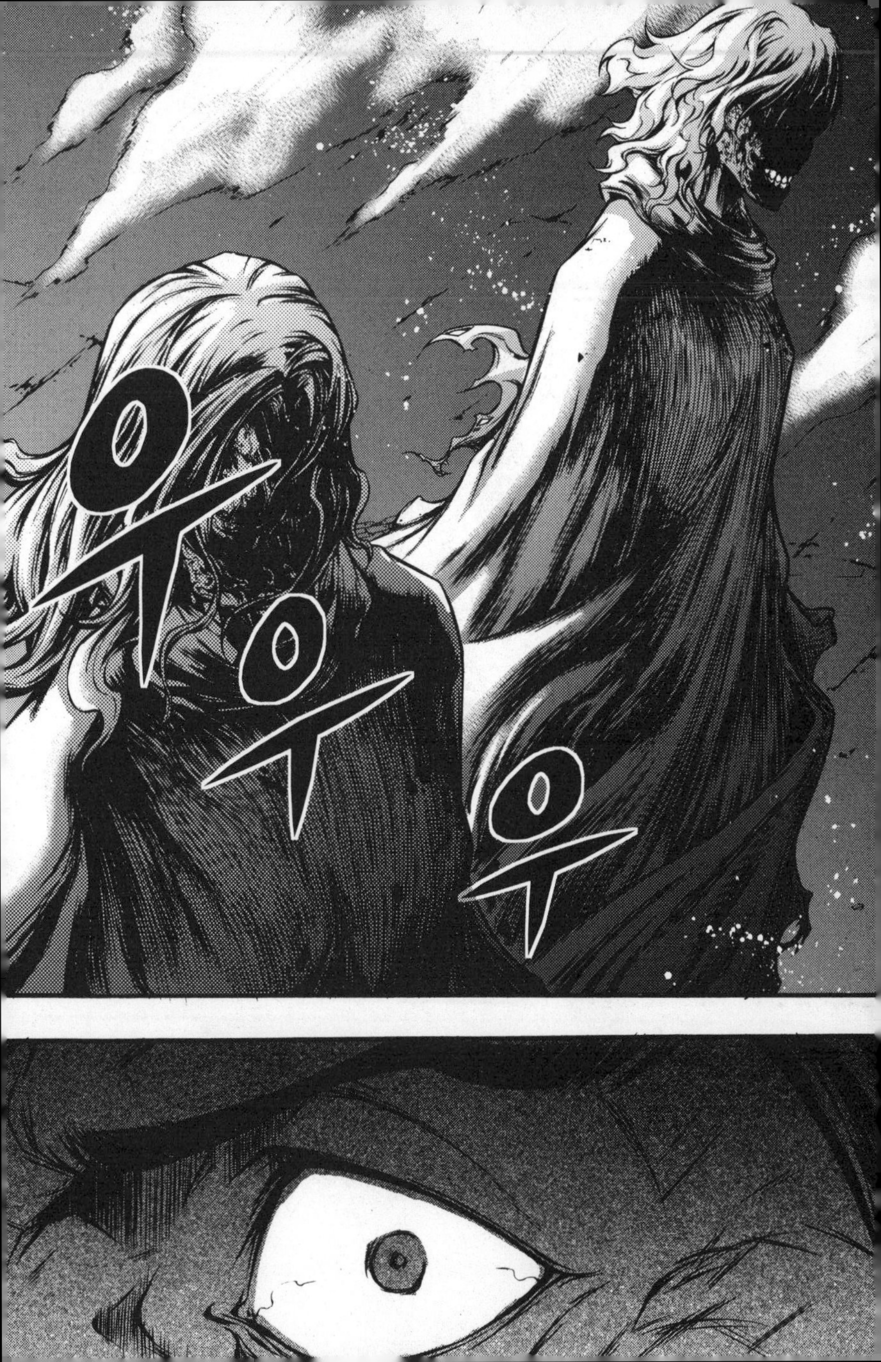
우우우

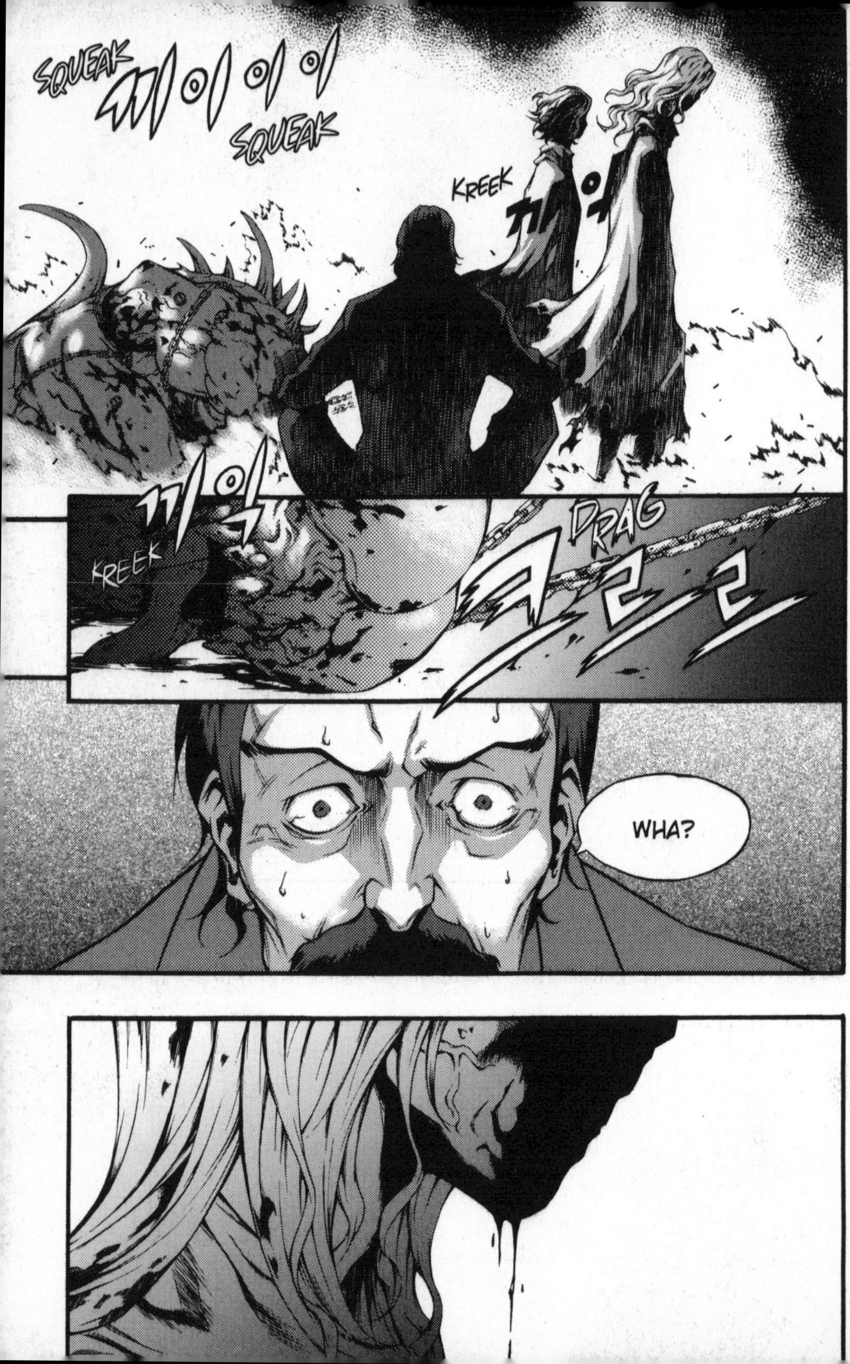
SQUEAK
끼이이이
SQUEAK
KREEK
까악
끼익
KREEK
DRAG
주르르
WHA?

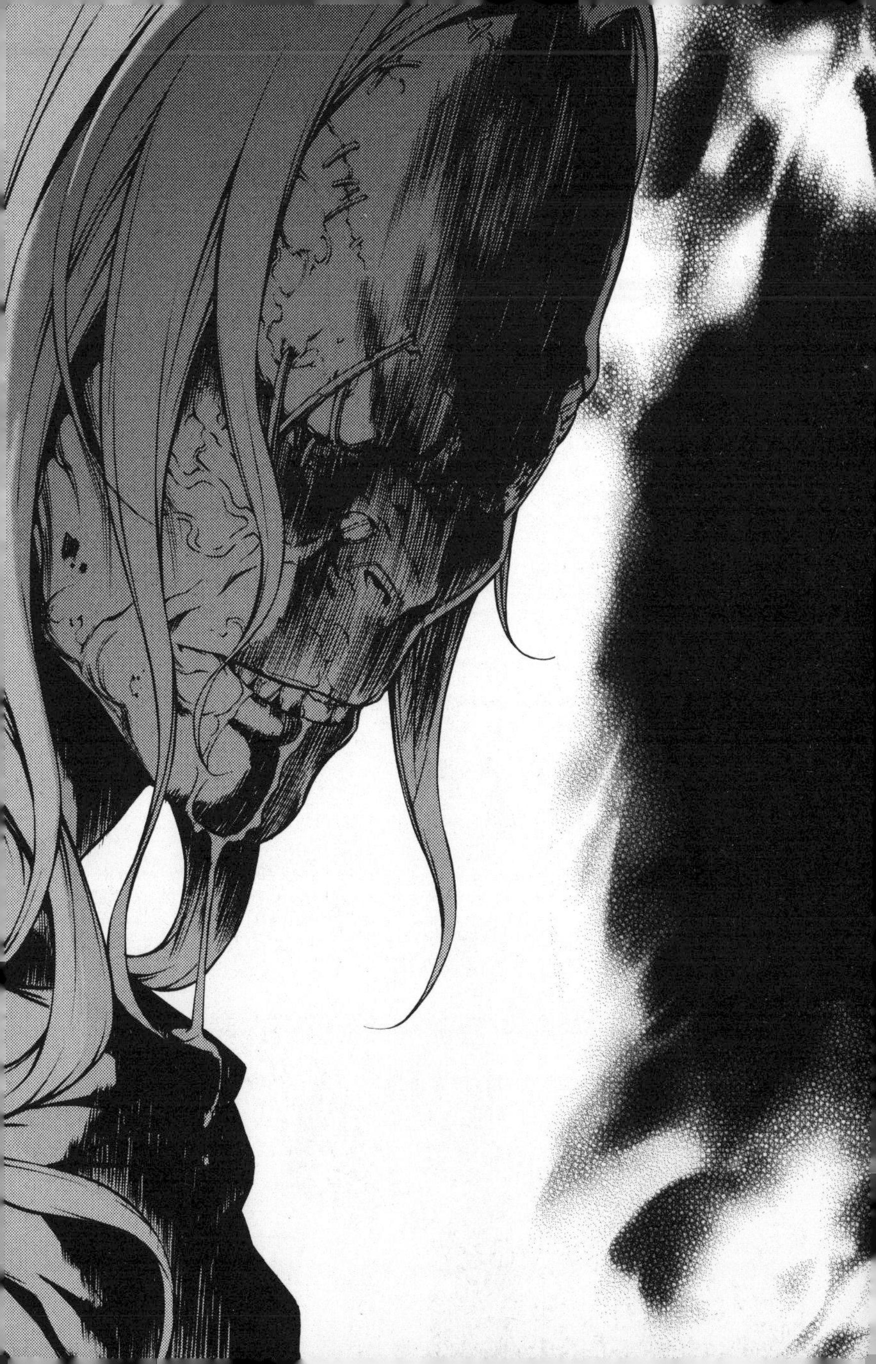

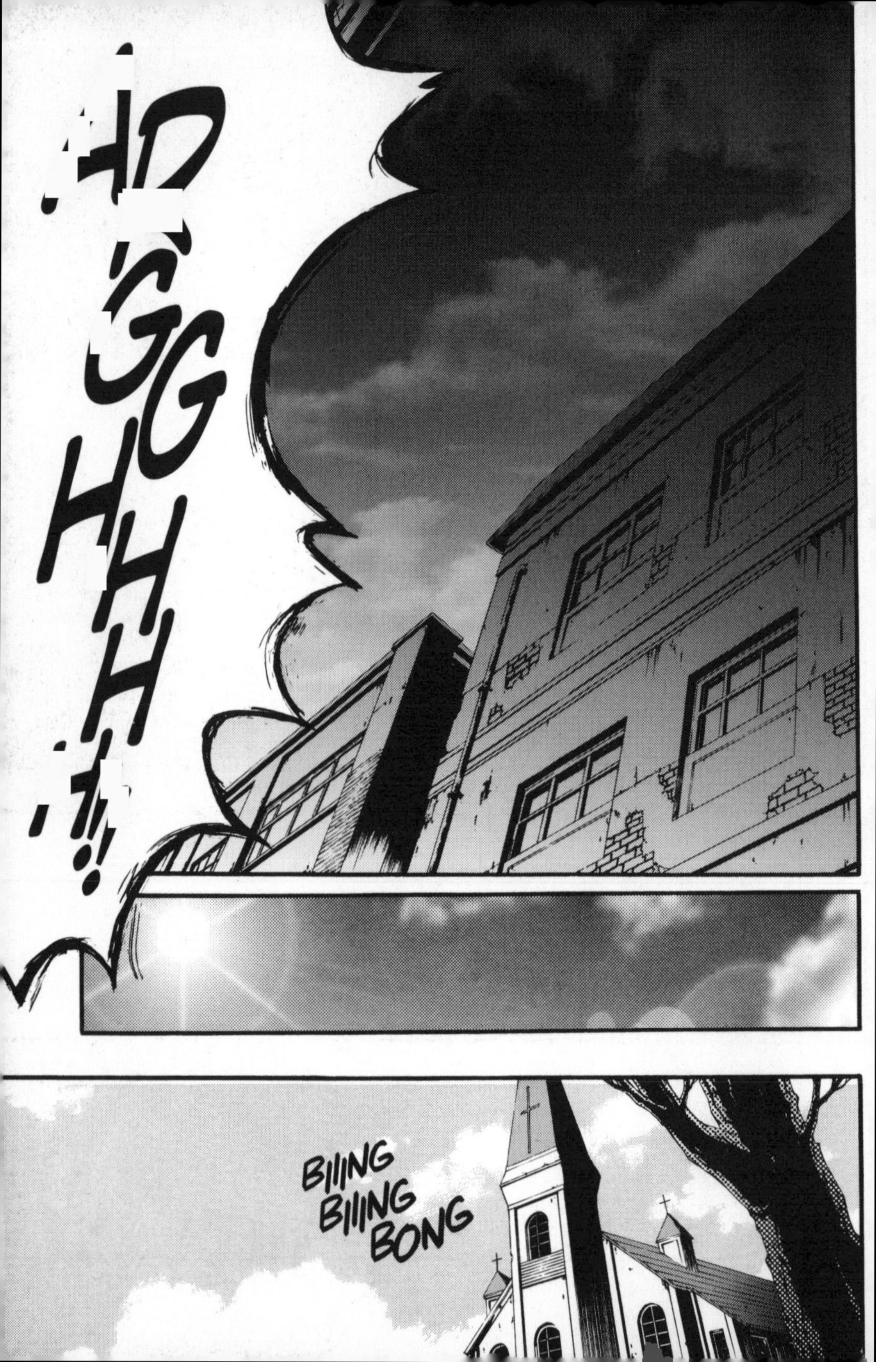
BIIING
BIIING
BONG

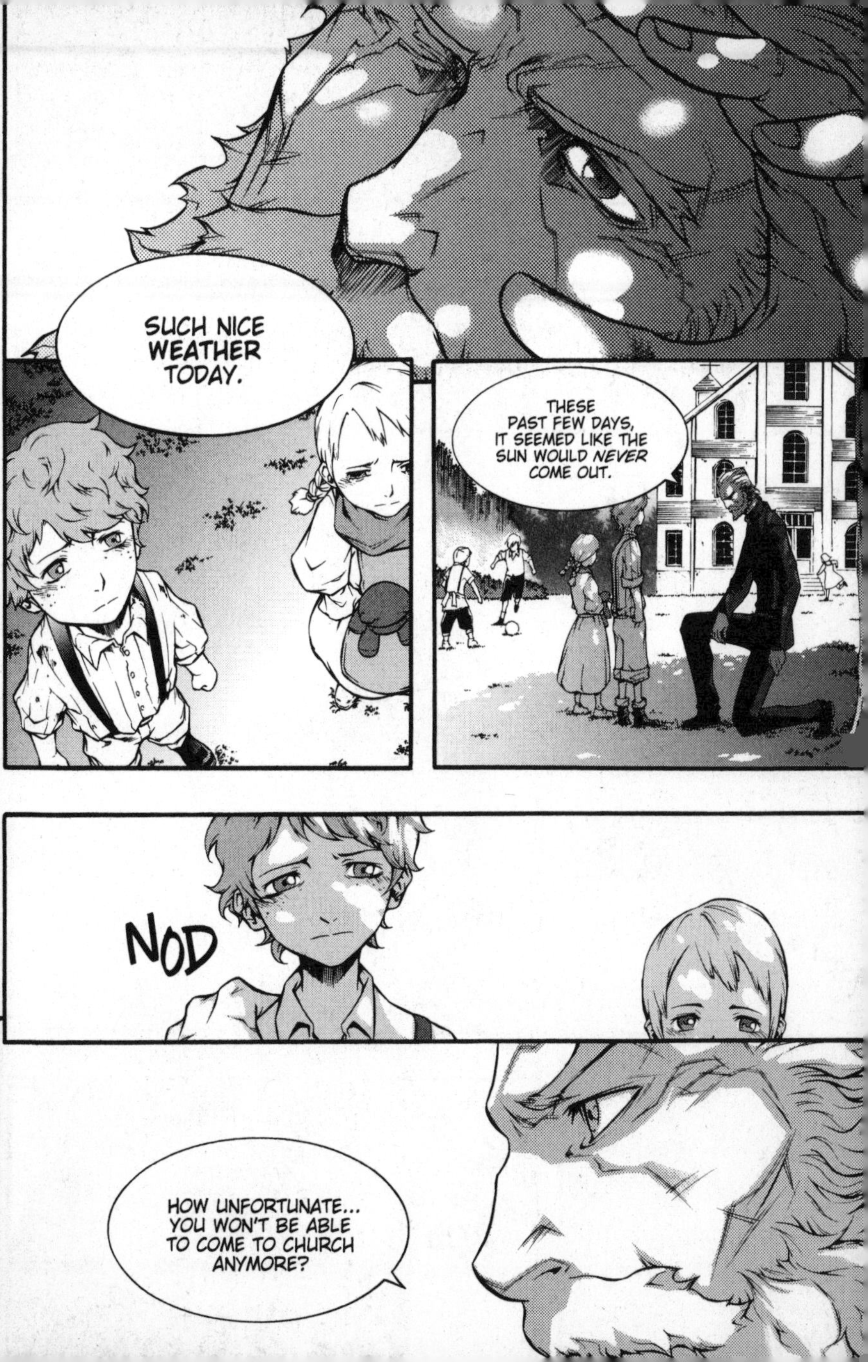
SUCH NICE WEATHER TODAY.
THESE PAST FEW DAYS, IT SEEMED LIKE THE SUN WOULD *NEVER* COME OUT.
NOD
HOW UNFORTUNATE... YOU WON'T BE ABLE TO COME TO CHURCH ANYMORE?

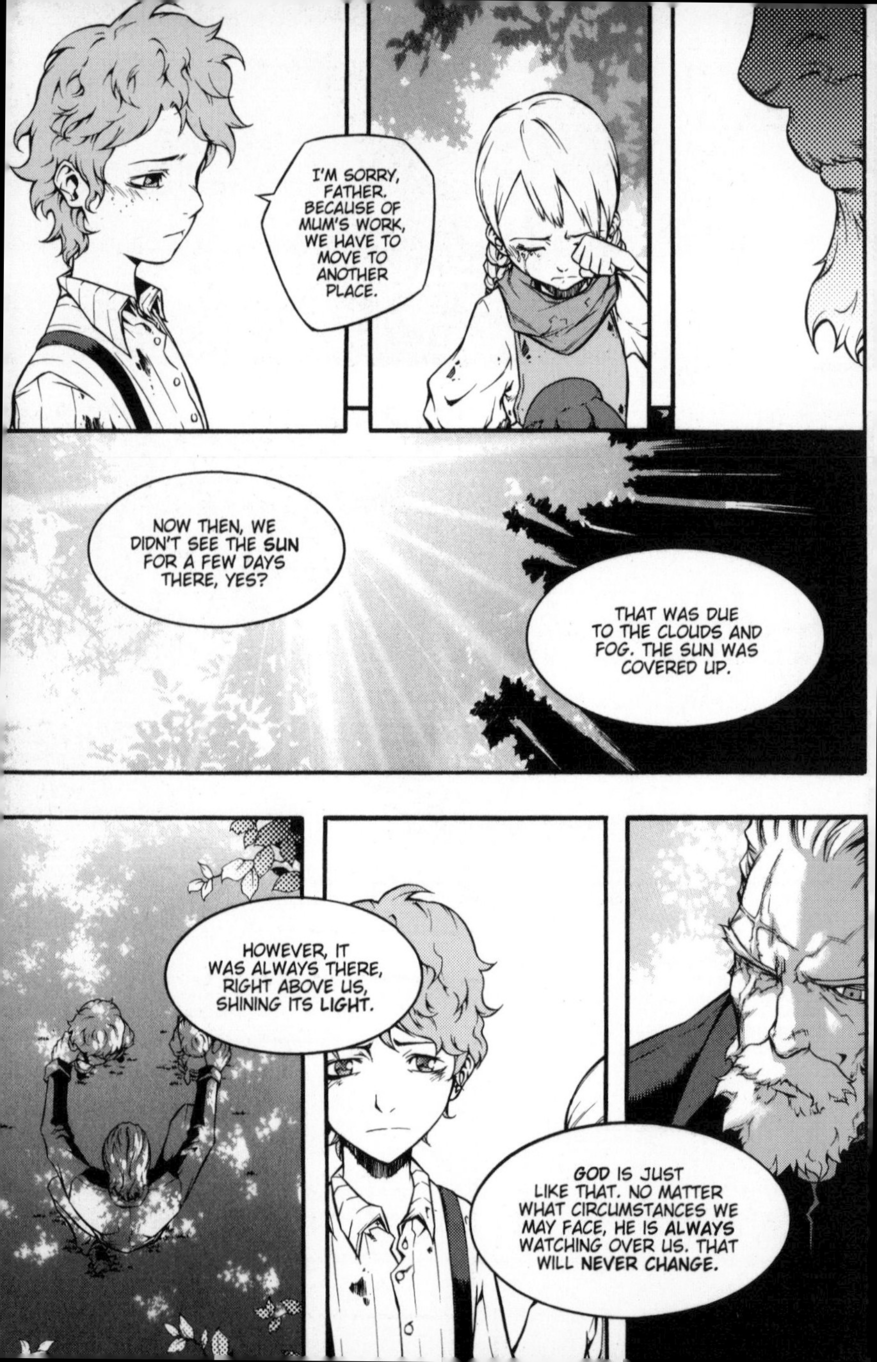
I'M SORRY, FATHER. BECAUSE OF MUM'S WORK, WE HAVE TO MOVE TO ANOTHER PLACE.
NOW THEN, WE DIDN'T SEE THE SUN FOR A FEW DAYS THERE, YES?
THAT WAS DUE TO THE CLOUDS AND FOG. THE SUN WAS COVERED UP.
HOWEVER, IT WAS ALWAYS THERE, RIGHT ABOVE US, SHINING ITS LIGHT.
GOD IS JUST LIKE THAT. NO MATTER WHAT CIRCUMSTANCES WE MAY FACE, HE IS ALWAYS WATCHING OVER US. THAT WILL NEVER CHANGE.

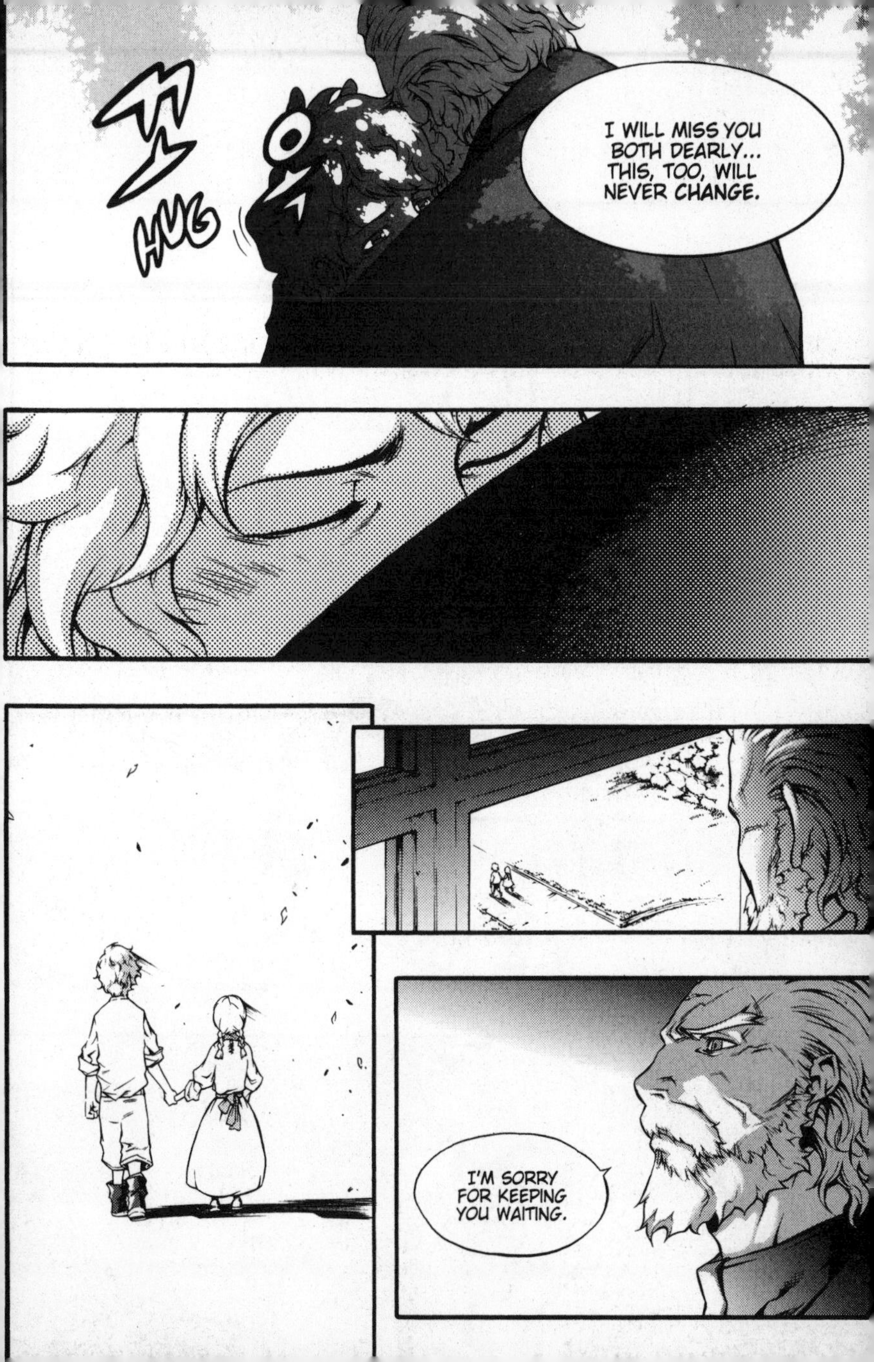
HUG
I WILL MISS YOU BOTH DEARLY... THIS, TOO, WILL NEVER CHANGE.
I'M SORRY FOR KEEPING YOU WAITING.

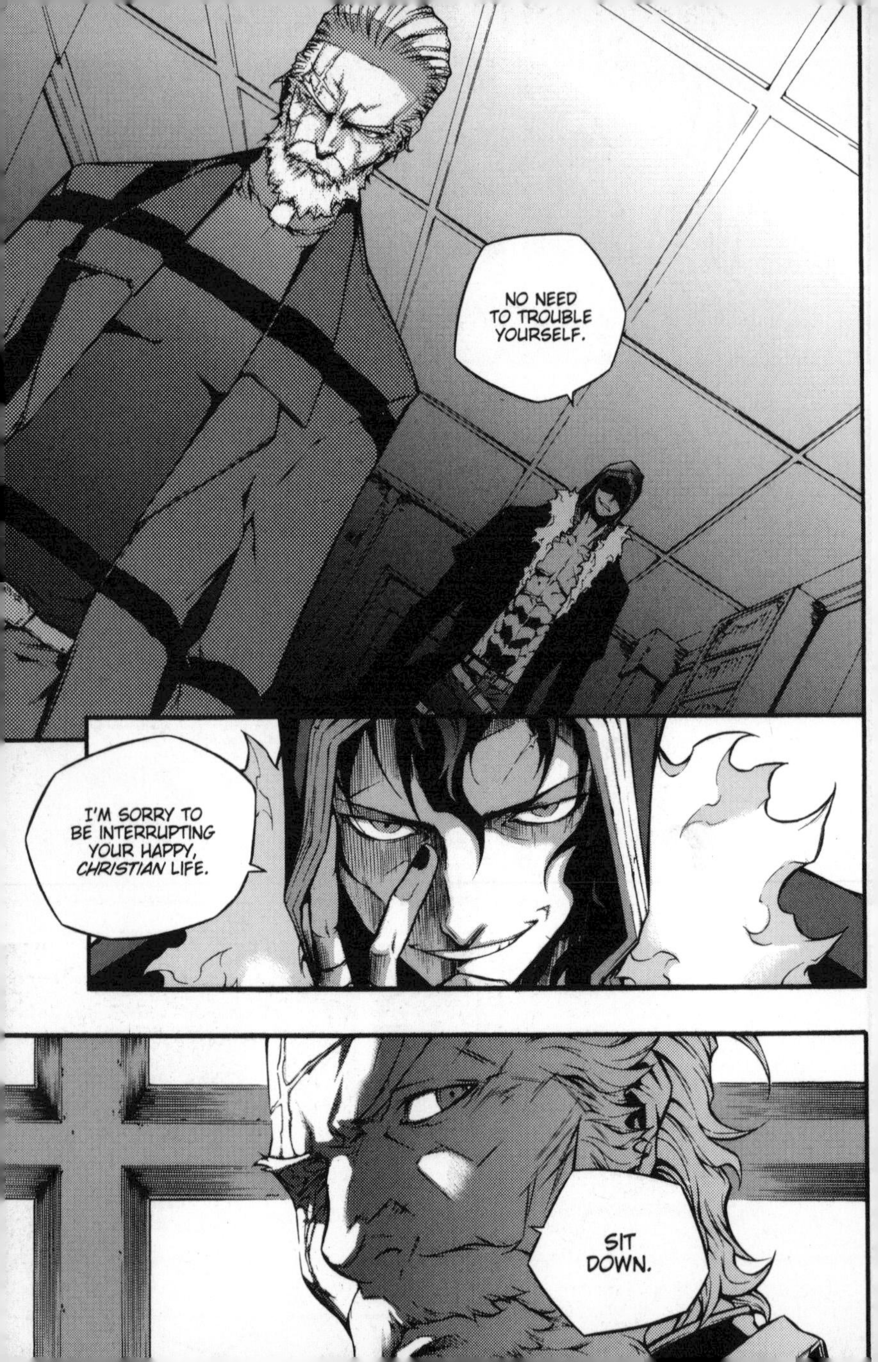
NO NEED TO TROUBLE YOURSELF.
I'M SORRY TO BE INTERRUPTING YOUR HAPPY, *CHRISTIAN* LIFE.
SIT DOWN.

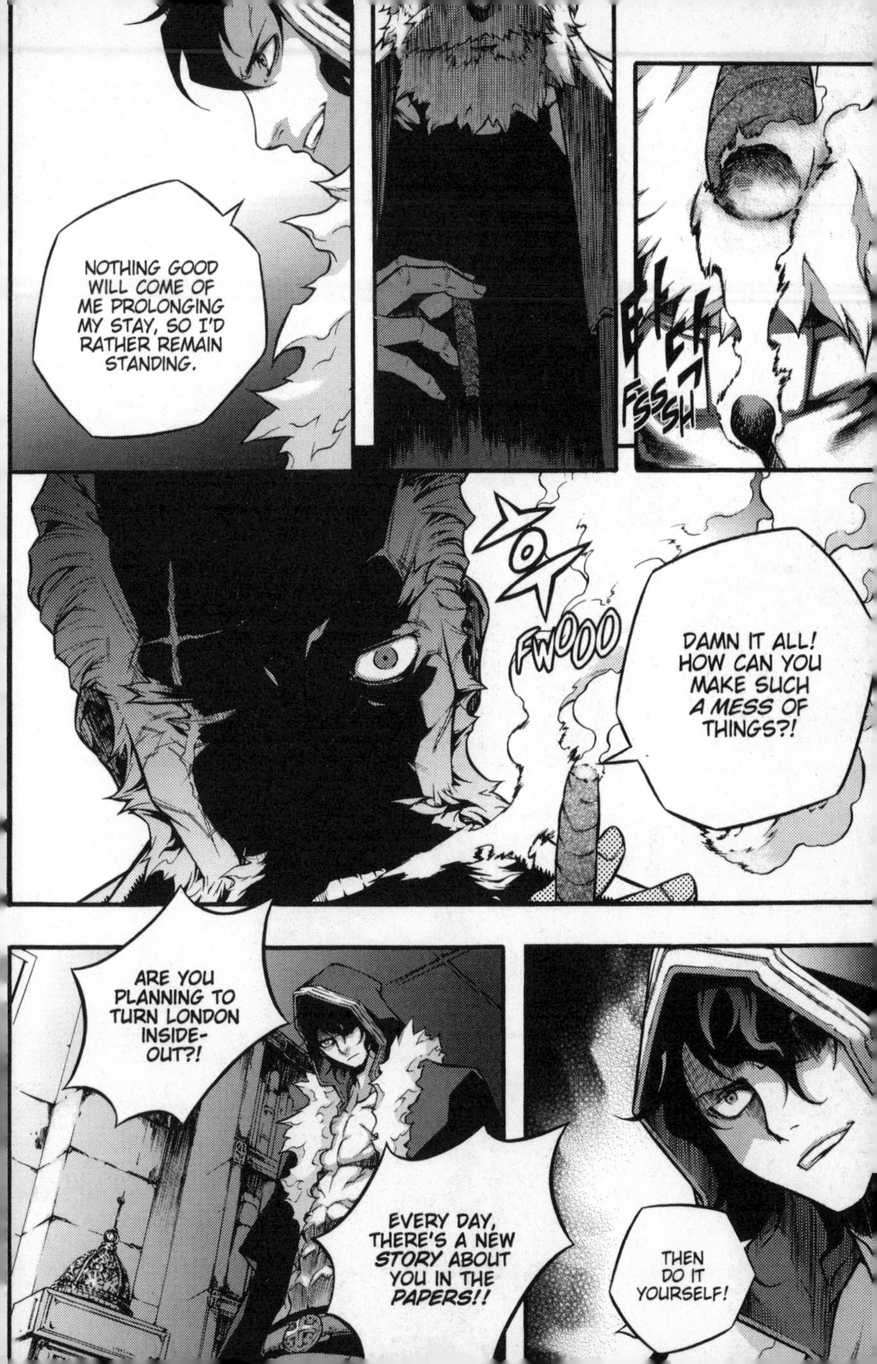
NOTHING GOOD WILL COME OF ME PROLONGING MY STAY, SO I'D RATHER REMAIN STANDING.
FSSSH
DAMN IT ALL! HOW CAN YOU MAKE SUCH A MESS OF THINGS?!
FWOOO
ARE YOU PLANNING TO TURN LONDON INSIDE-OUT?!
EVERY DAY, THERE'S A NEW STORY ABOUT YOU IN THE PAPERS!!
THEN DO IT YOURSELF!

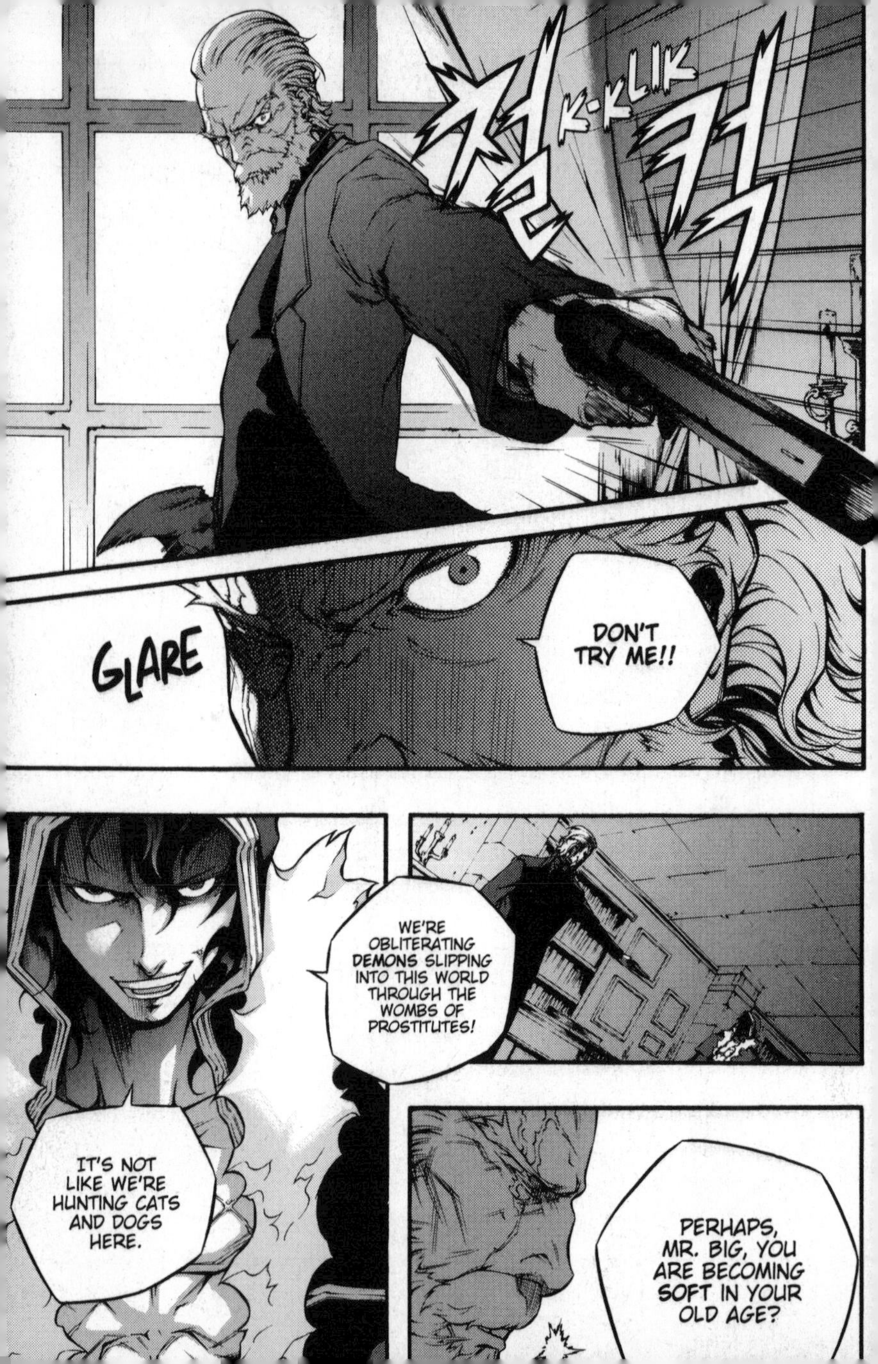
K-KLIK
GLARE
DON'T TRY ME!!
WE'RE OBLITERATING DEMONS SLIPPING INTO THIS WORLD THROUGH THE WOMBS OF PROSTITUTES!
IT'S NOT LIKE WE'RE HUNTING CATS AND DOGS HERE.
PERHAPS, MR. BIG, YOU ARE BECOMING SOFT IN YOUR OLD AGE?

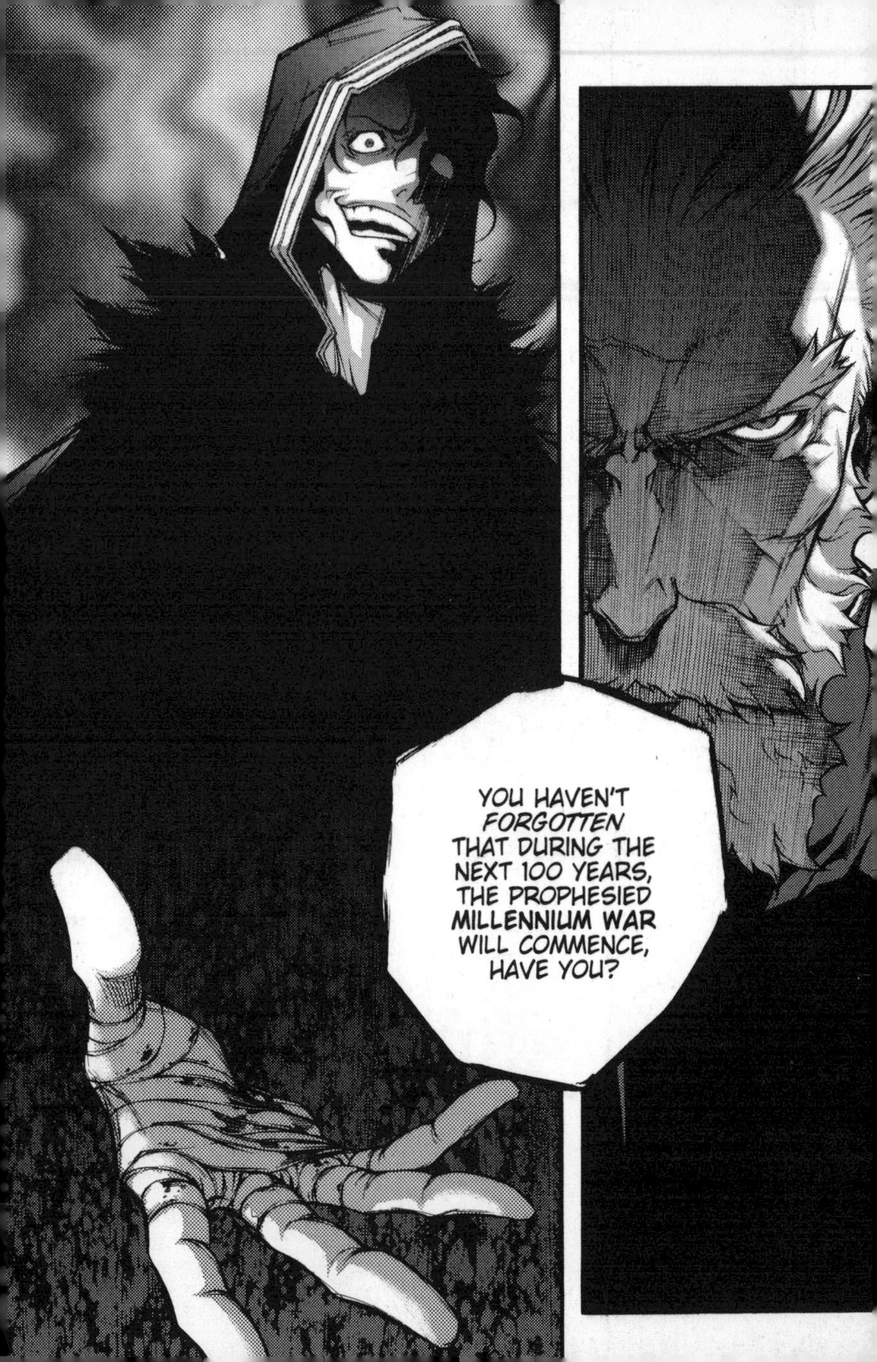
YOU HAVEN'T *FORGOTTEN* THAT DURING THE NEXT 100 YEARS, THE PROPHESIED MILLENNIUM WAR WILL COMMENCE, HAVE YOU?

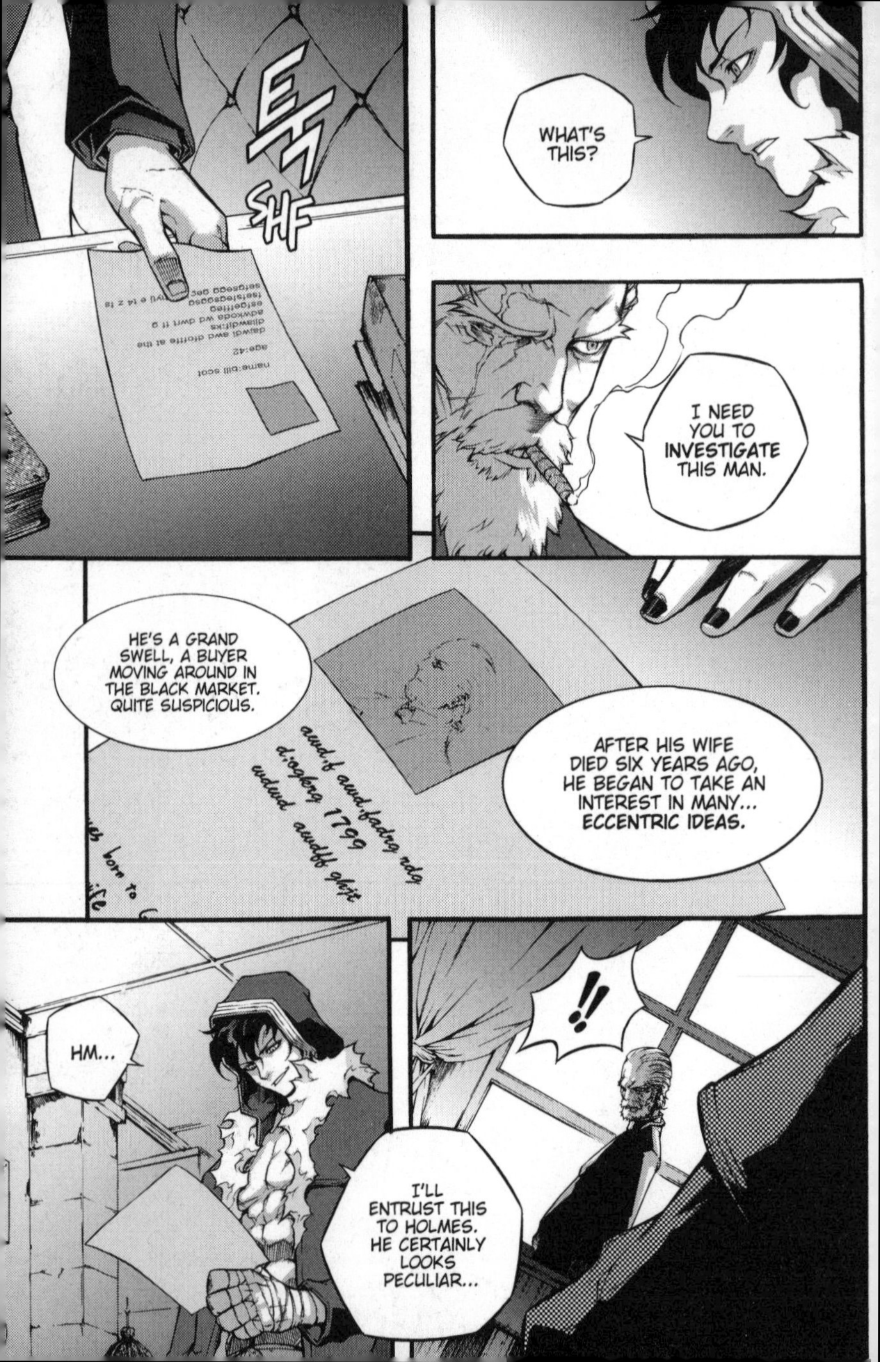
SHF
WHAT'S THIS?
I NEED YOU TO INVESTIGATE THIS MAN.
HE'S A GRAND SWELL, A BUYER MOVING AROUND IN THE BLACK MARKET. QUITE SUSPICIOUS.
AFTER HIS WIFE DIED SIX YEARS AGO, HE BEGAN TO TAKE AN INTEREST IN MANY... ECCENTRIC IDEAS.
HM...
!!
I'LL ENTRUST THIS TO HOLMES. HE CERTAINLY LOOKS PECULIAR...

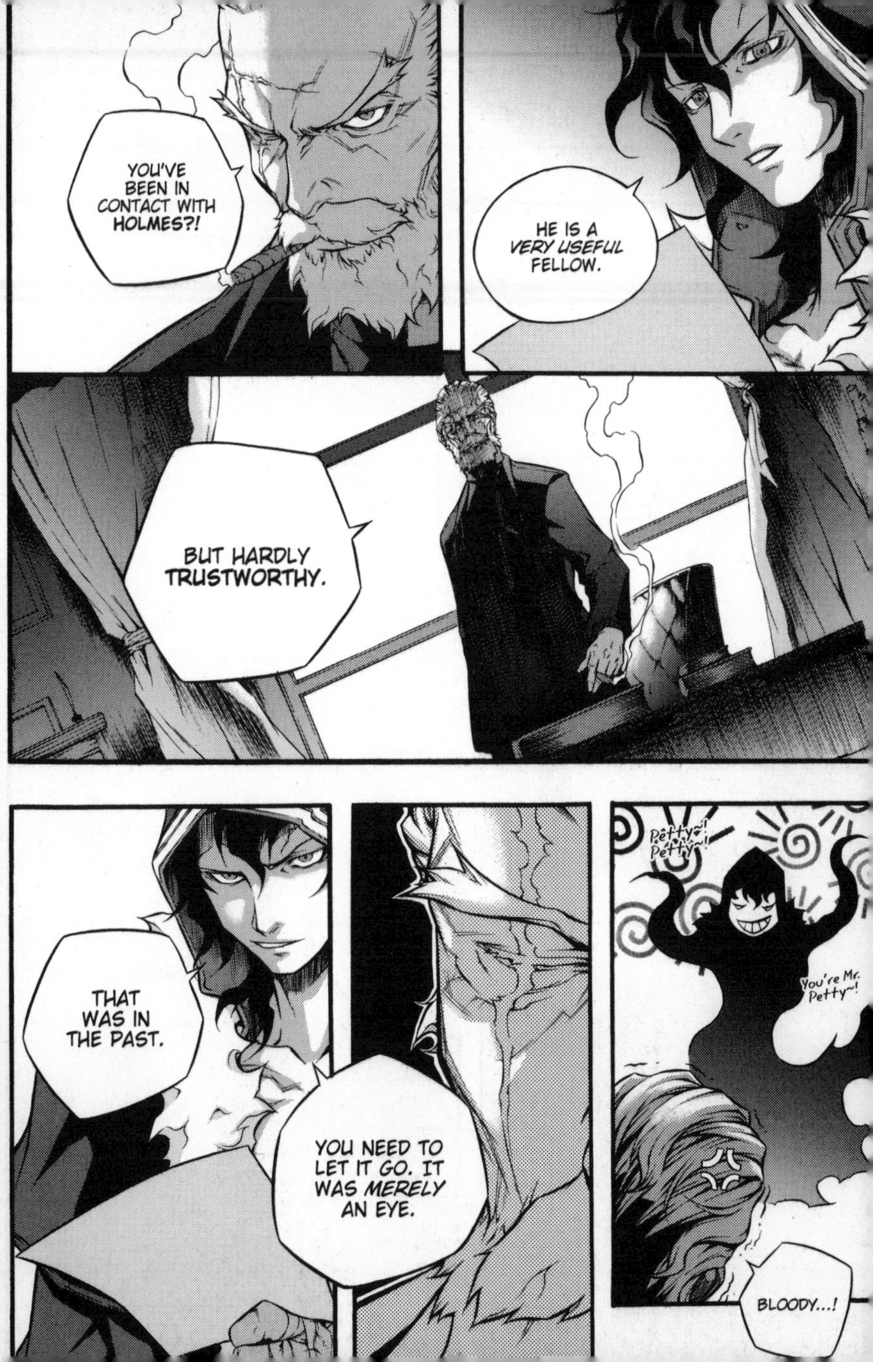
YOU'VE BEEN IN CONTACT WITH HOLMES?!
HE IS A *VERY USEFUL* FELLOW.
BUT HARDLY TRUSTWORTHY.
THAT WAS IN THE PAST.
YOU NEED TO LET IT GO. IT WAS *MERELY* AN EYE.
Petty~! Petty~!
You're Mr. Petty~!
BLOODY...!

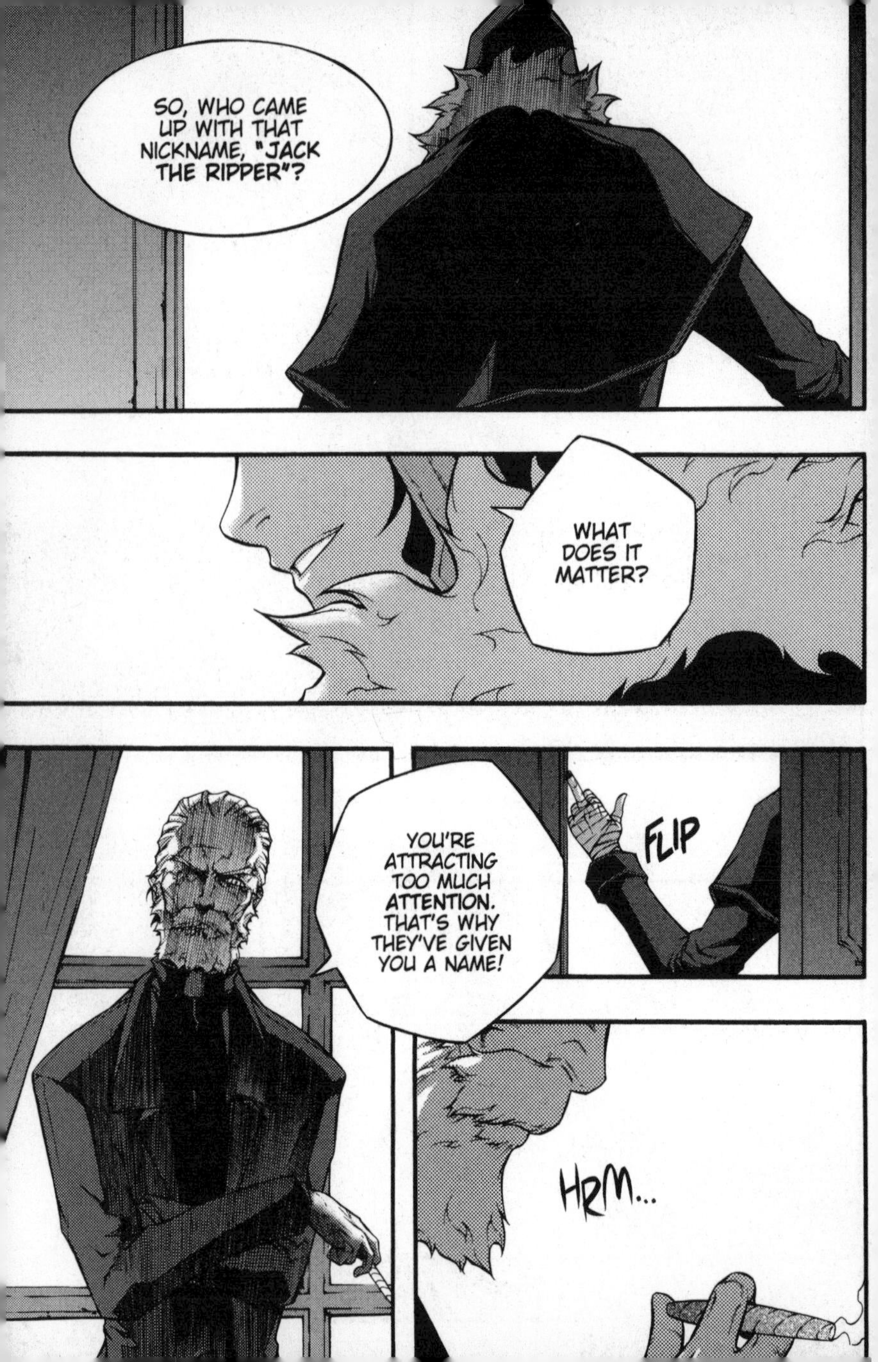
SO, WHO CAME UP WITH THAT NICKNAME, "JACK THE RIPPER"?
WHAT DOES IT MATTER?
YOU'RE ATTRACTING TOO MUCH ATTENTION. THAT'S WHY THEY'VE GIVEN YOU A NAME!
FLIP
HRM...

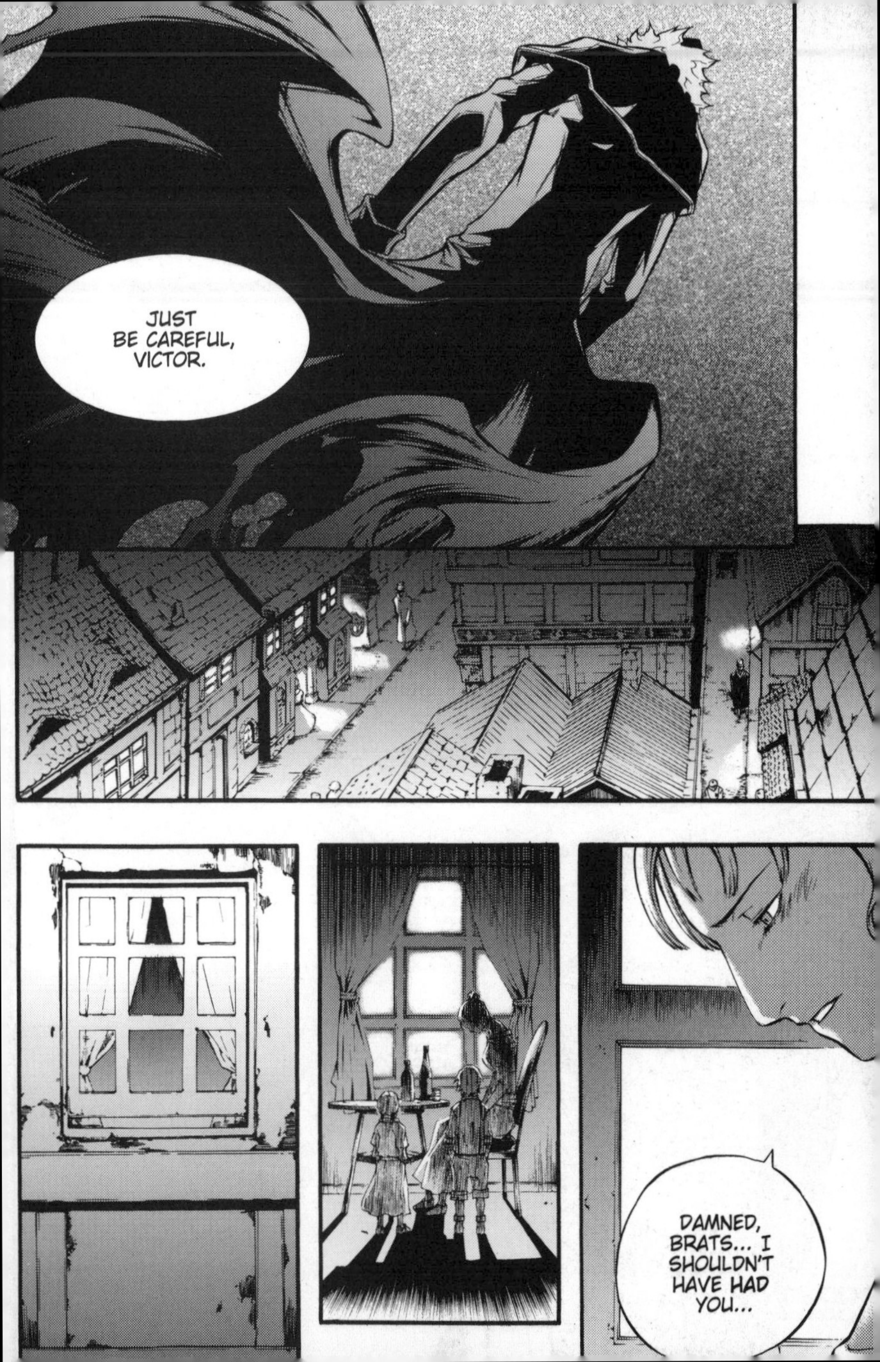
JUST BE CAREFUL, VICTOR.
DAMNED, BRATS... I SHOULDN'T HAVE HAD YOU...

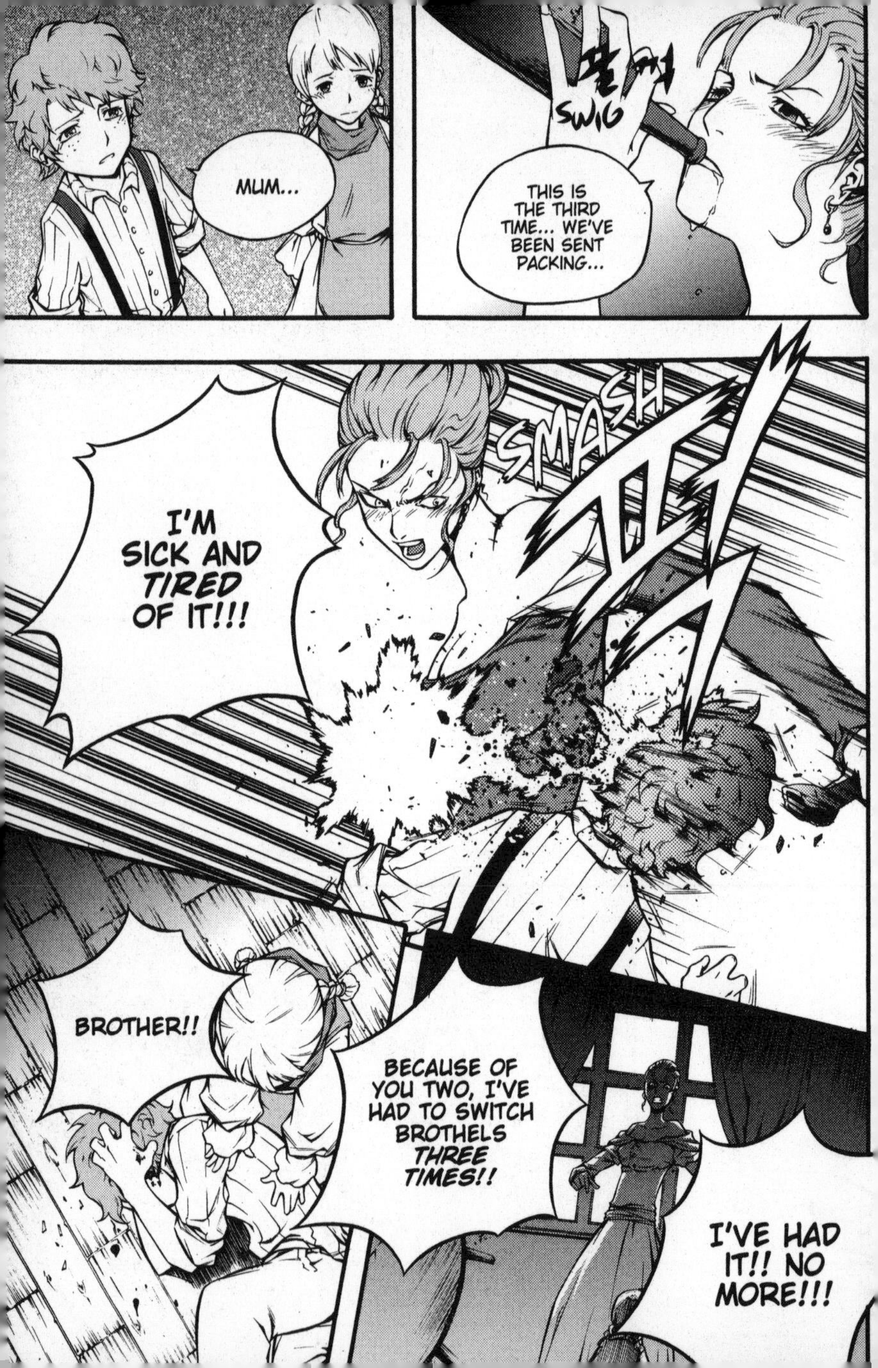
MUM...
SWIG
THIS IS THE THIRD TIME... WE'VE BEEN SENT PACKING...
I'M SICK AND TIRED OF IT!!!
SMASH
BROTHER!!
BECAUSE OF YOU TWO, I'VE HAD TO SWITCH BROTHELS THREE TIMES!!
I'VE HAD IT!! NO MORE!!!

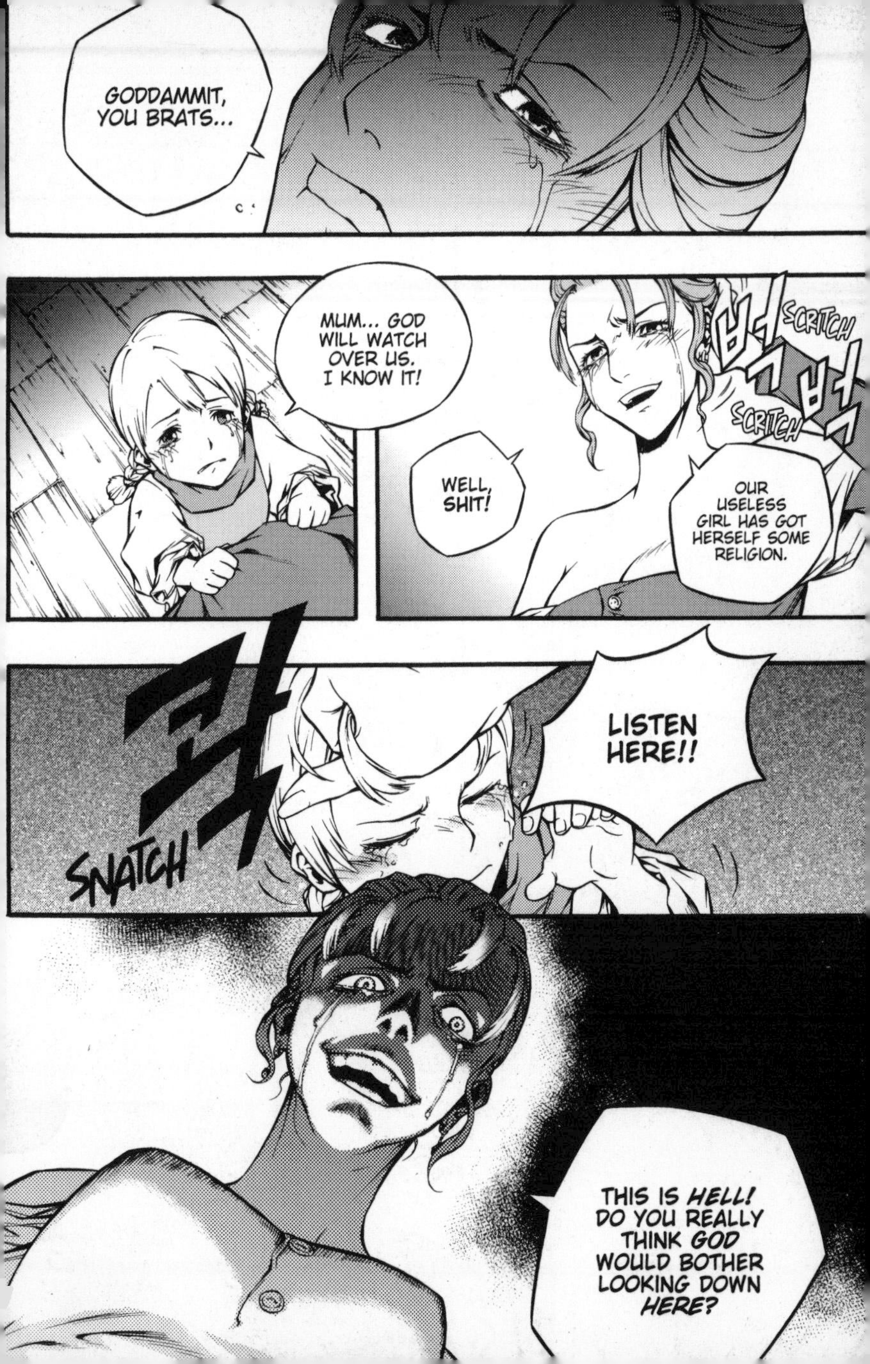
GODDAMMIT, YOU BRATS...
MUM... GOD WILL WATCH OVER US. I KNOW IT!
SCRITCH
SCRITCH
WELL, SHIT!
OUR USELESS GIRL HAS GOT HERSELF SOME RELIGION.
SNATCH
LISTEN HERE!!
THIS IS *HELL!* DO YOU REALLY THINK *GOD* WOULD BOTHER LOOKING DOWN *HERE?*

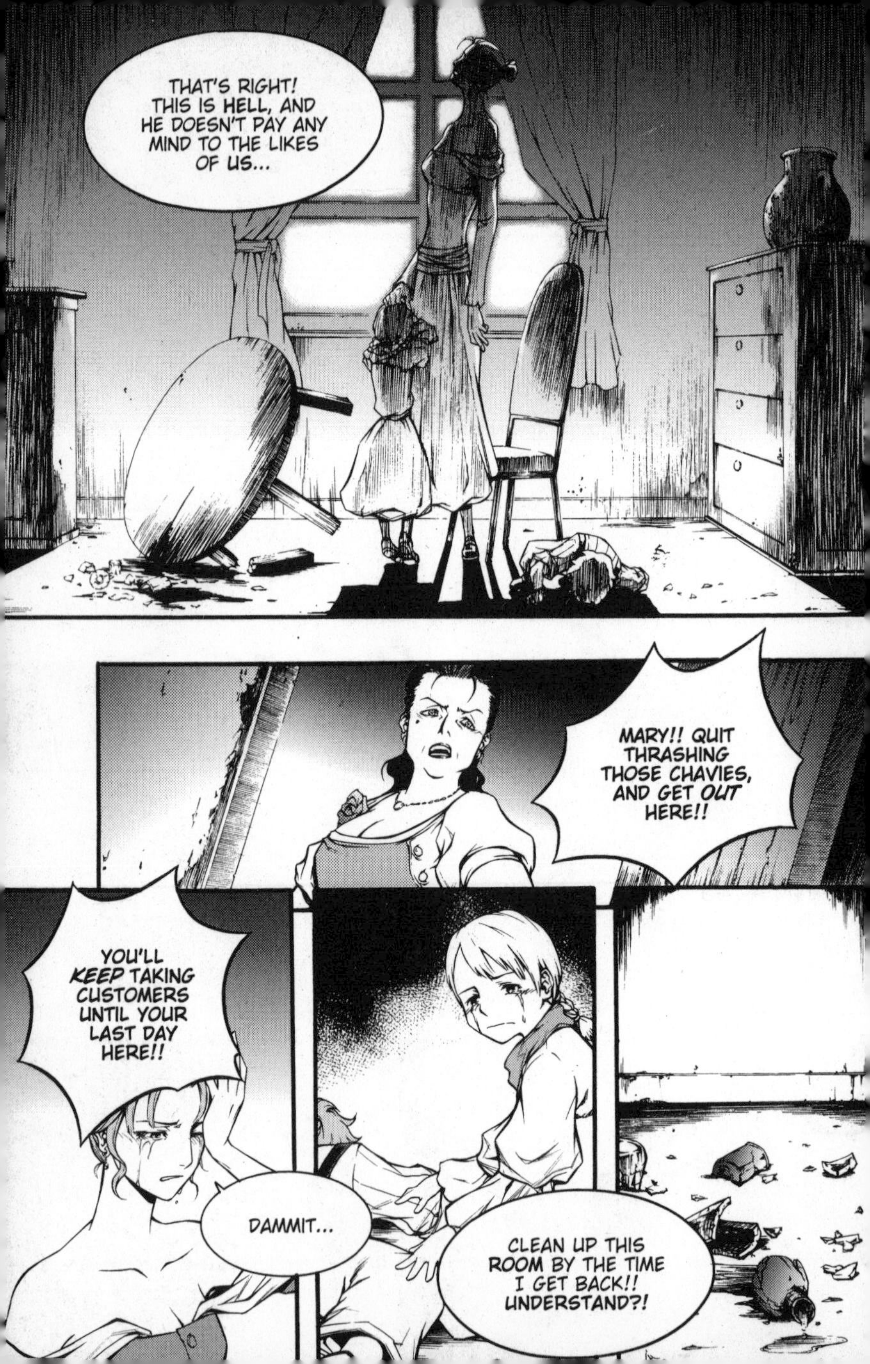
THAT'S RIGHT! THIS IS HELL, AND HE DOESN'T PAY ANY MIND TO THE LIKES OF US...
MARY!! QUIT THRASHING THOSE CHAVIES, AND GET OUT HERE!!
YOU'LL KEEP TAKING CUSTOMERS UNTIL YOUR LAST DAY HERE!!
DAMMIT...
CLEAN UP THIS ROOM BY THE TIME I GET BACK!! UNDERSTAND?!

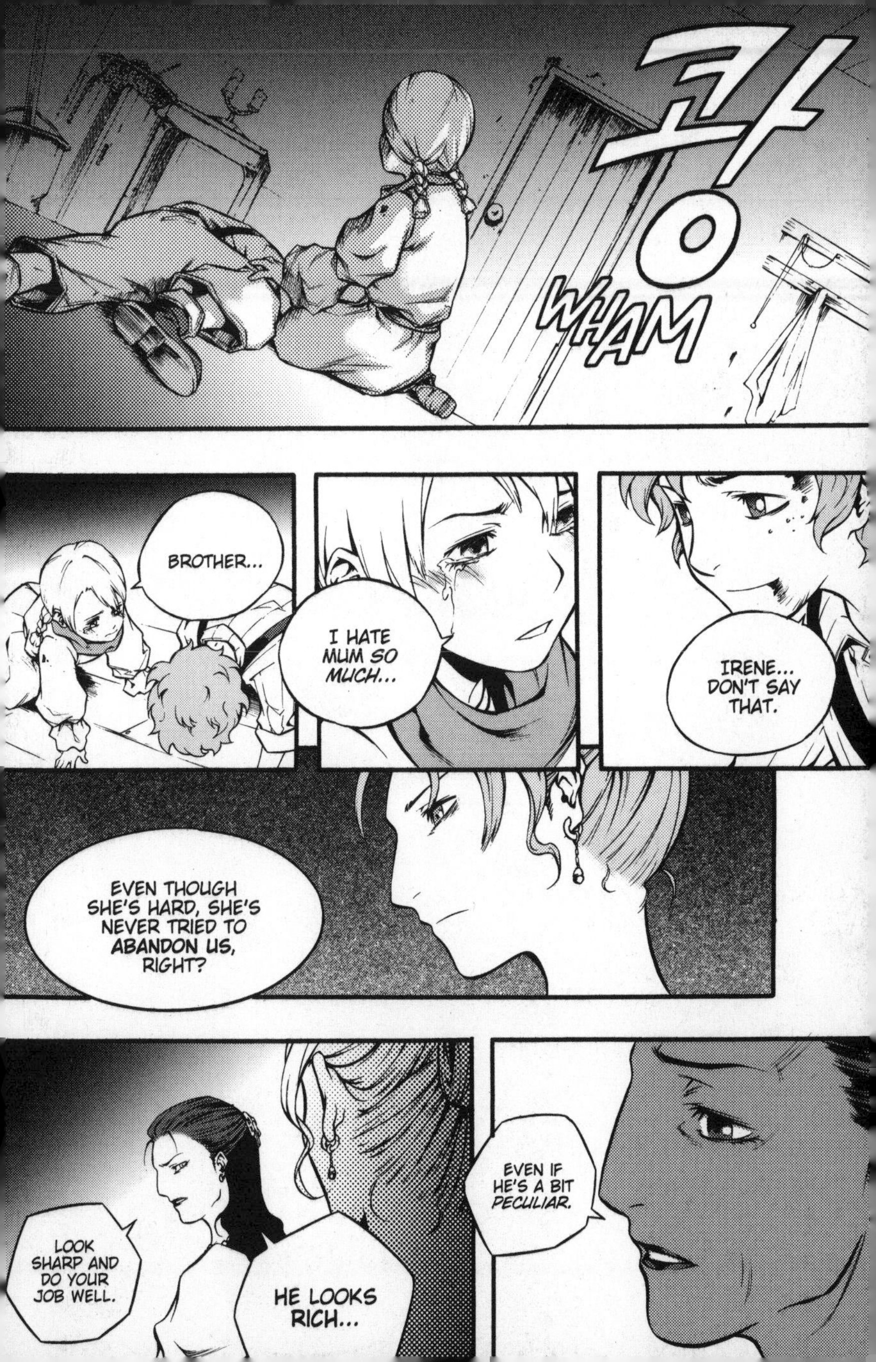

쾅
WHAM
BROTHER...
I HATE MUM SO MUCH...
IRENE... DON'T SAY THAT.
EVEN THOUGH SHE'S HARD, SHE'S NEVER TRIED TO ABANDON US, RIGHT?
EVEN IF HE'S A BIT *PECULIAR*.
HE LOOKS RICH...
LOOK SHARP AND DO YOUR JOB WELL.

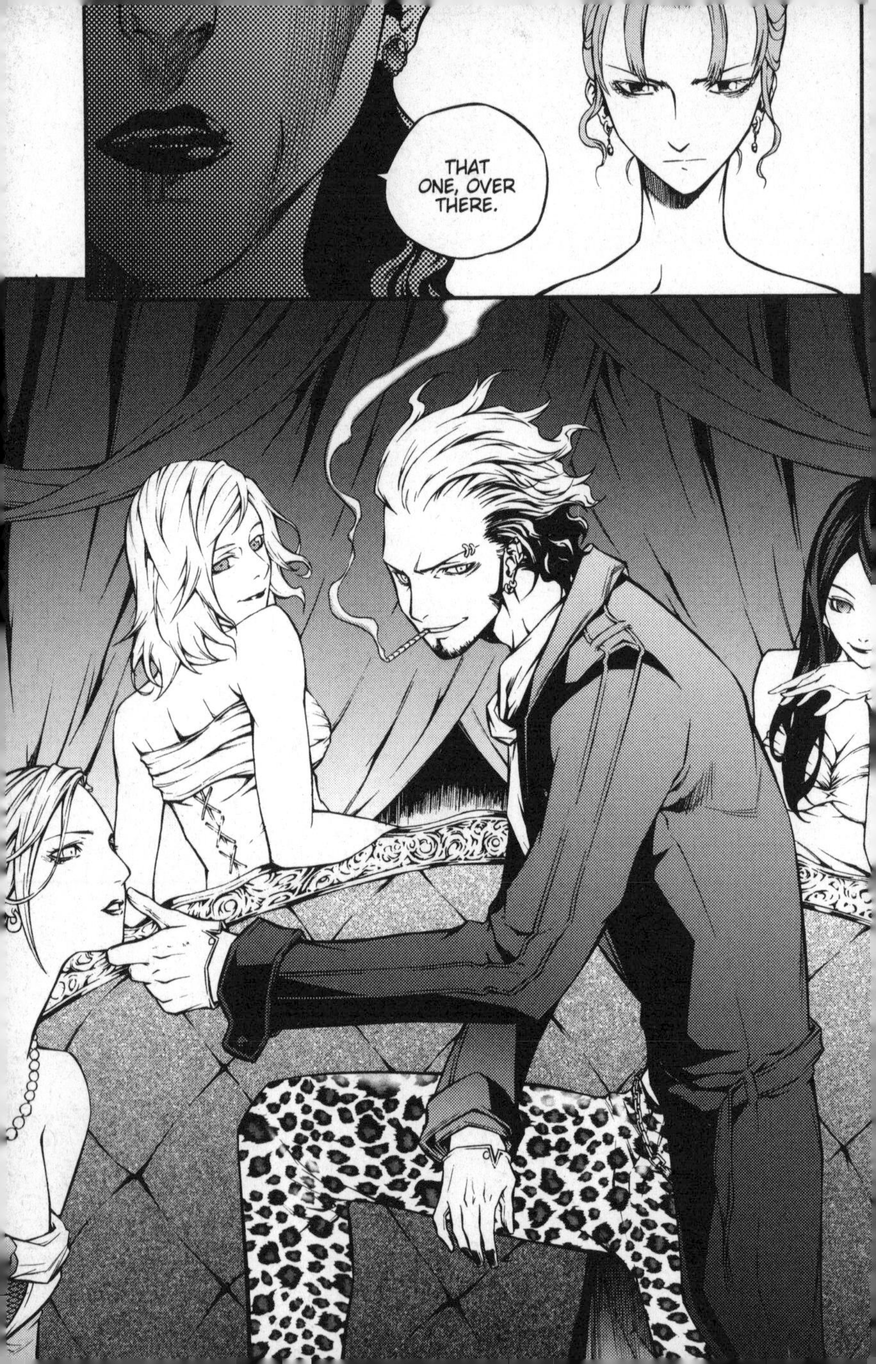
THAT ONE, OVER THERE.

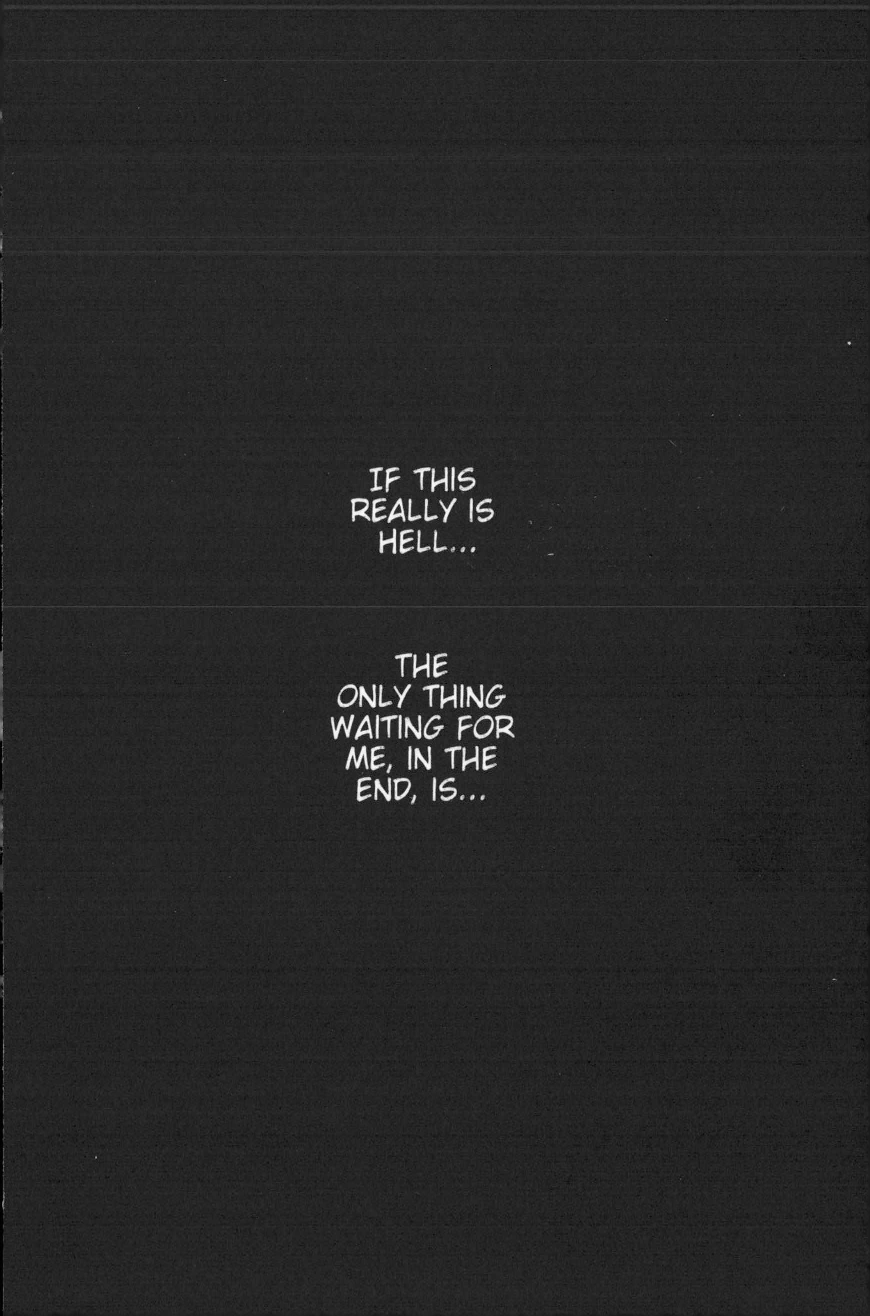
IF THIS REALLY IS HELL...
THE ONLY THING WAITING FOR ME, IN THE END, IS...

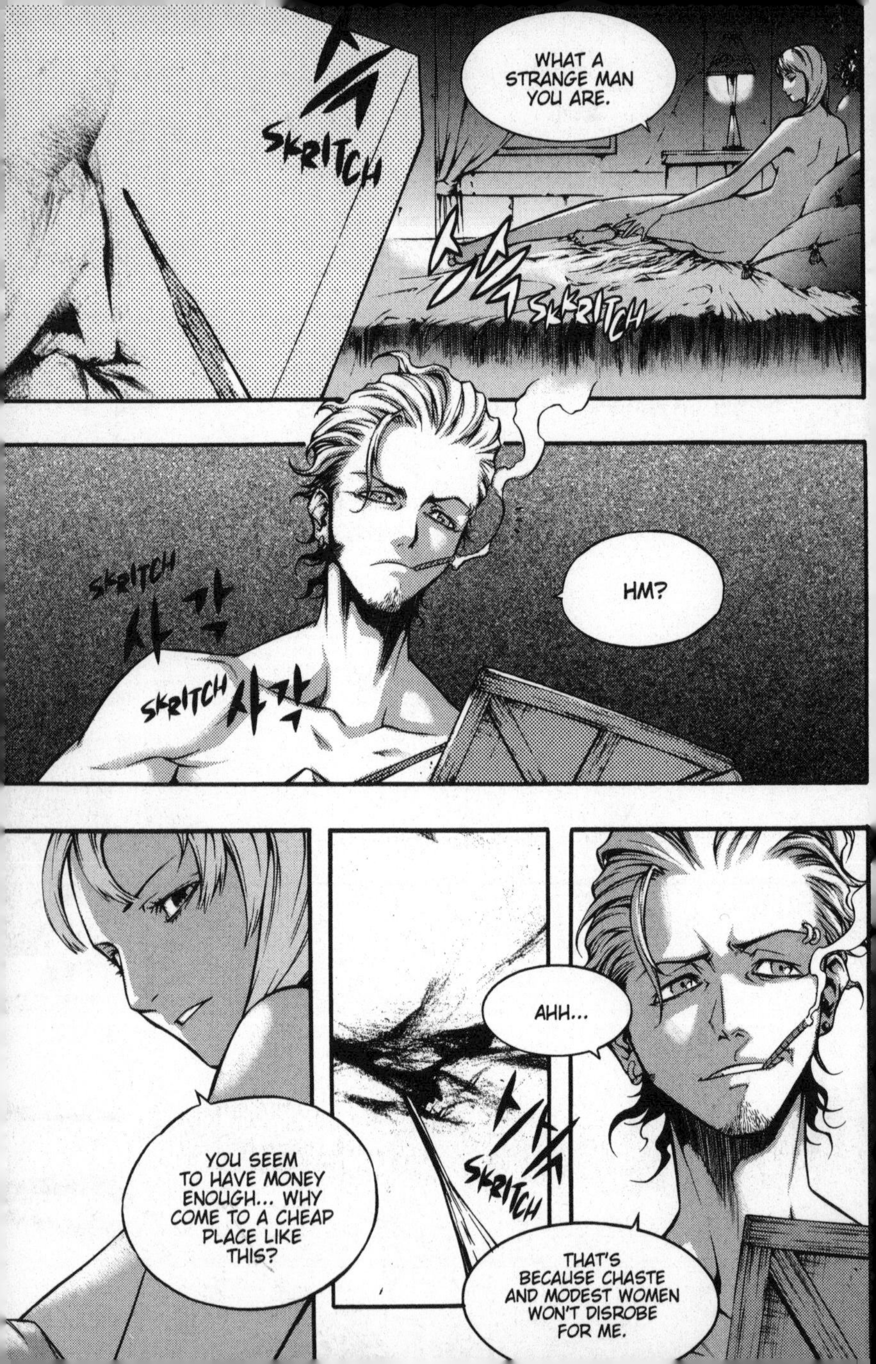
SKRITCH
WHAT A STRANGE MAN YOU ARE.
SKRITCH
SKRITCH
사각
SKRITCH
사각
HM?
YOU SEEM TO HAVE MONEY ENOUGH... WHY COME TO A CHEAP PLACE LIKE THIS?
AHH...
SKRITCH
THAT'S BECAUSE CHASTE AND MODEST WOMEN WON'T DISROBE FOR ME.

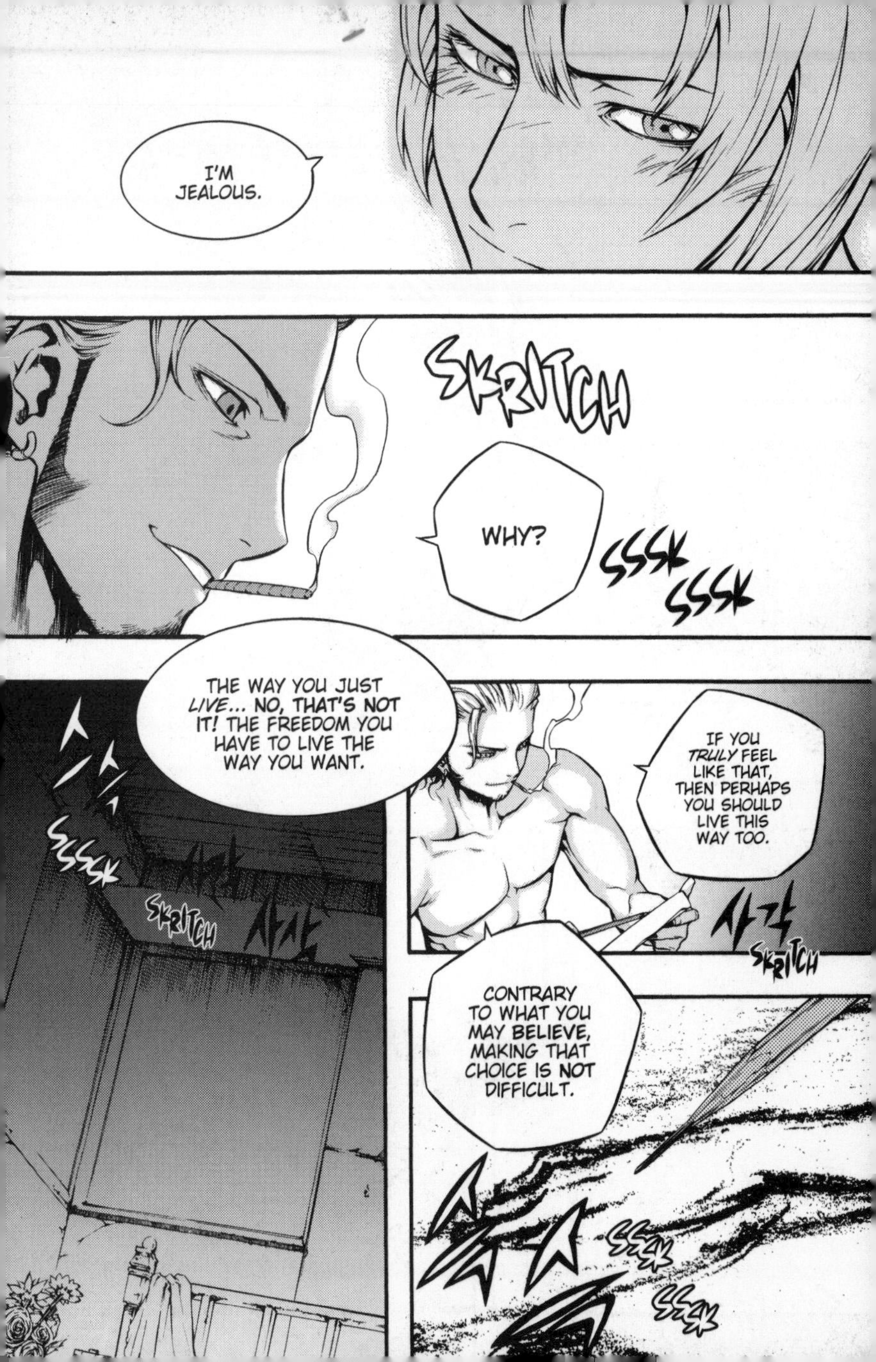
I'M JEALOUS.
SKRITCH
WHY?
SSSK SSSK
THE WAY YOU JUST *LIVE*... NO, THAT'S NOT IT! THE FREEDOM YOU HAVE TO LIVE THE WAY YOU WANT.
IF YOU *TRULY* FEEL LIKE THAT, THEN PERHAPS YOU SHOULD LIVE THIS WAY TOO.
SSSSK
SKRITCH
SKRITCH
CONTRARY TO WHAT YOU MAY BELIEVE, MAKING THAT CHOICE IS NOT DIFFICULT.

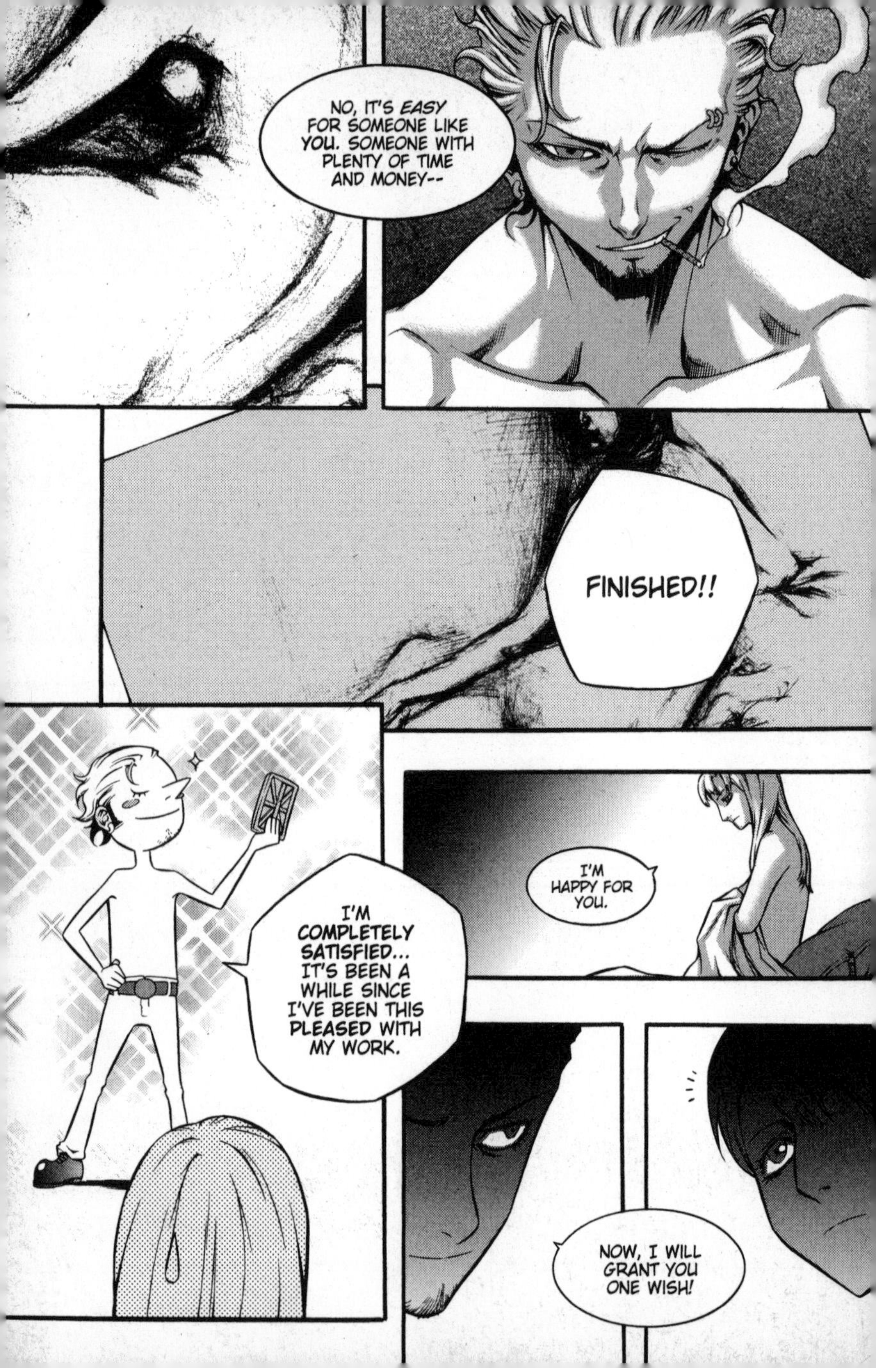
NO, IT'S *EASY* FOR SOMEONE LIKE YOU. SOMEONE WITH PLENTY OF TIME AND MONEY--
FINISHED!!
I'M HAPPY FOR YOU.
I'M COMPLETELY SATISFIED... IT'S BEEN A WHILE SINCE I'VE BEEN THIS PLEASED WITH MY WORK.
NOW, I WILL GRANT YOU ONE WISH!

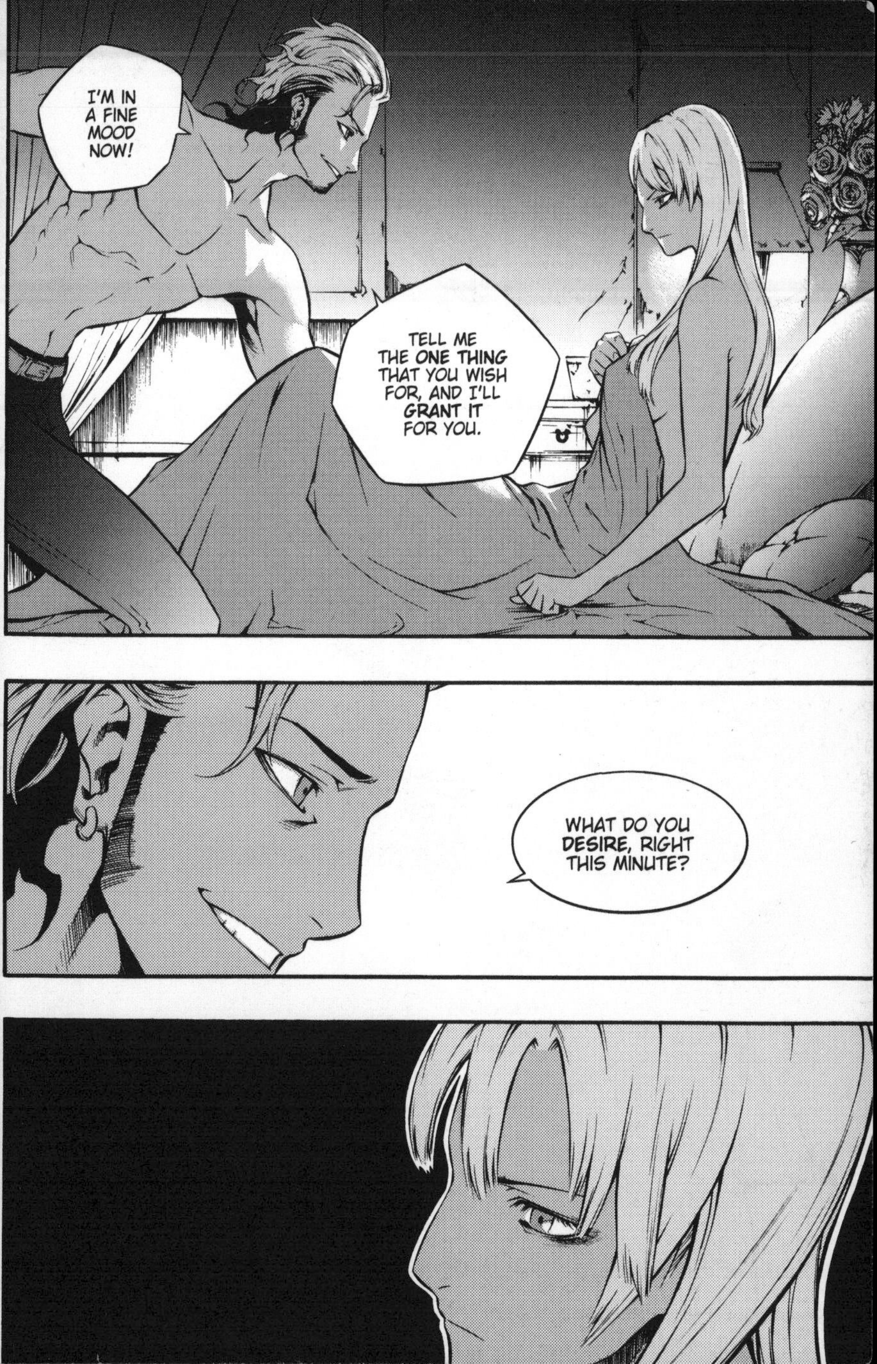
I'M IN A FINE MOOD NOW!
TELL ME THE ONE THING THAT YOU WISH FOR, AND I'LL GRANT IT FOR YOU.
WHAT DO YOU DESIRE, RIGHT THIS MINUTE?

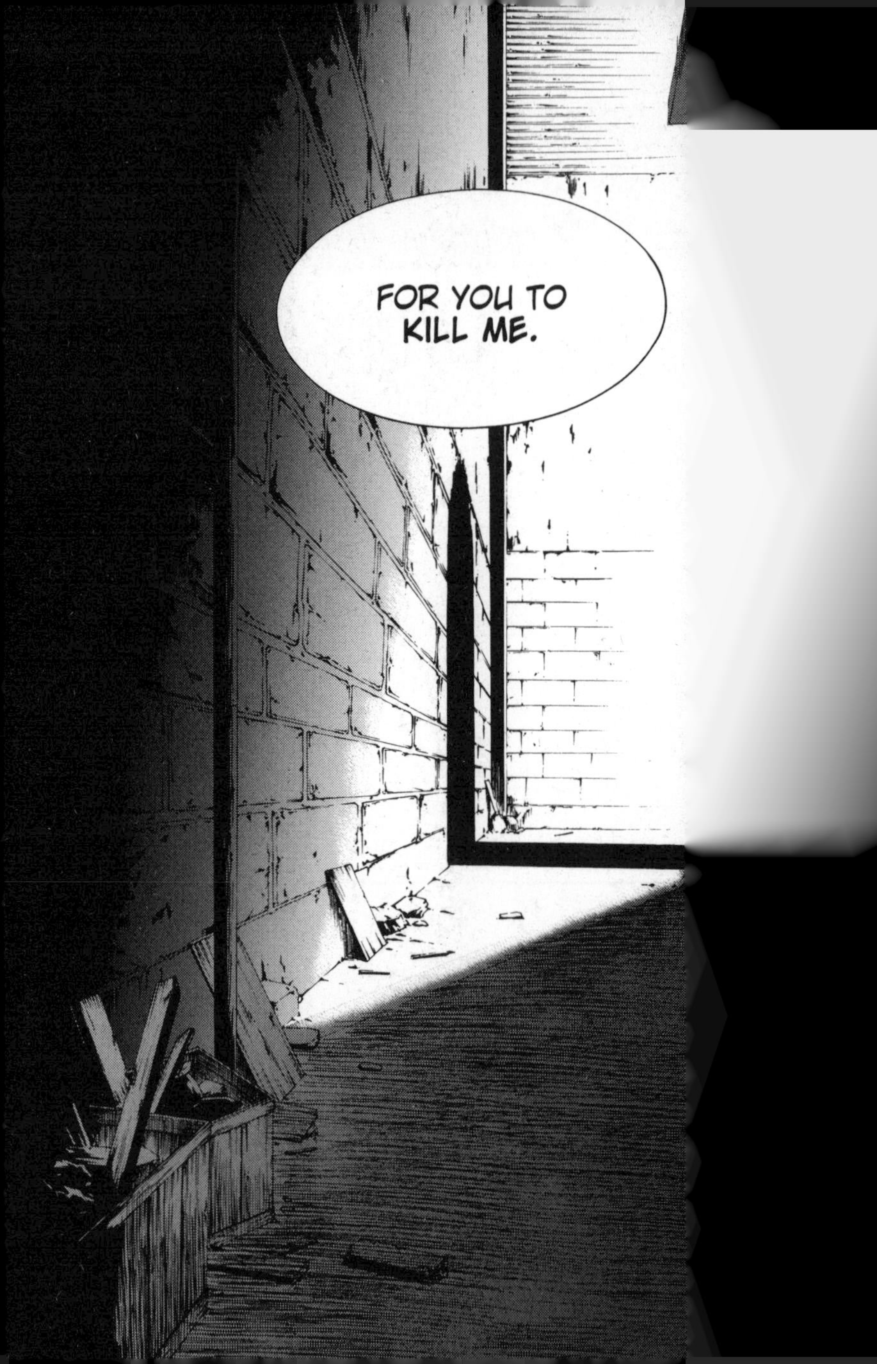
FOR YOU TO KILL ME.

EPISODE 8

HUNTERS (3)

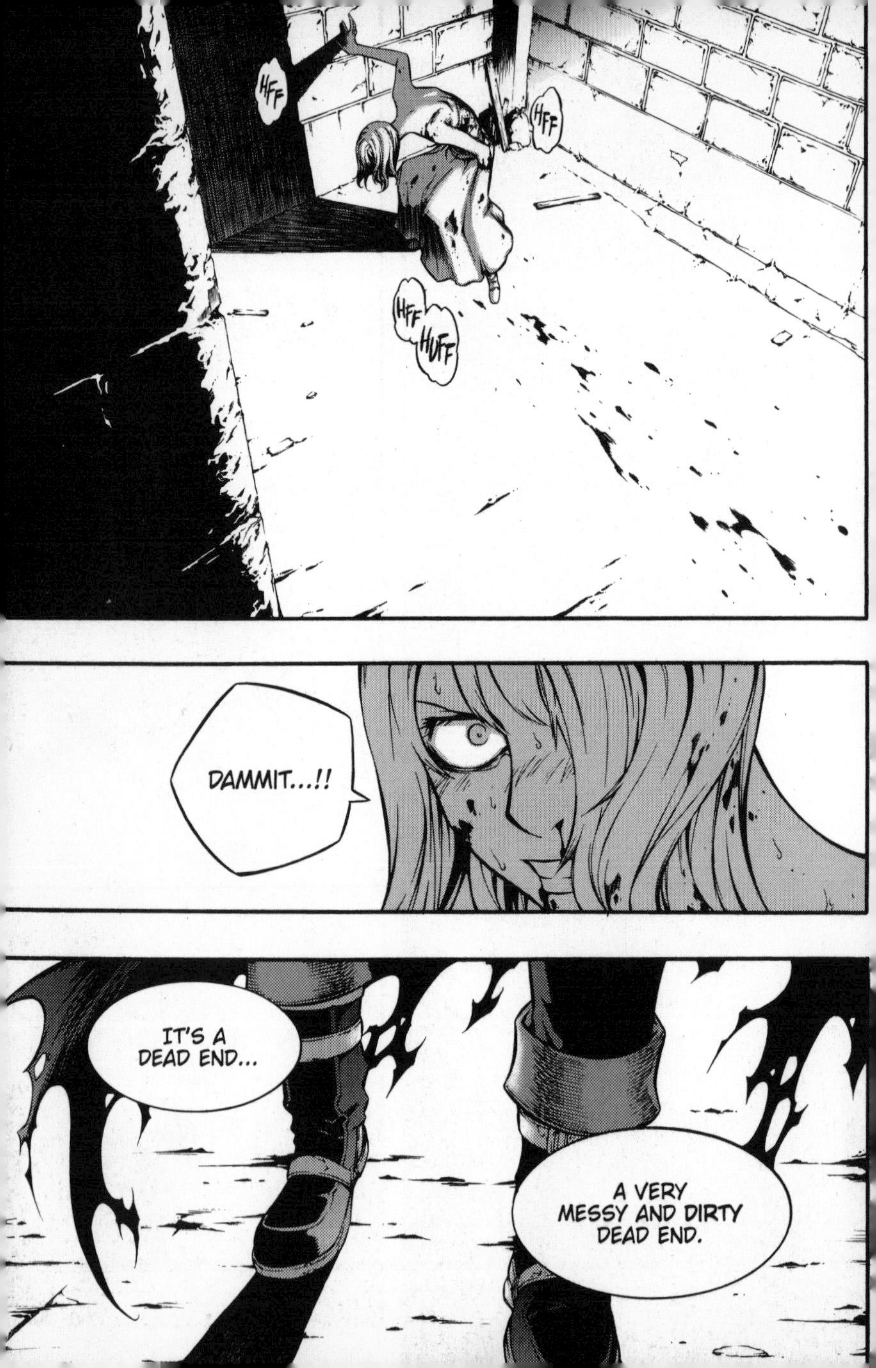
HFF
HFF
HFF
HUFF
DAMMIT...!!
IT'S A DEAD END...
A VERY MESSY AND DIRTY DEAD END.

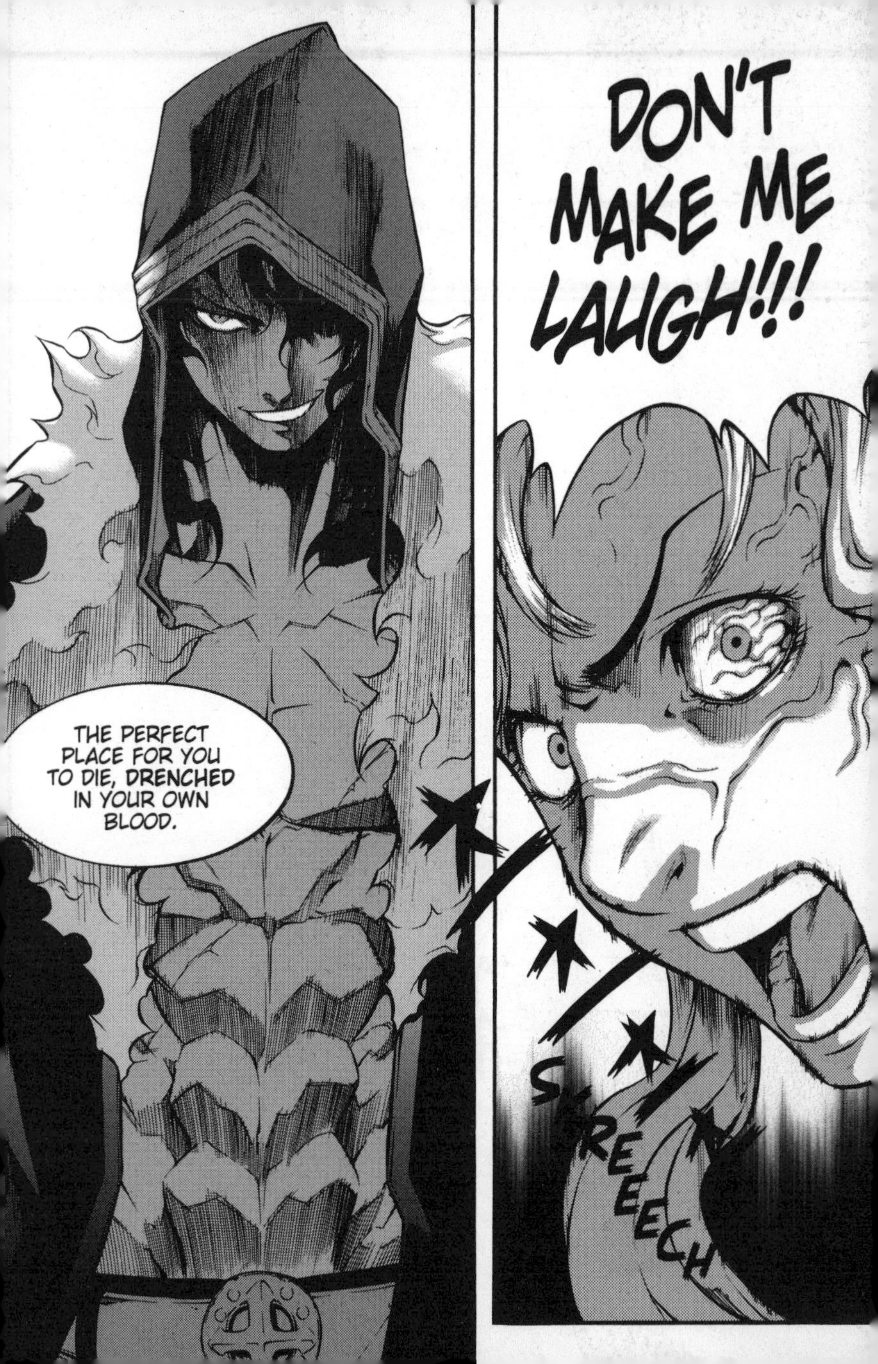
THE PERFECT PLACE FOR YOU TO DIE, DRENCHED IN YOUR OWN BLOOD.
DON'T MAKE ME LAUGH!!!
SKREEECH

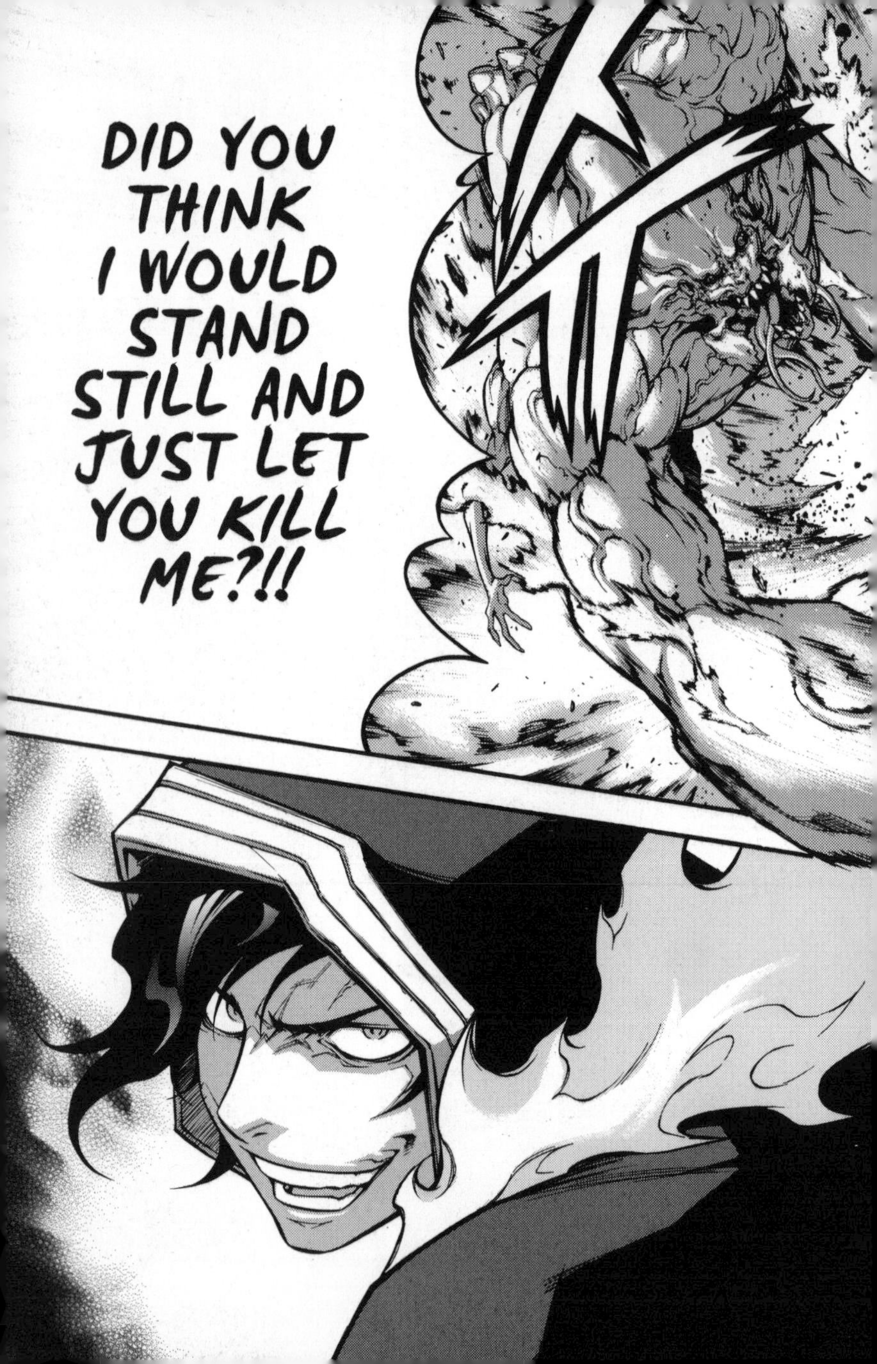
DID YOU THINK I WOULD STAND STILL AND JUST LET YOU KILL ME?!!

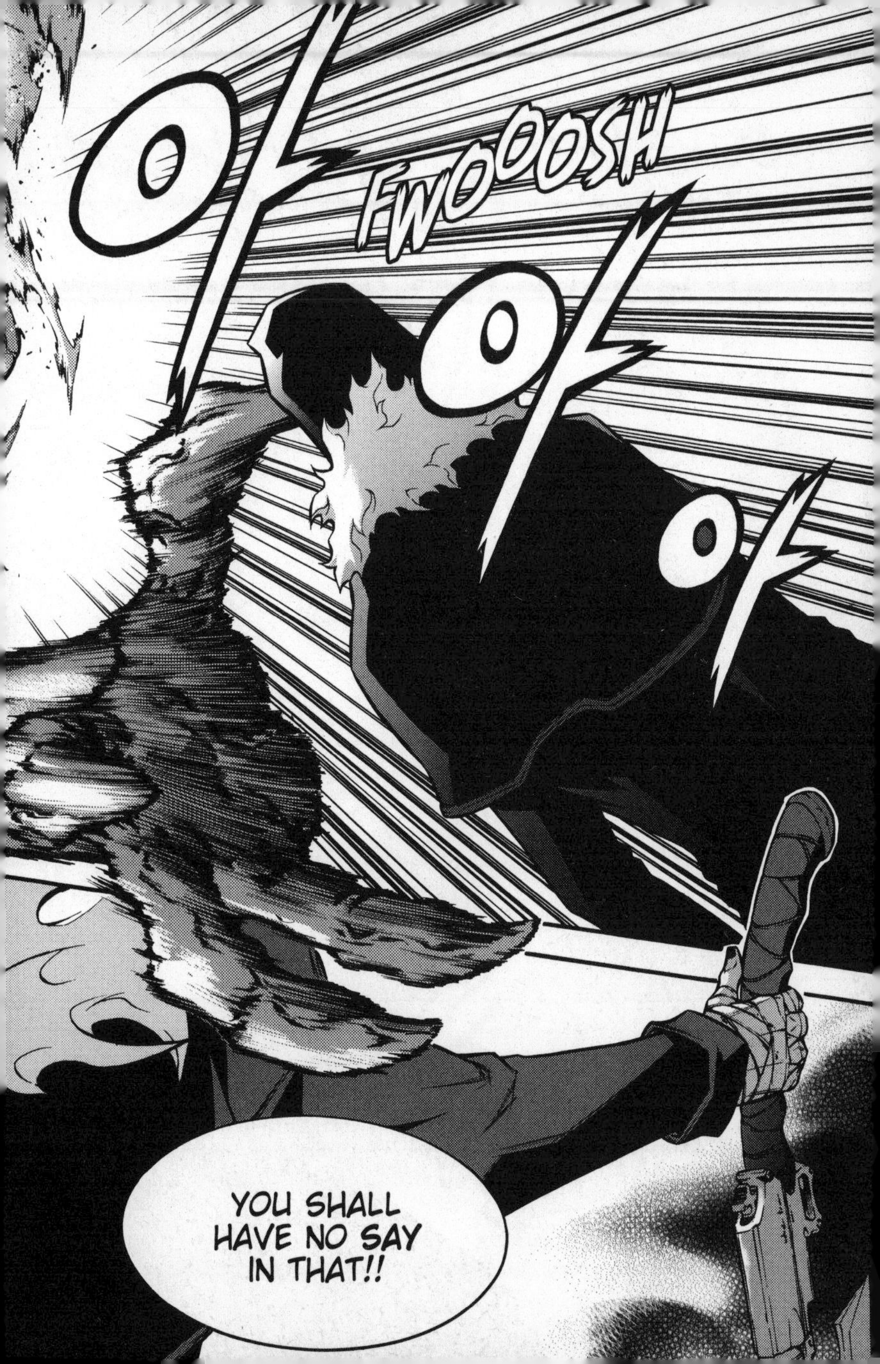
FWOOOSH
YOU SHALL HAVE NO SAY IN THAT!!

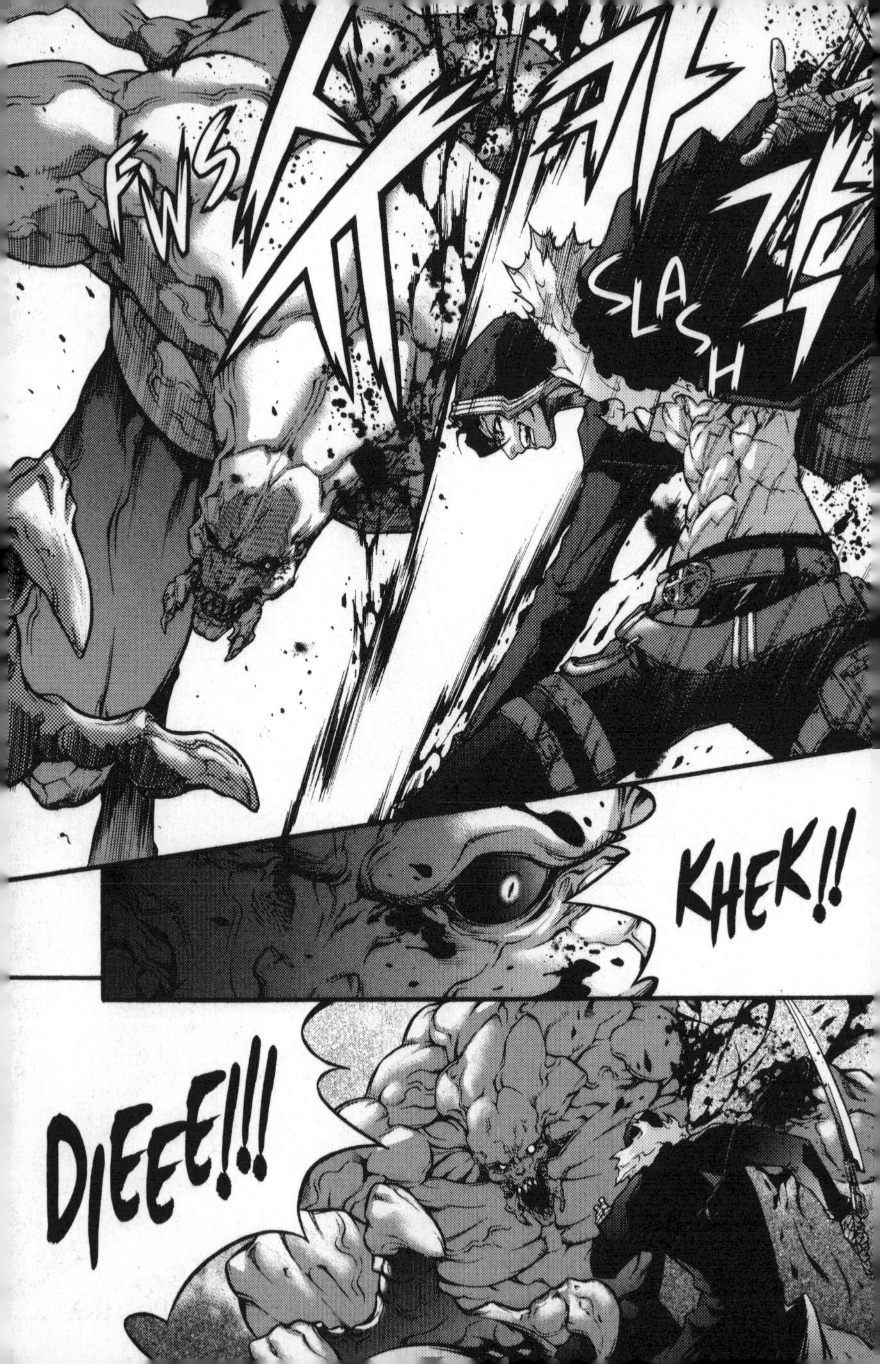
FWS
SLASH
KHEK!!
DIEEE!!!

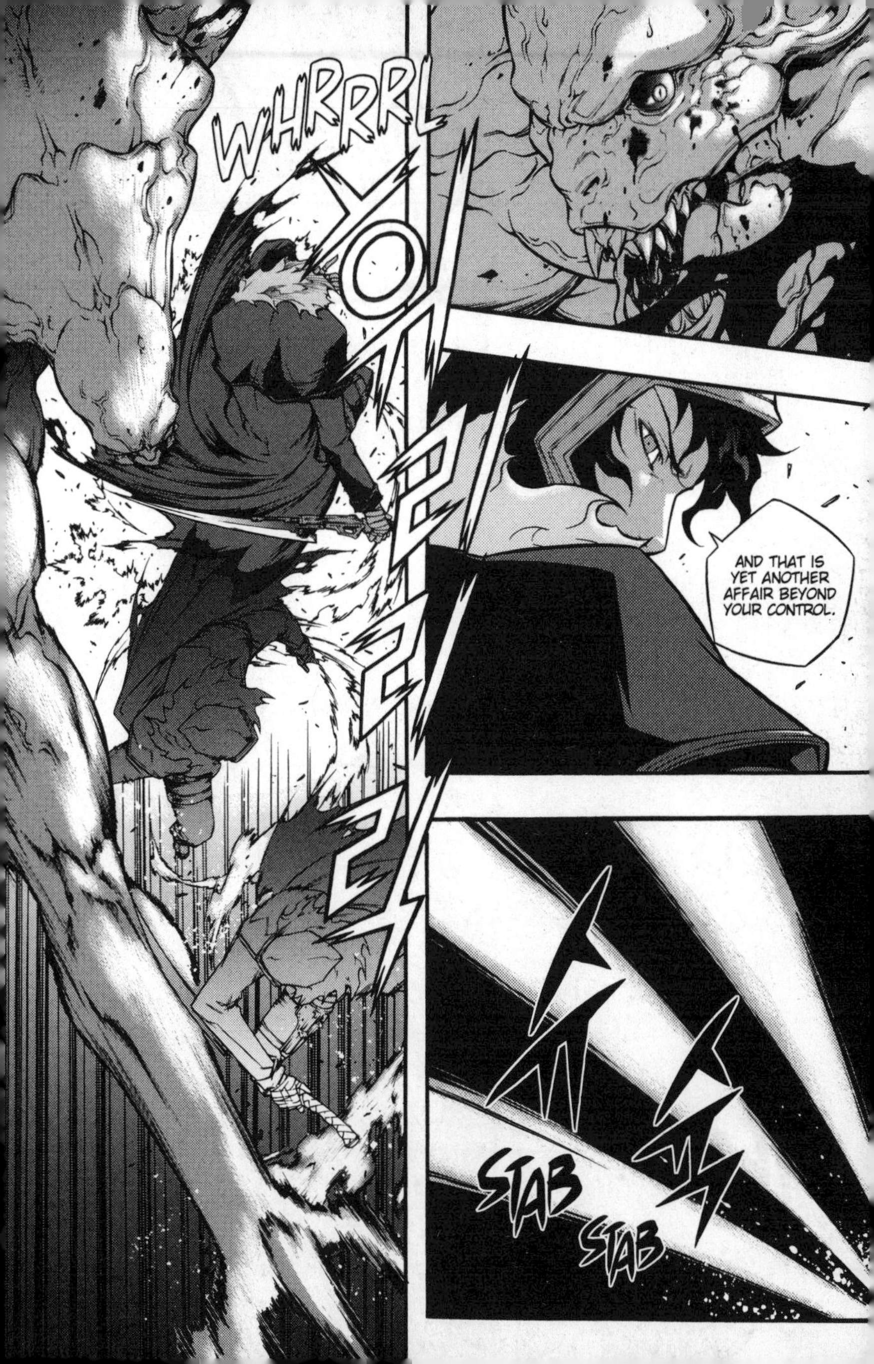
WHRRRL
AND THAT IS YET ANOTHER AFFAIR BEYOND YOUR CONTROL.
STAB
STAB

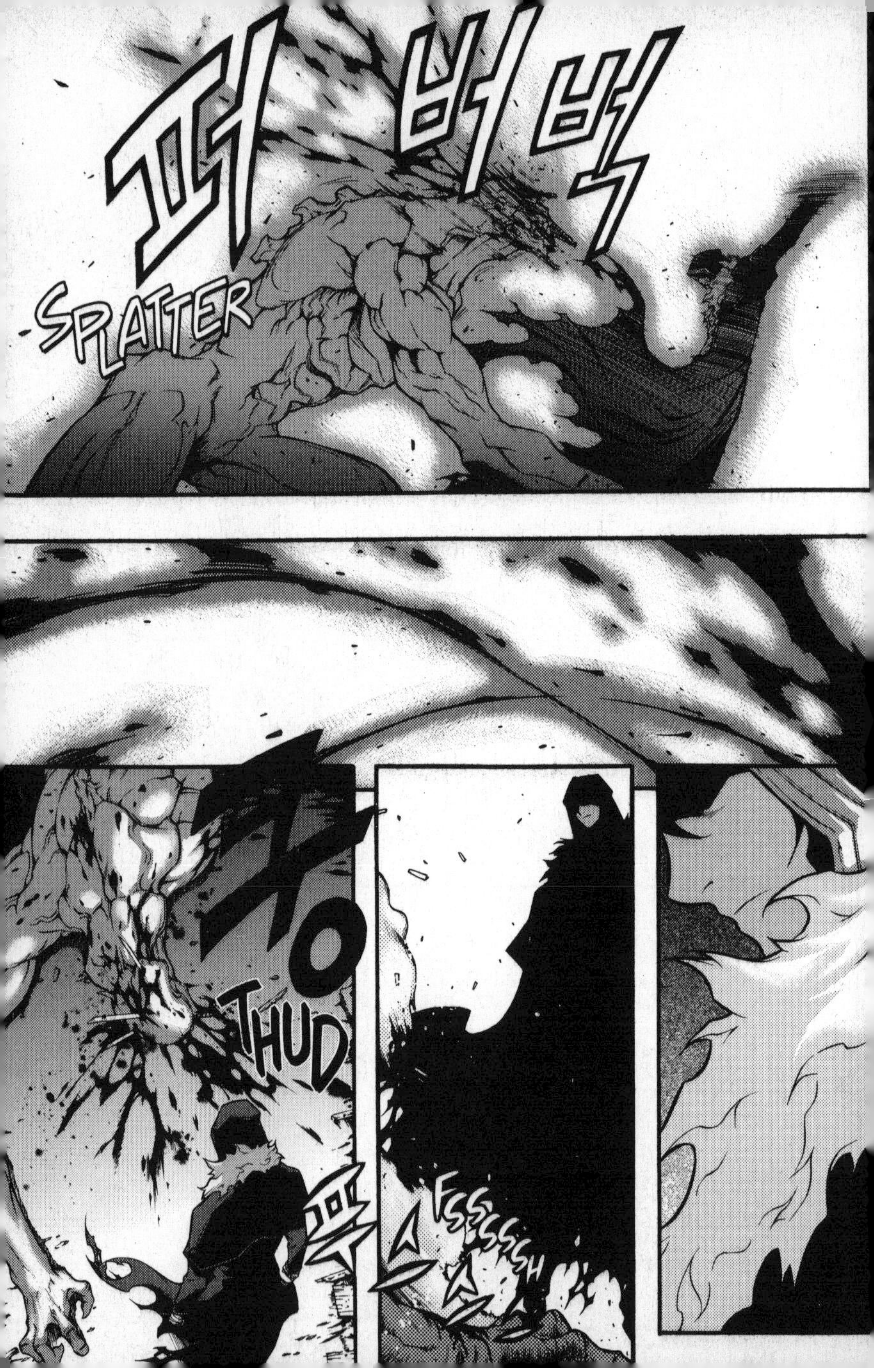
SPLATTER
THUD
FSSSSSSH

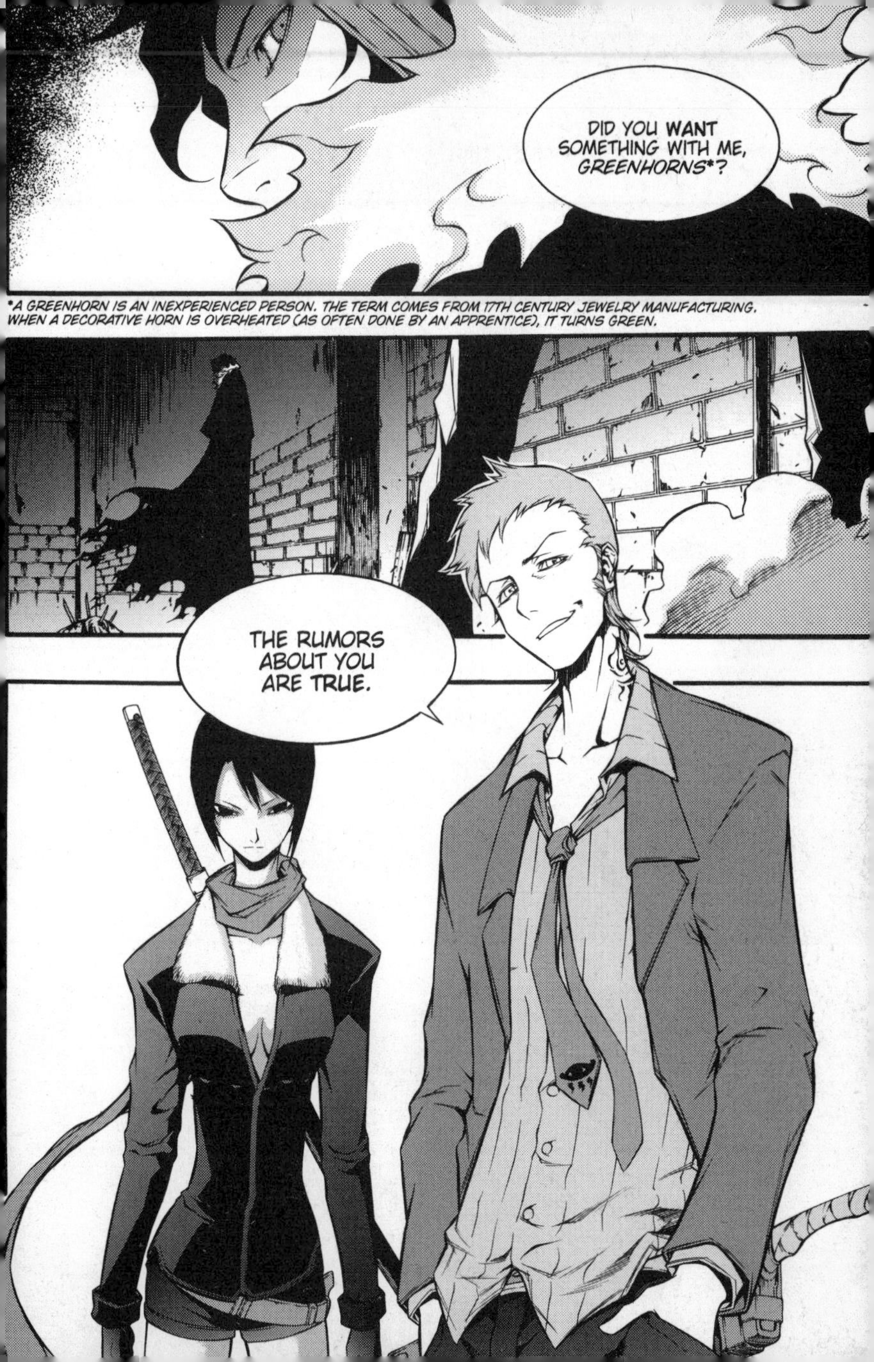
DID YOU WANT SOMETHING WITH ME, GREENHORNS*?
*A GREENHORN IS AN INEXPERIENCED PERSON. THE TERM COMES FROM 17TH CENTURY JEWELRY MANUFACTURING. WHEN A DECORATIVE HORN IS OVERHEATED (AS OFTEN DONE BY AN APPRENTICE), IT TURNS GREEN.
THE RUMORS ABOUT YOU ARE TRUE.

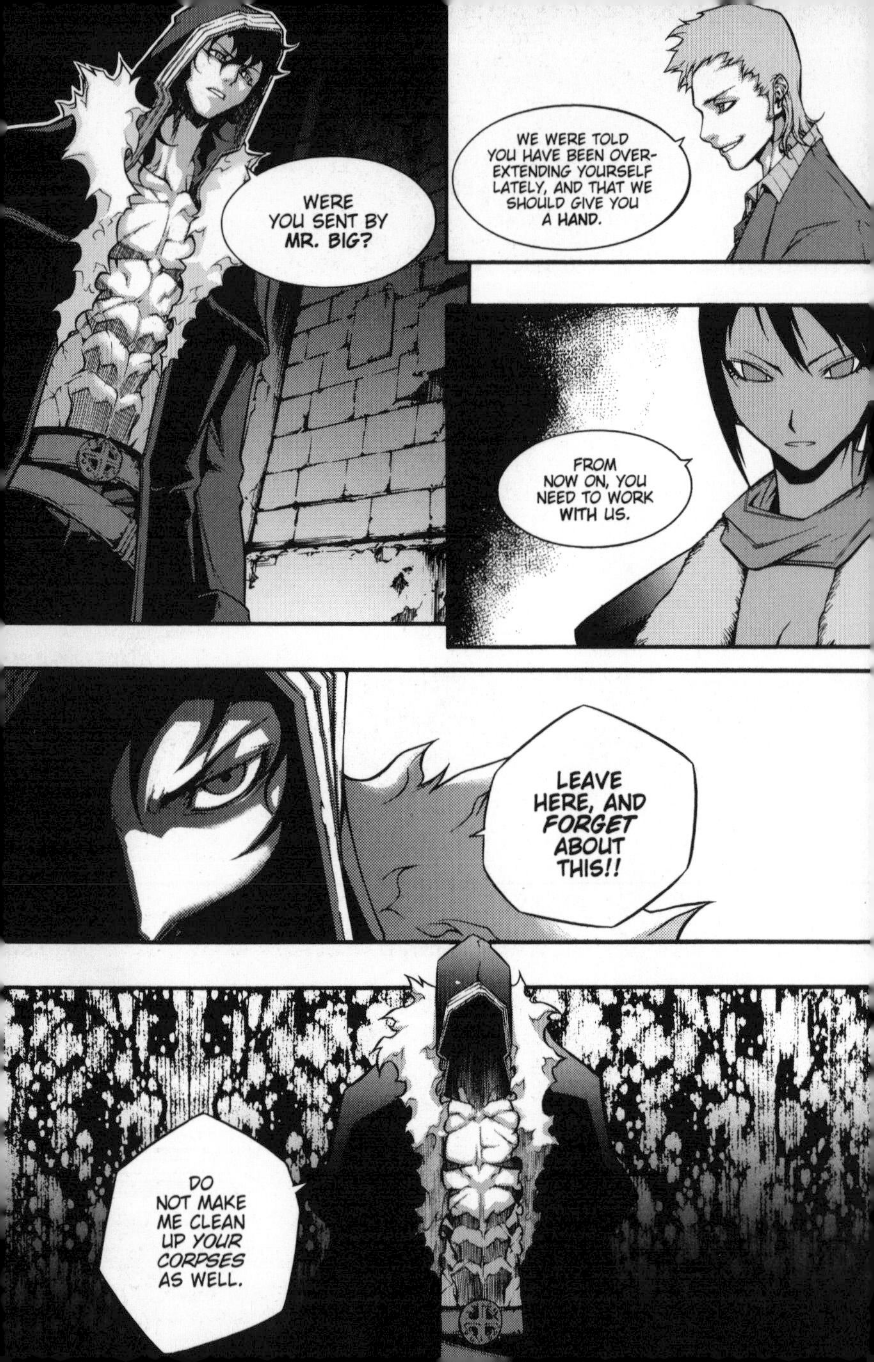
WERE YOU SENT BY MR. BIG?
WE WERE TOLD YOU HAVE BEEN OVER-EXTENDING YOURSELF LATELY, AND THAT WE SHOULD GIVE YOU A HAND.
FROM NOW ON, YOU NEED TO WORK WITH US.
LEAVE HERE, AND *FORGET* ABOUT THIS!!
DO NOT MAKE ME CLEAN UP *YOUR CORPSES* AS WELL.

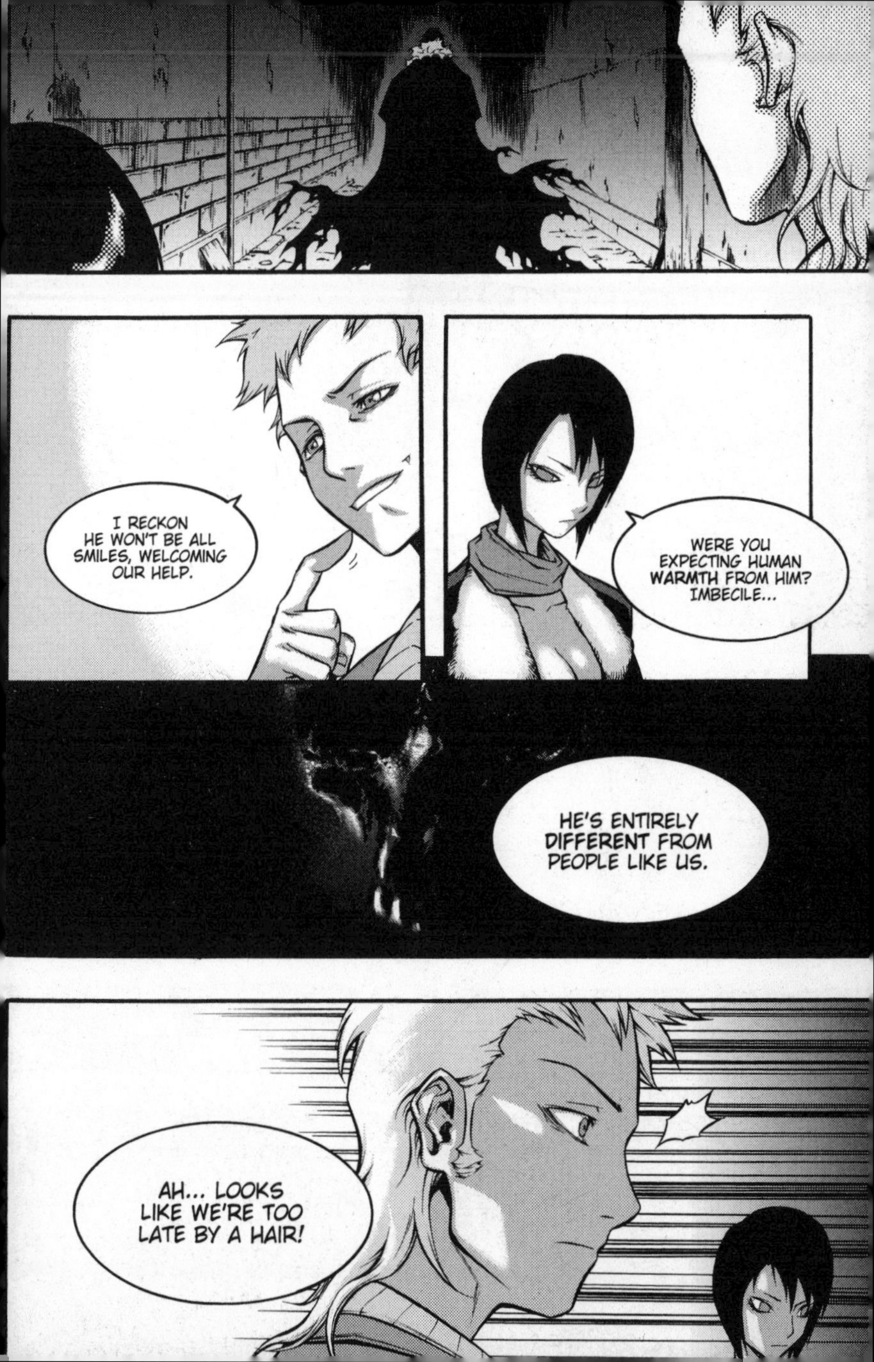
I RECKON HE WON'T BE ALL SMILES, WELCOMING OUR HELP.
WERE YOU EXPECTING HUMAN WARMTH FROM HIM? IMBECILE...
HE'S ENTIRELY DIFFERENT FROM PEOPLE LIKE US.
AH... LOOKS LIKE WE'RE TOO LATE BY A HAIR!

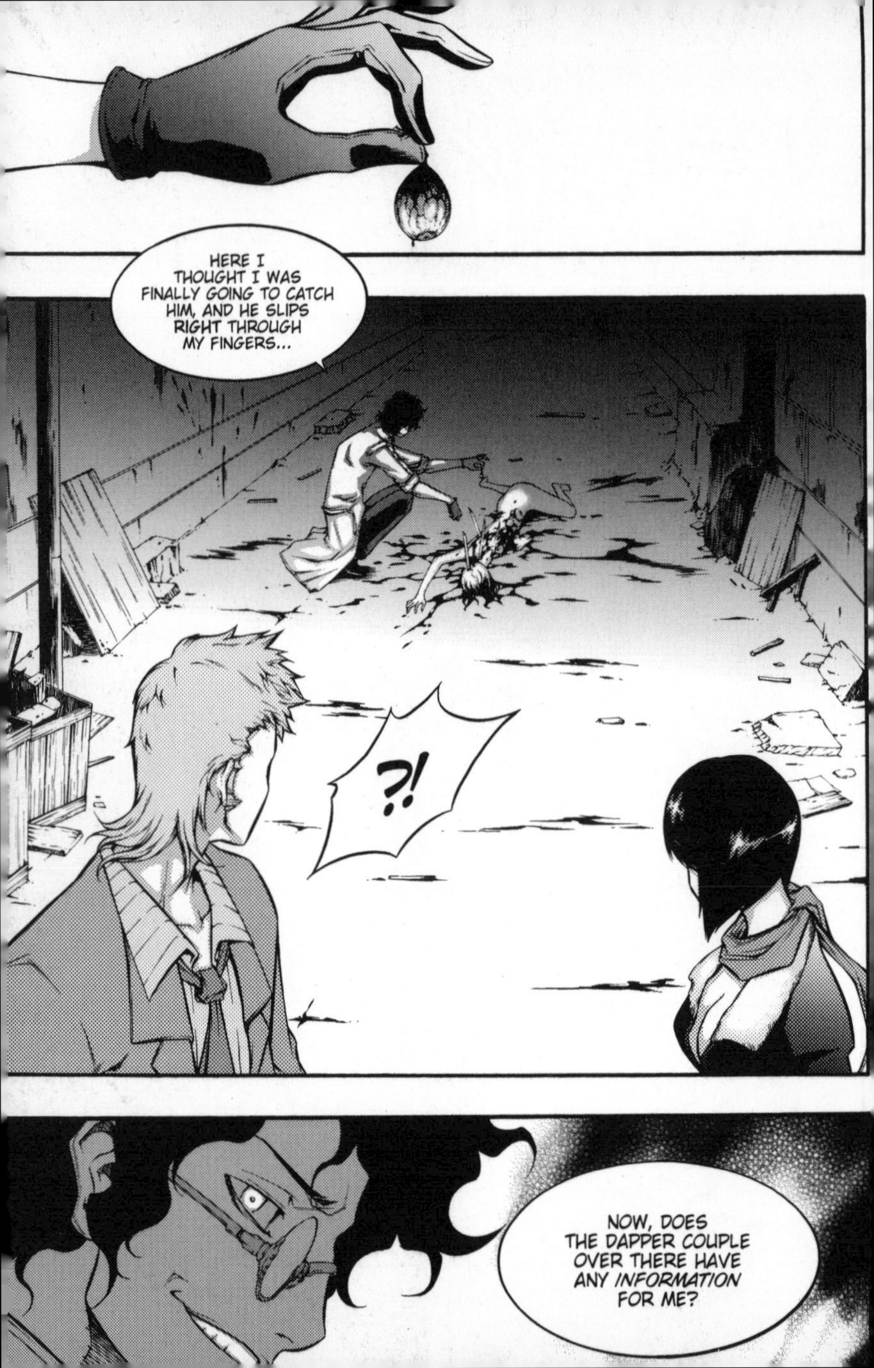
HERE I THOUGHT I WAS FINALLY GOING TO CATCH HIM, AND HE SLIPS RIGHT THROUGH MY FINGERS...
?!
NOW, DOES THE DAPPER COUPLE OVER THERE HAVE ANY *INFORMATION* FOR ME?

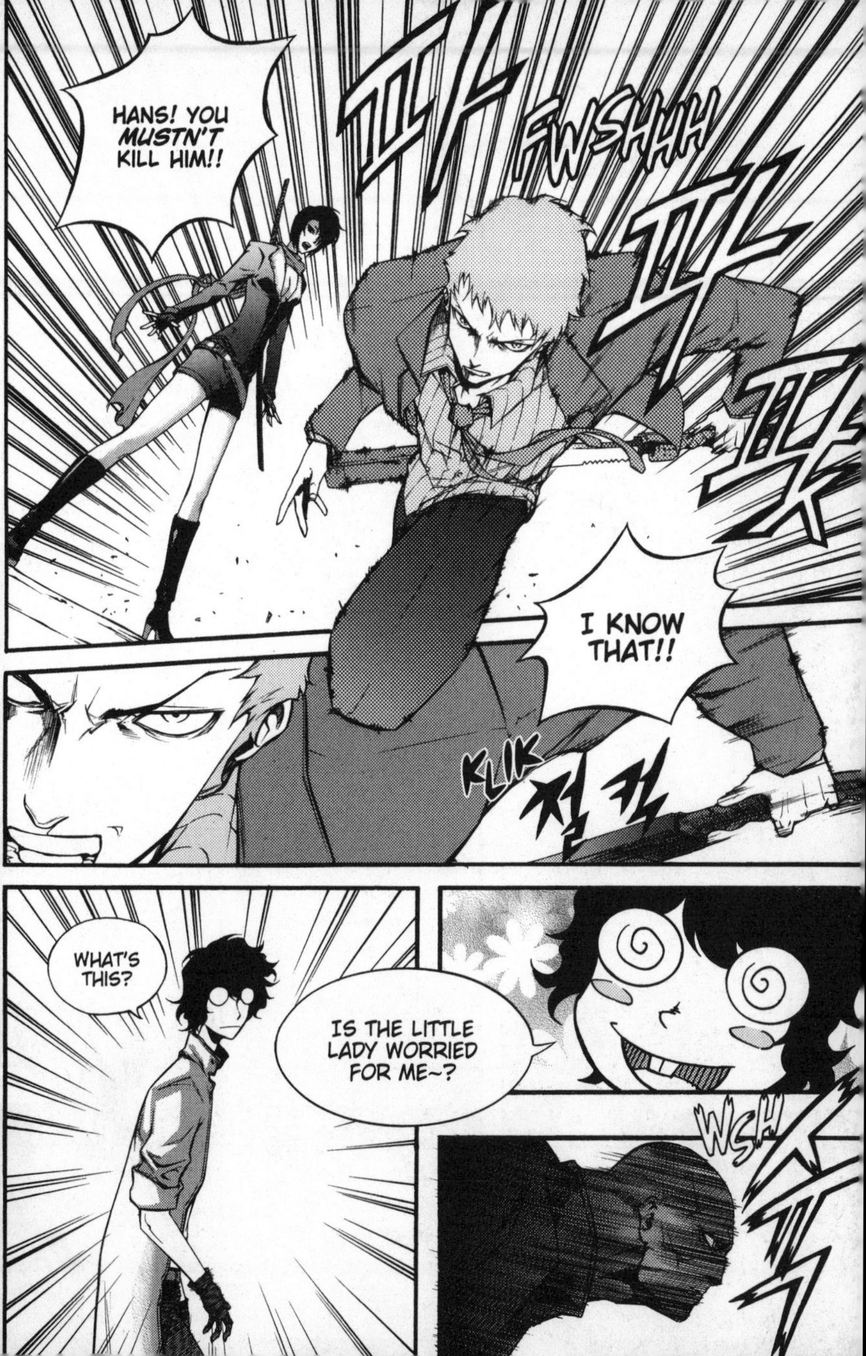
HANS! YOU MUSTN'T KILL HIM!!
FWSHHH
I KNOW THAT!!
KLIK
WHAT'S THIS?
IS THE LITTLE LADY WORRIED FOR ME~?
WSH

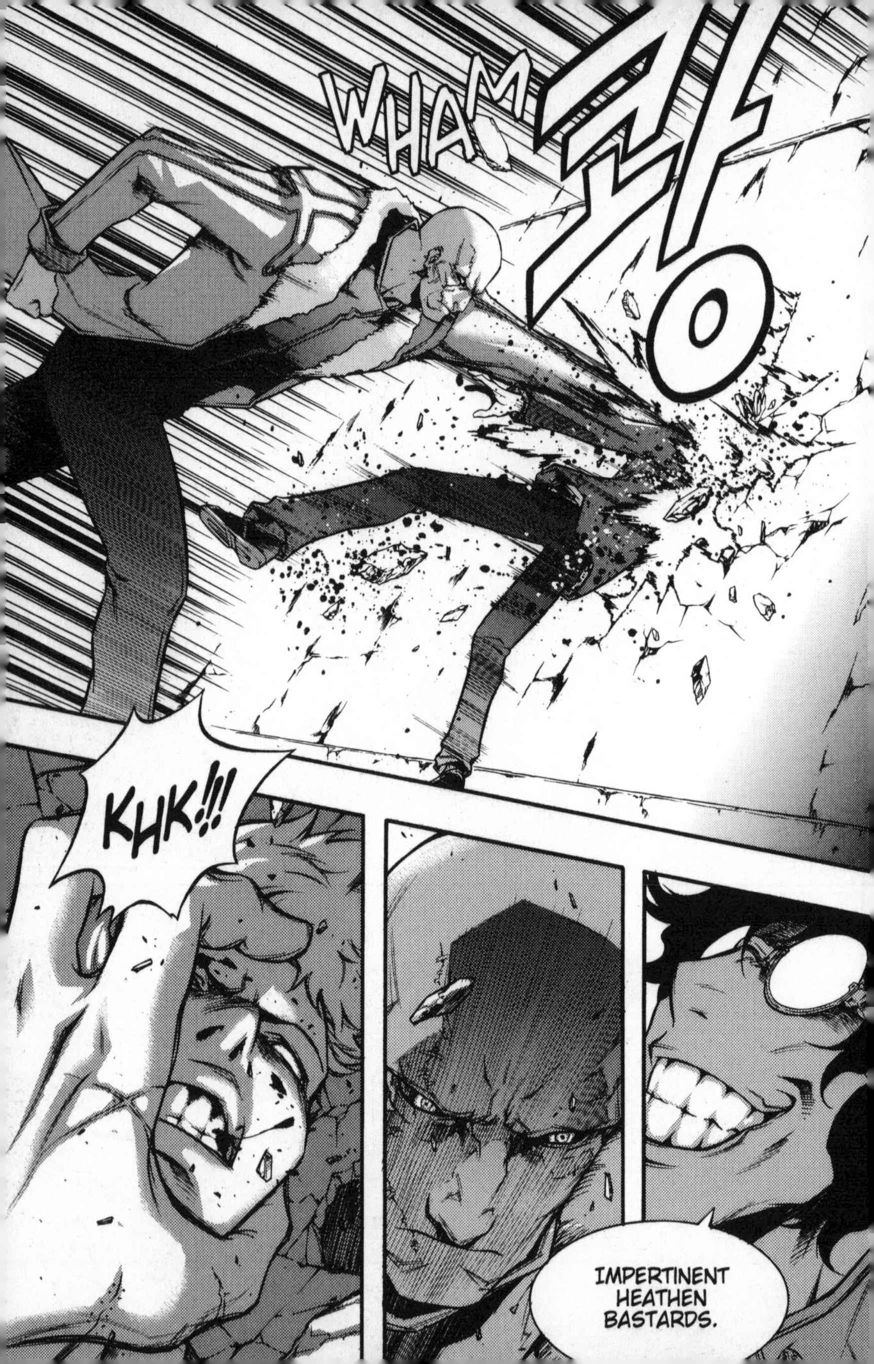
WHAM
ZAK
KHK!!!
IMPERTINENT HEATHEN BASTARDS.

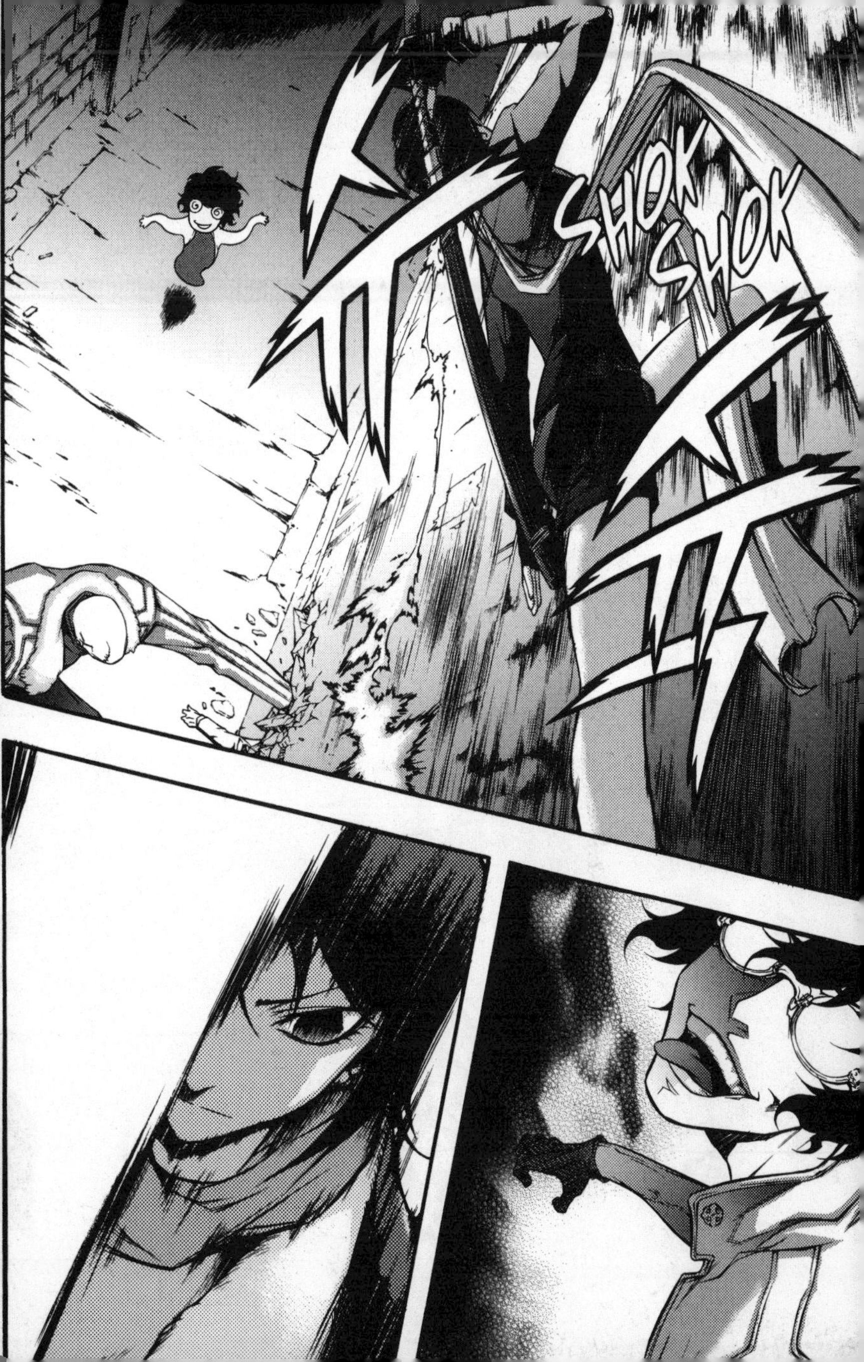
SHOK SHOK

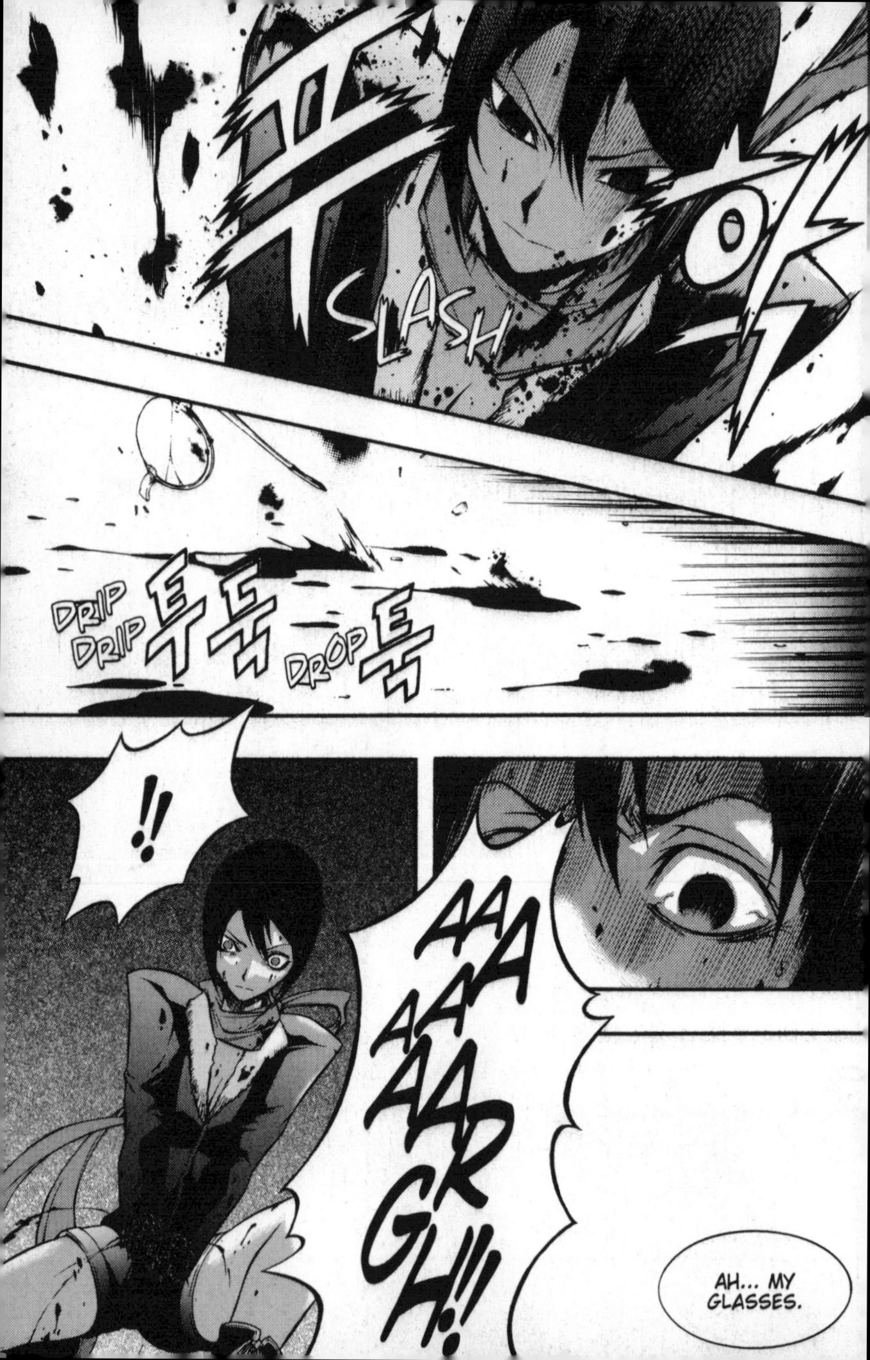
SLASH
DRIP
DRIP
DROP
!!
AAAAAAAARGH!!
AH... MY GLASSES.

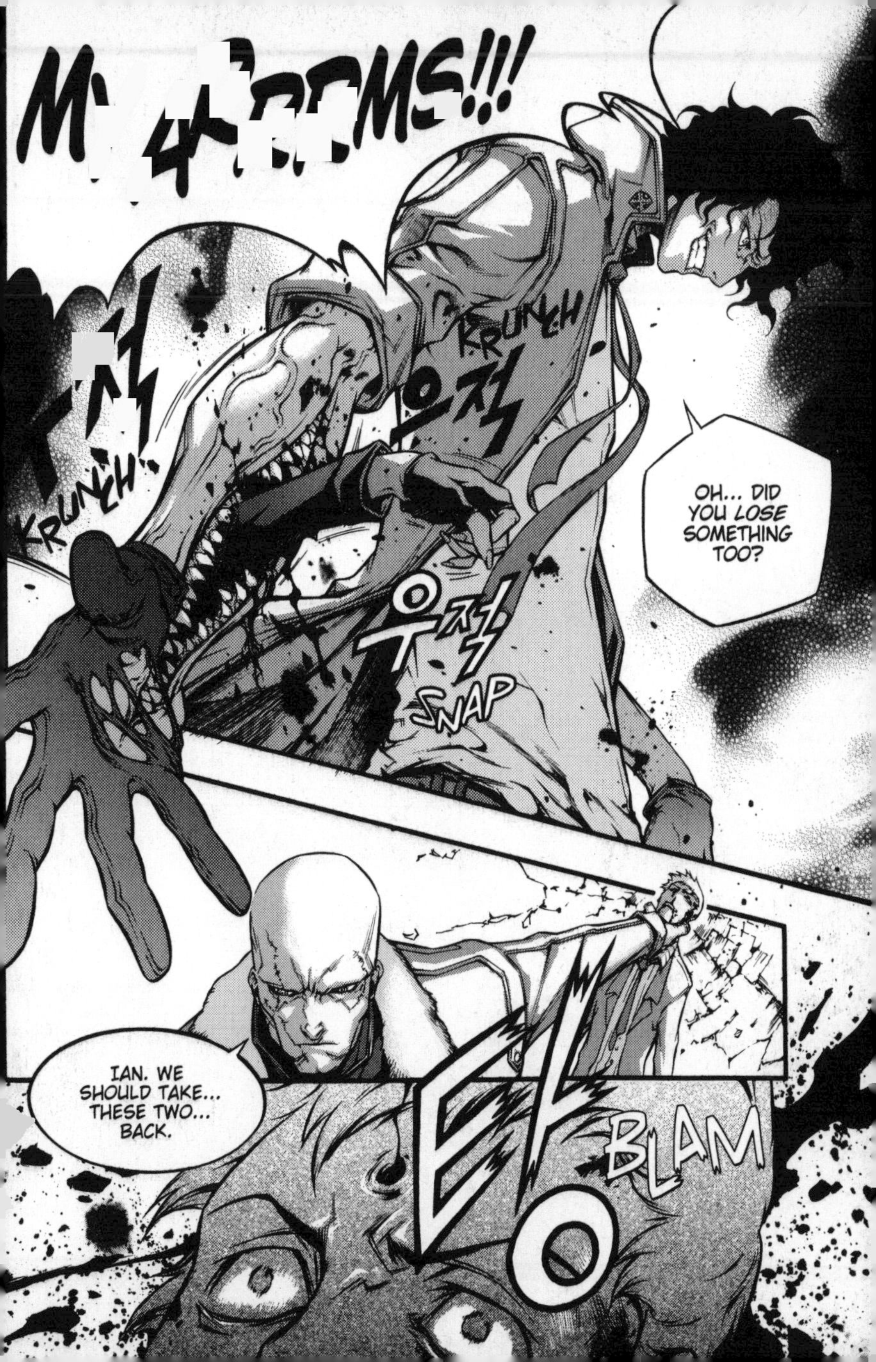
KRUNCH
KRUNCH
OH... DID YOU LOSE SOMETHING TOO?
SNAP
IAN. WE SHOULD TAKE... THESE TWO... BACK.
BLAM

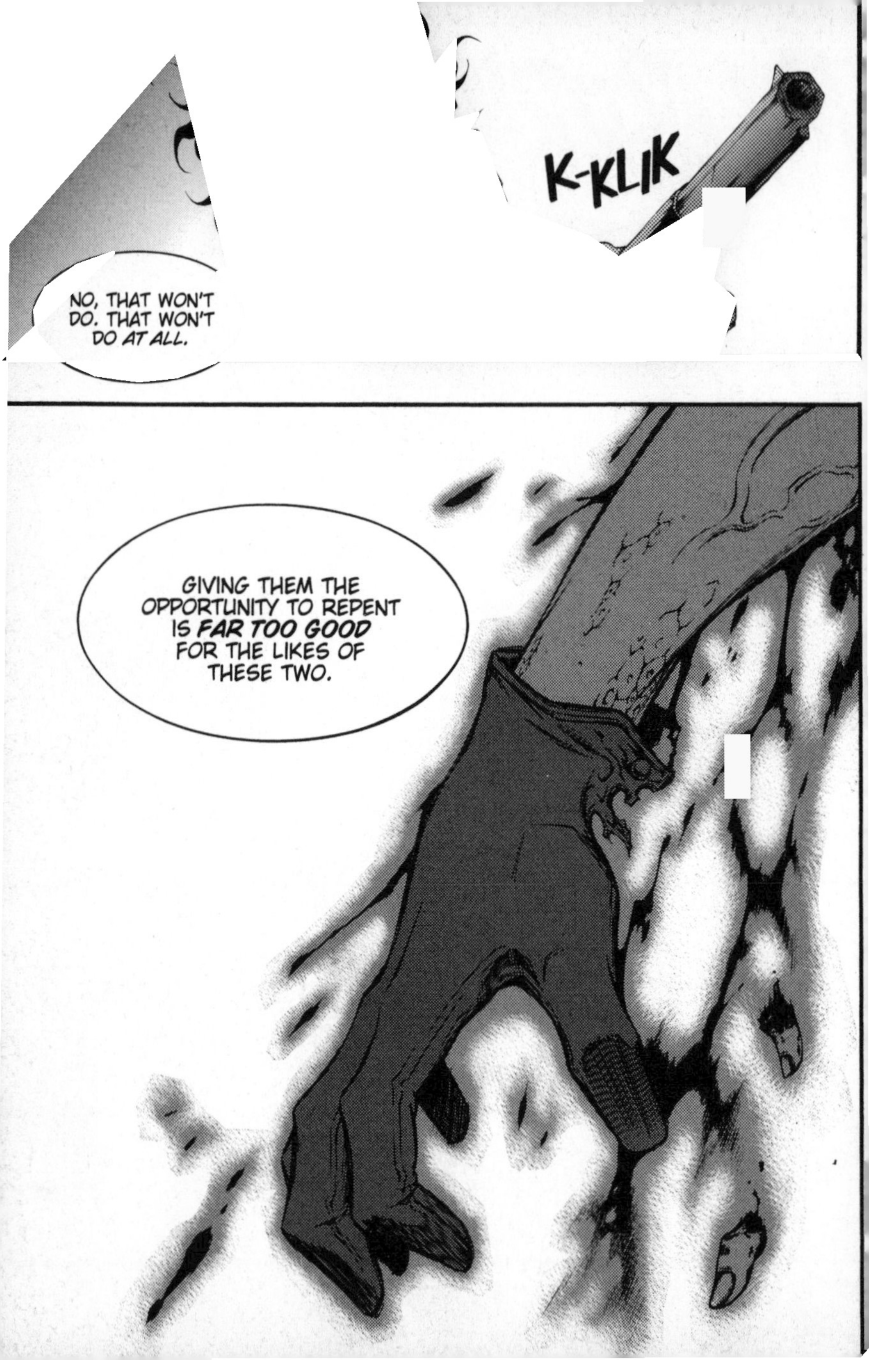
K-KLIK
NO, THAT WON'T DO. THAT WON'T DO AT ALL.
GIVING THEM THE OPPORTUNITY TO REPENT IS FAR TOO GOOD FOR THE LIKES OF THESE TWO.

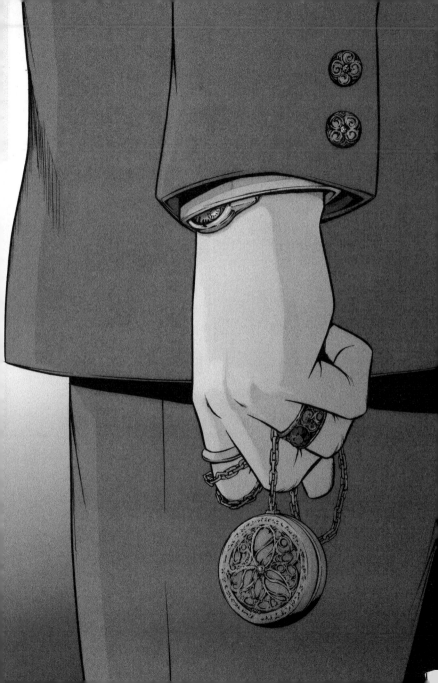

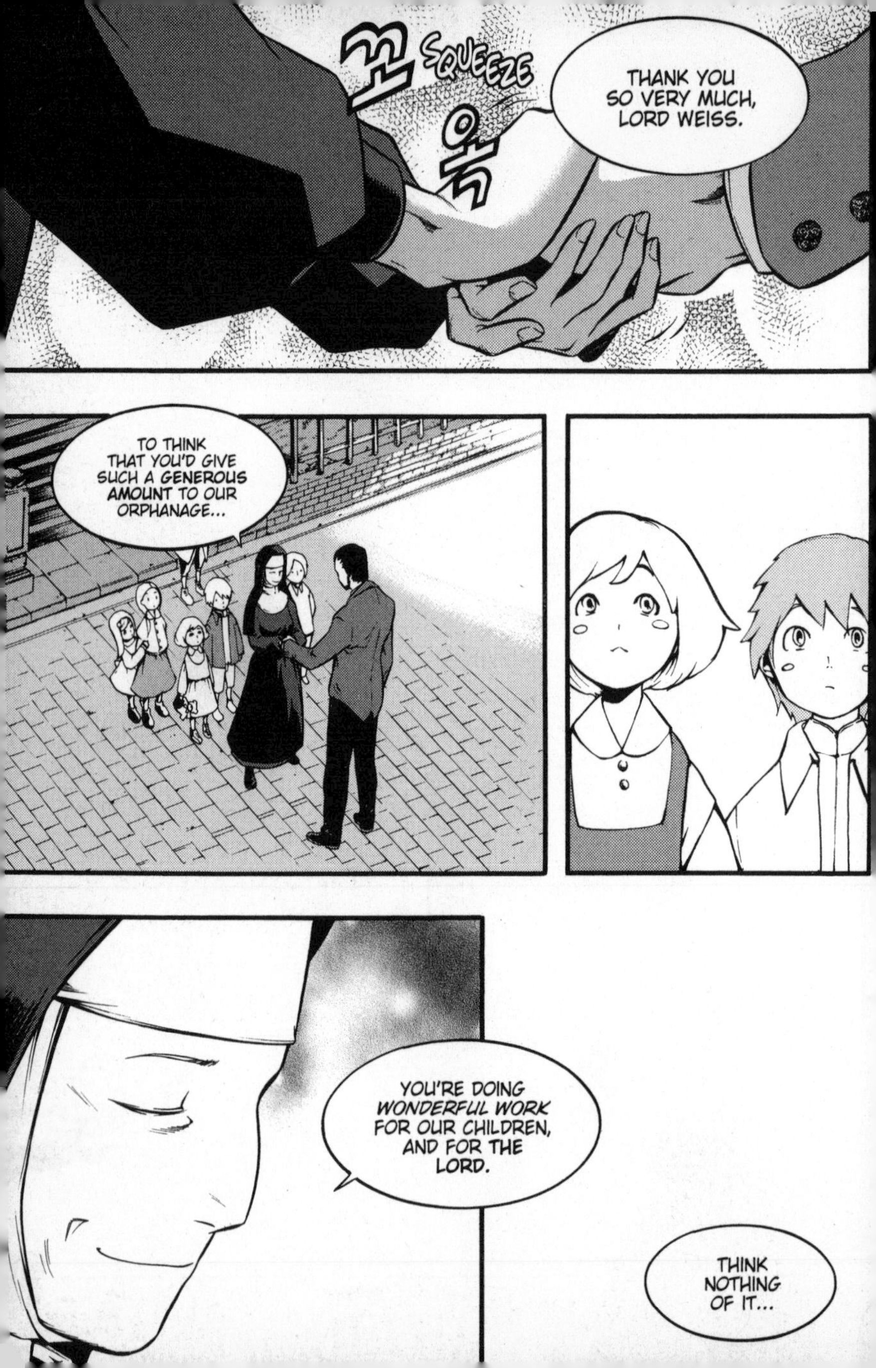
꼬옥
SQUEEZE
THANK YOU SO VERY MUCH, LORD WEISS.
TO THINK THAT YOU'D GIVE SUCH A GENEROUS AMOUNT TO OUR ORPHANAGE...
YOU'RE DOING WONDERFUL WORK FOR OUR CHILDREN, AND FOR THE LORD.
THINK NOTHING OF IT...

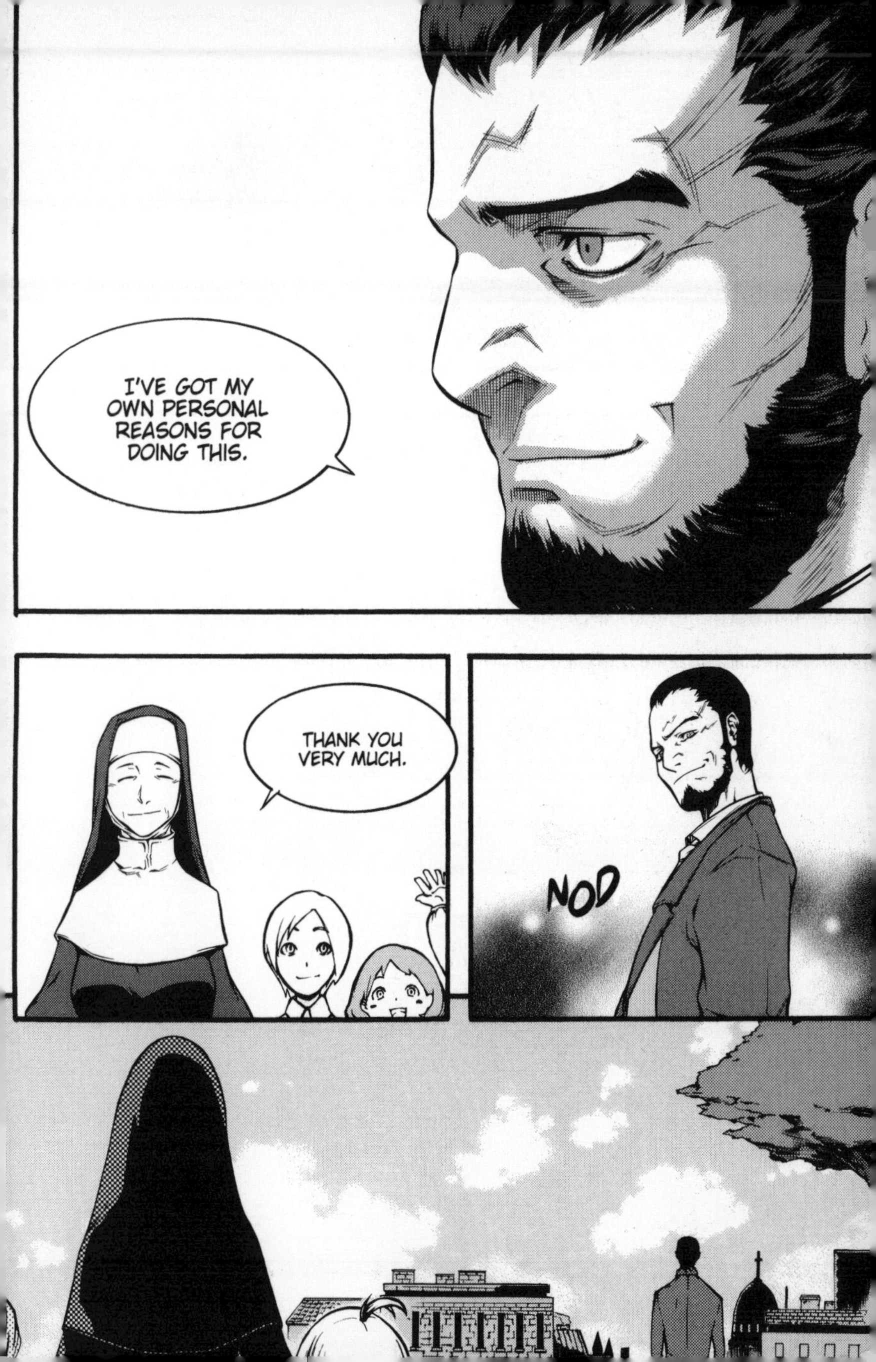
I'VE GOT MY OWN PERSONAL REASONS FOR DOING THIS.
THANK YOU VERY MUCH.
NOD

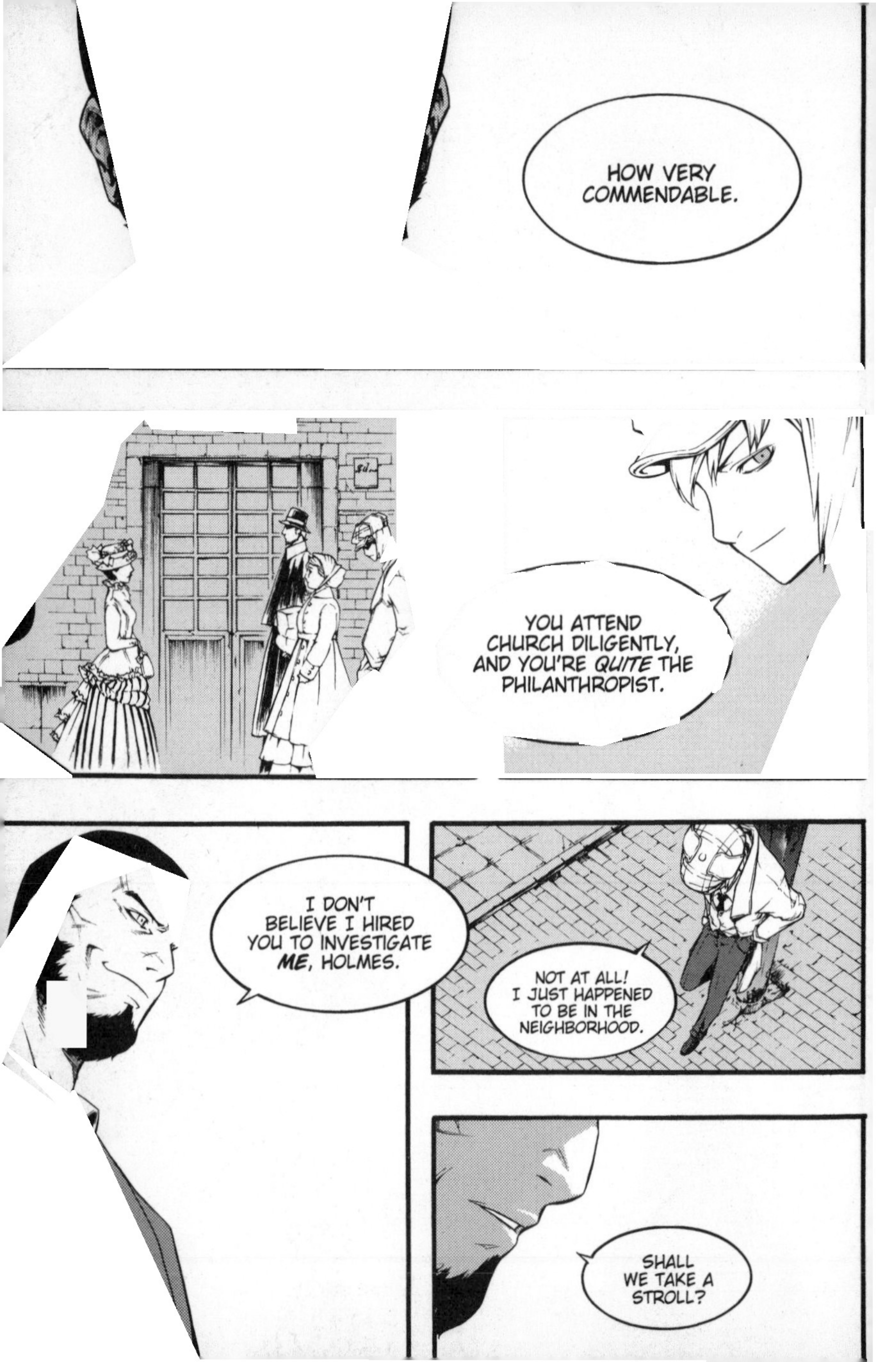
HOW VERY COMMENDABLE.
YOU ATTEND CHURCH DILIGENTLY, AND YOU'RE *QUITE* THE PHILANTHROPIST.
I DON'T BELIEVE I HIRED YOU TO INVESTIGATE ***ME***, HOLMES.
NOT AT ALL! I JUST HAPPENED TO BE IN THE NEIGHBORHOOD.
SHALL WE TAKE A STROLL?

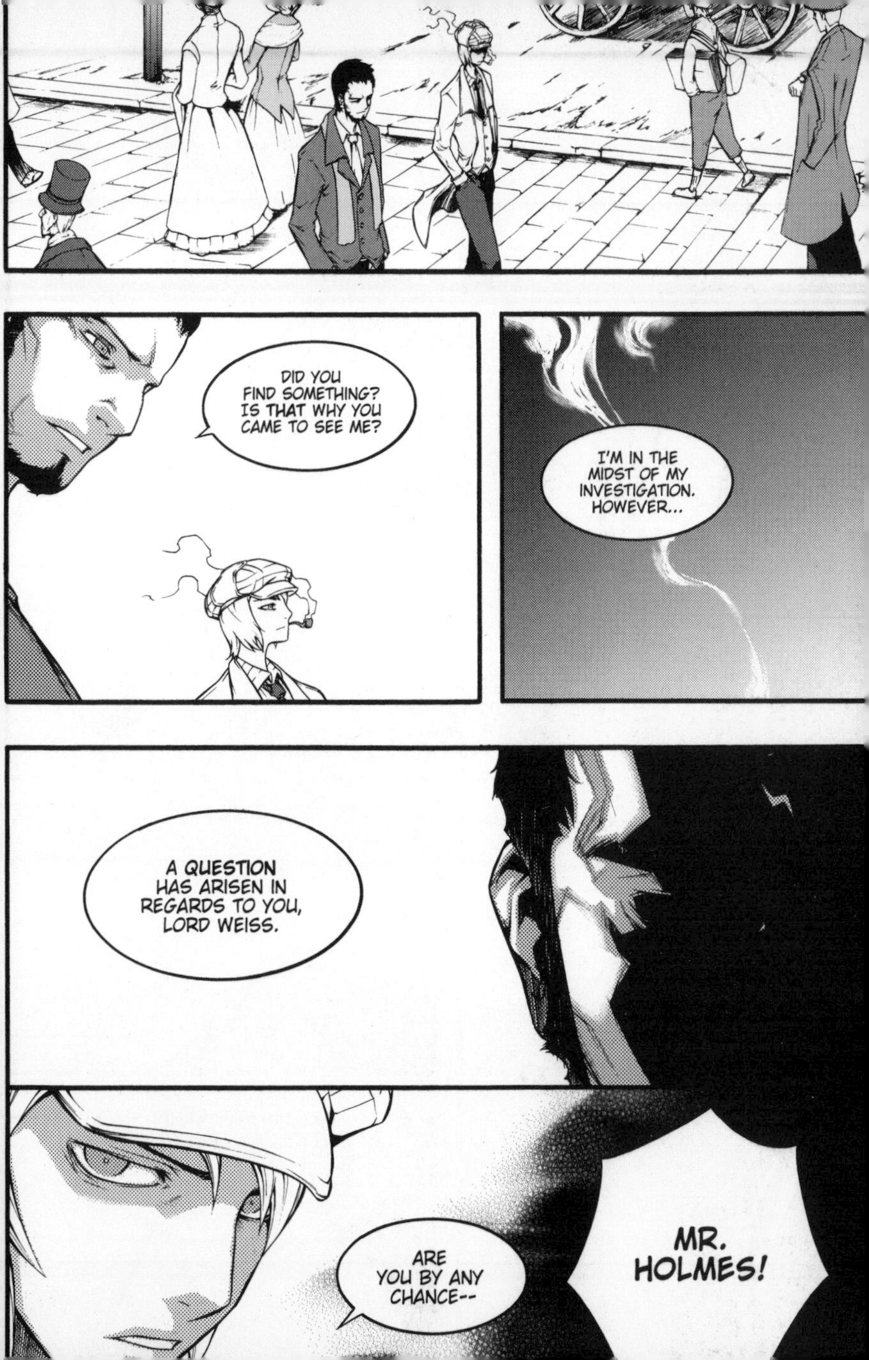
DID YOU FIND SOMETHING? IS THAT WHY YOU CAME TO SEE ME?
I'M IN THE MIDST OF MY INVESTIGATION. HOWEVER...
A QUESTION HAS ARISEN IN REGARDS TO YOU, LORD WEISS.
ARE YOU BY ANY CHANCE--
MR. HOLMES!

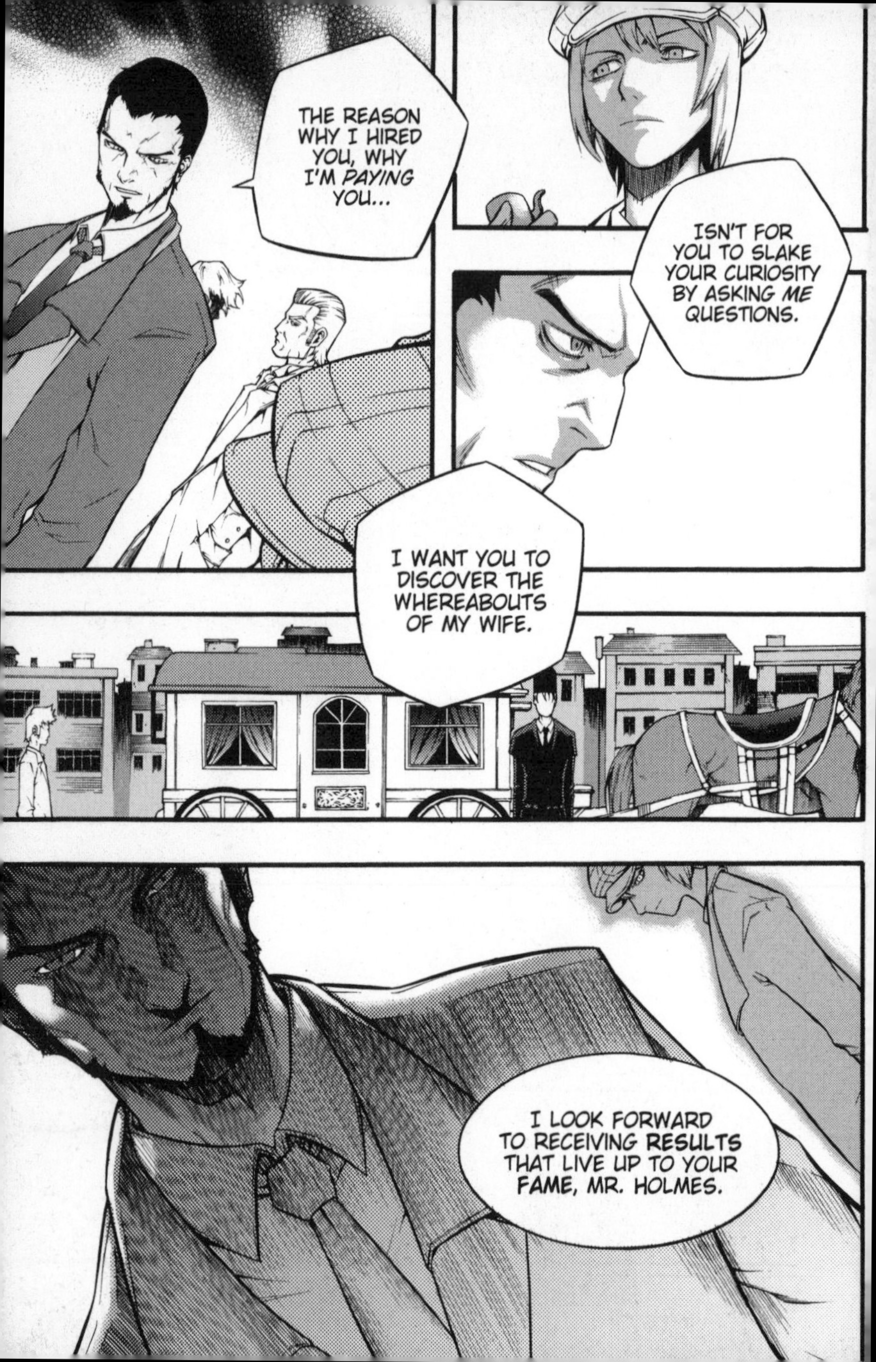
THE REASON WHY I HIRED YOU, WHY I'M *PAYING* YOU...
ISN'T FOR YOU TO SLAKE YOUR CURIOSITY BY ASKING *ME* QUESTIONS.
I WANT YOU TO DISCOVER THE WHEREABOUTS OF MY WIFE.
I LOOK FORWARD TO RECEIVING **RESULTS** THAT LIVE UP TO YOUR **FAME**, MR. HOLMES.

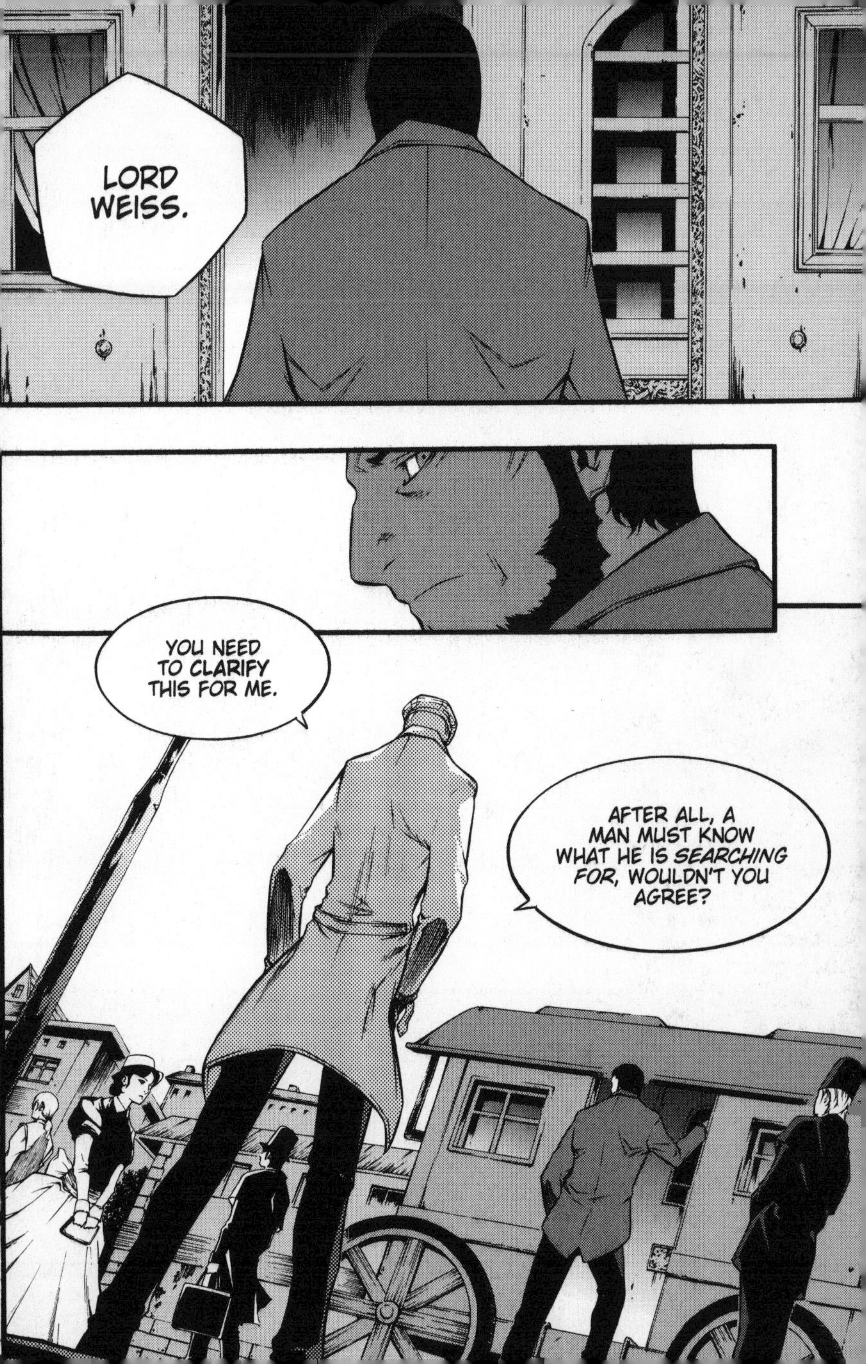
LORD WEISS.
YOU NEED TO CLARIFY THIS FOR ME.
AFTER ALL, A MAN MUST KNOW WHAT HE IS *SEARCHING FOR*, WOULDN'T YOU AGREE?

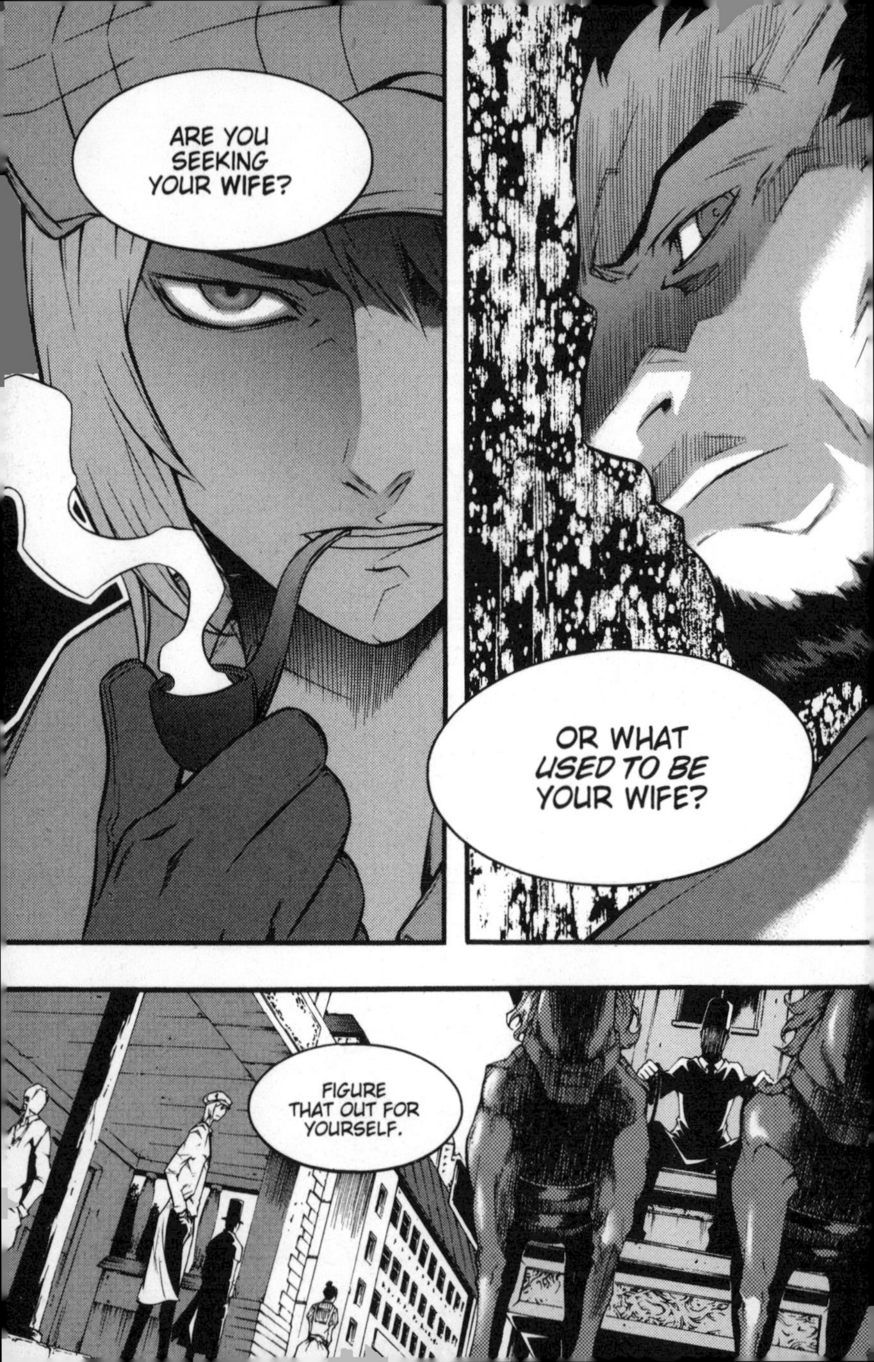
ARE YOU SEEKING YOUR WIFE?
OR WHAT *USED TO BE* YOUR WIFE?
FIGURE THAT OUT FOR YOURSELF.

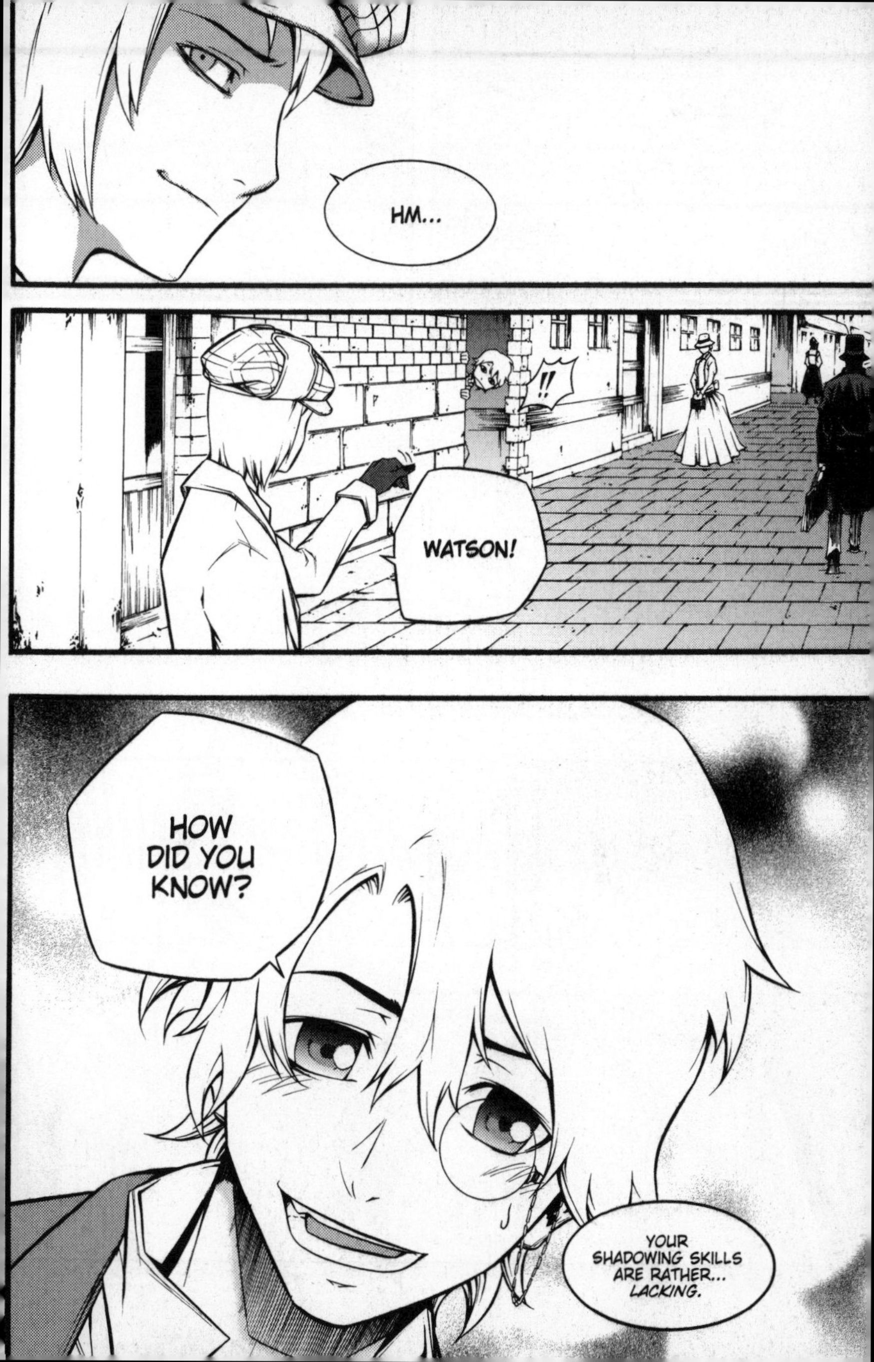
HM...
WATSON!
!!
HOW DID YOU KNOW?
YOUR SHADOWING SKILLS ARE RATHER... *LACKING.*

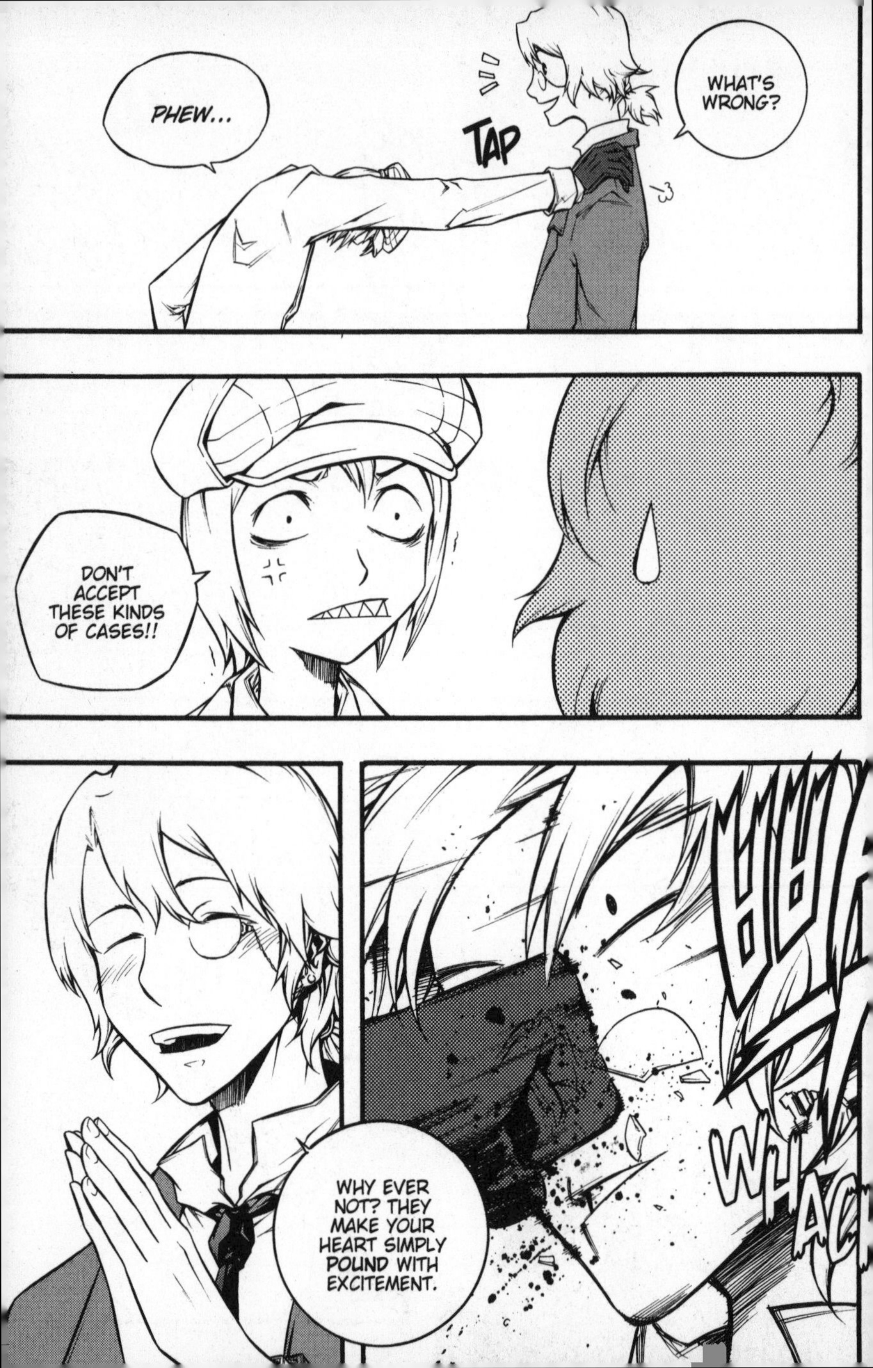
PHEW...
TAP
WHAT'S WRONG?
DON'T ACCEPT THESE KINDS OF CASES!!
WHY EVER NOT? THEY MAKE YOUR HEART SIMPLY POUND WITH EXCITEMENT.
WHAC

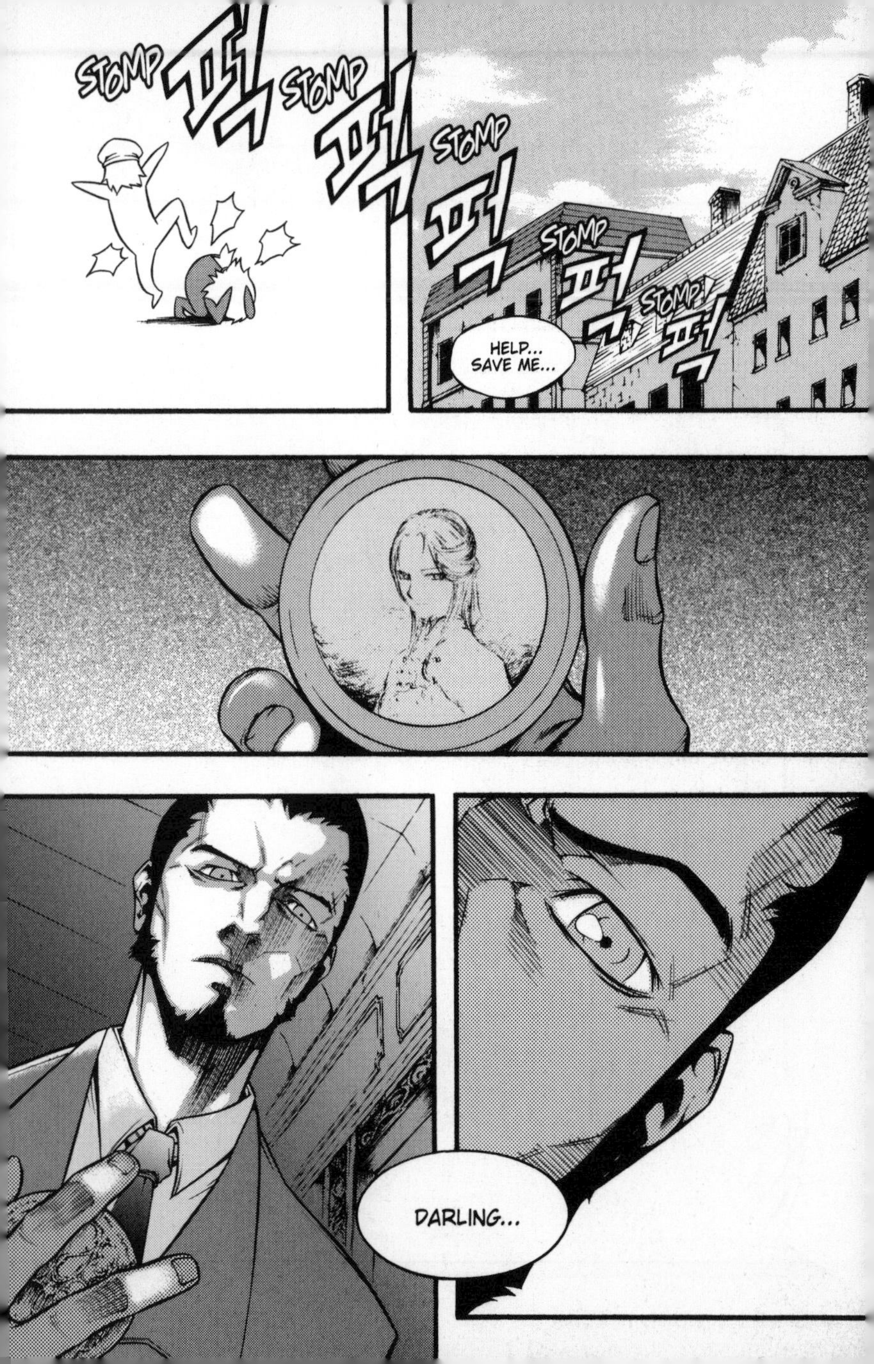
STOMP
퍽
STOMP
퍽
STOMP
퍽
STOMP
퍽
STOMP!
퍽
HELP... SAVE ME...
DARLING...

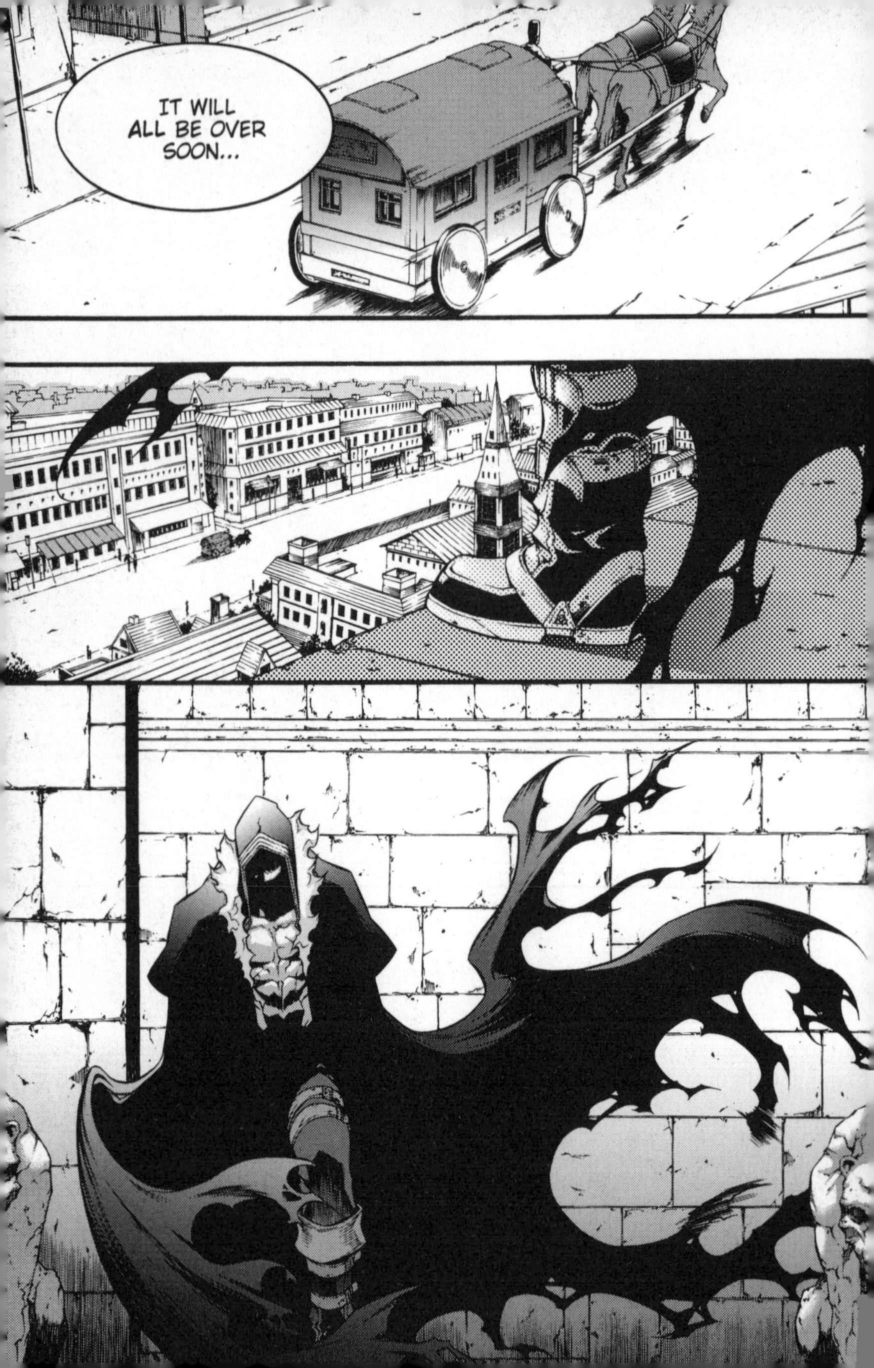
IT WILL ALL BE OVER SOON...

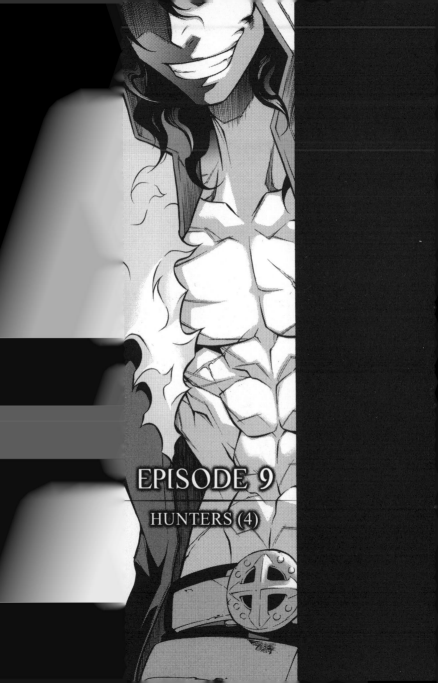

EPISODE 9

HUNTERS (4)

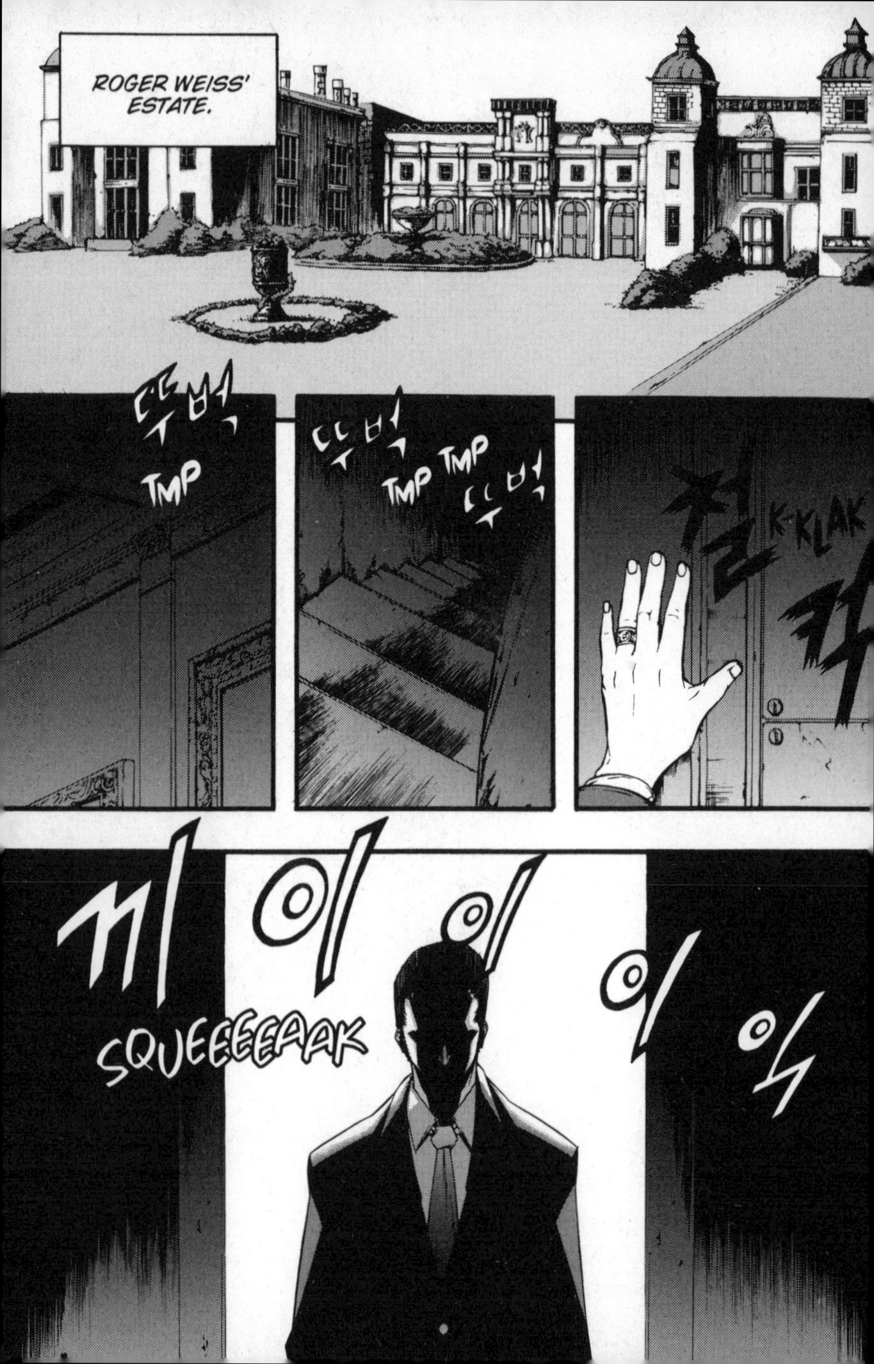
ROGER WEISS' ESTATE.
뚜벅
TMP
뚜벅
TMP TMP
뚜벅
K-KLAK
끼이이이익
SQUEEEEEAAK

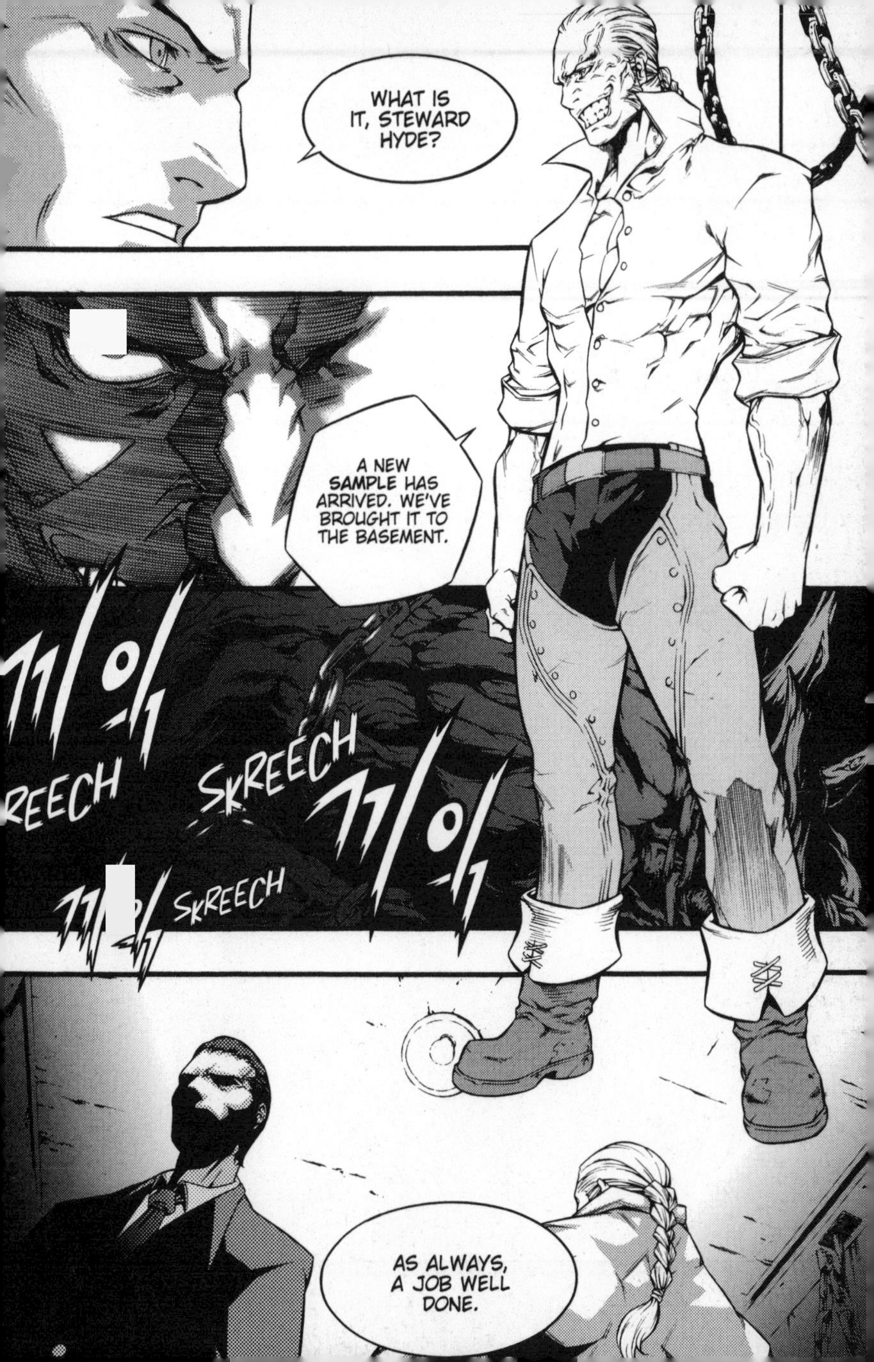
WHAT IS IT, STEWARD HYDE?
A NEW SAMPLE HAS ARRIVED. WE'VE BROUGHT IT TO THE BASEMENT.
REECH
SKREECH
SKREECH
AS ALWAYS, A JOB WELL DONE.

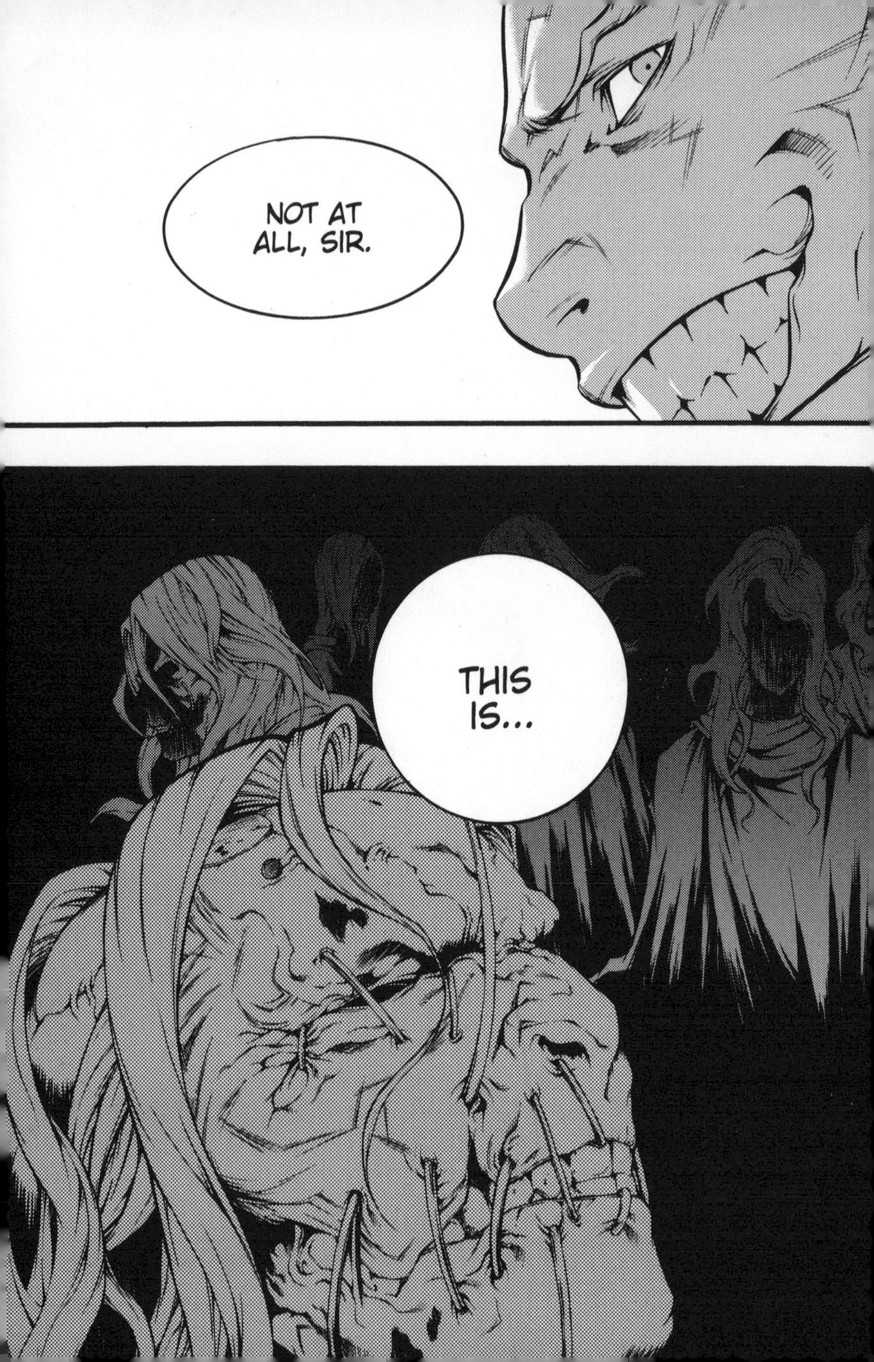
NOT AT ALL, SIR.
THIS IS...

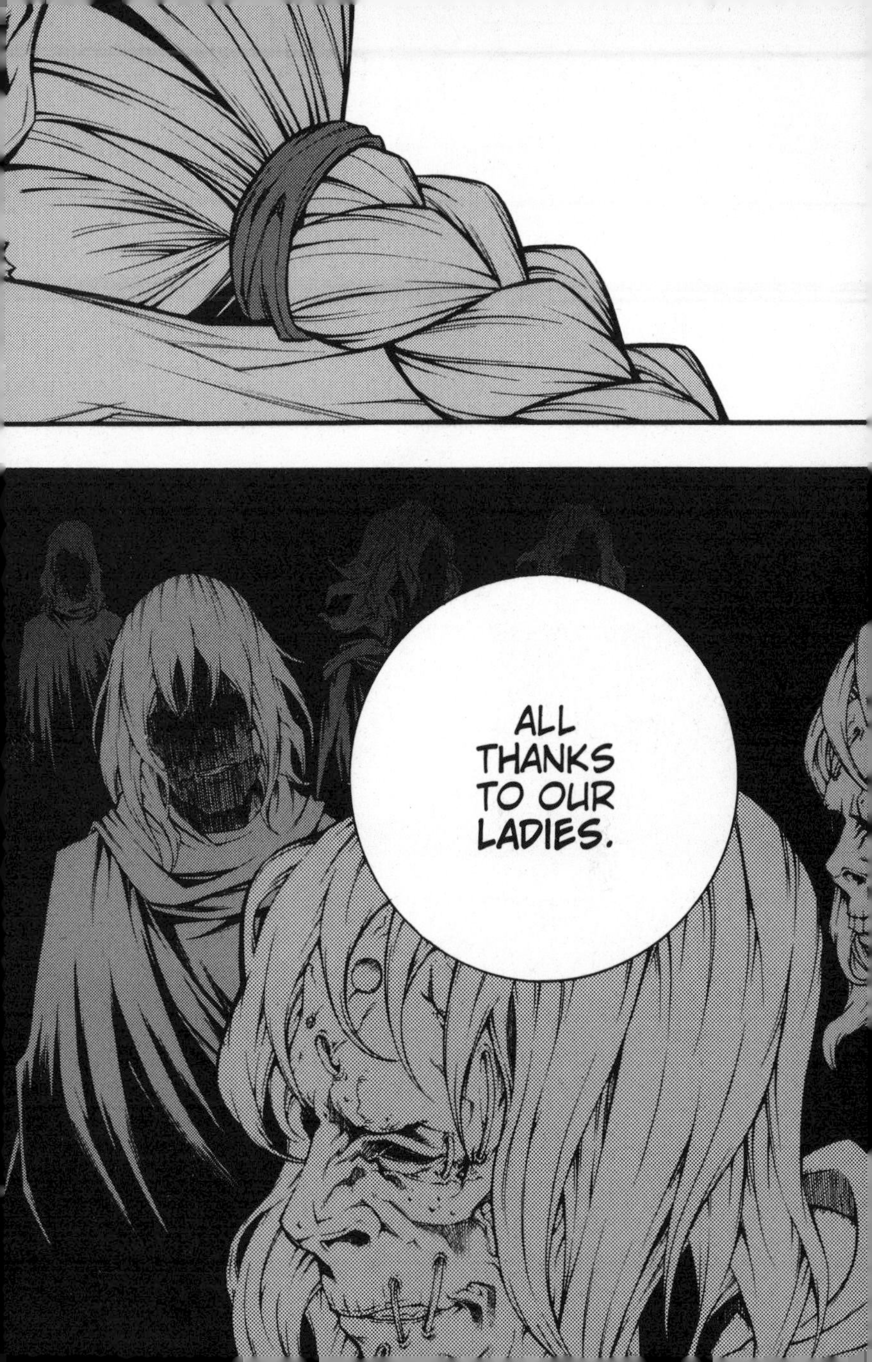
ALL THANKS TO OUR LADIES.

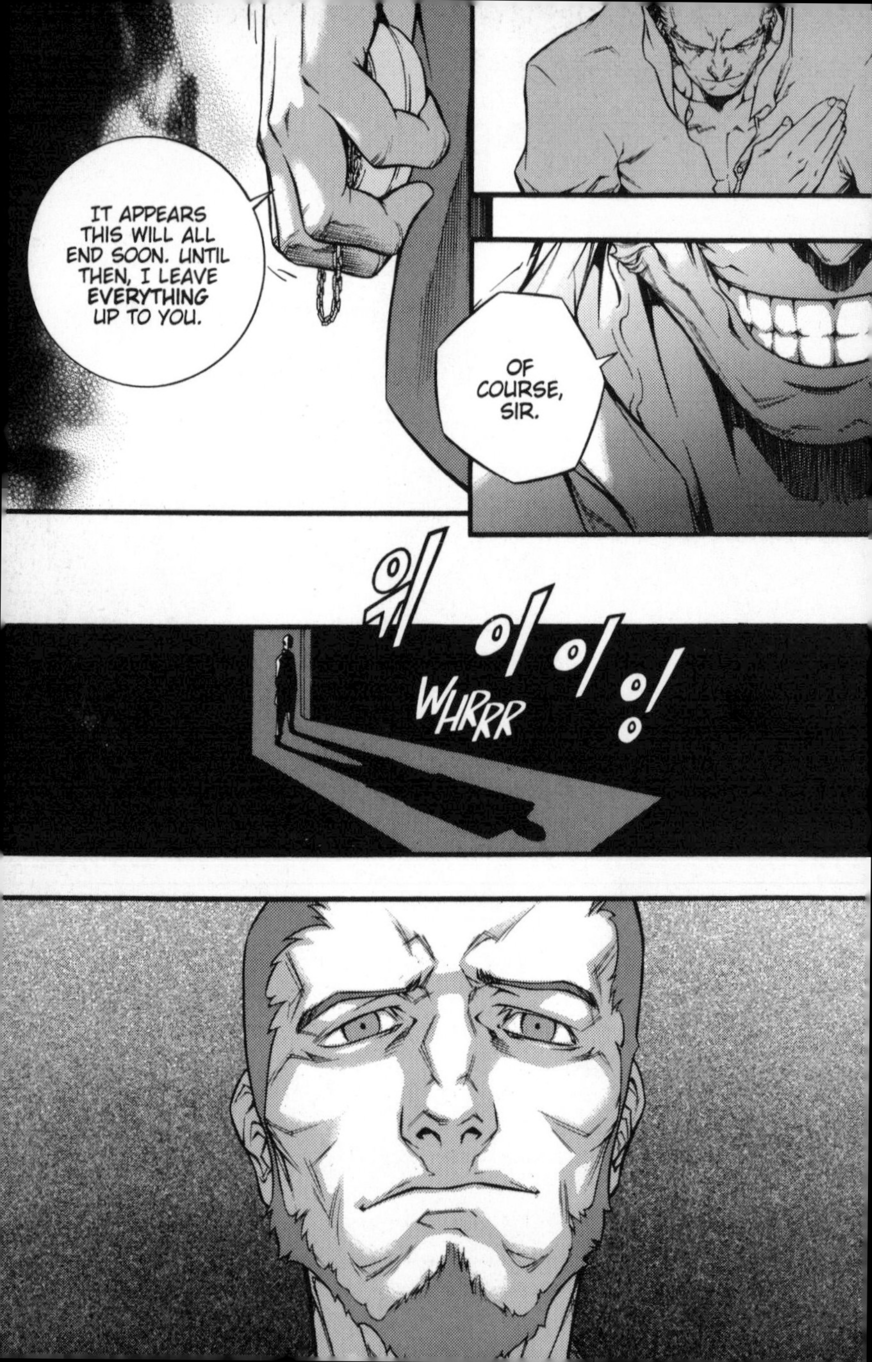
IT APPEARS THIS WILL ALL END SOON. UNTIL THEN, I LEAVE EVERYTHING UP TO YOU.
OF COURSE, SIR.
웨이이잉!
WHRRR

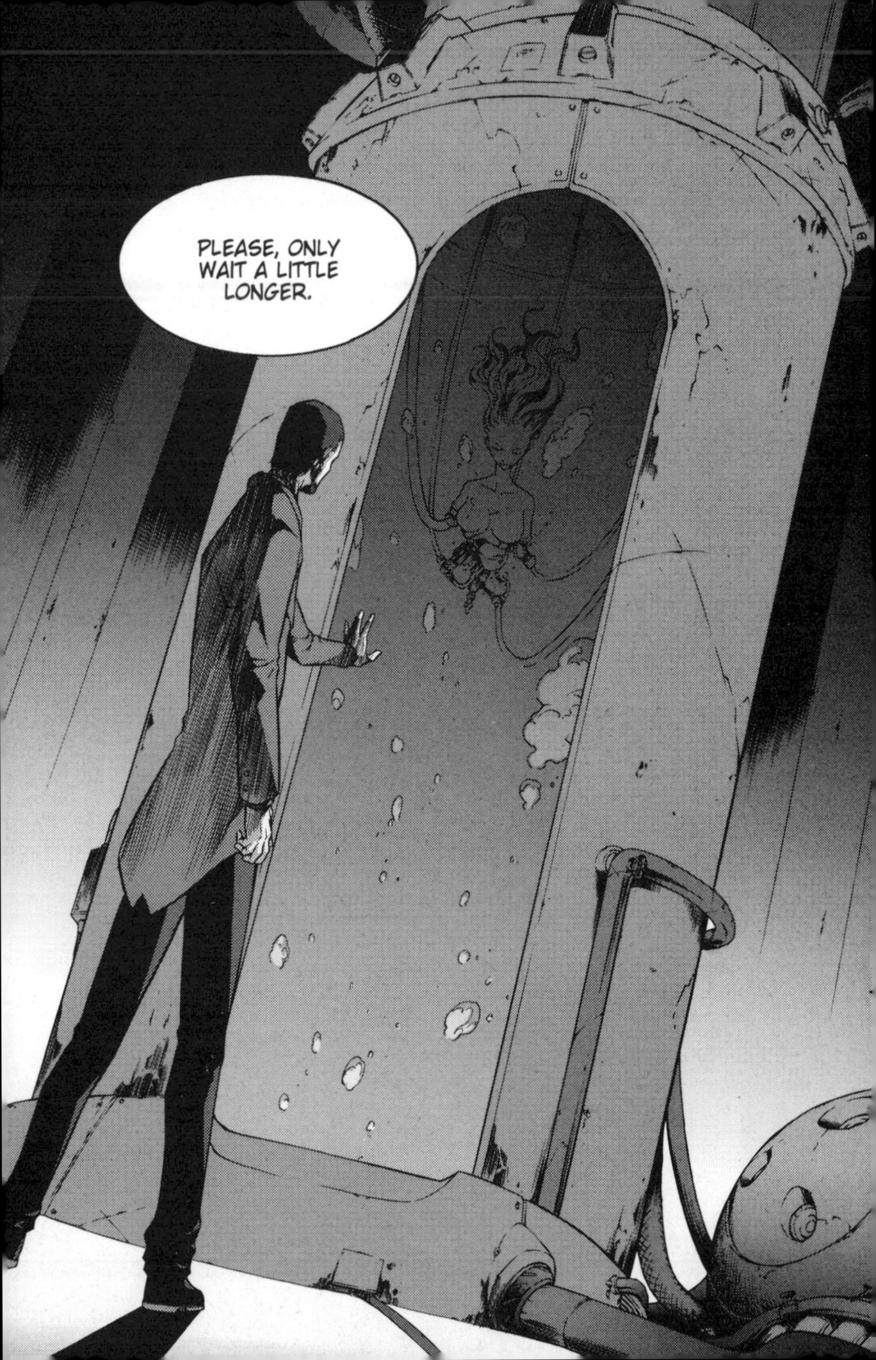
PLEASE, ONLY WAIT A LITTLE LONGER.

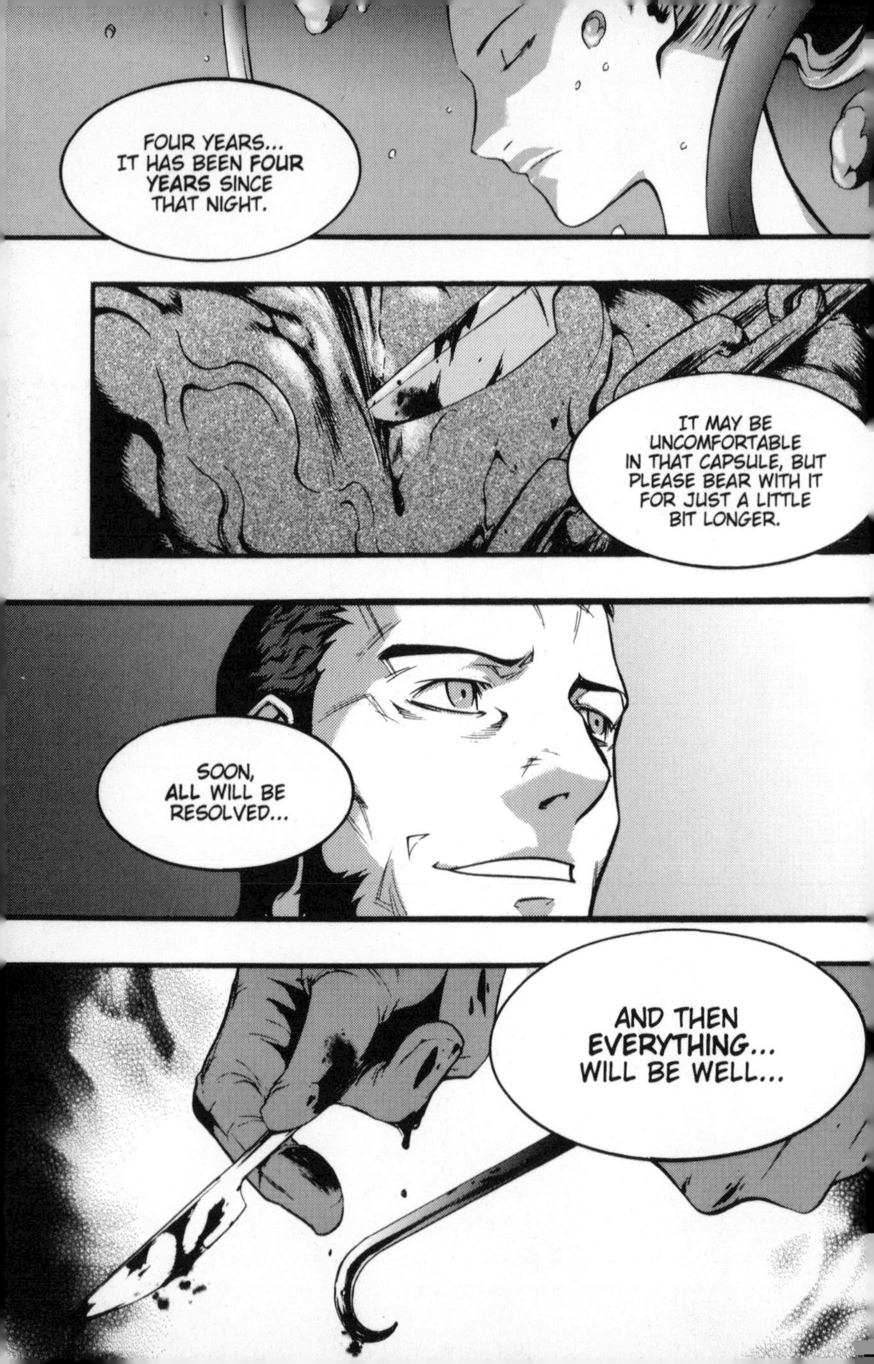
FOUR YEARS... IT HAS BEEN FOUR YEARS SINCE THAT NIGHT.
IT MAY BE UNCOMFORTABLE IN THAT CAPSULE, BUT PLEASE BEAR WITH IT FOR JUST A LITTLE BIT LONGER.
SOON, ALL WILL BE RESOLVED...
AND THEN EVERYTHING... WILL BE WELL...

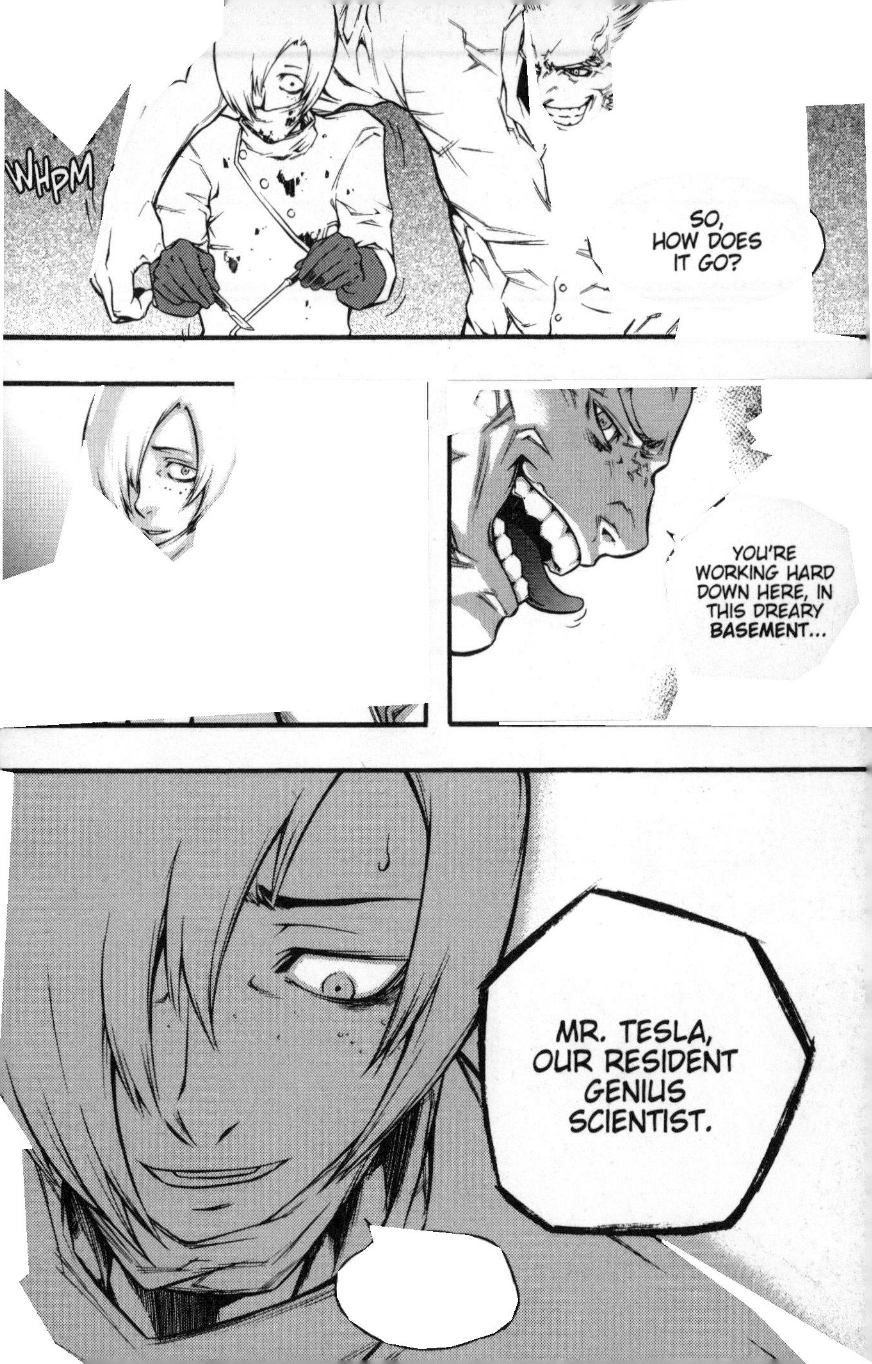
WHPM
SO, HOW DOES IT GO?
YOU'RE WORKING HARD DOWN HERE, IN THIS DREARY BASEMENT...
MR. TESLA, OUR RESIDENT GENIUS SCIENTIST.

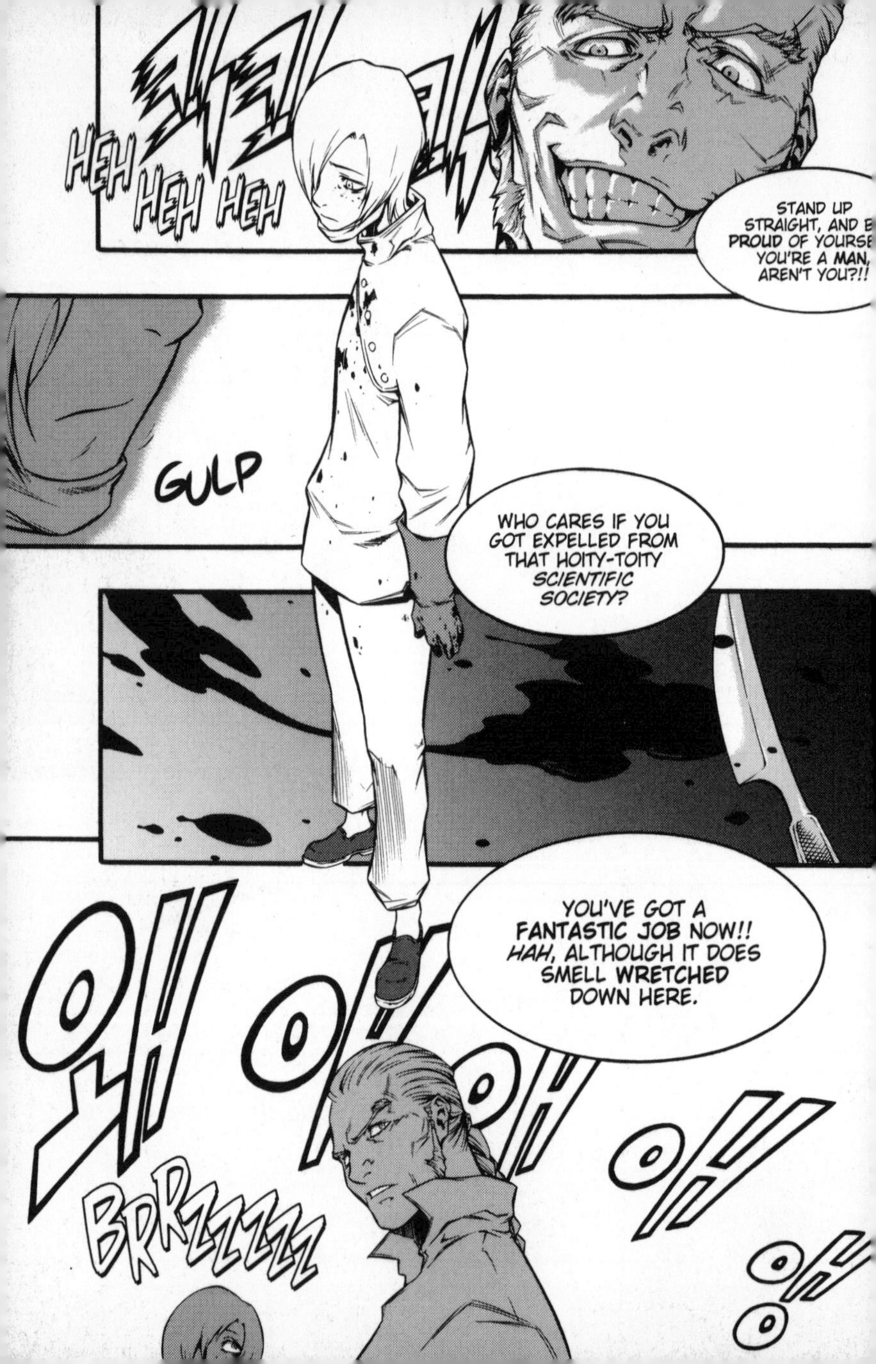
HEH HEH HEH HEH
STAND UP STRAIGHT, AND B PROUD OF YOURSE YOU'RE A MAN, AREN'T YOU?!!
GULP
WHO CARES IF YOU GOT EXPELLED FROM THAT HOITY-TOITY *SCIENTIFIC SOCIETY*?
YOU'VE GOT A FANTASTIC JOB NOW!! *HAH*, ALTHOUGH IT DOES SMELL WRETCHED DOWN HERE.
OH HOH HOH OH OH
BRRZZZZZ

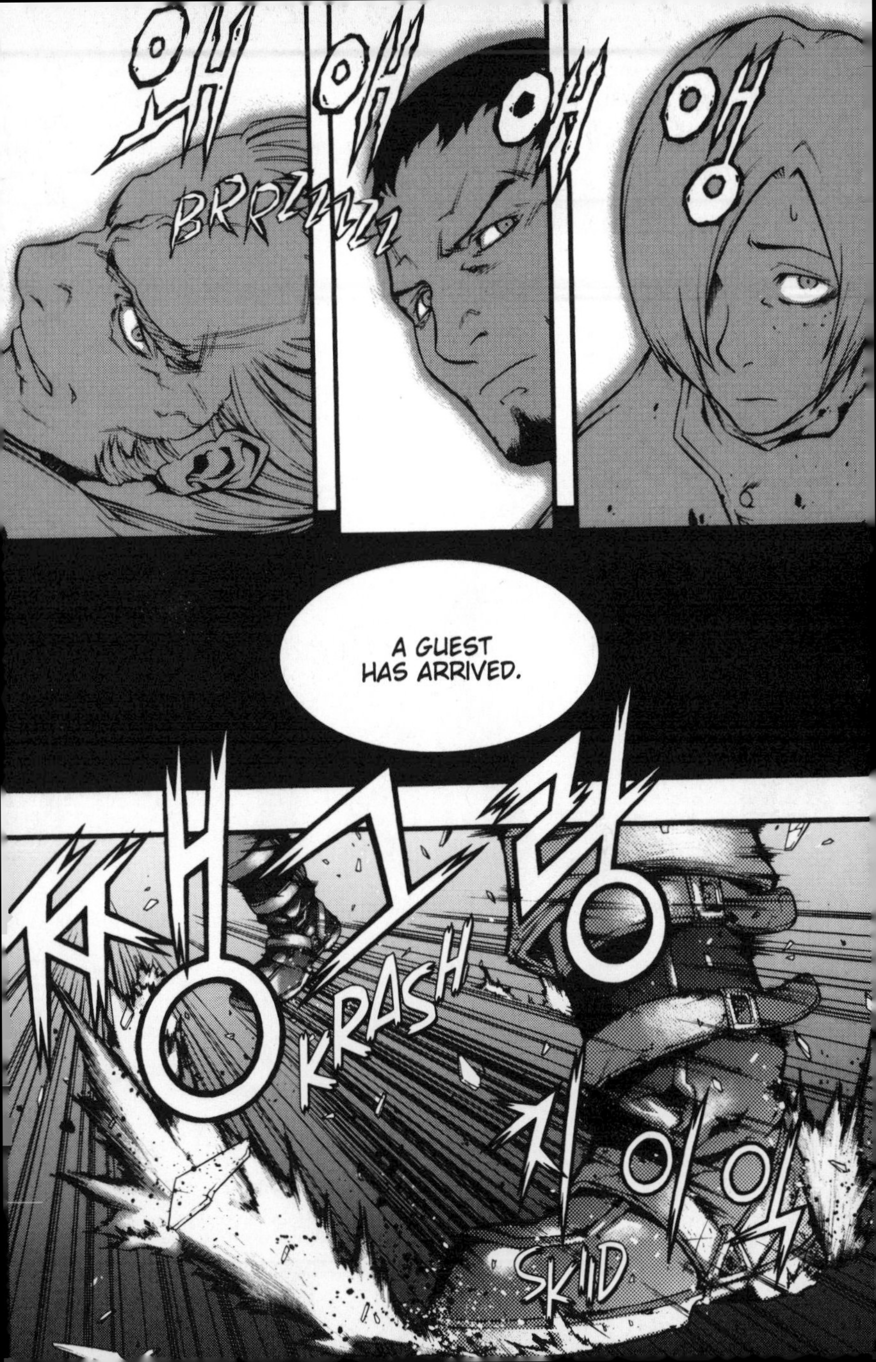
OH OH OH OH
BRRZZZZZZ
A GUEST HAS ARRIVED.
KRASH
SKID

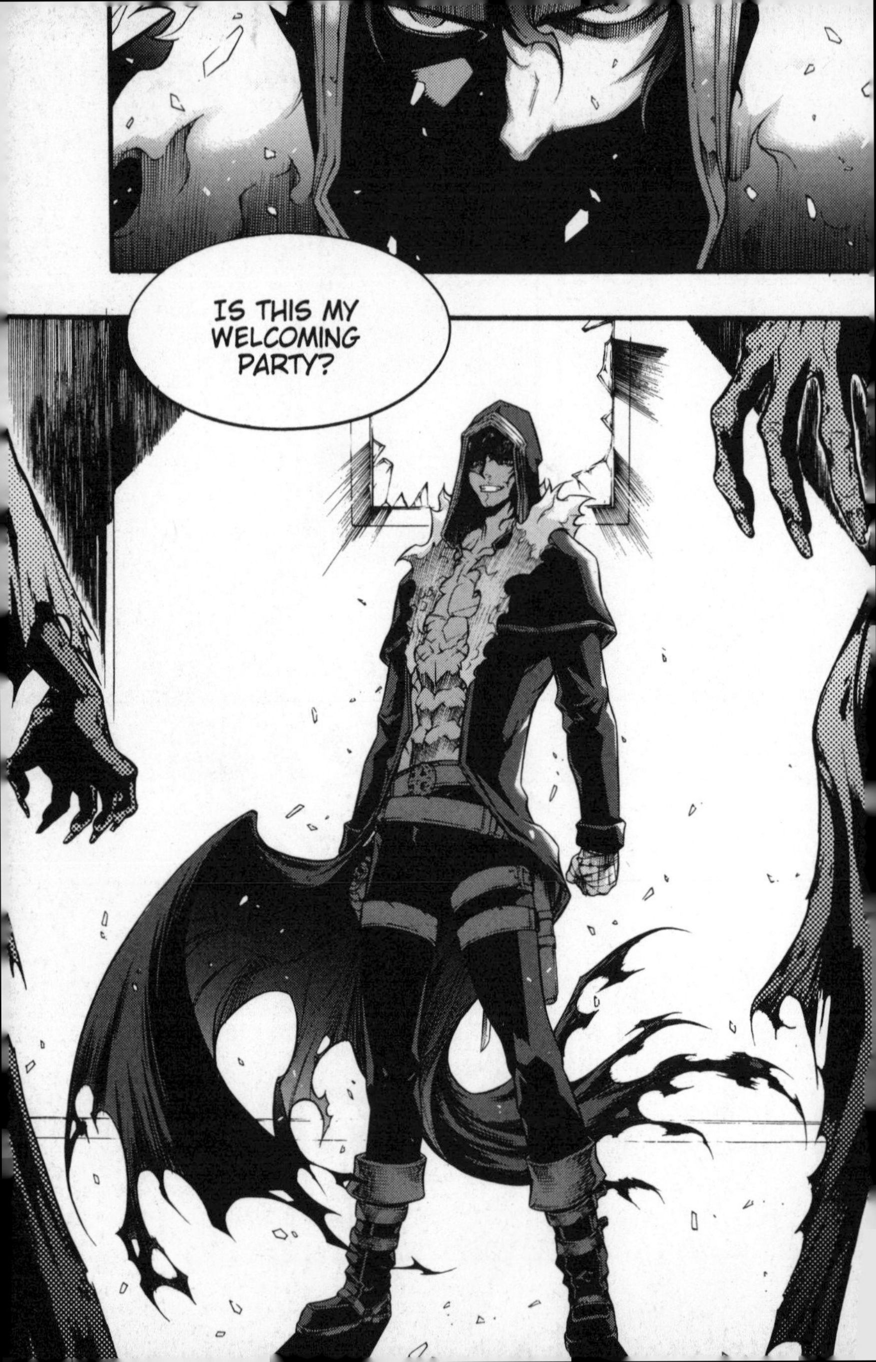
IS THIS MY WELCOMING PARTY?

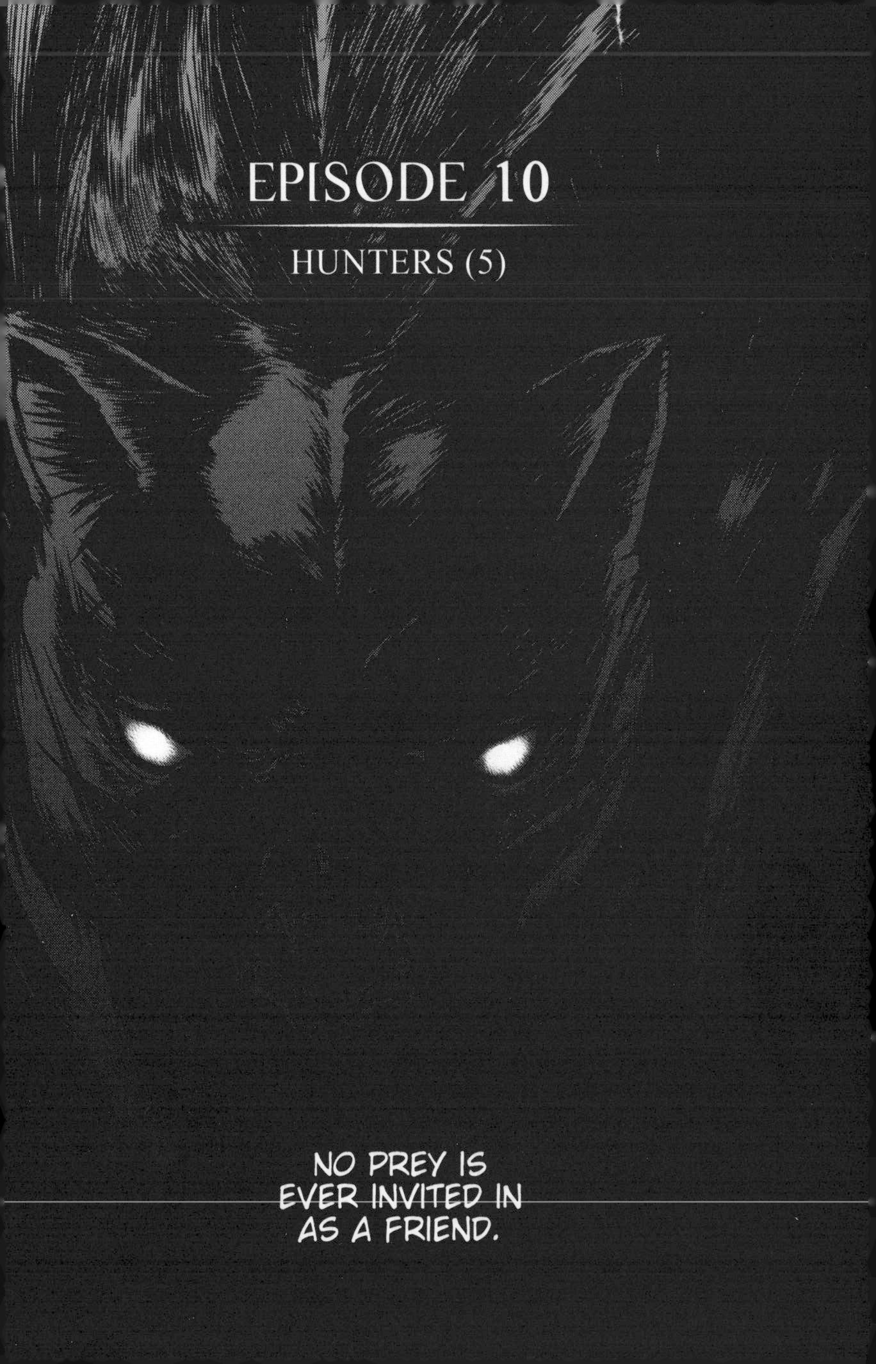
EPISODE 10
HUNTERS (5)
NO PREY IS EVER INVITED IN AS A FRIEND.

THE RICH HAVE SUCH UNUSUAL TRINKETS IN THEIR *GARRETS**.

*A GARRET IS A SMALL ATTIC, USUALLY IN A STATE OF DISREPA[IR]

ARE THESE ABANDONED TOYS, TOSSED AWAY IN BOREDOM?

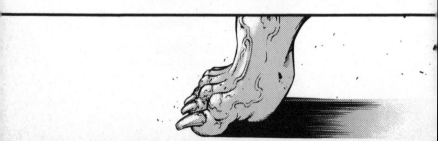

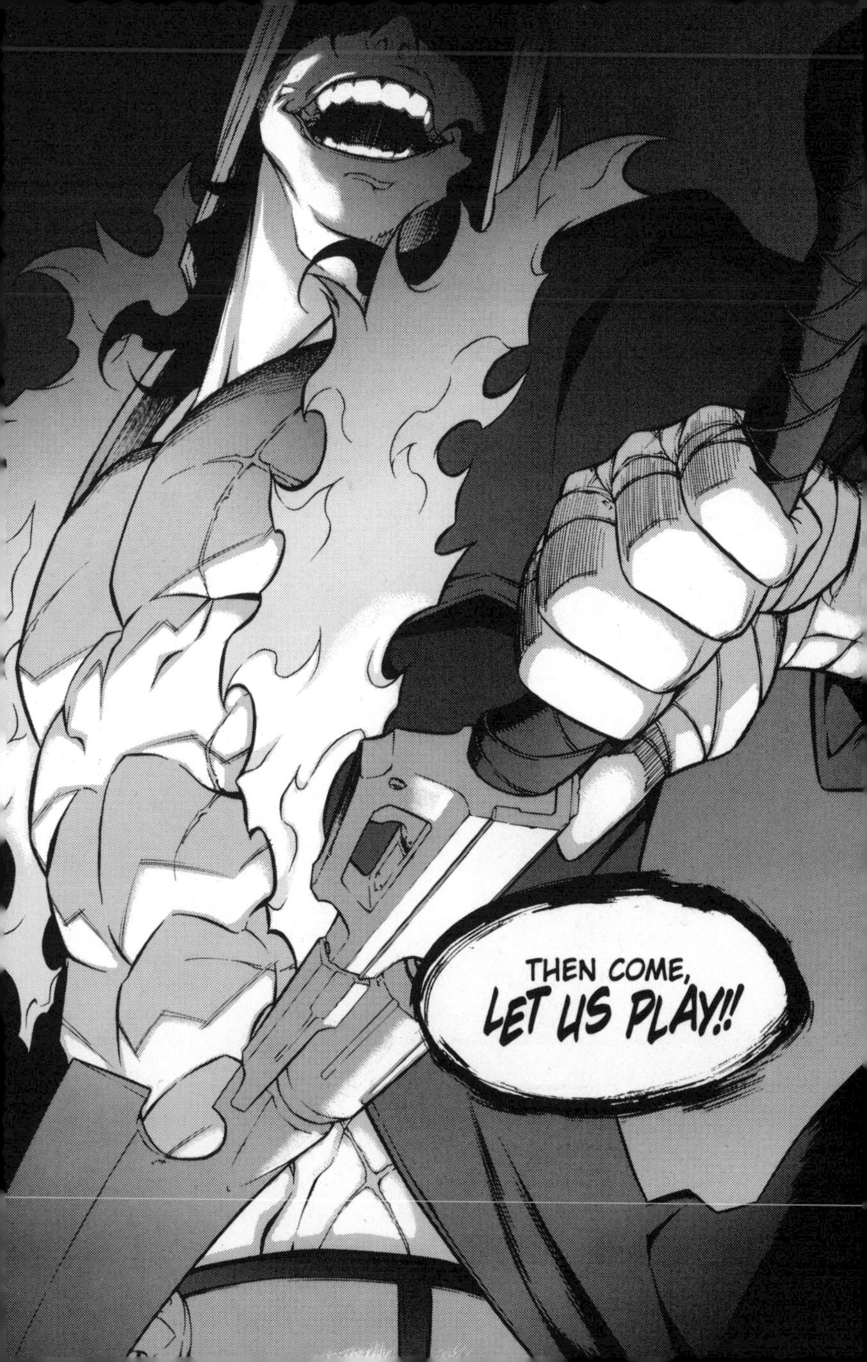
THEN COME,
LET US PLAY!!

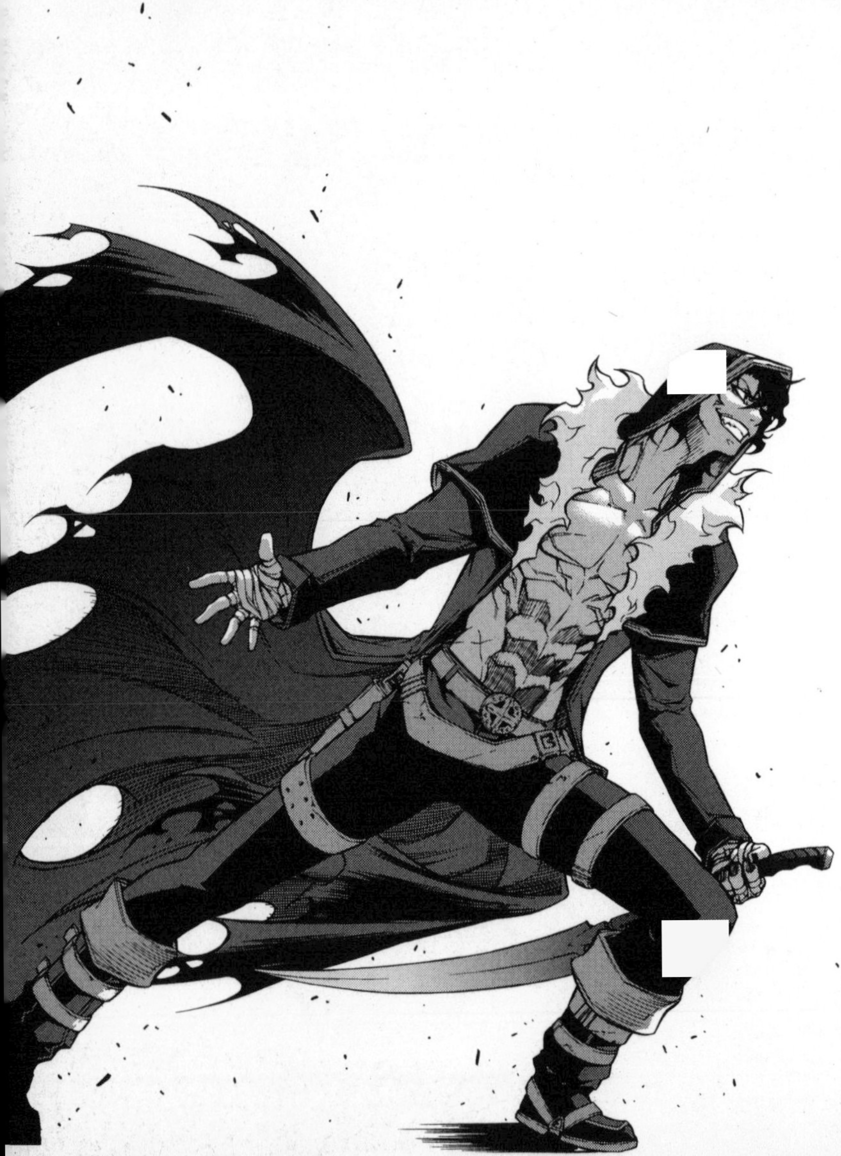

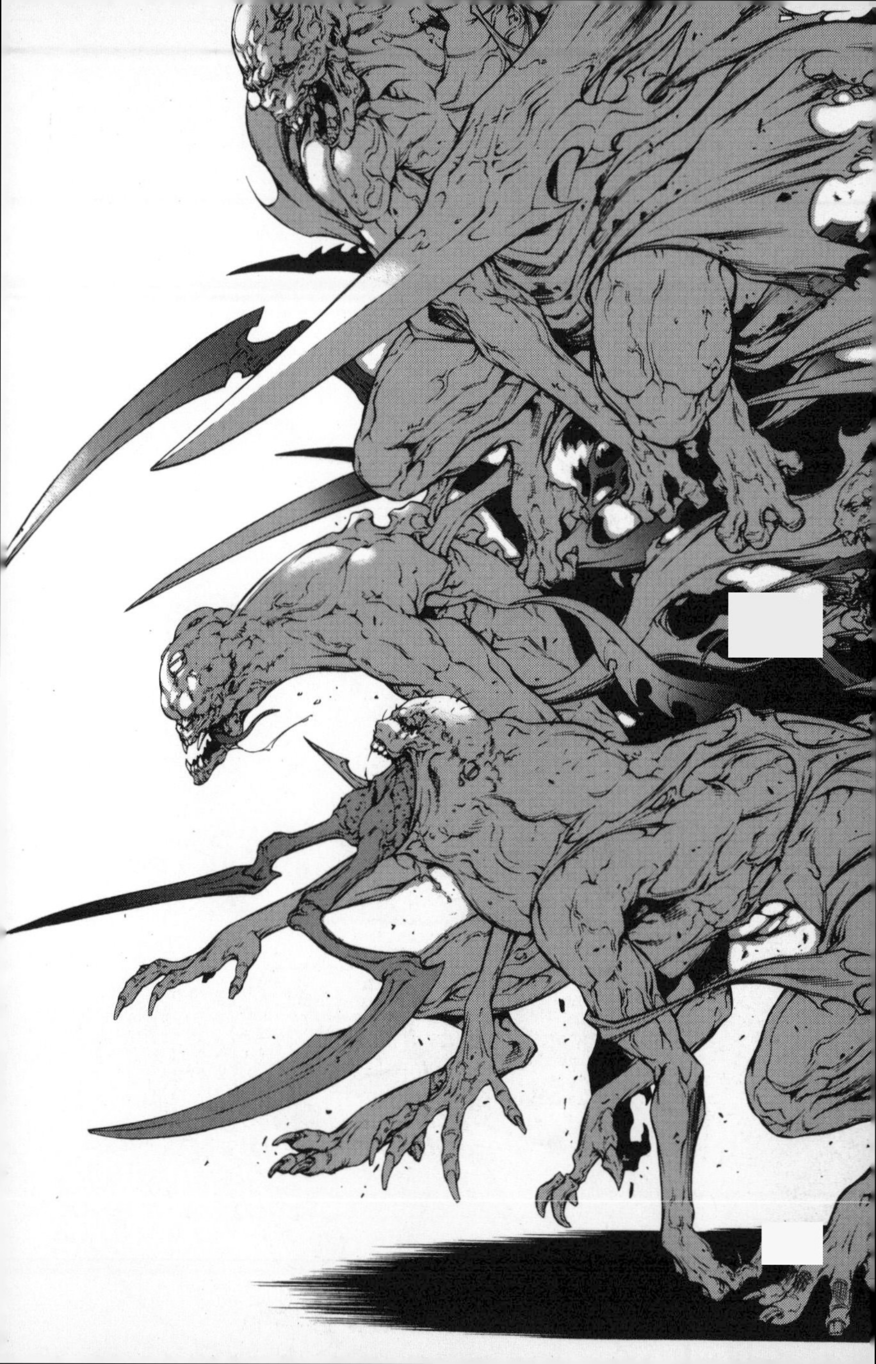

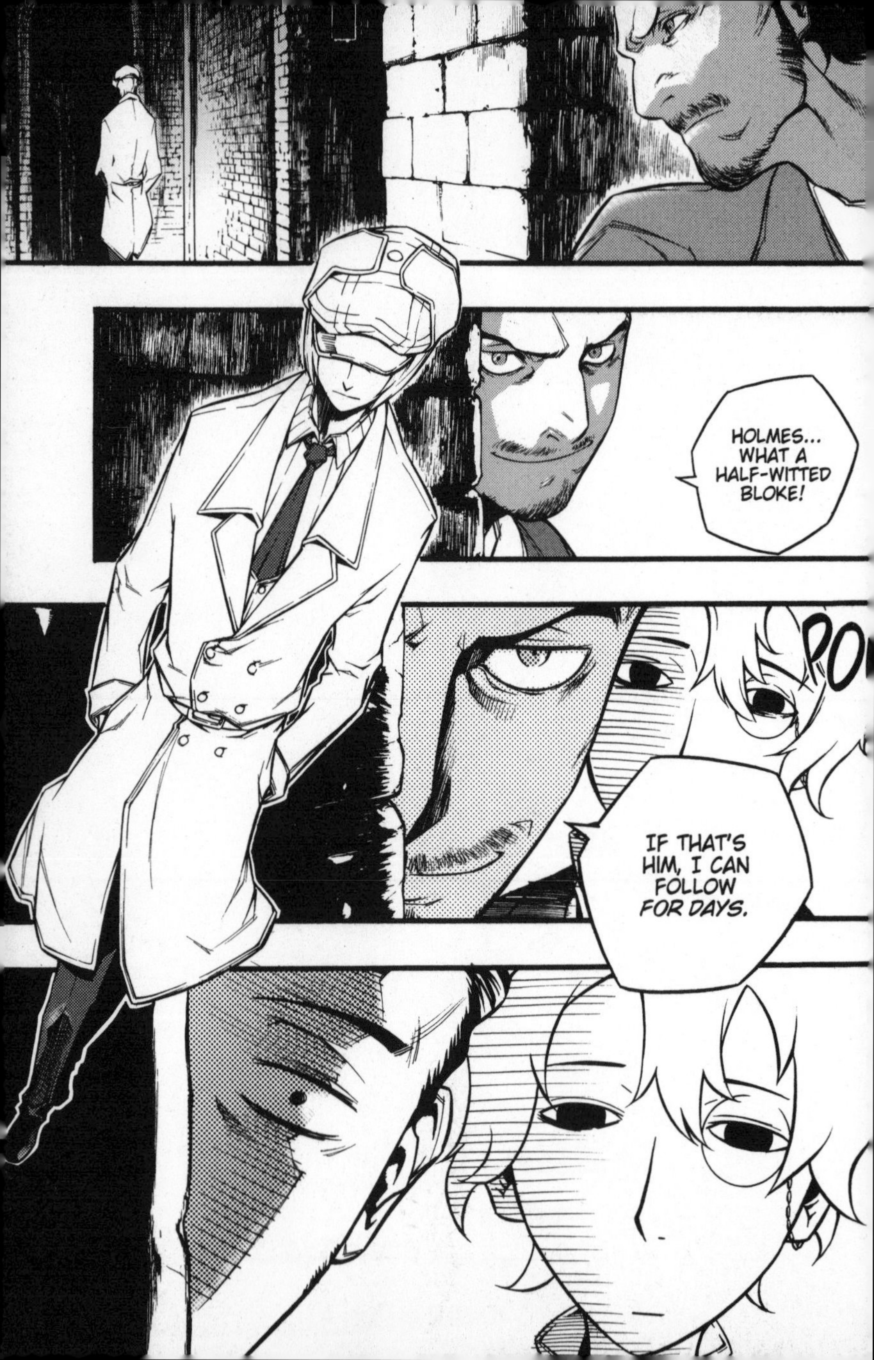
HOLMES... WHAT A HALF-WITTED BLOKE!
IF THAT'S HIM, I CAN FOLLOW FOR DAYS.

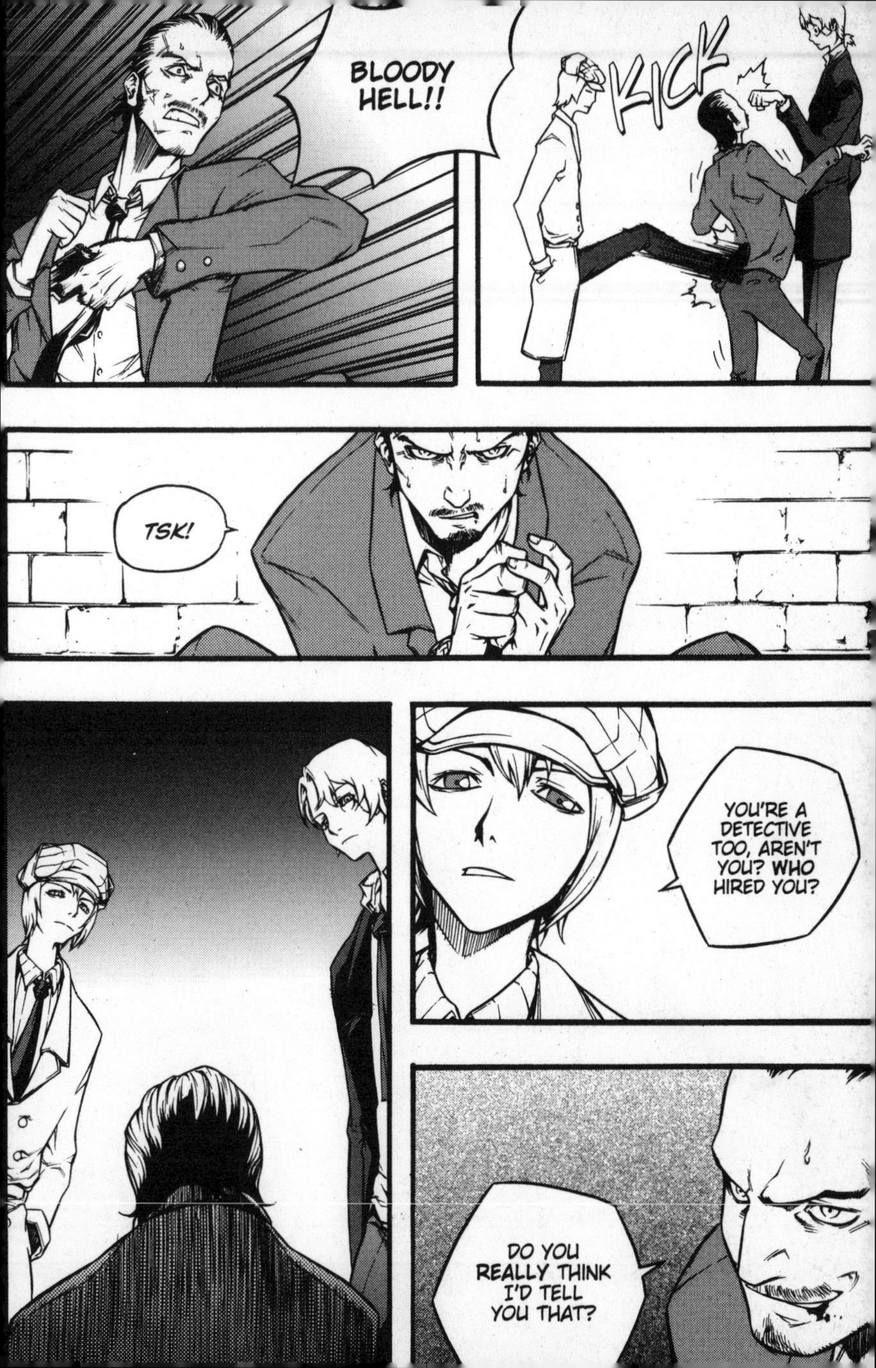
BLOODY HELL!!
KICK
TSK!
YOU'RE A DETECTIVE TOO, AREN'T YOU? WHO HIRED YOU?
DO YOU REALLY THINK I'D TELL YOU THAT?

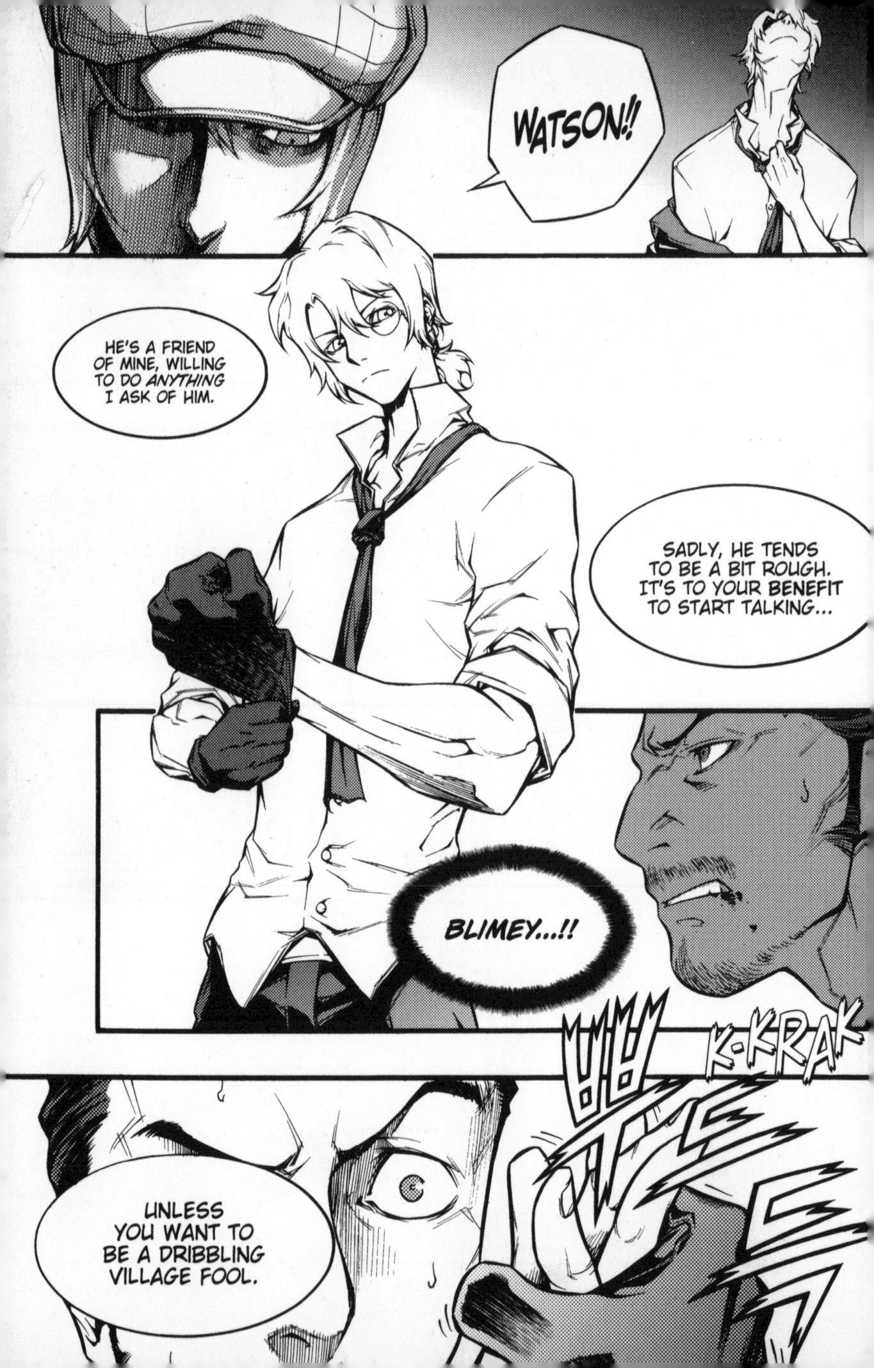
WATSON!!
HE'S A FRIEND OF MINE, WILLING TO DO *ANYTHING* I ASK OF HIM.
SADLY, HE TENDS TO BE A BIT ROUGH. IT'S TO YOUR BENEFIT TO START TALKING...
BLIMEY...!!
K-KRAK
UNLESS YOU WANT TO BE A DRIBBLING VILLAGE FOOL.

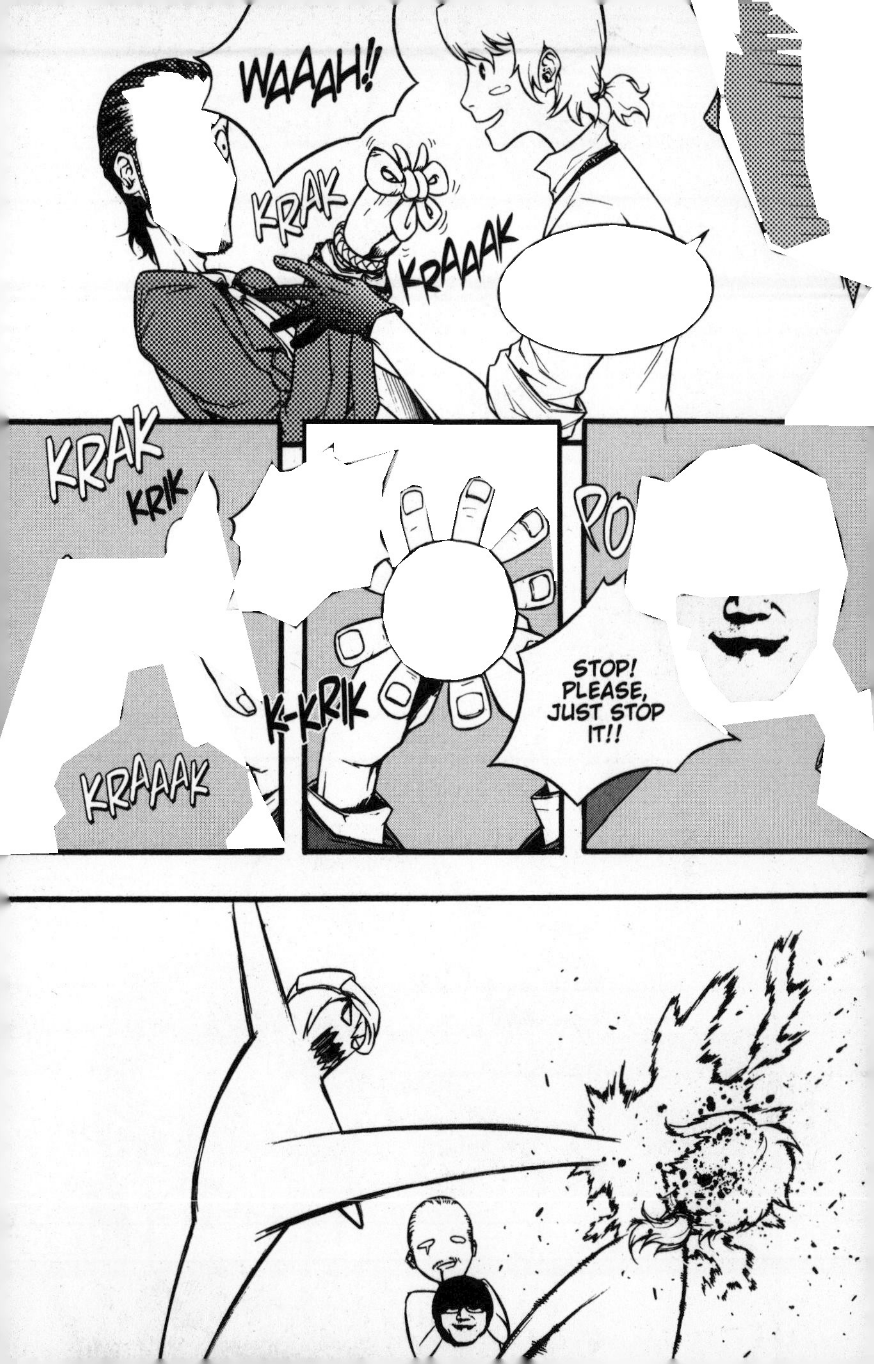
WAAAH!!
KRAK
KRAAAK
KRAK
KRIK
KRAAAK
K-KRIK
PO
STOP! PLEASE, JUST STOP IT!!

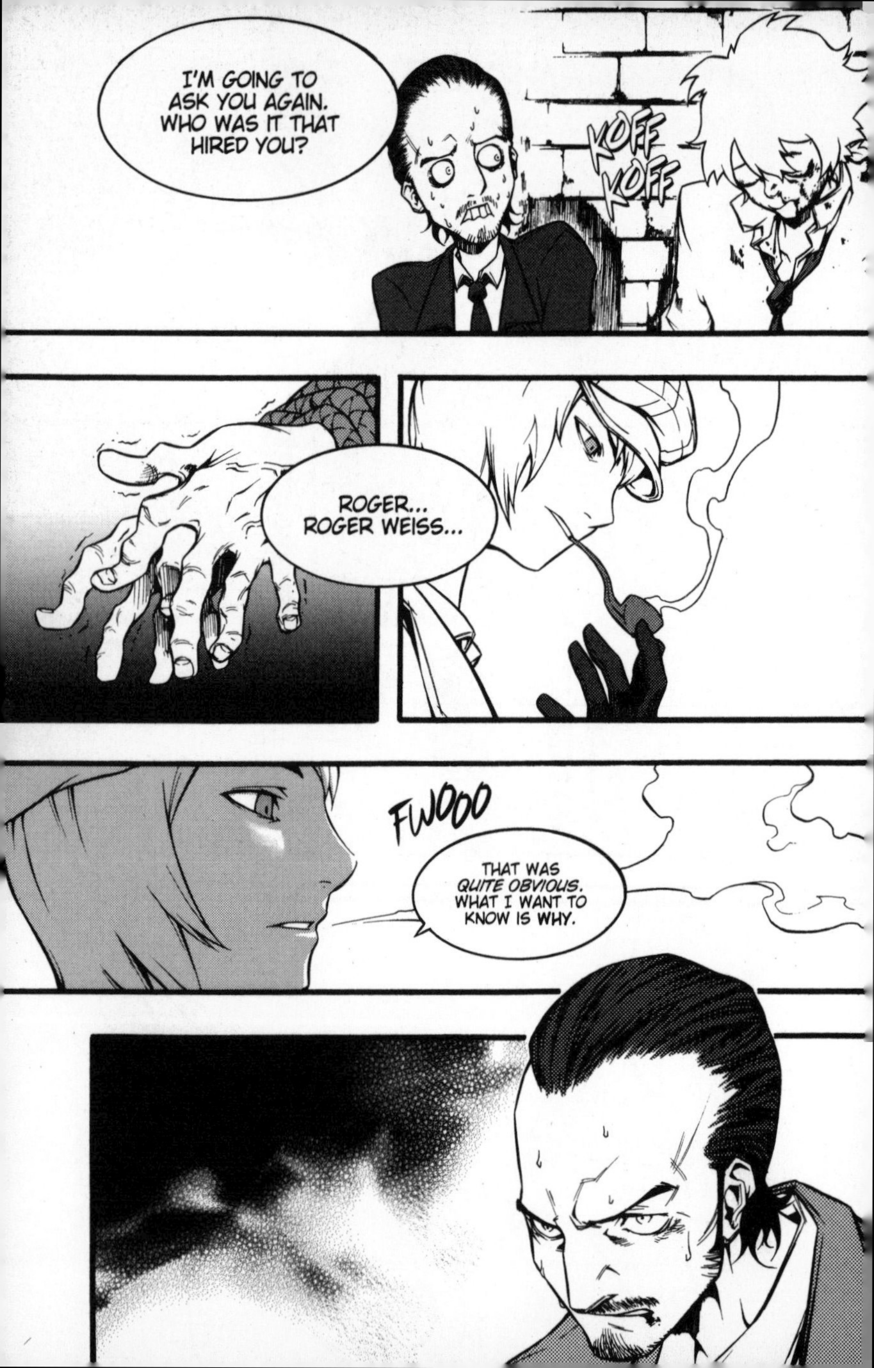
I'M GOING TO ASK YOU AGAIN. WHO WAS IT THAT HIRED YOU?
KOFF KOFF
ROGER... ROGER WEISS...
FWOOO
THAT WAS *QUITE OBVIOUS*. WHAT I WANT TO KNOW IS WHY.

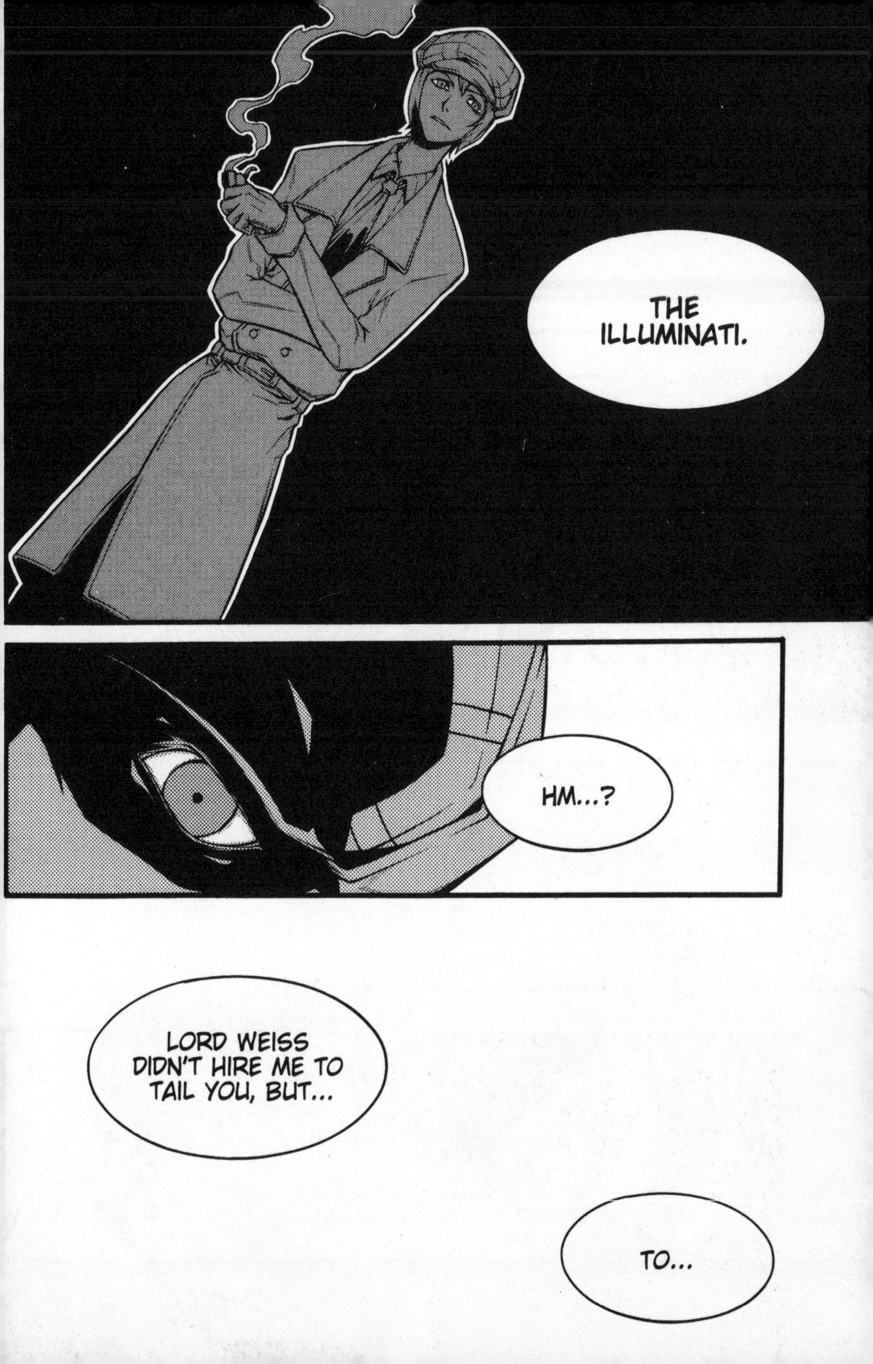

THE ILLUMINATI.
HM...?
LORD WEISS DIDN'T HIRE ME TO TAIL YOU, BUT...
TO...

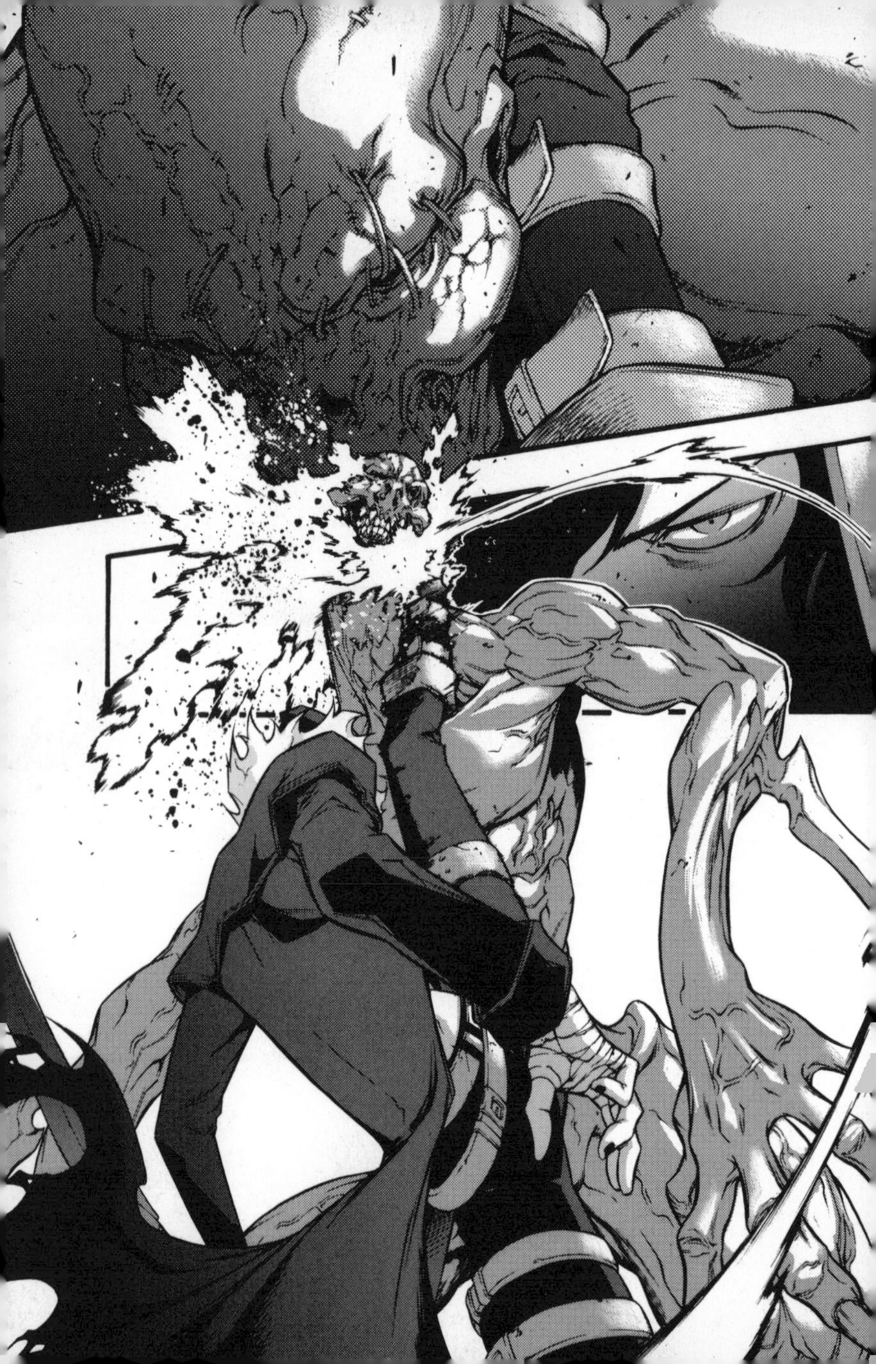

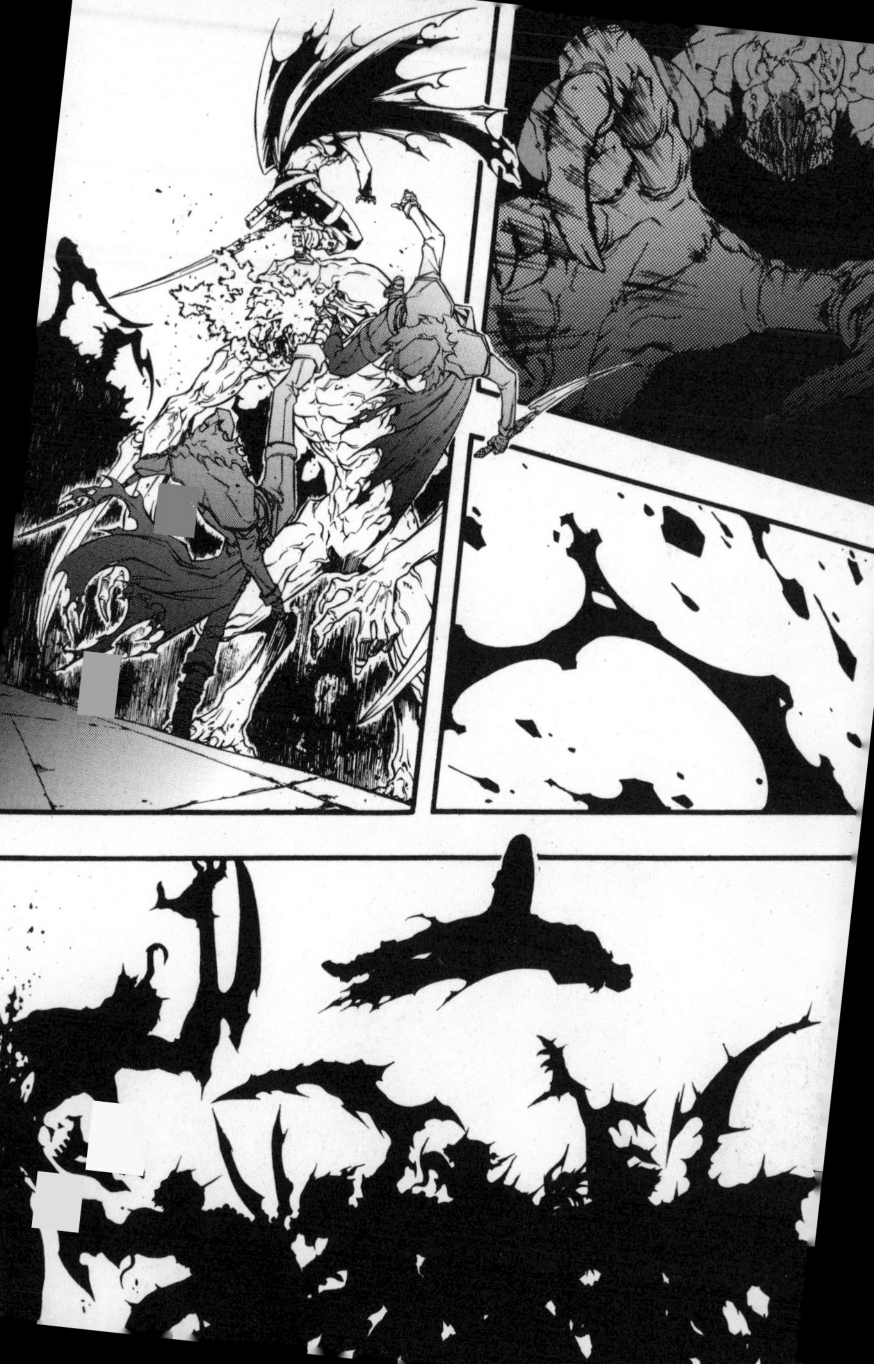

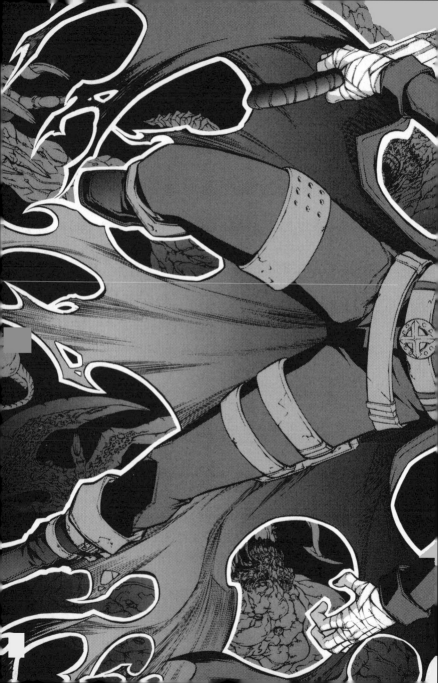

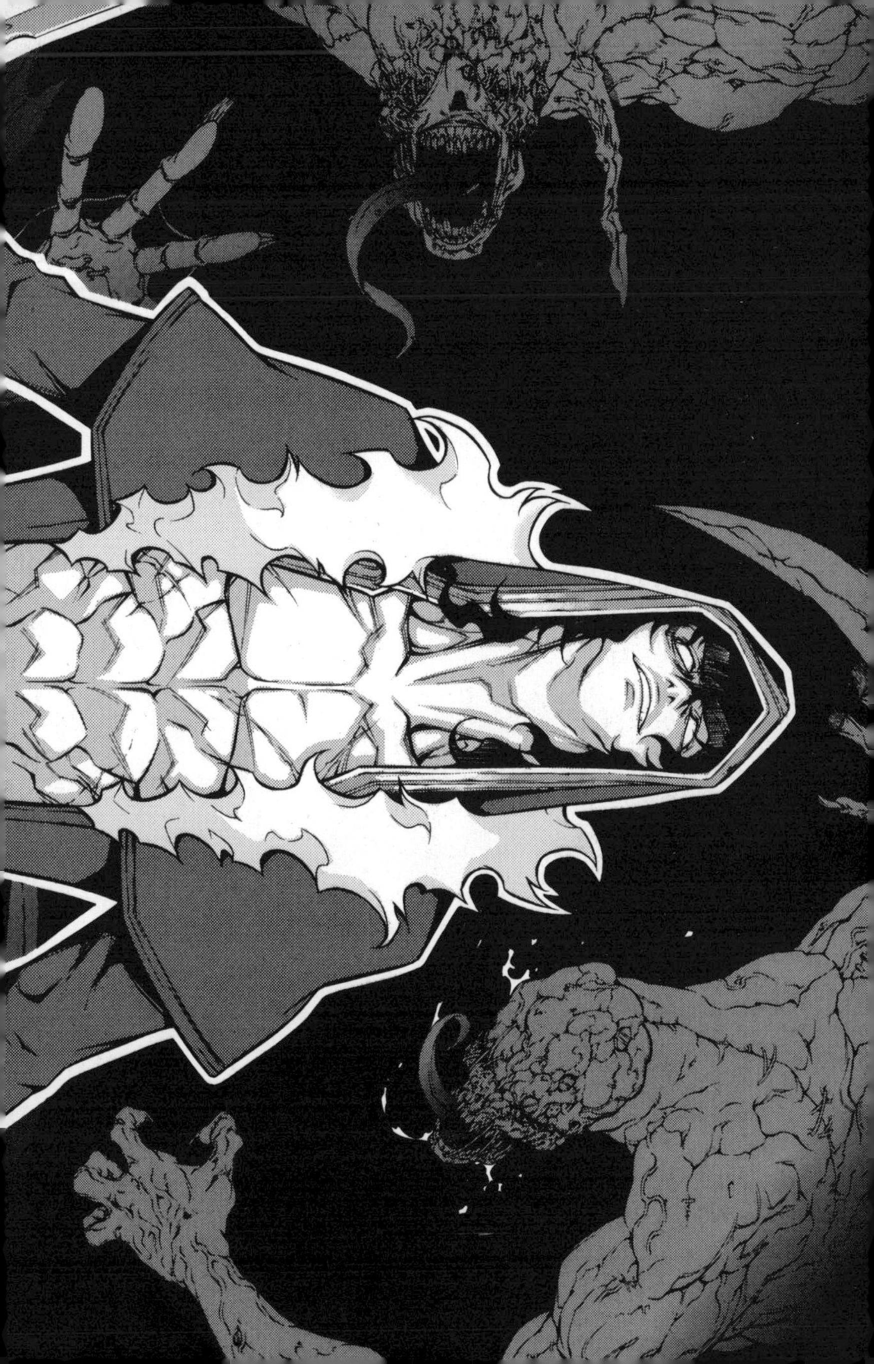

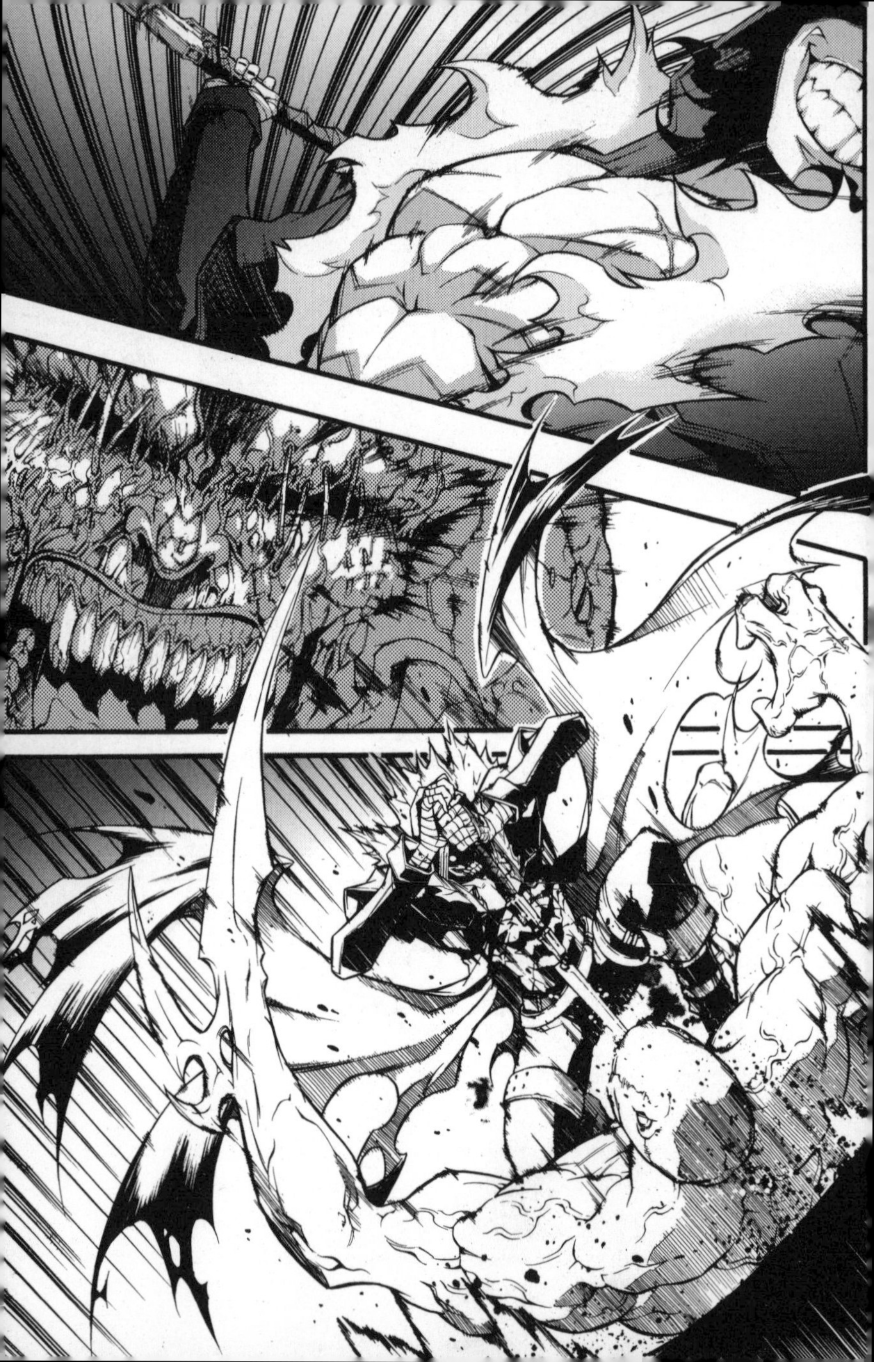

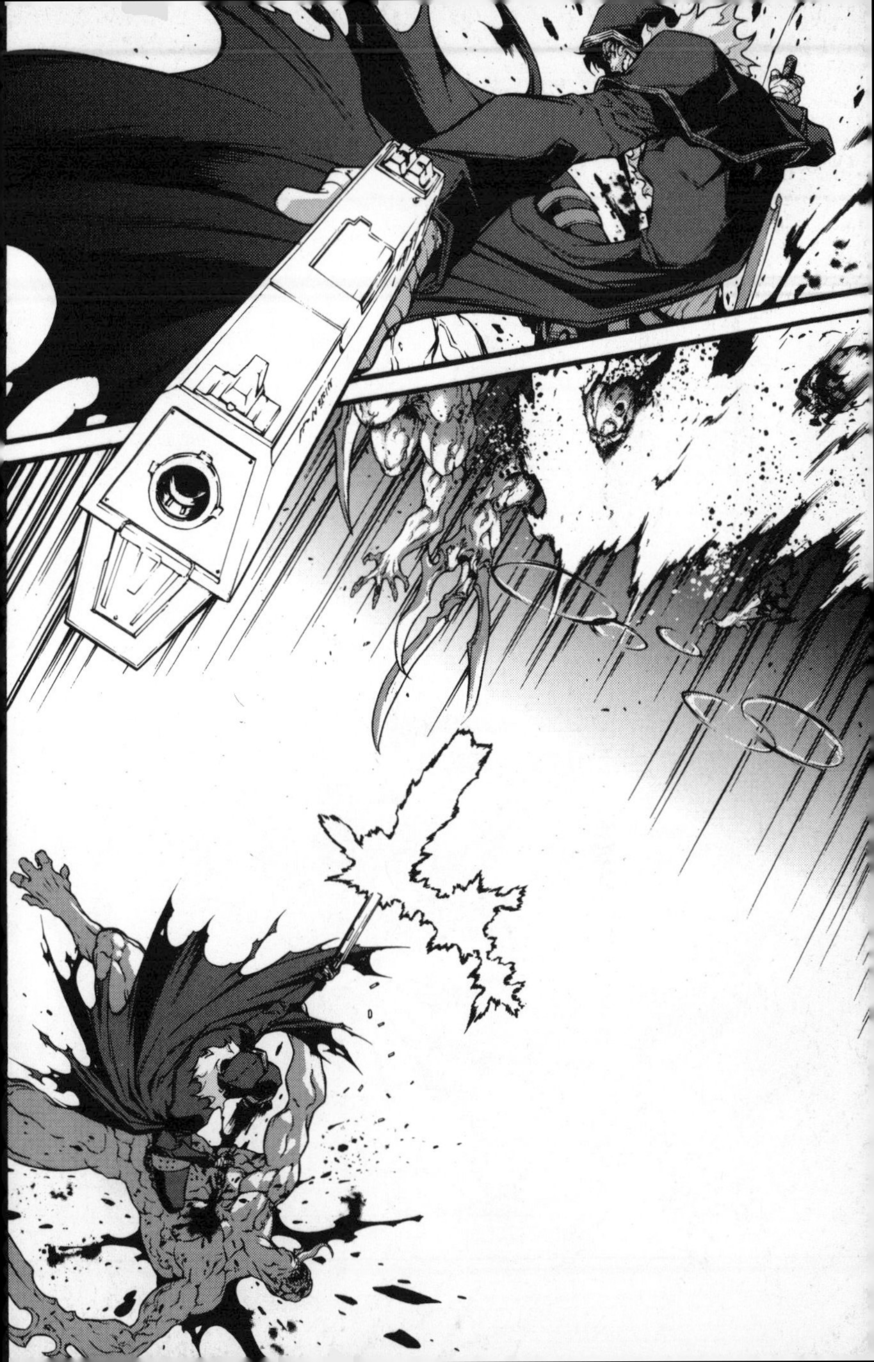

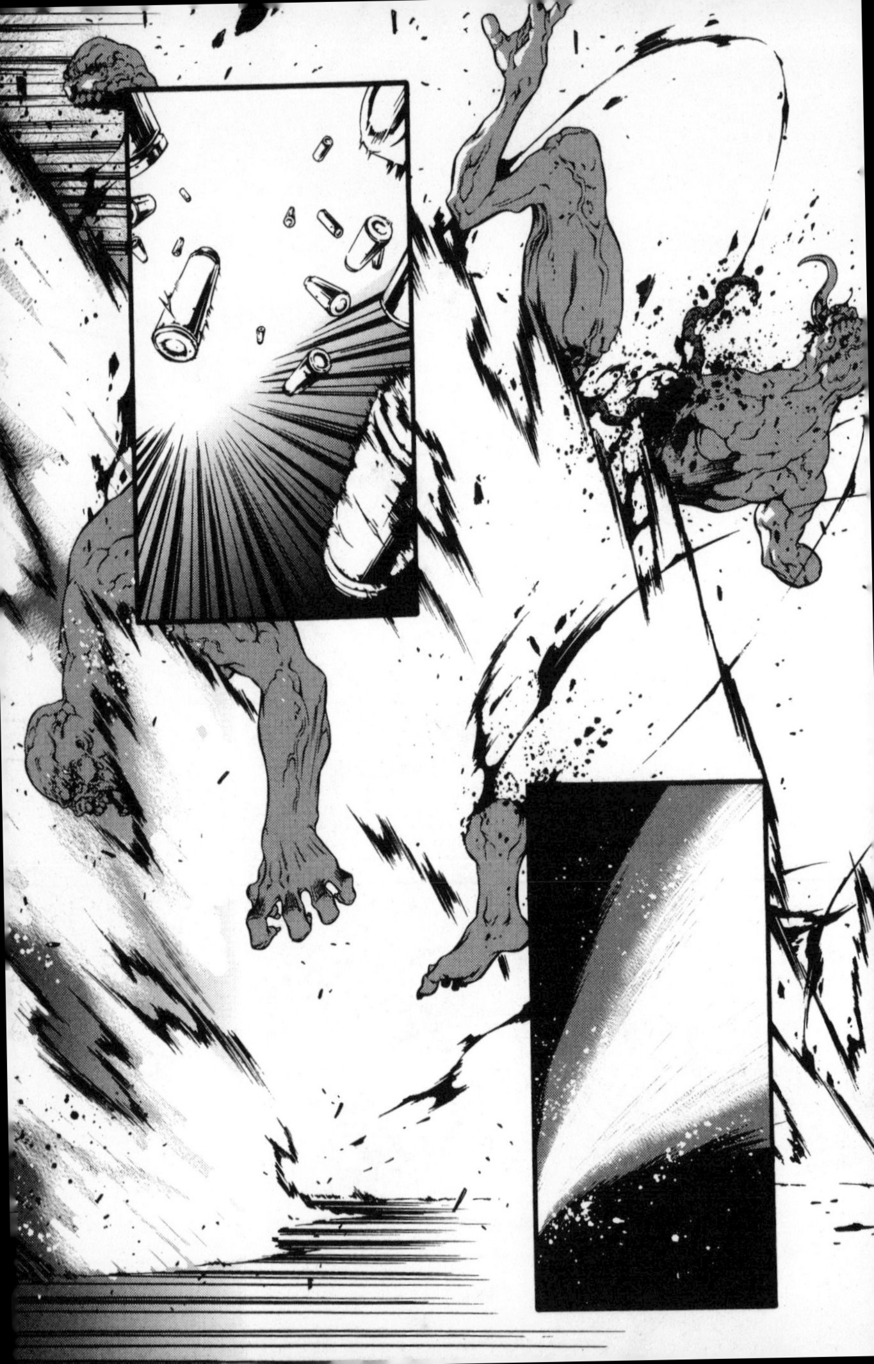

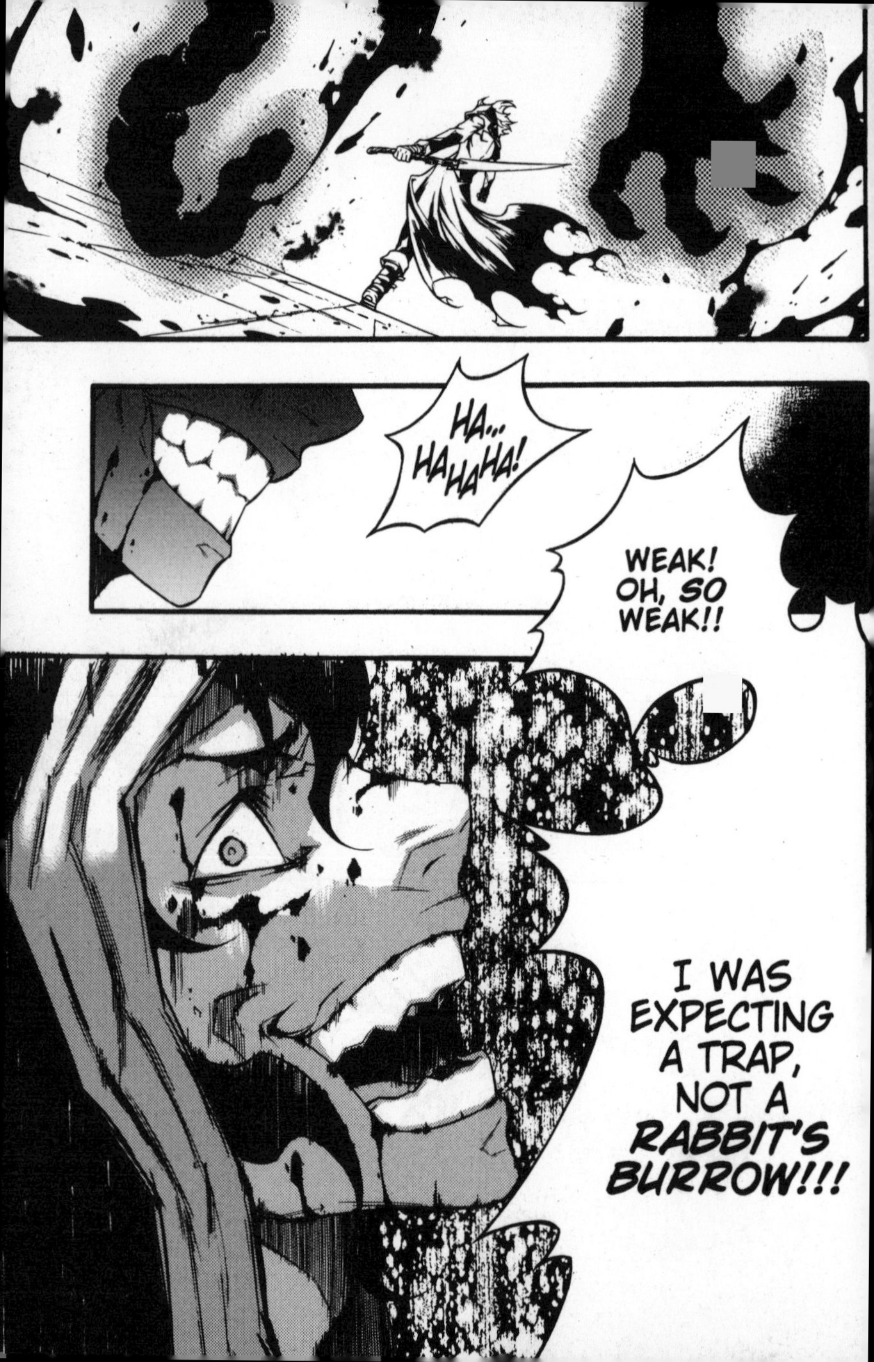
HA... HAHAHA!
WEAK! OH, SO WEAK!!
I WAS EXPECTING A TRAP, NOT A RABBIT'S BURROW!!!

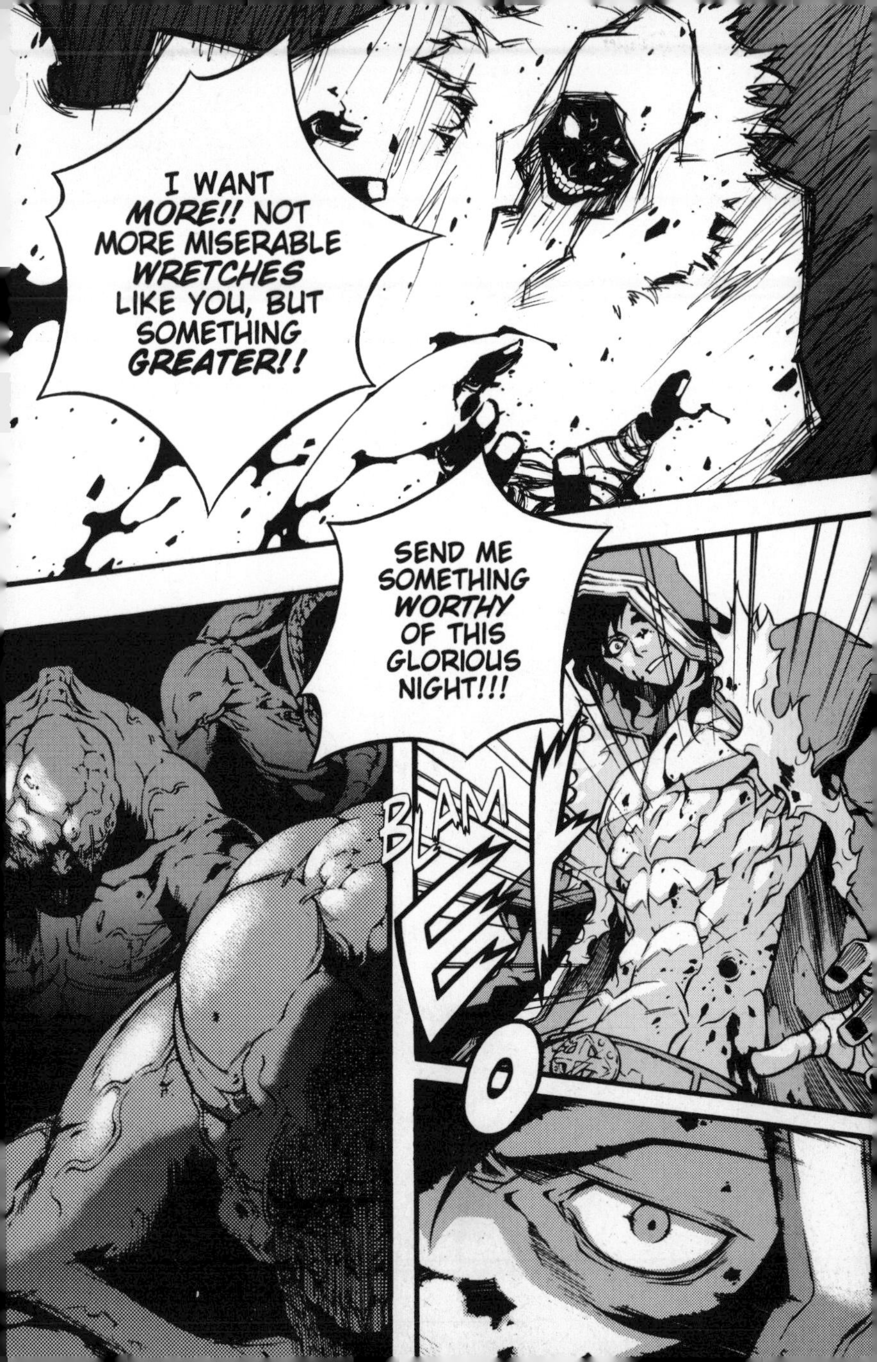
I WANT MORE!! NOT MORE MISERABLE WRETCHES LIKE YOU, BUT SOMETHING GREATER!!
SEND ME SOMETHING WORTHY OF THIS GLORIOUS NIGHT!!!
BLAM

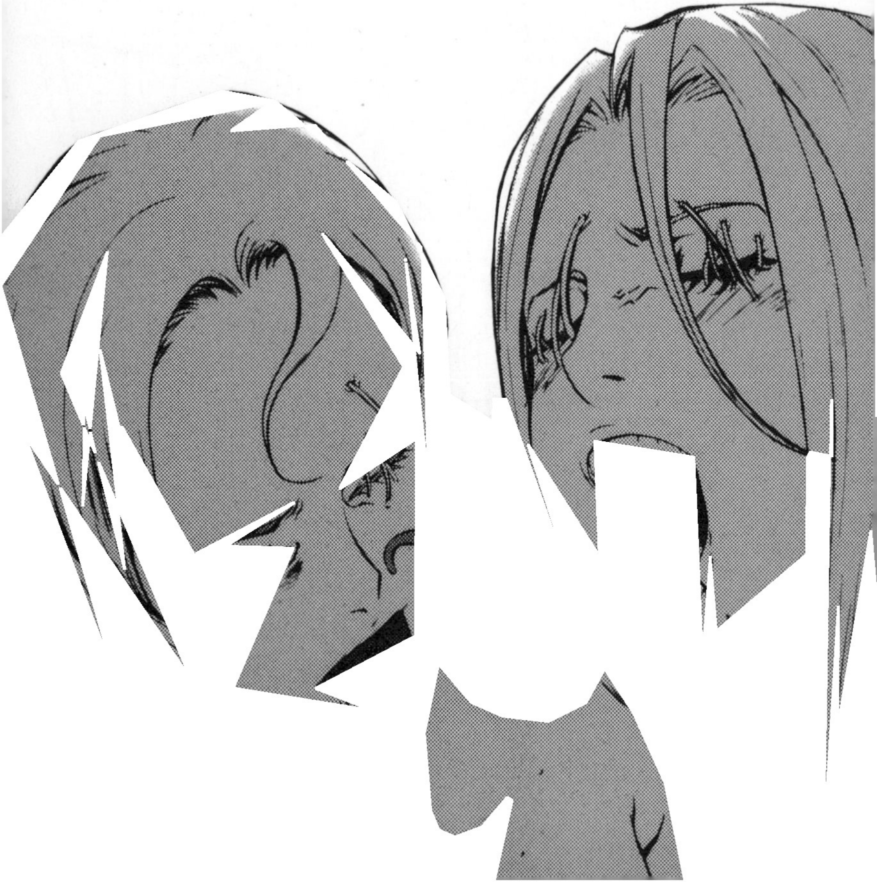

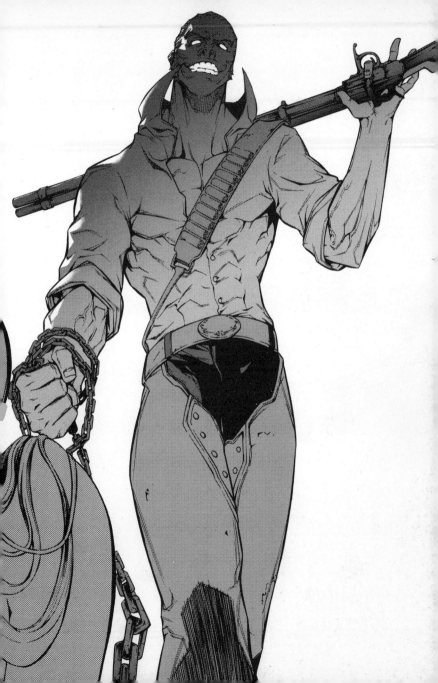

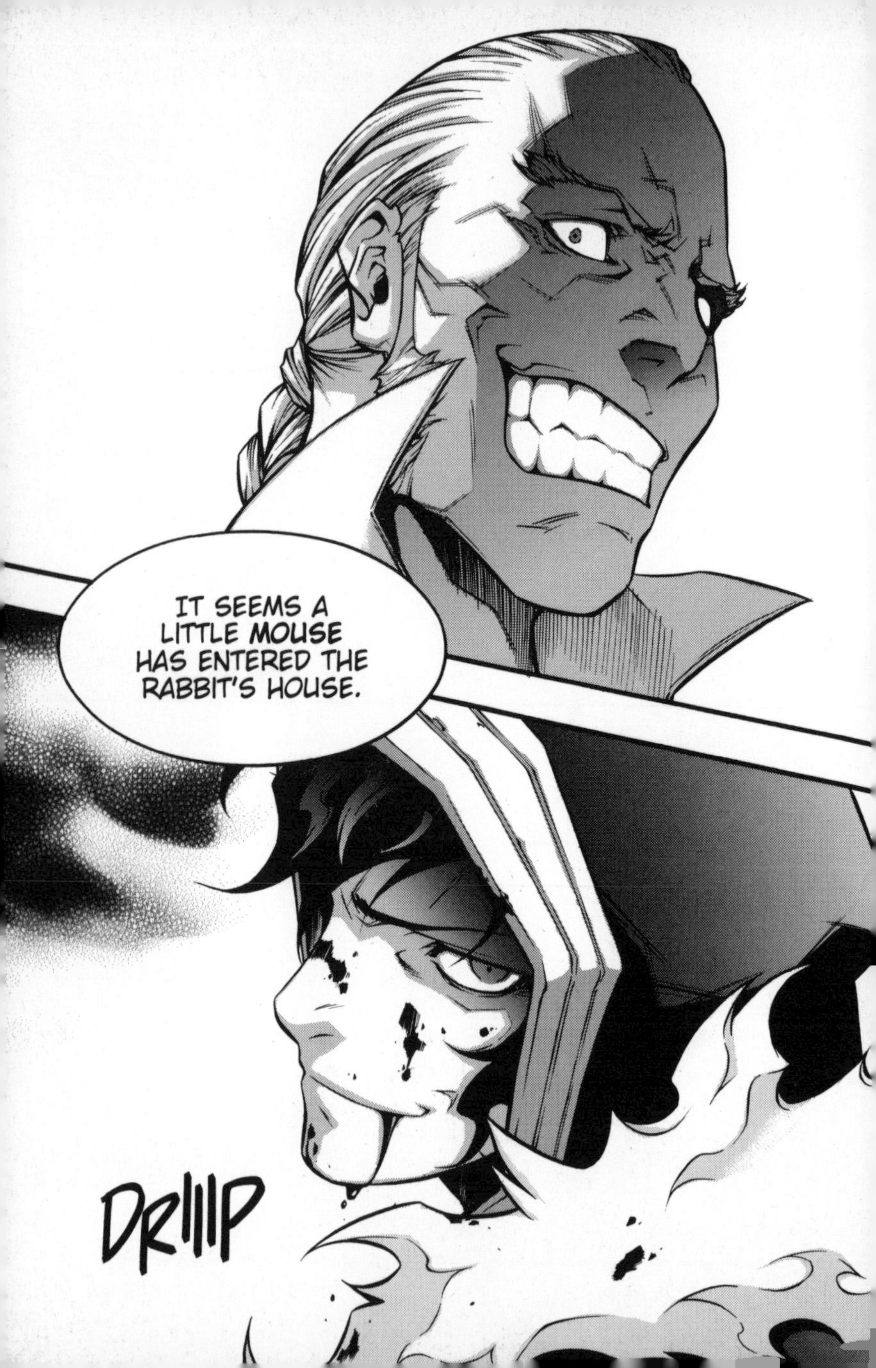
IT SEEMS A LITTLE MOUSE HAS ENTERED THE RABBIT'S HOUSE.
DRIIIP

EPISODE 11

HUNTERS (6)

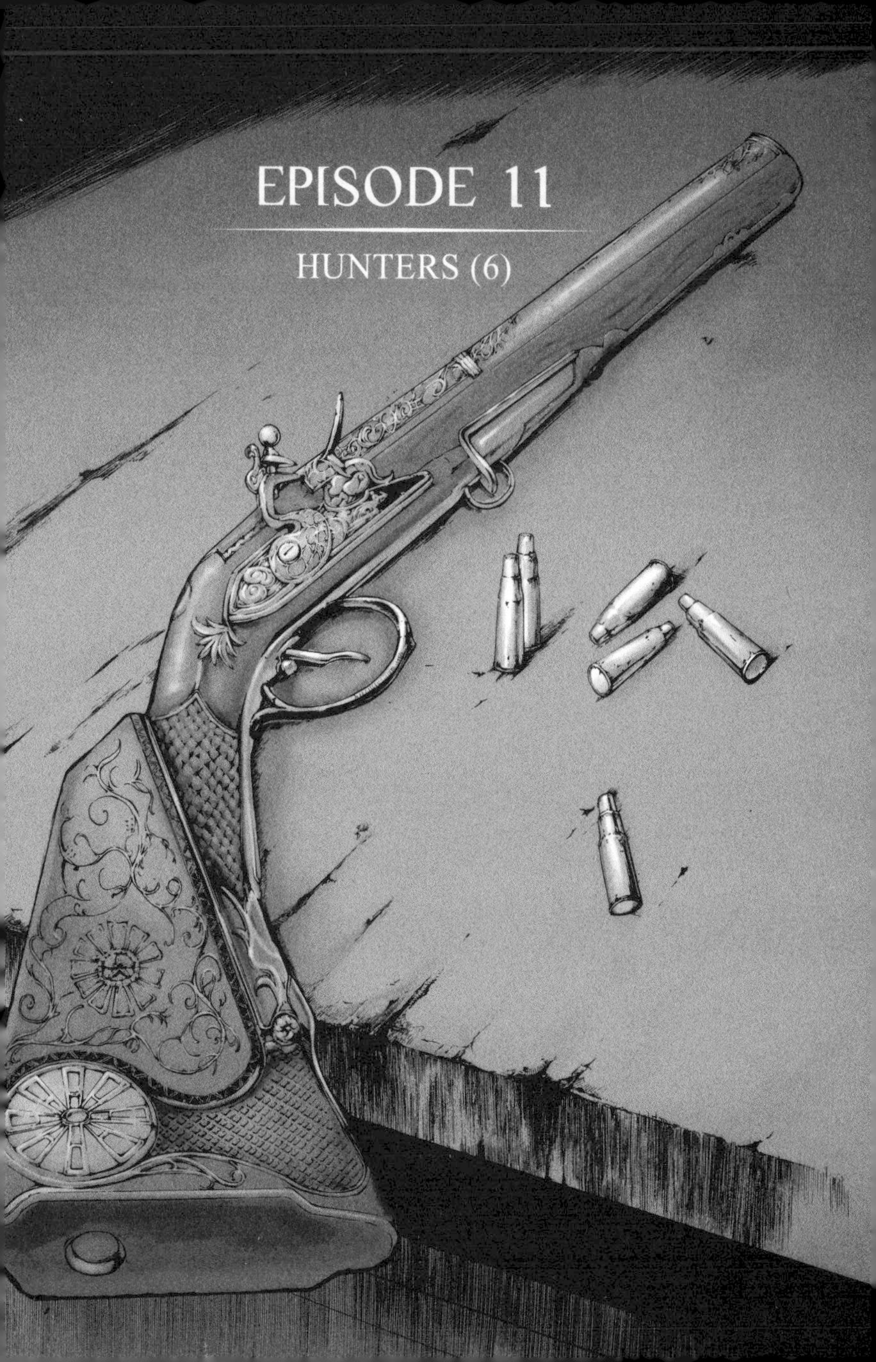

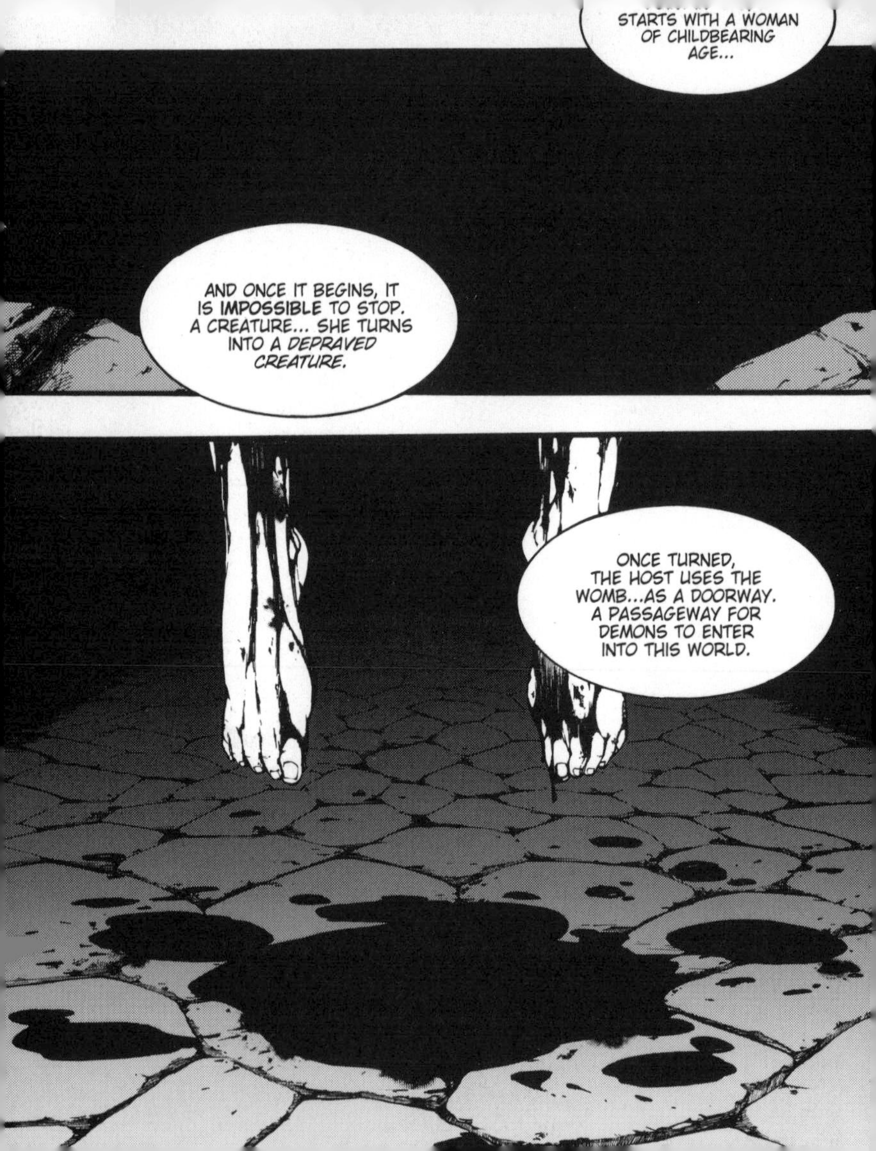
STARTS WITH A WOMAN OF CHILDBEARING AGE...
AND ONCE IT BEGINS, IT IS **IMPOSSIBLE** TO STOP. A CREATURE... SHE TURNS INTO A *DEPRAVED CREATURE.*
ONCE TURNED, THE HOST USES THE WOMB...AS A DOORWAY. A PASSAGEWAY FOR DEMONS TO ENTER INTO THIS WORLD.

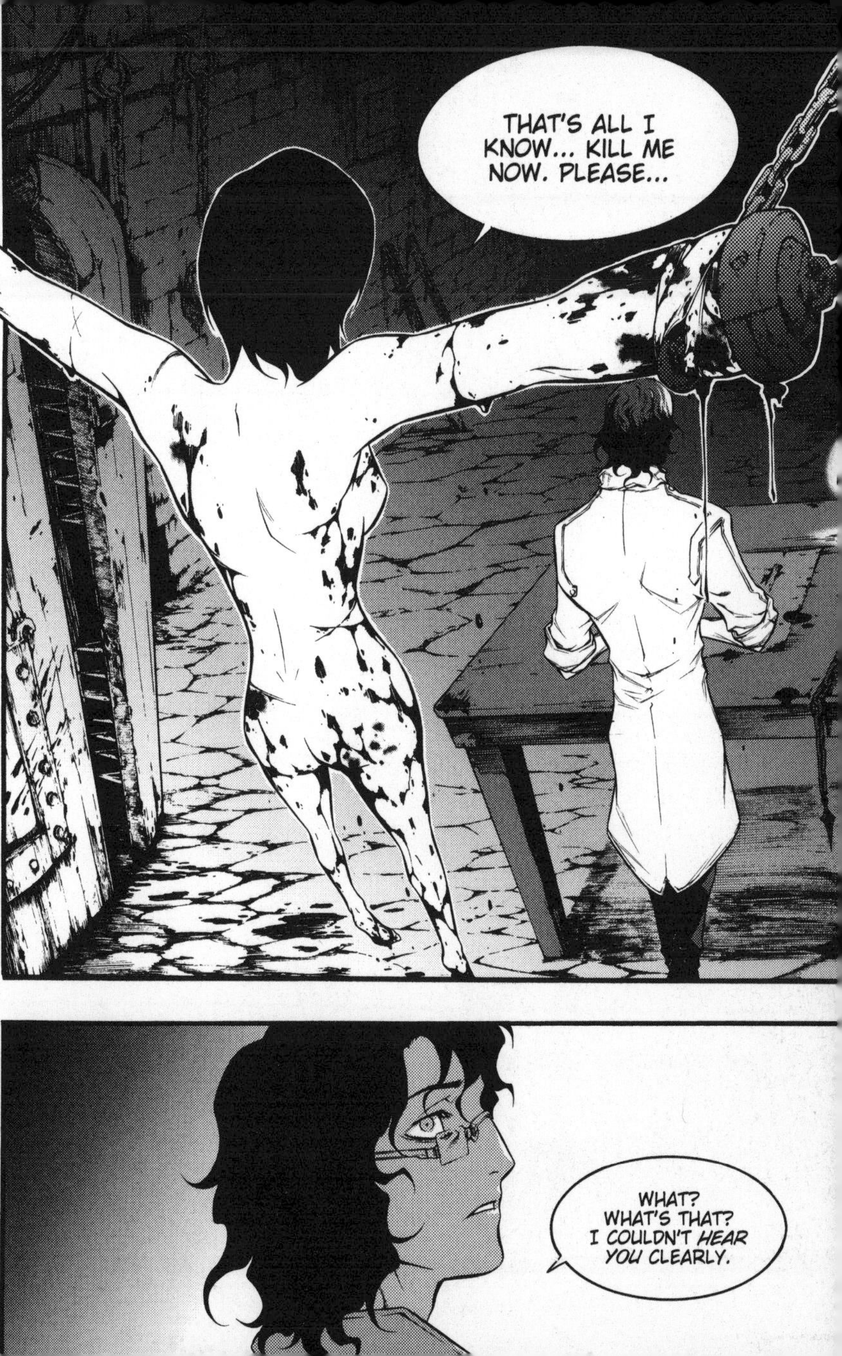
THAT'S ALL I KNOW... KILL ME NOW. PLEASE...
WHAT? WHAT'S THAT? I COULDN'T *HEAR YOU* CLEARLY.

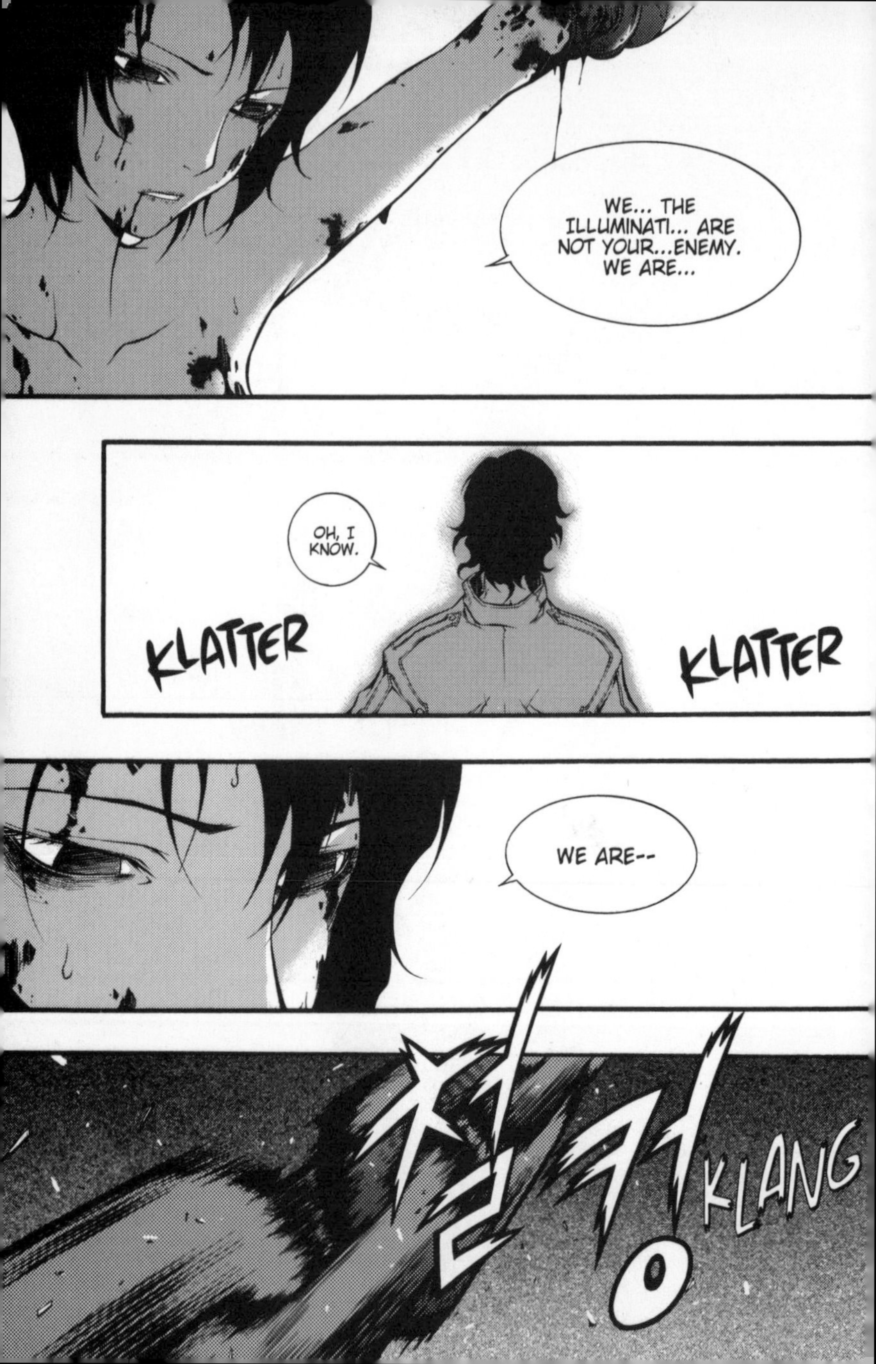
WE... THE ILLUMINATI... ARE NOT YOUR...ENEMY. WE ARE...
OH, I KNOW.
KLATTER
KLATTER
WE ARE--
KLANG

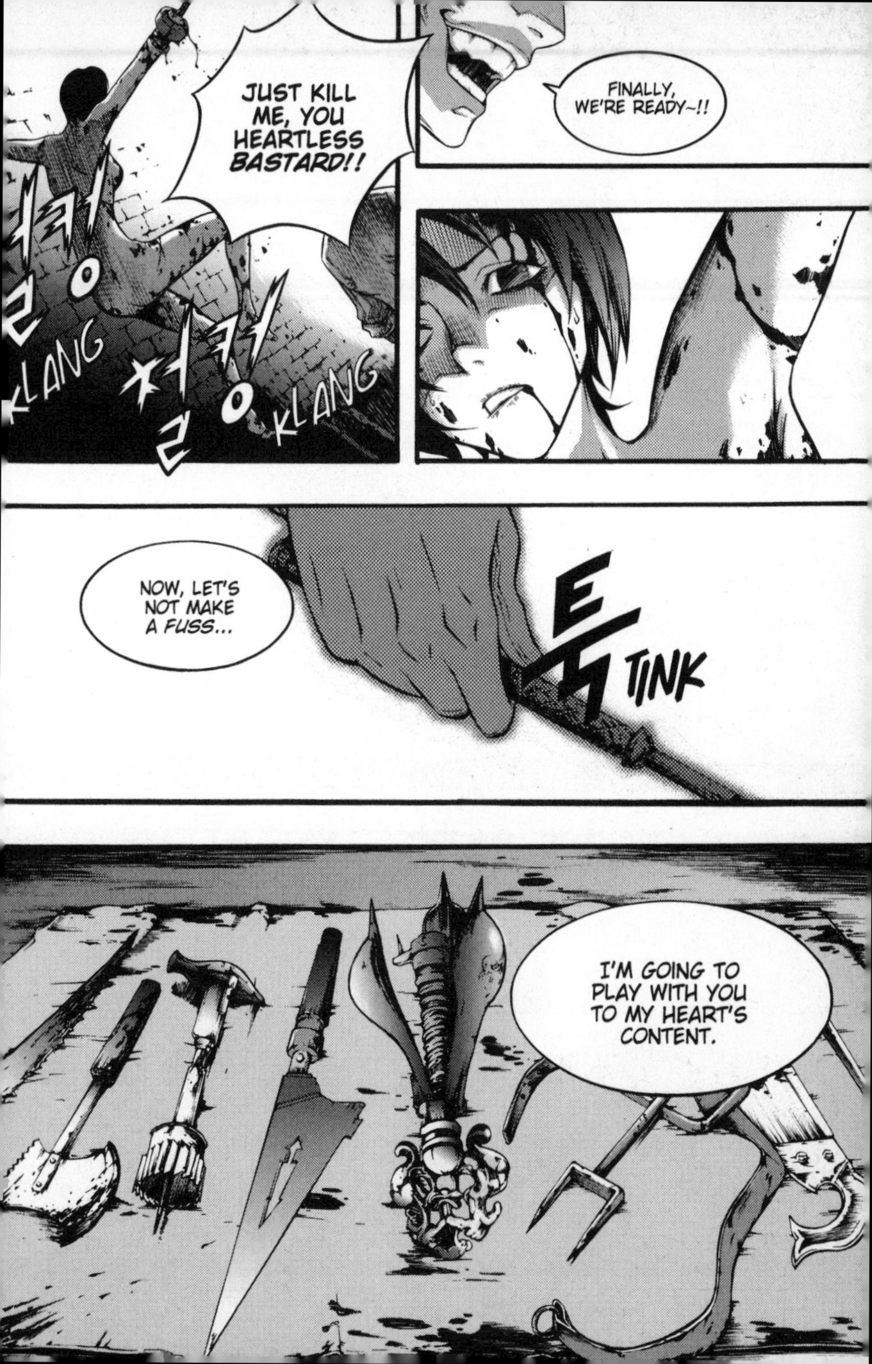

JUST KILL ME, YOU HEARTLESS *BASTARD!!*
FINALLY, WE'RE READY~!!
KLANG
KLANG
NOW, LET'S NOT MAKE A *FUSS...*
TINK
I'M GOING TO PLAY WITH YOU TO MY HEART'S CONTENT.

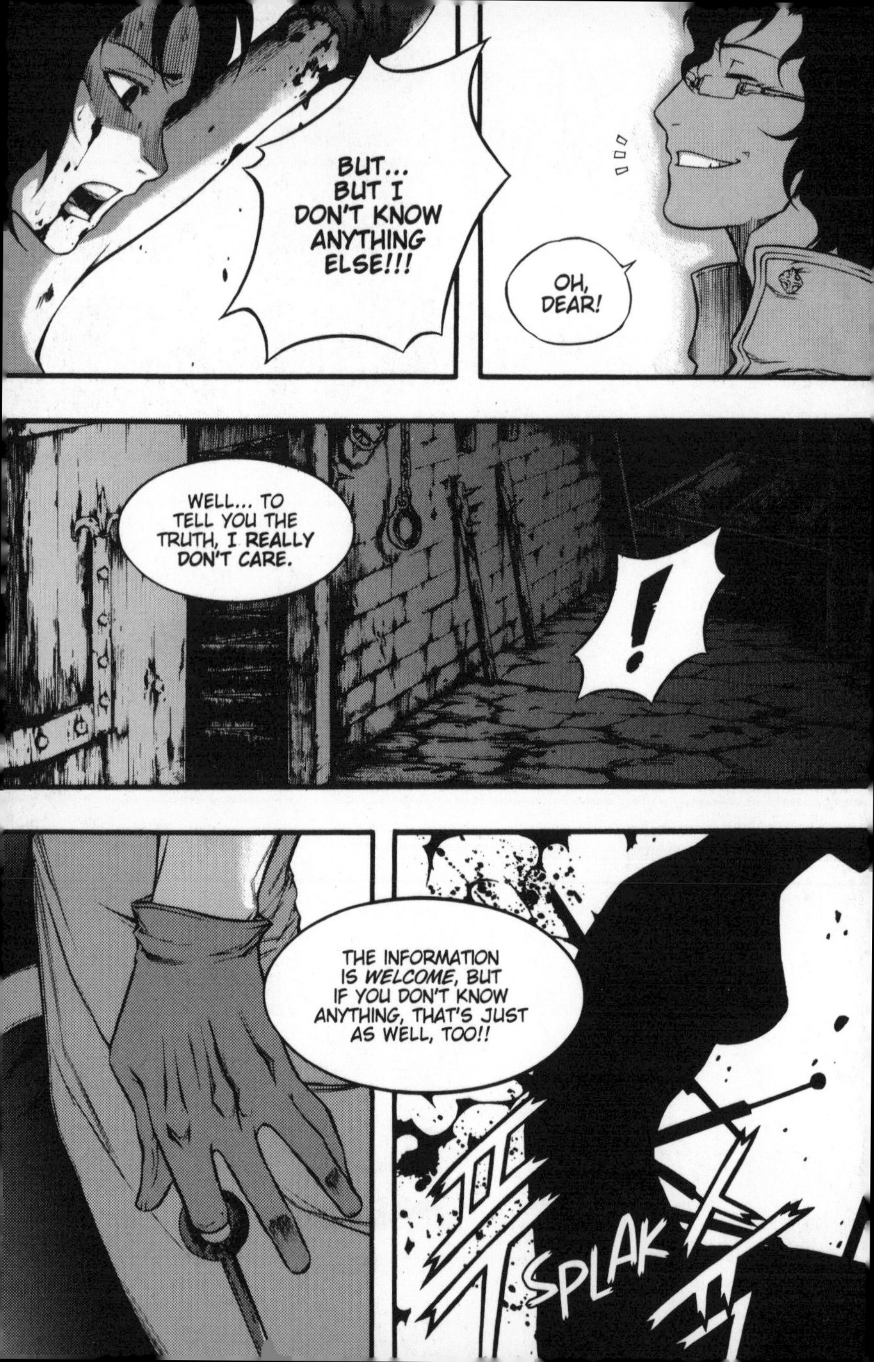
BUT... BUT I DON'T KNOW ANYTHING ELSE!!!
OH, DEAR!
WELL... TO TELL YOU THE TRUTH, I REALLY DON'T CARE.
!
THE INFORMATION IS *WELCOME*, BUT IF YOU DON'T KNOW ANYTHING, THAT'S JUST AS WELL, TOO!!
SPLAK

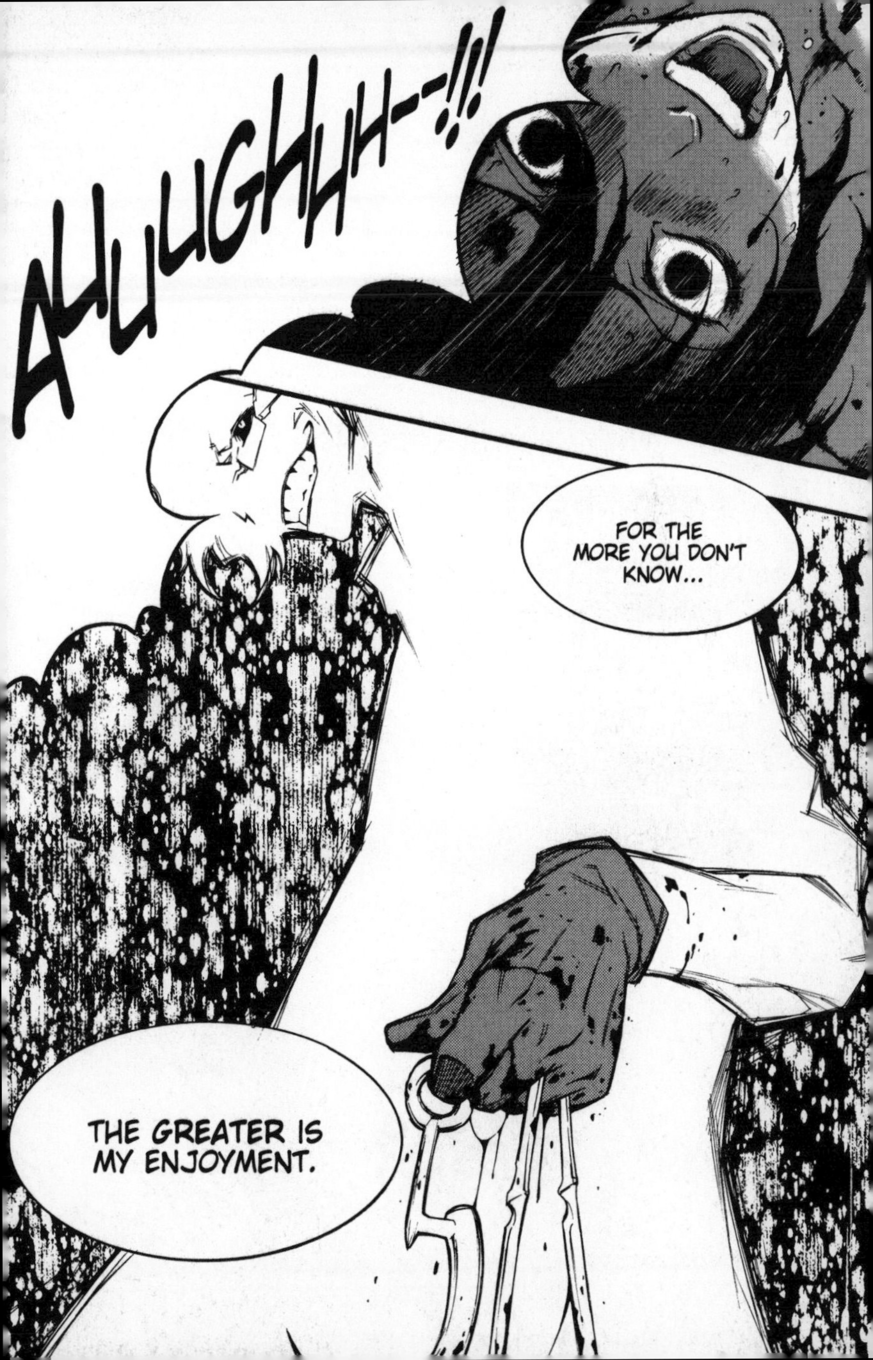
AUUGHHH--!!!
FOR THE MORE YOU DON'T KNOW...
THE GREATER IS MY ENJOYMENT.

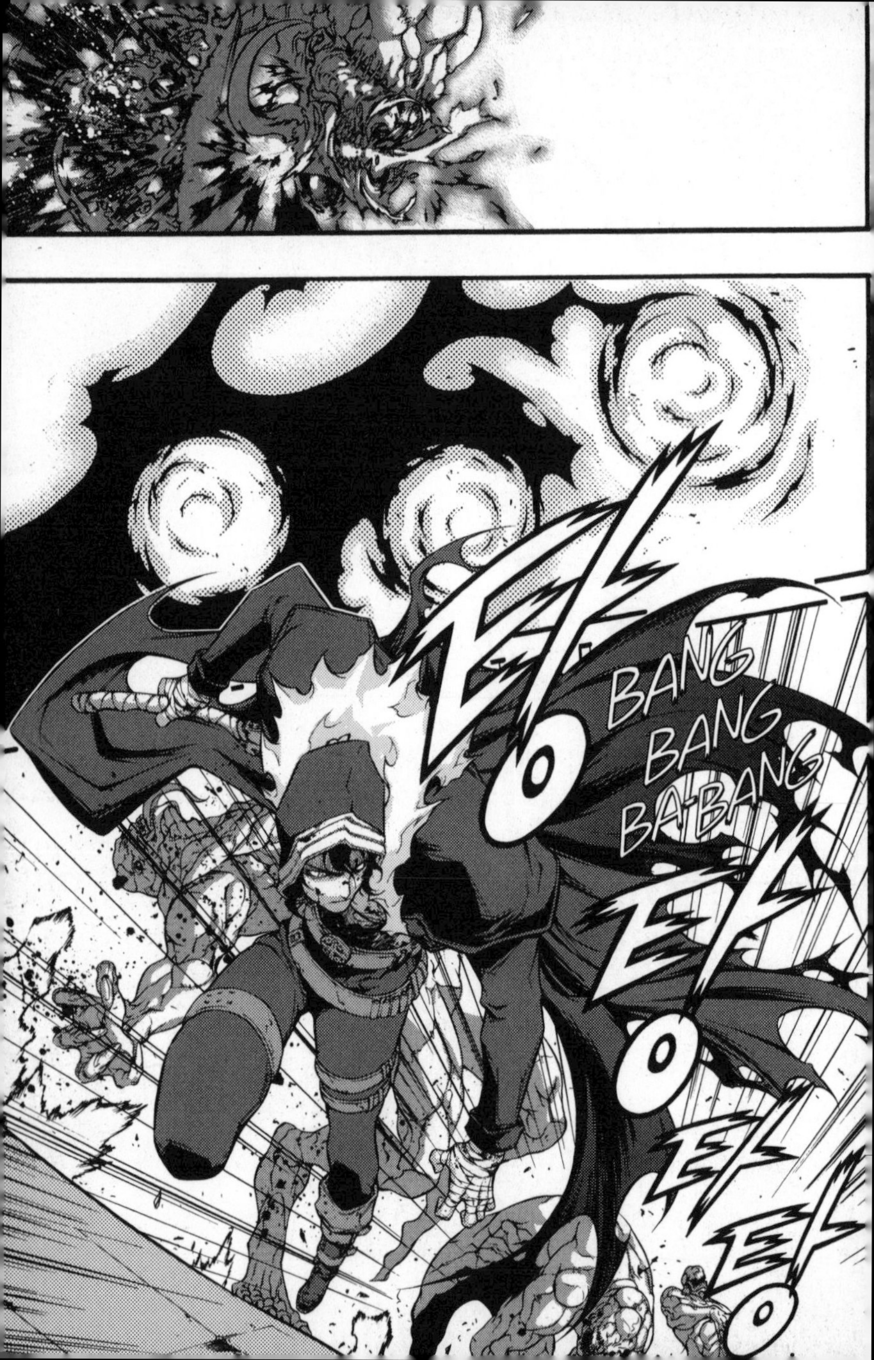
BANG
BANG
BA-BANG

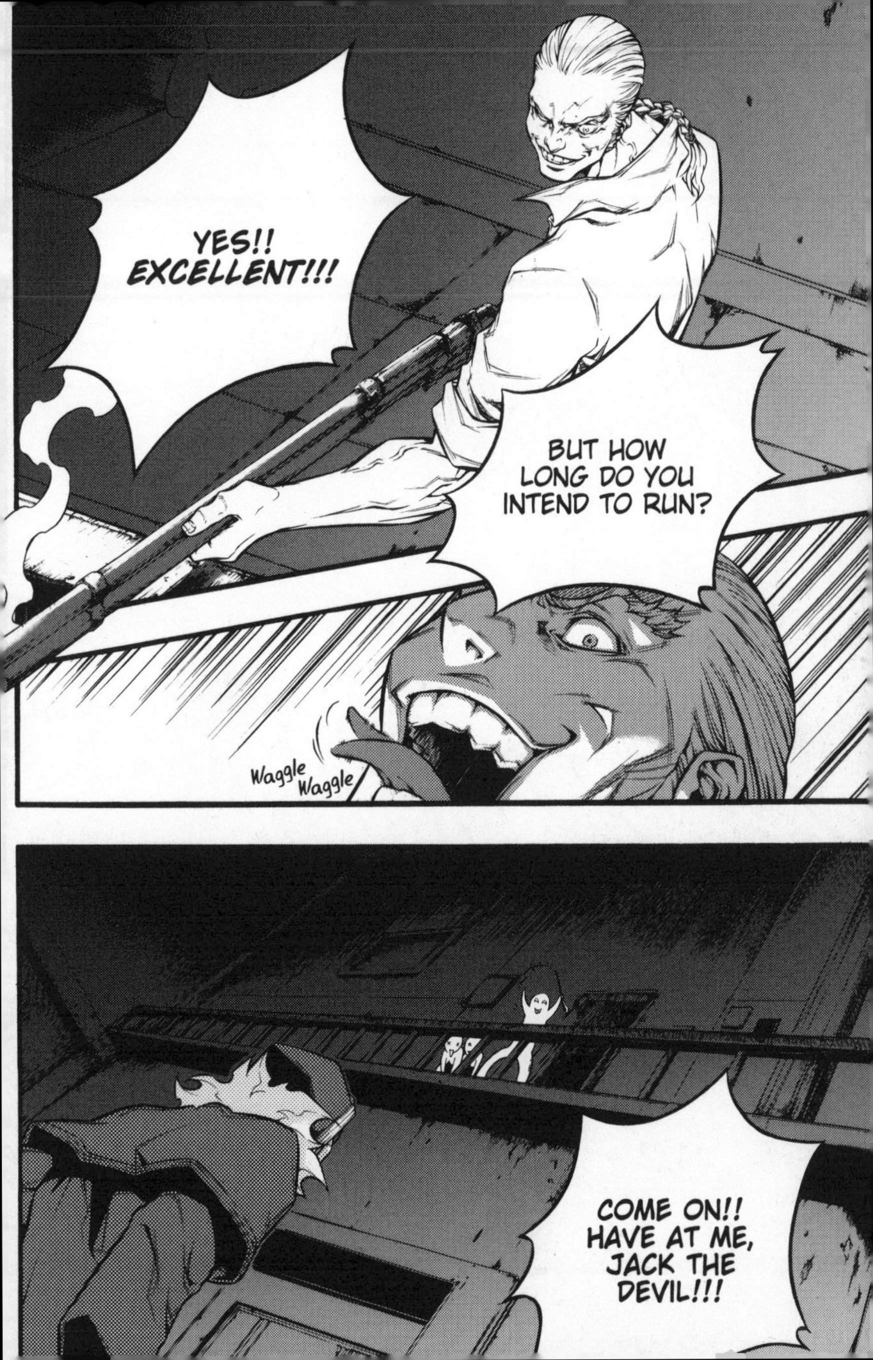
YES!! EXCELLENT!!!
BUT HOW LONG DO YOU INTEND TO RUN?
Waggle Waggle
COME ON!! HAVE AT ME, JACK THE DEVIL!!!

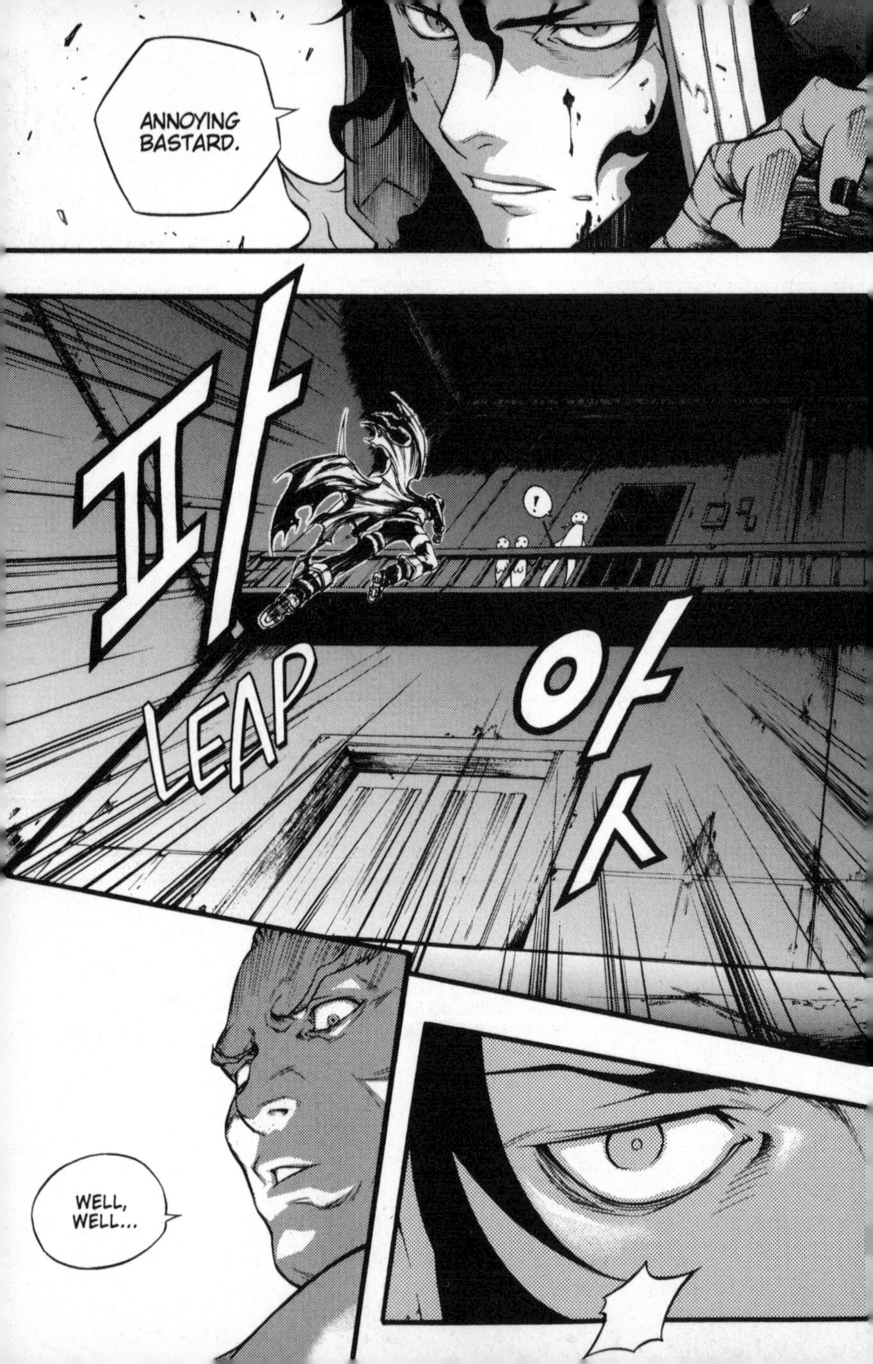
ANNOYING BASTARD.
LEAP
!
WELL, WELL...

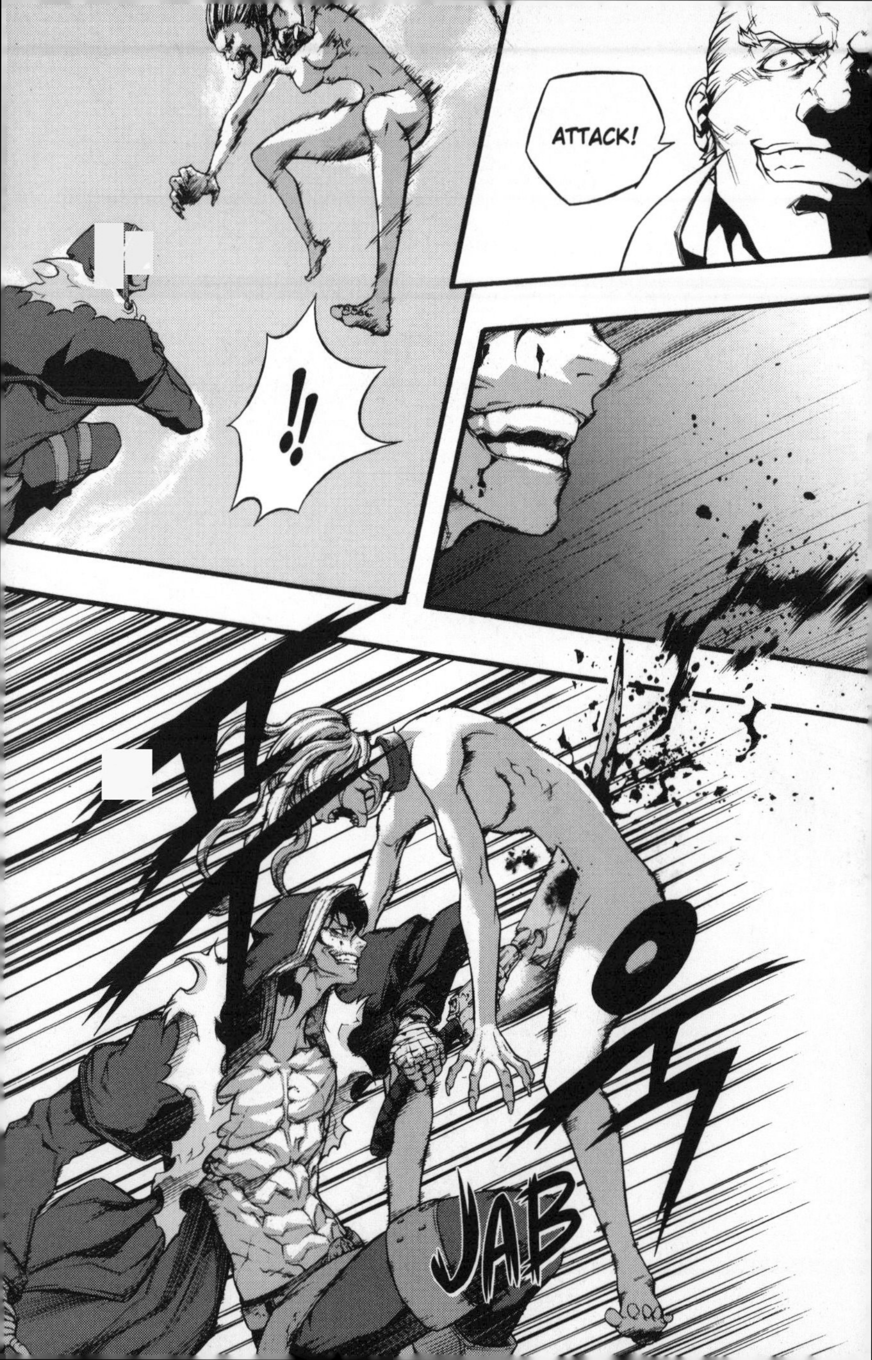

ATTACK!
!!
JAB

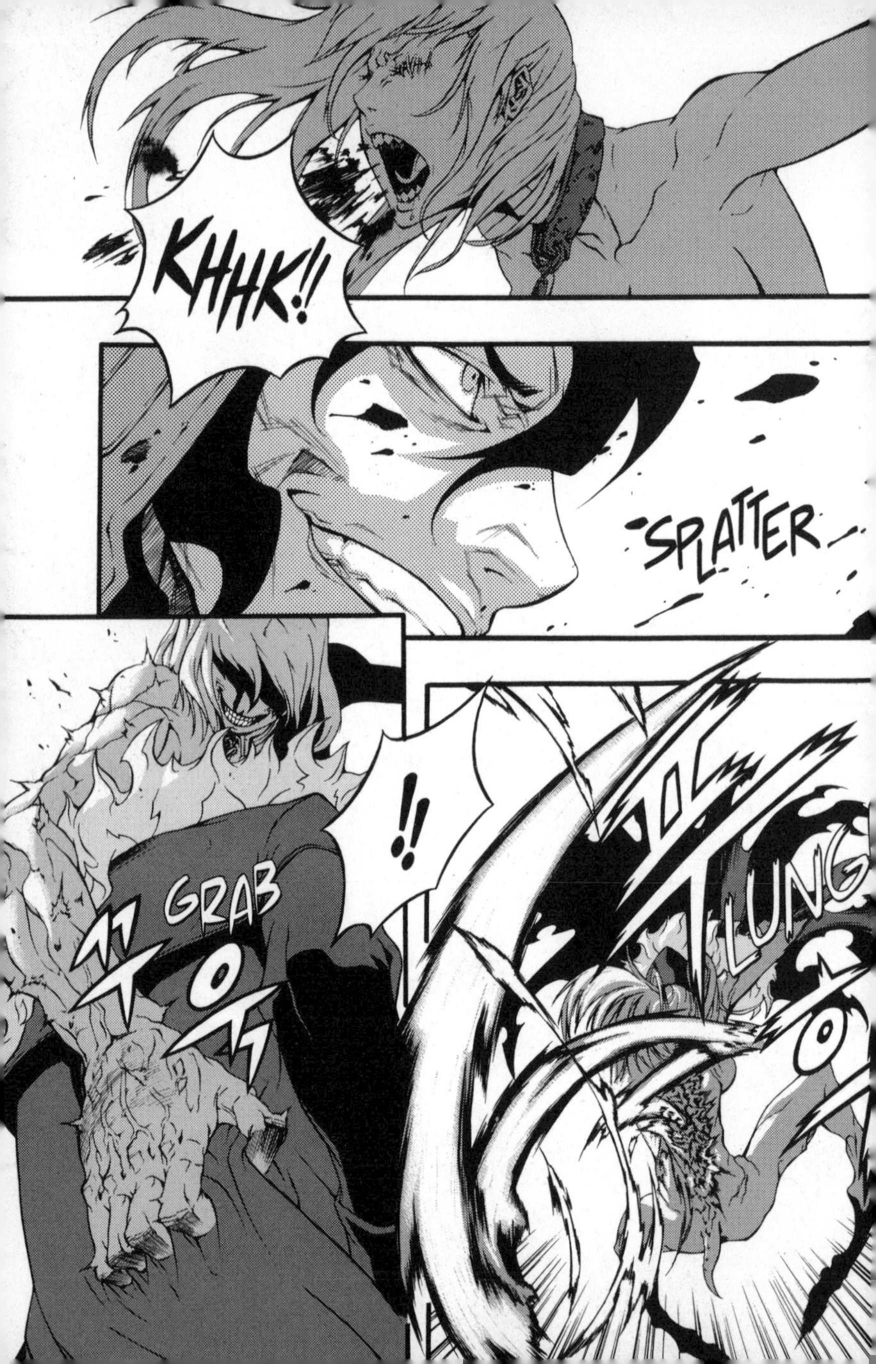
KHHK!!
SPLATTER
!!
GRAB

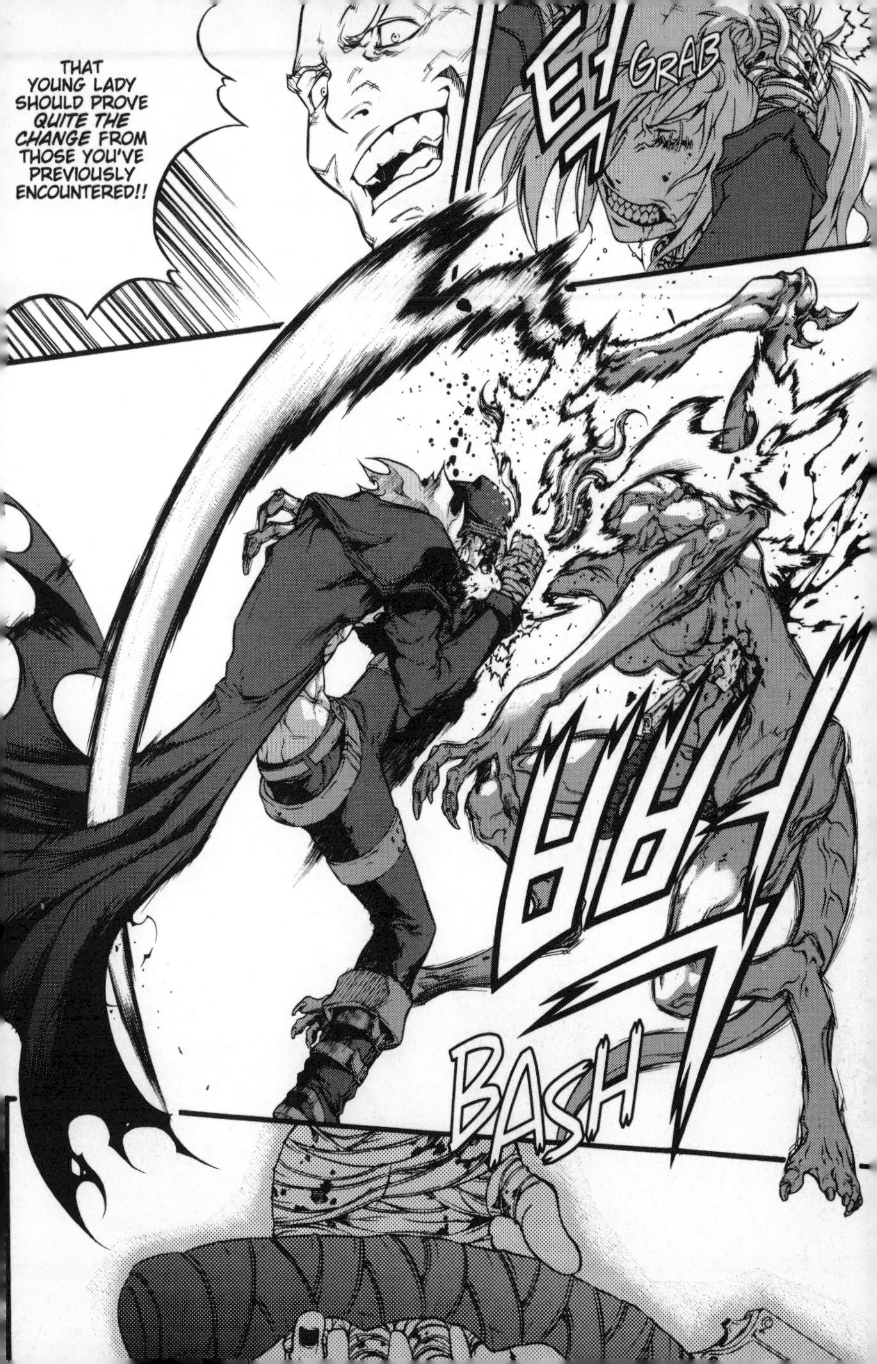
THAT YOUNG LADY SHOULD PROVE *QUITE THE CHANGE* FROM THOSE YOU'VE PREVIOUSLY ENCOUNTERED!!
GRAB
BASH

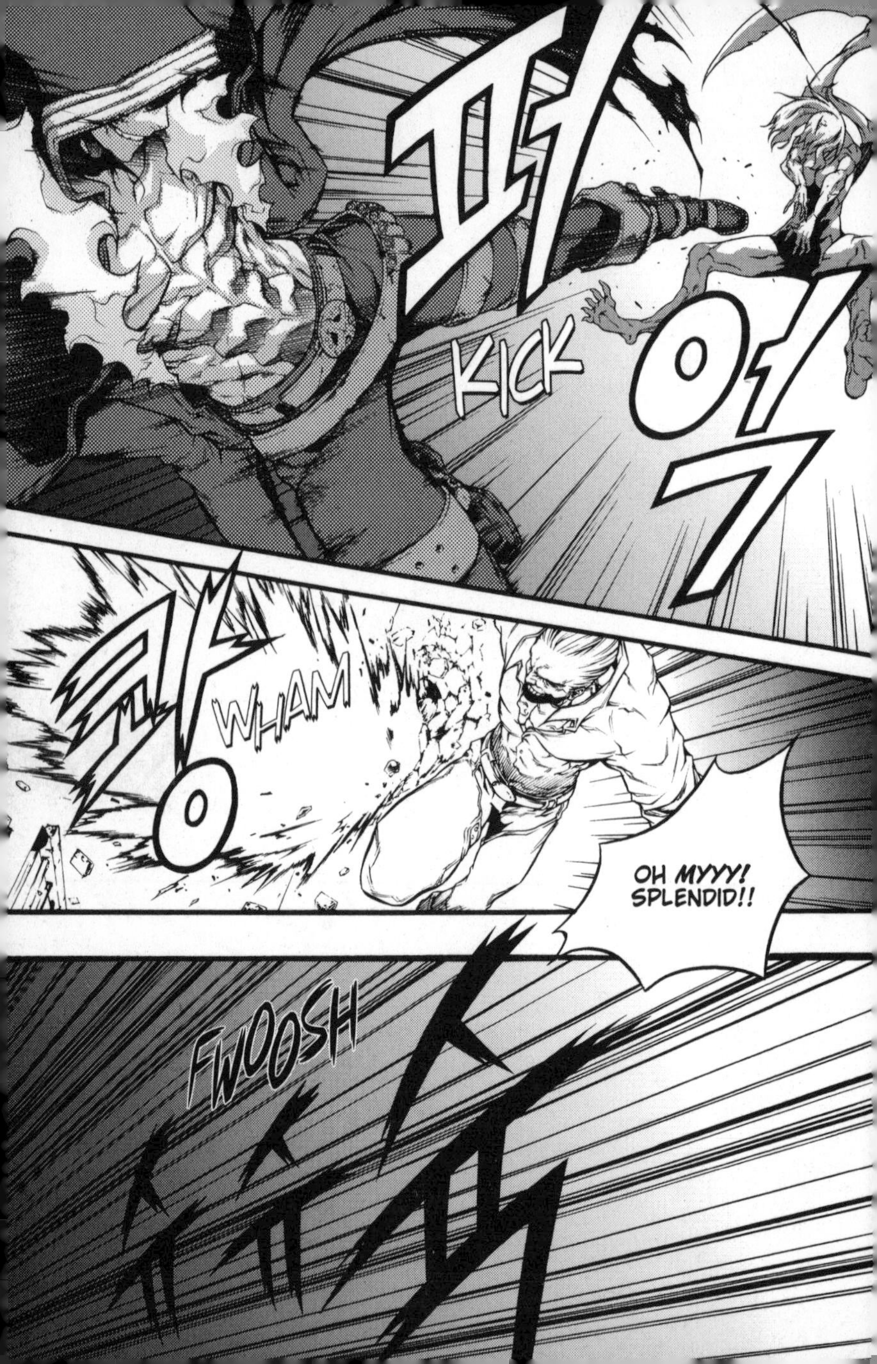
KICK
WHAM
OH MYYY!
SPLENDID!!
FWOOSH

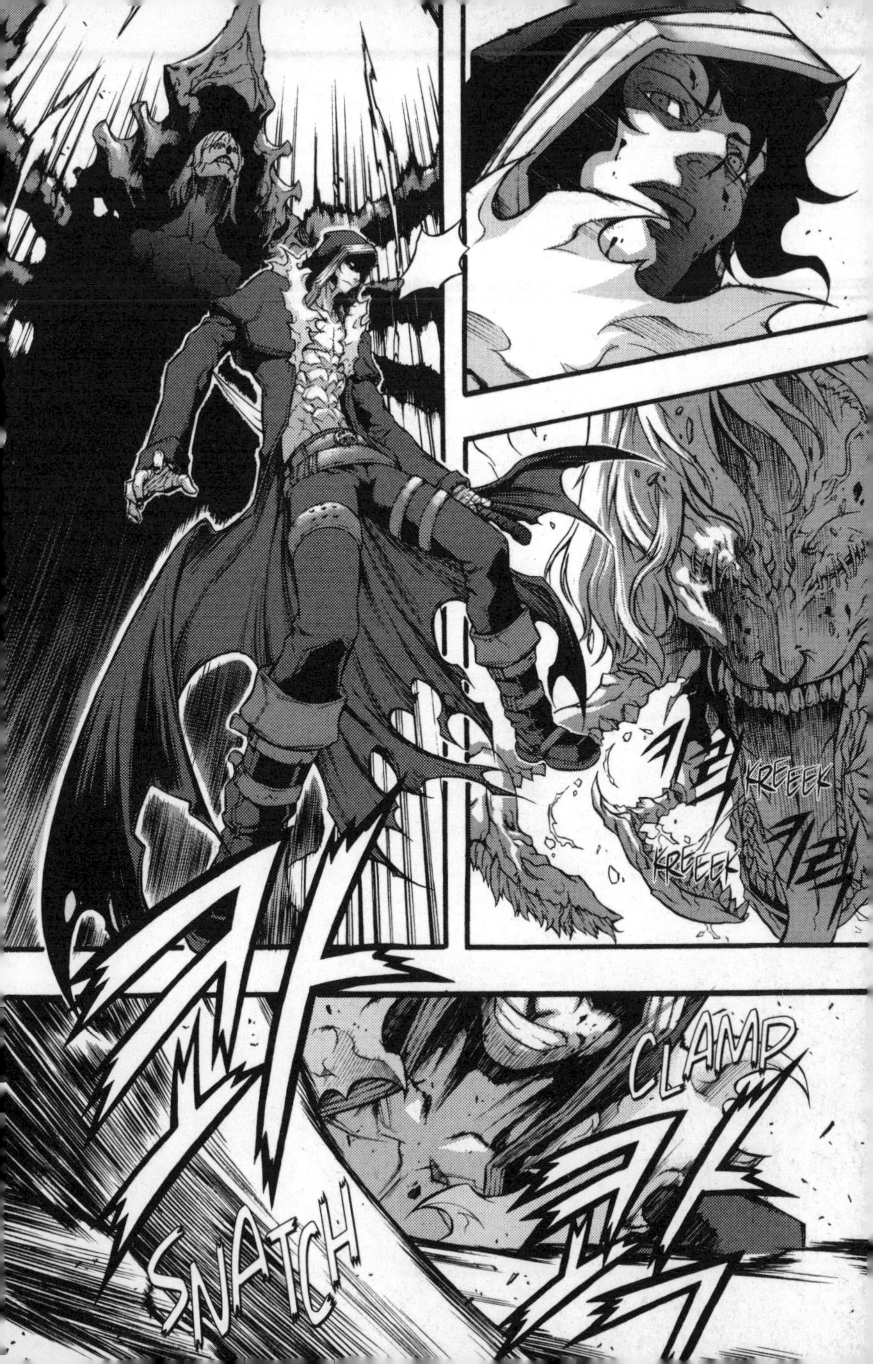

KREEEK
KREEEK
CLAMP
SNATCH

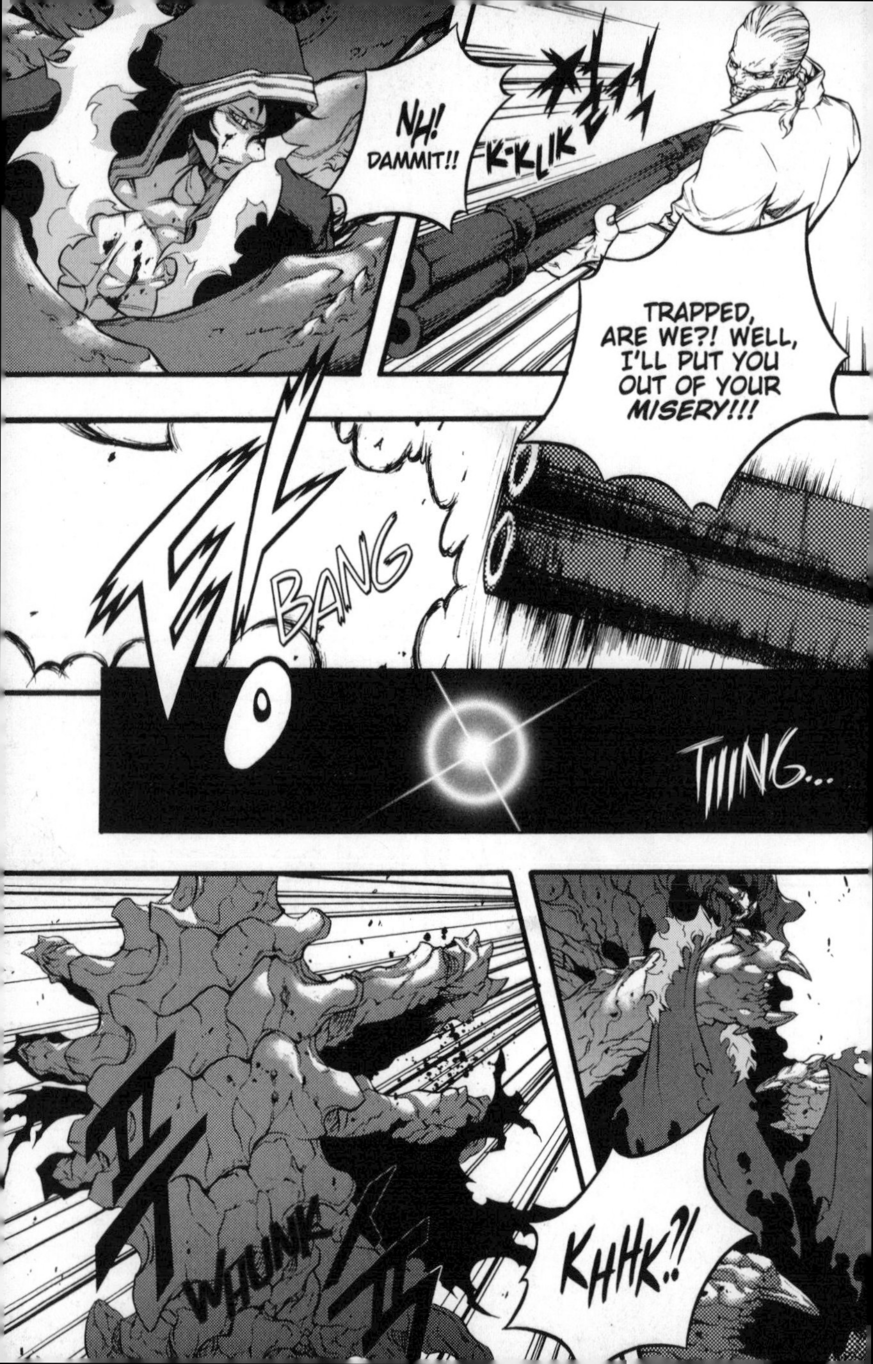
NH! DAMMIT!!
K-KLIK
TRAPPED, ARE WE?! WELL, I'LL PUT YOU OUT OF YOUR *MISERY!!!*
BANG
TIIING...
WHUNK
KHHK?!

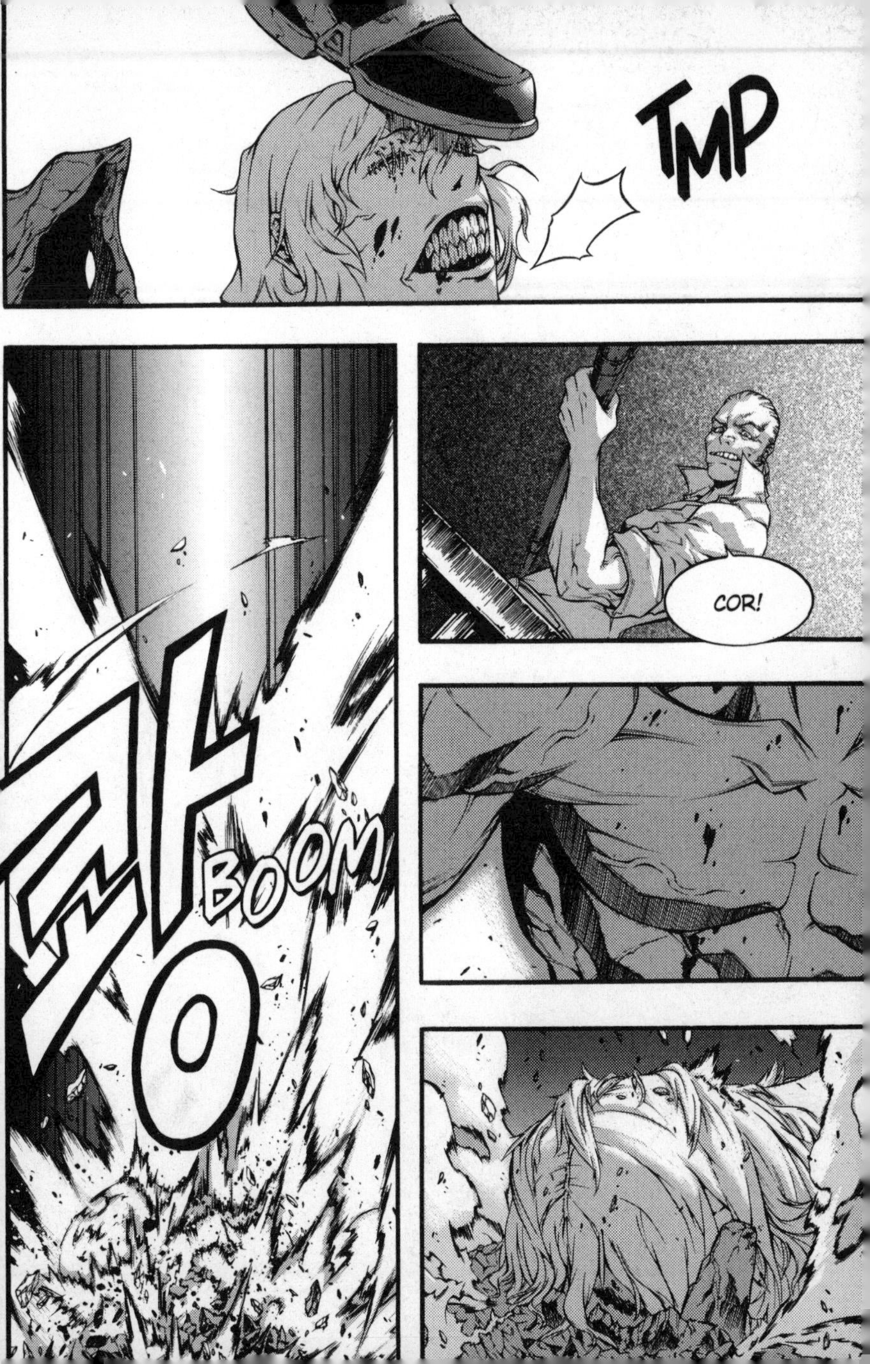
TMP
BOOM
COR!

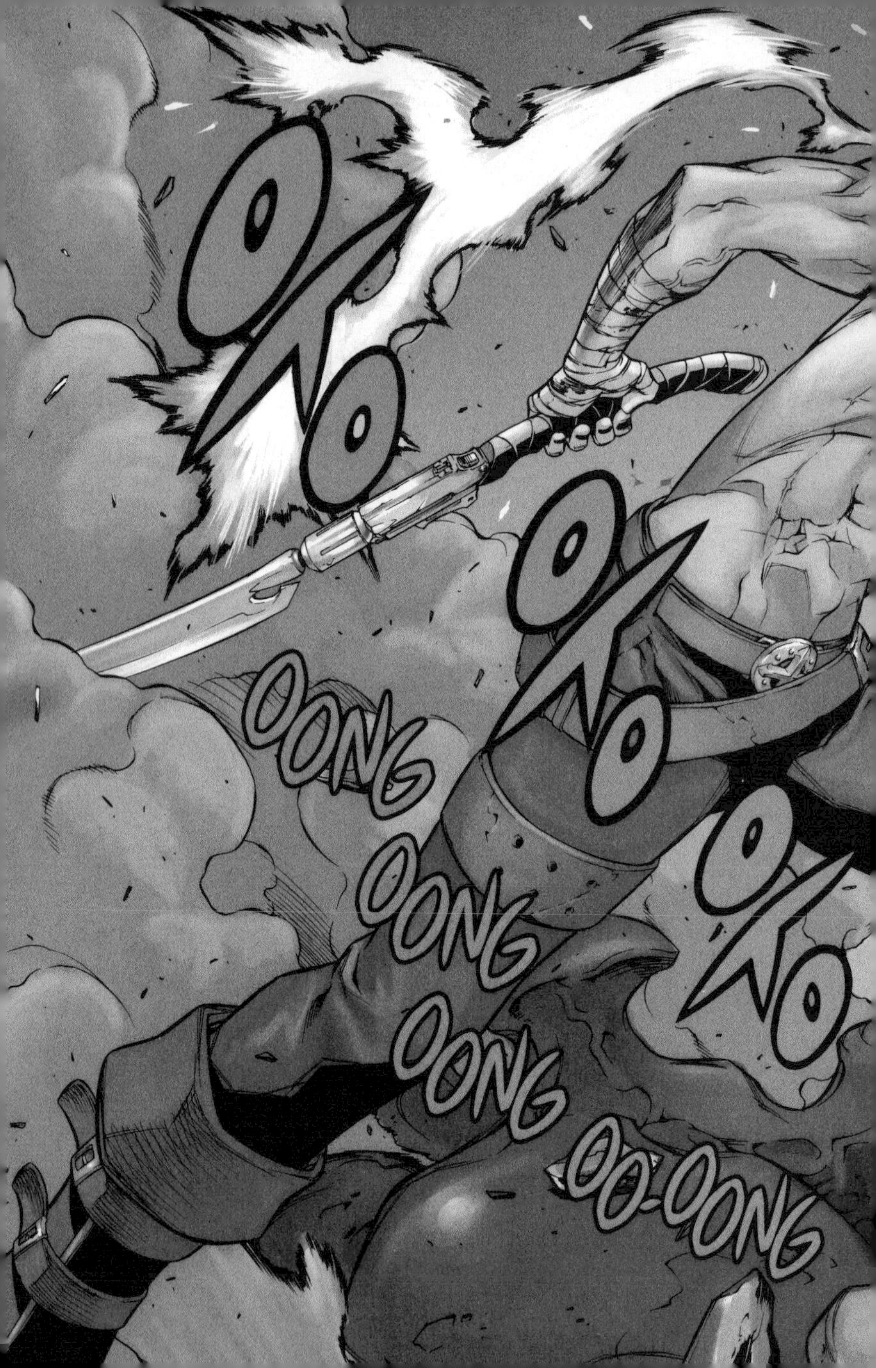

OOOO
OOONG
OOONG
OOONG
OO-OONG

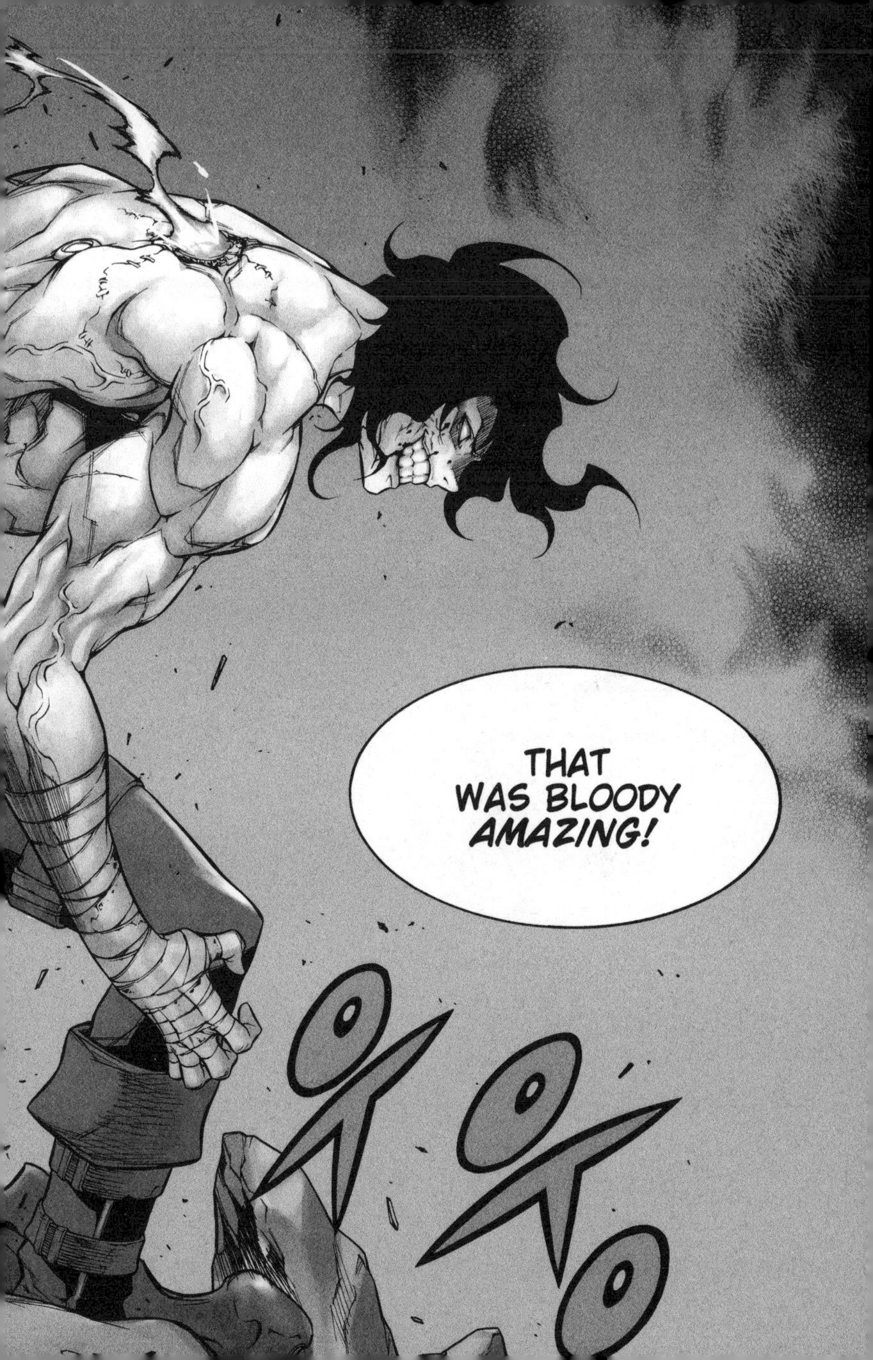
THAT WAS BLOODY AMAZING!

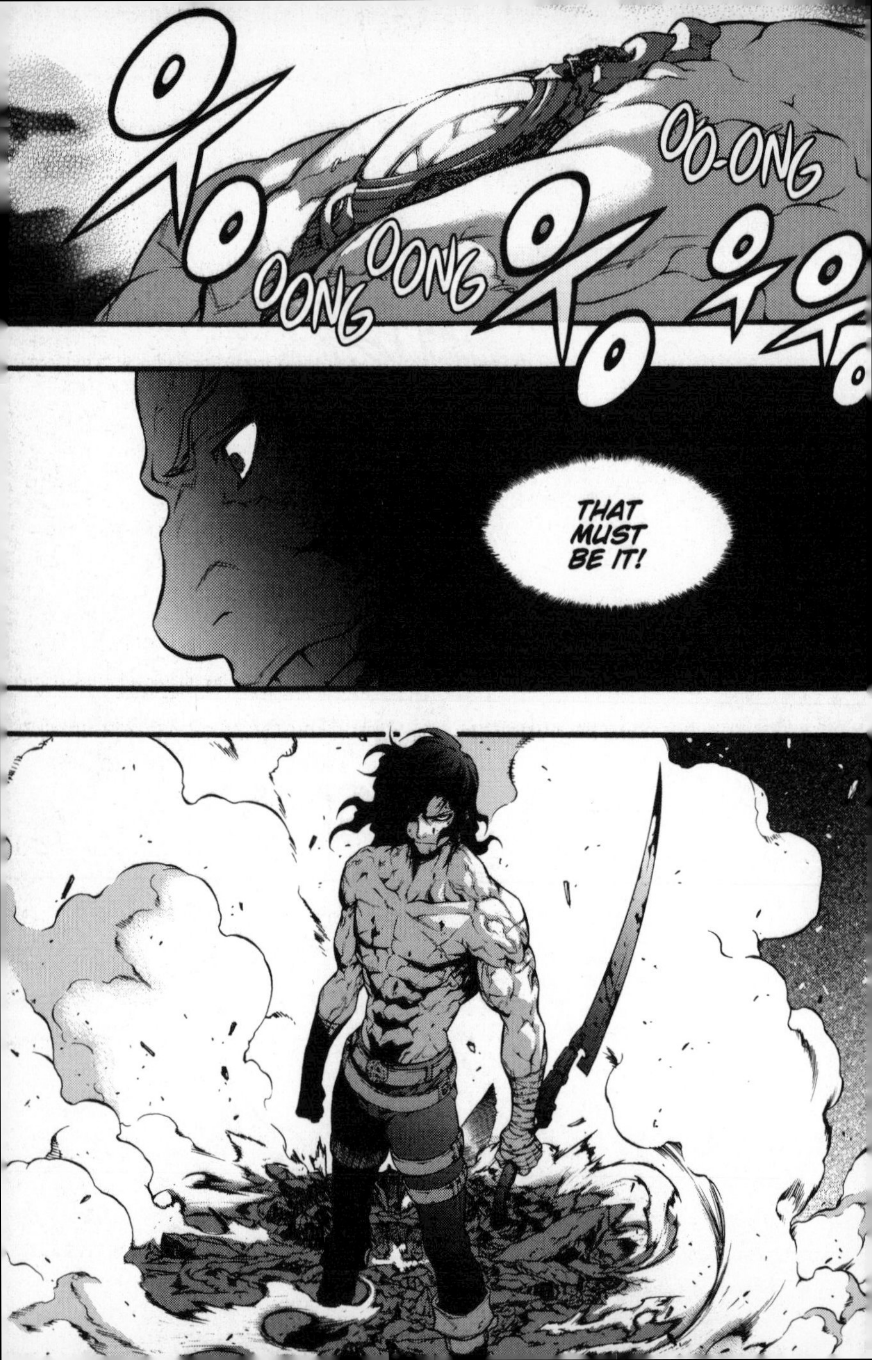
OONG OONG
OO-ONG
THAT MUST BE IT!

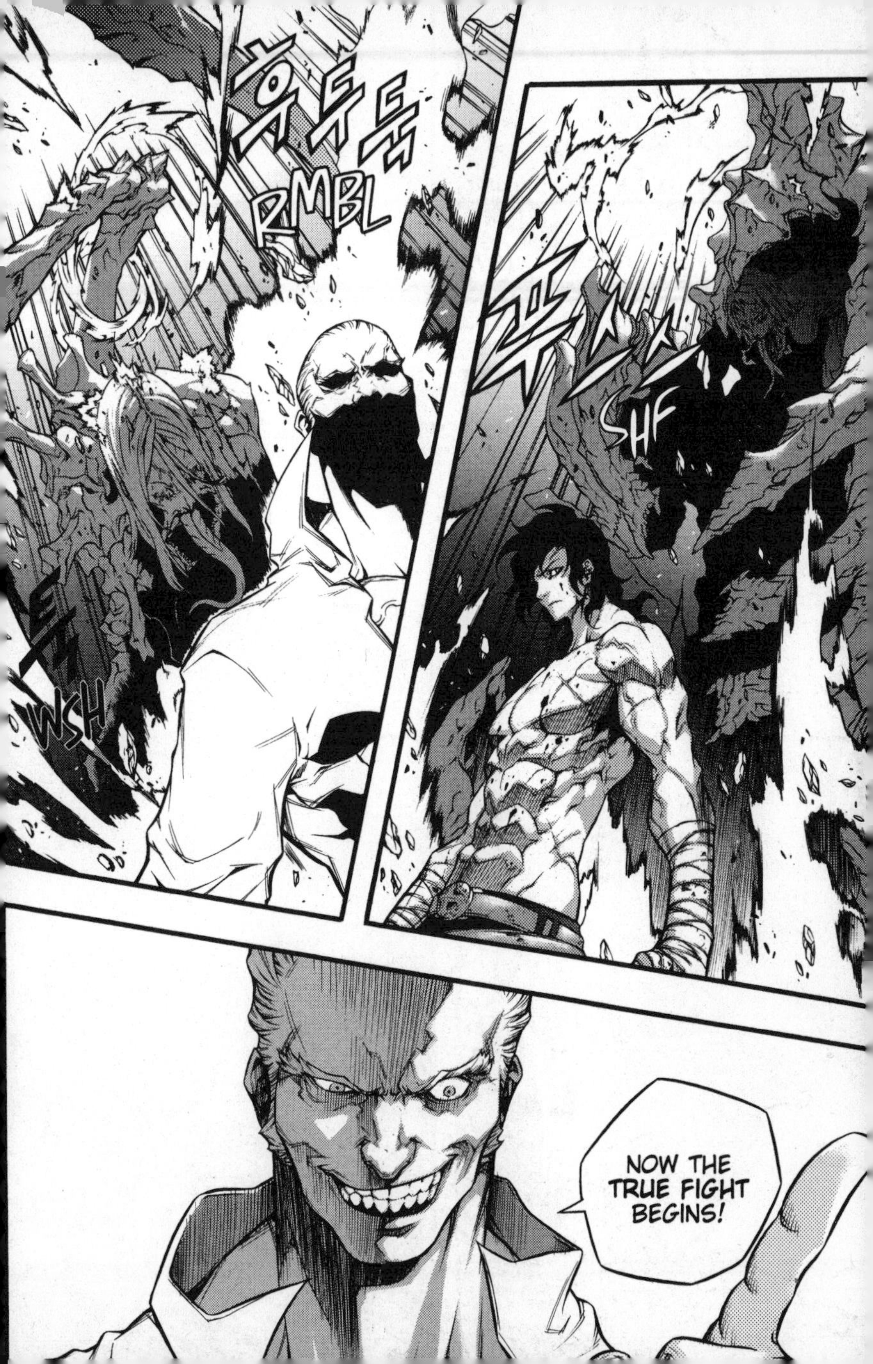
RMBL
SHF
WSH
NOW THE TRUE FIGHT BEGINS!

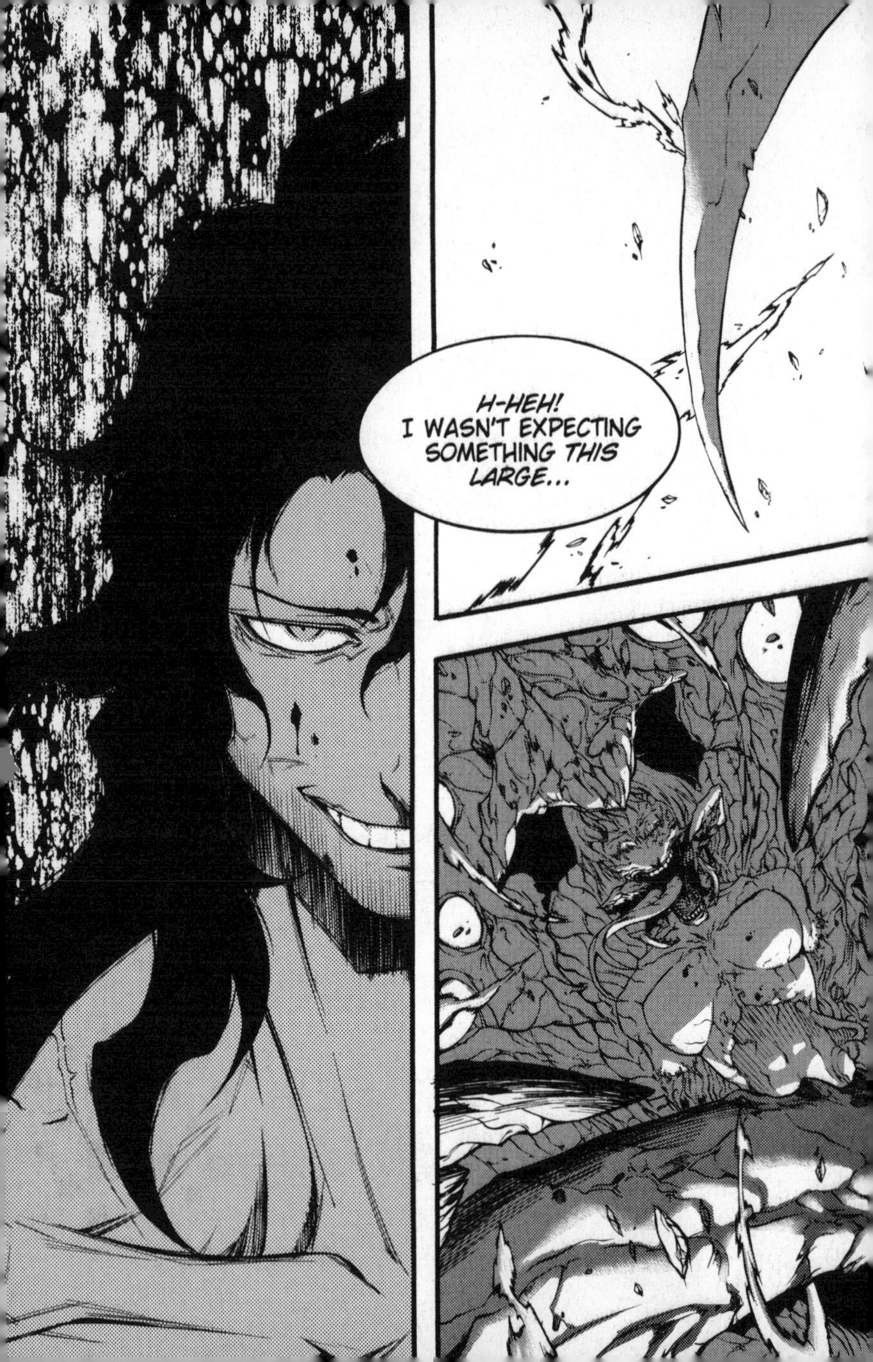
H-HEH!
I WASN'T EXPECTING SOMETHING THIS LARGE...

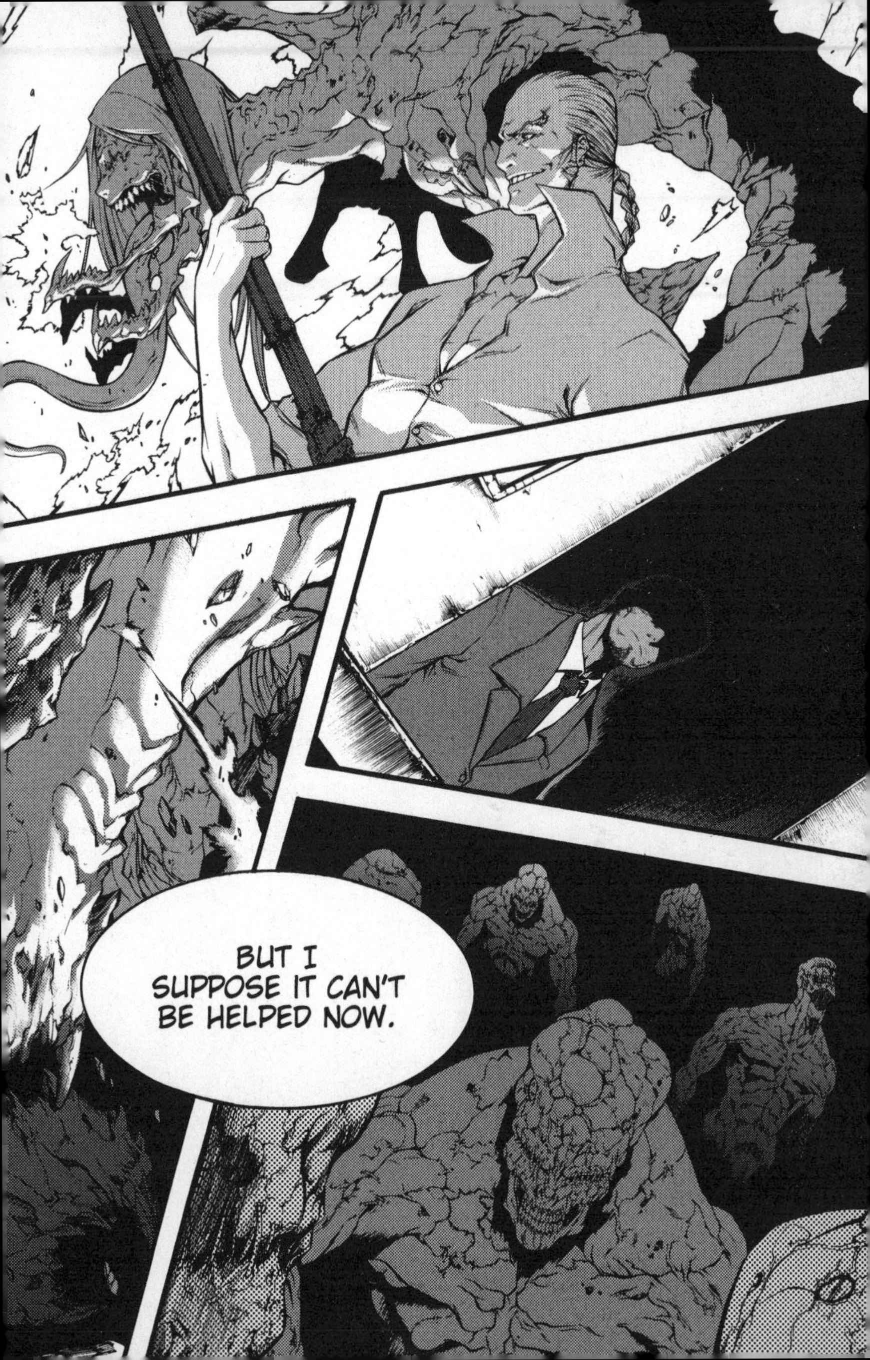
BUT I SUPPOSE IT CAN'T BE HELPED NOW.

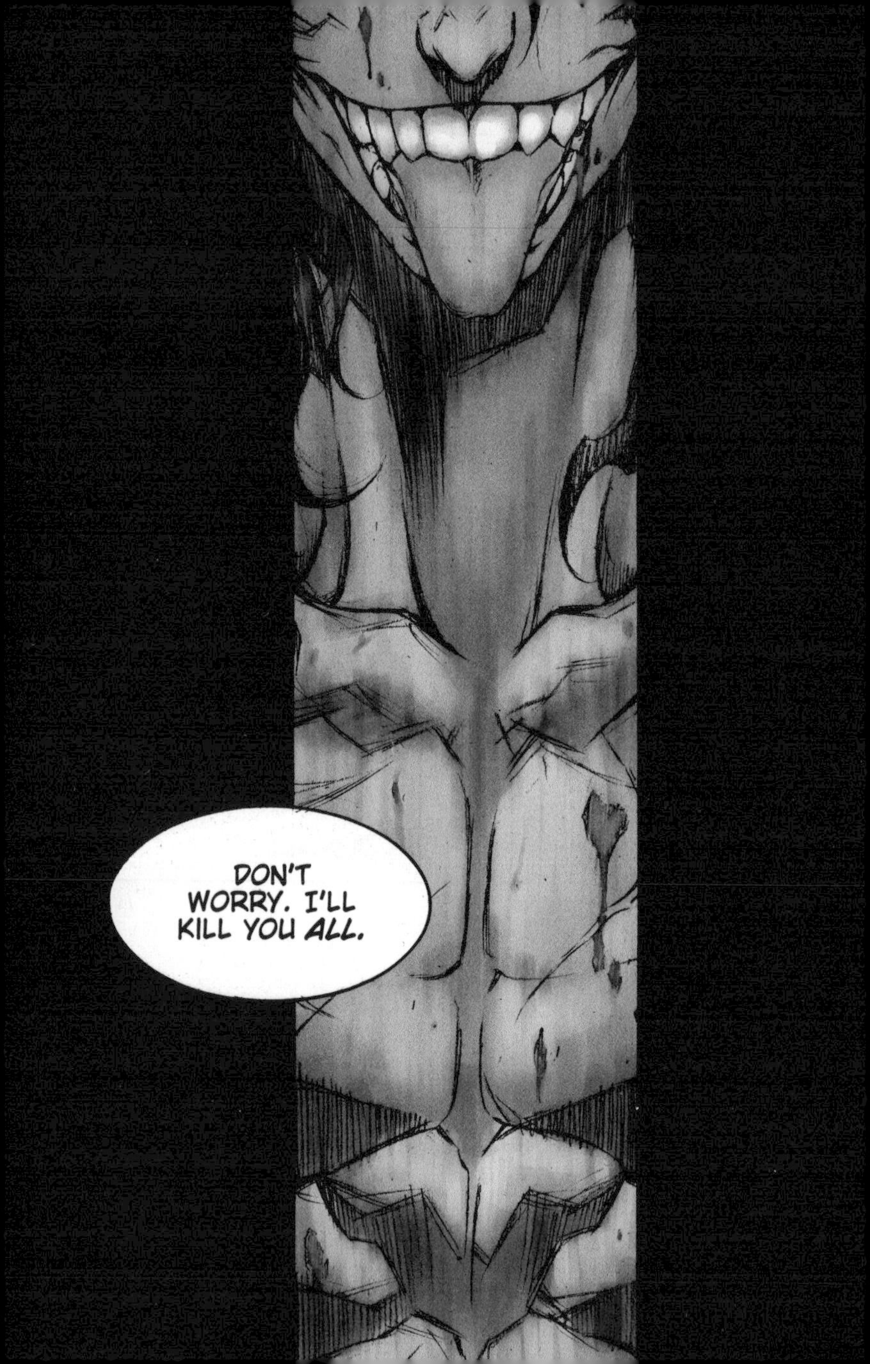
DON'T WORRY. I'LL KILL YOU ALL.

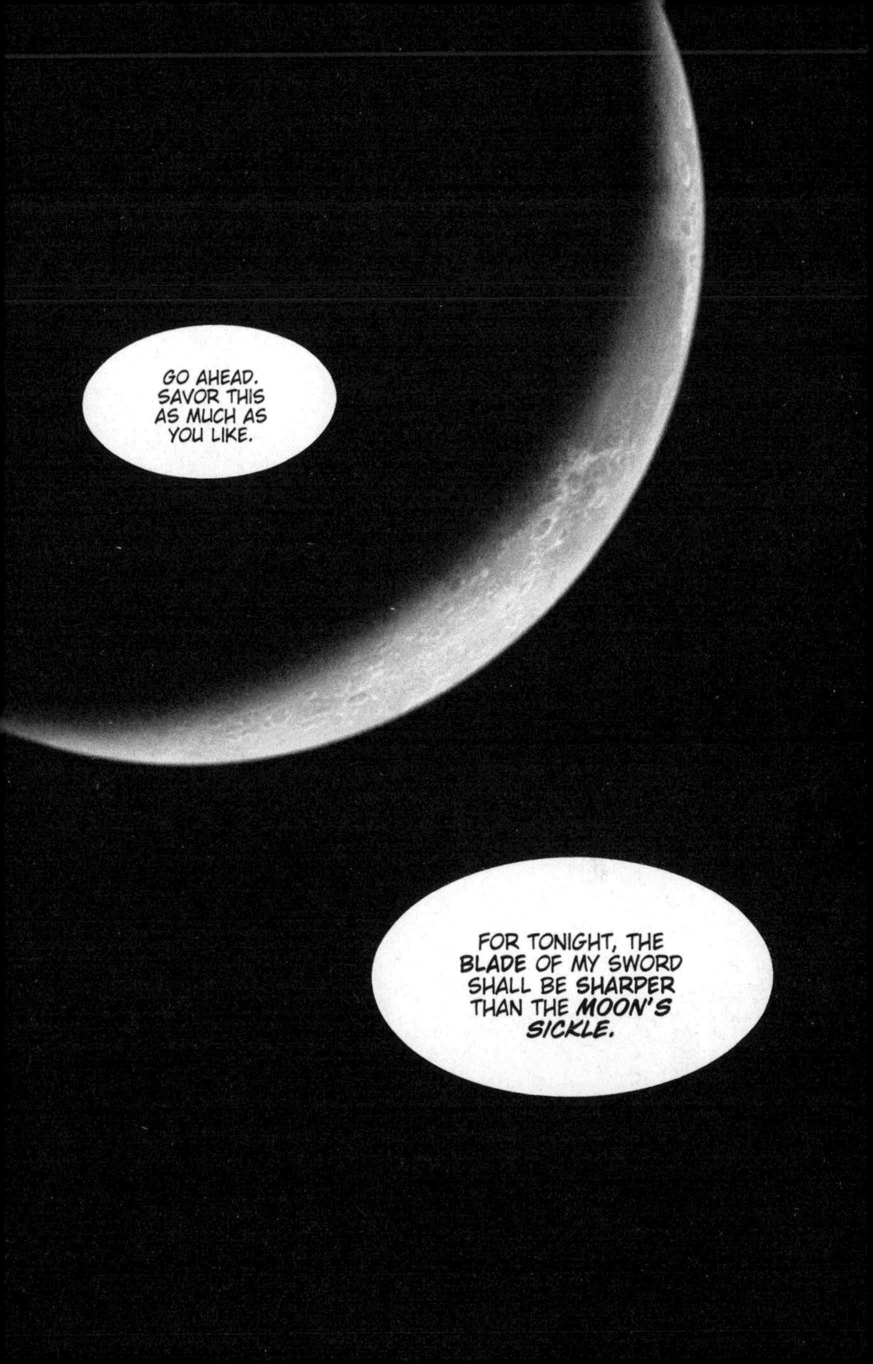
GO AHEAD. SAVOR THIS AS MUCH AS YOU LIKE.
FOR TONIGHT, THE BLADE OF MY SWORD SHALL BE SHARPER THAN THE *MOON'S SICKLE.*

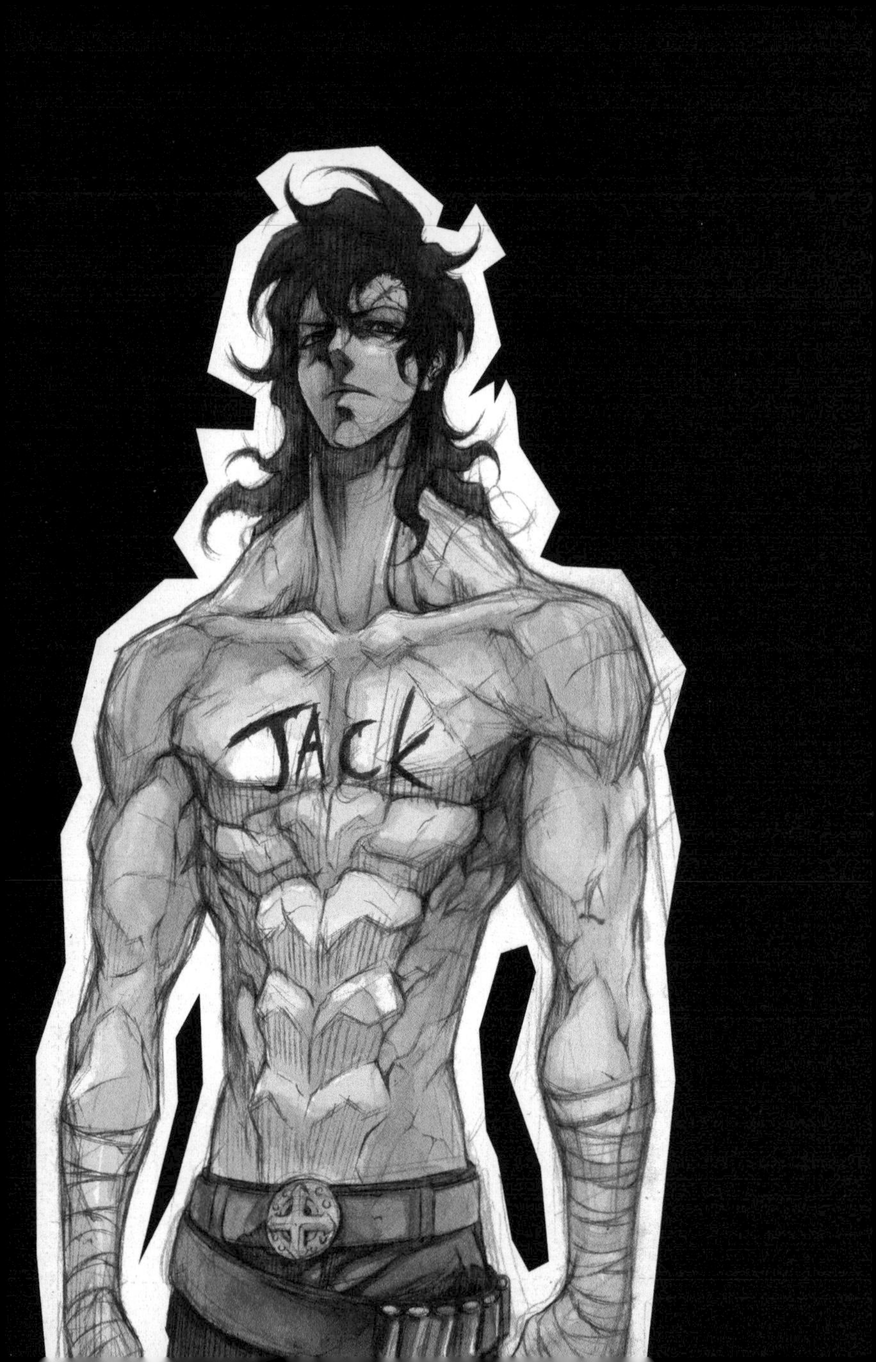
JACK

EPISODE 12

HUNTERS (7)

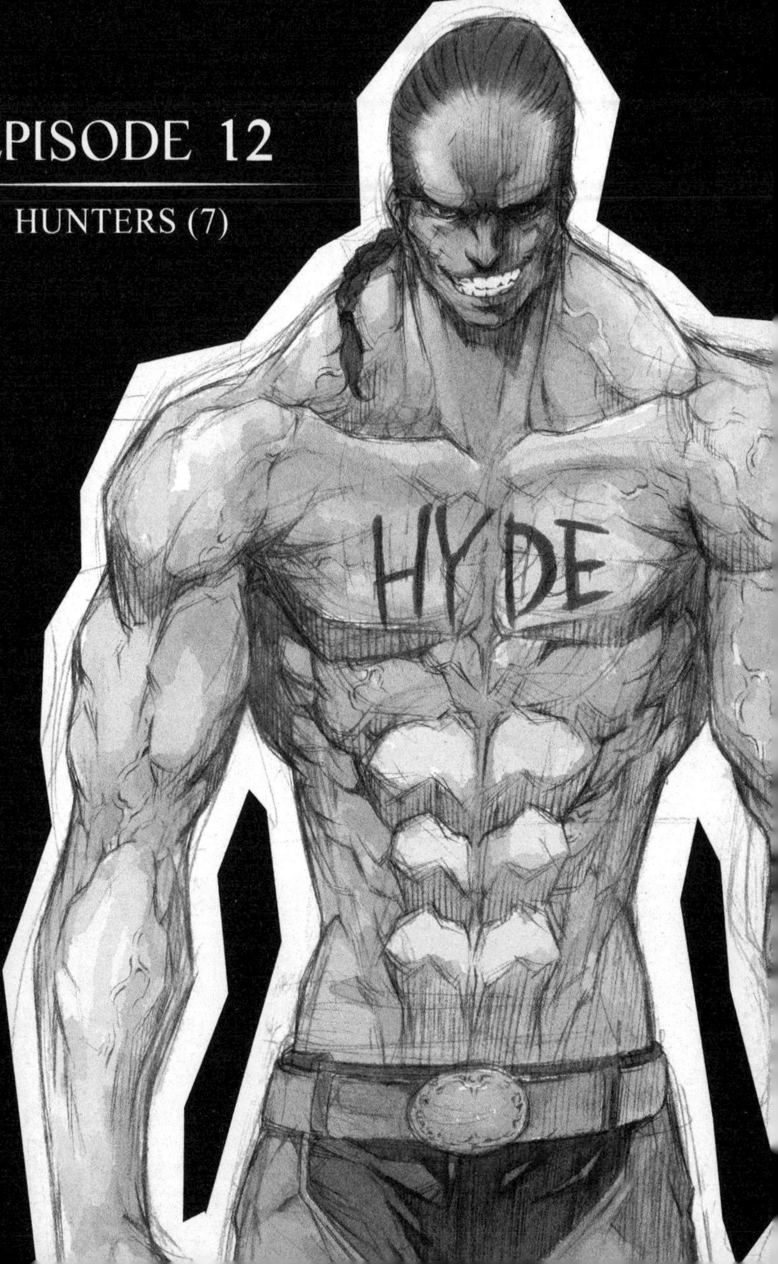
HYDE

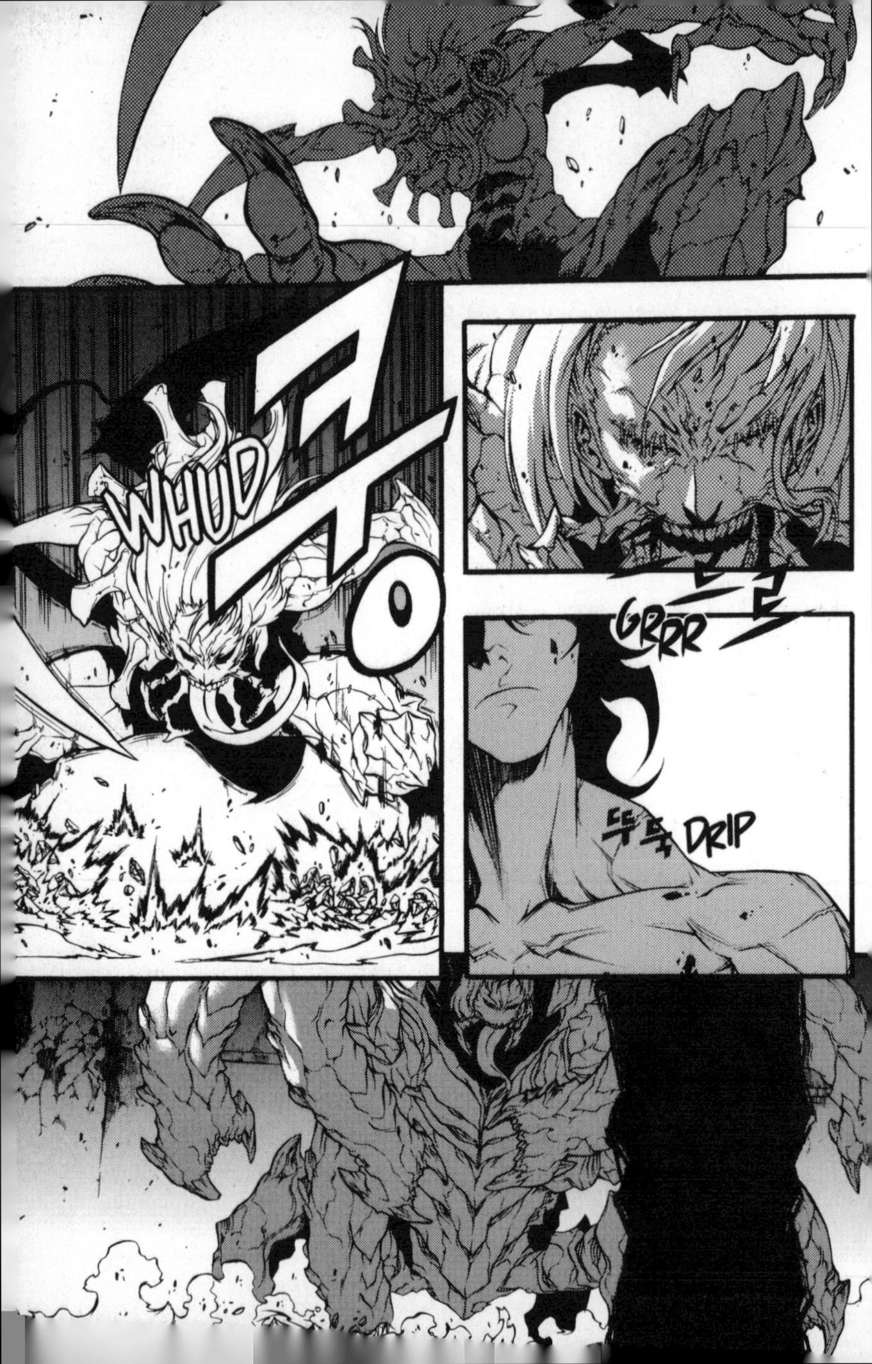
WHUD
GRRR
뚝뚝 DRIP

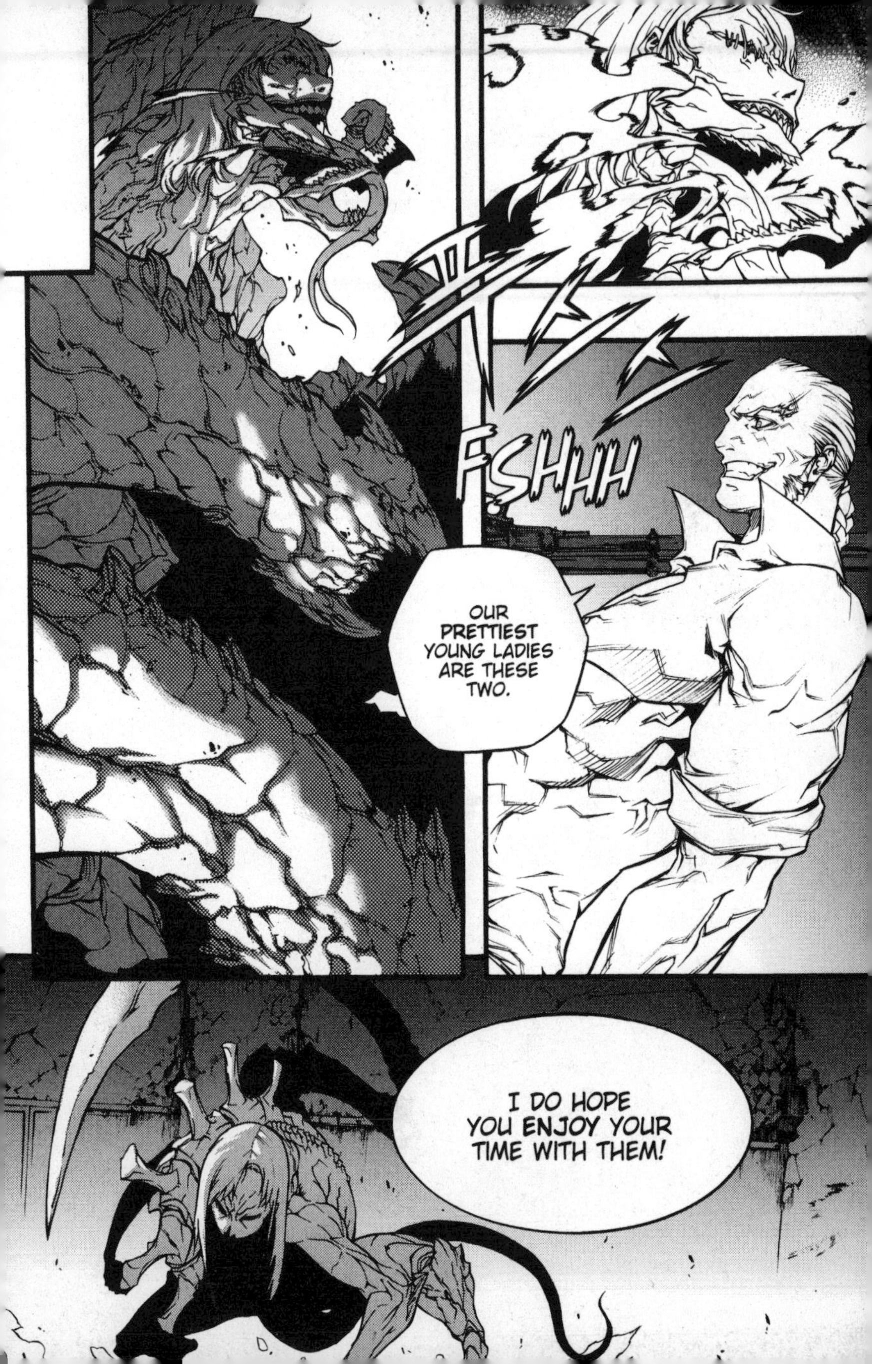
FSHHH
OUR PRETTIEST YOUNG LADIES ARE THESE TWO.
I DO HOPE YOU ENJOY YOUR TIME WITH THEM!

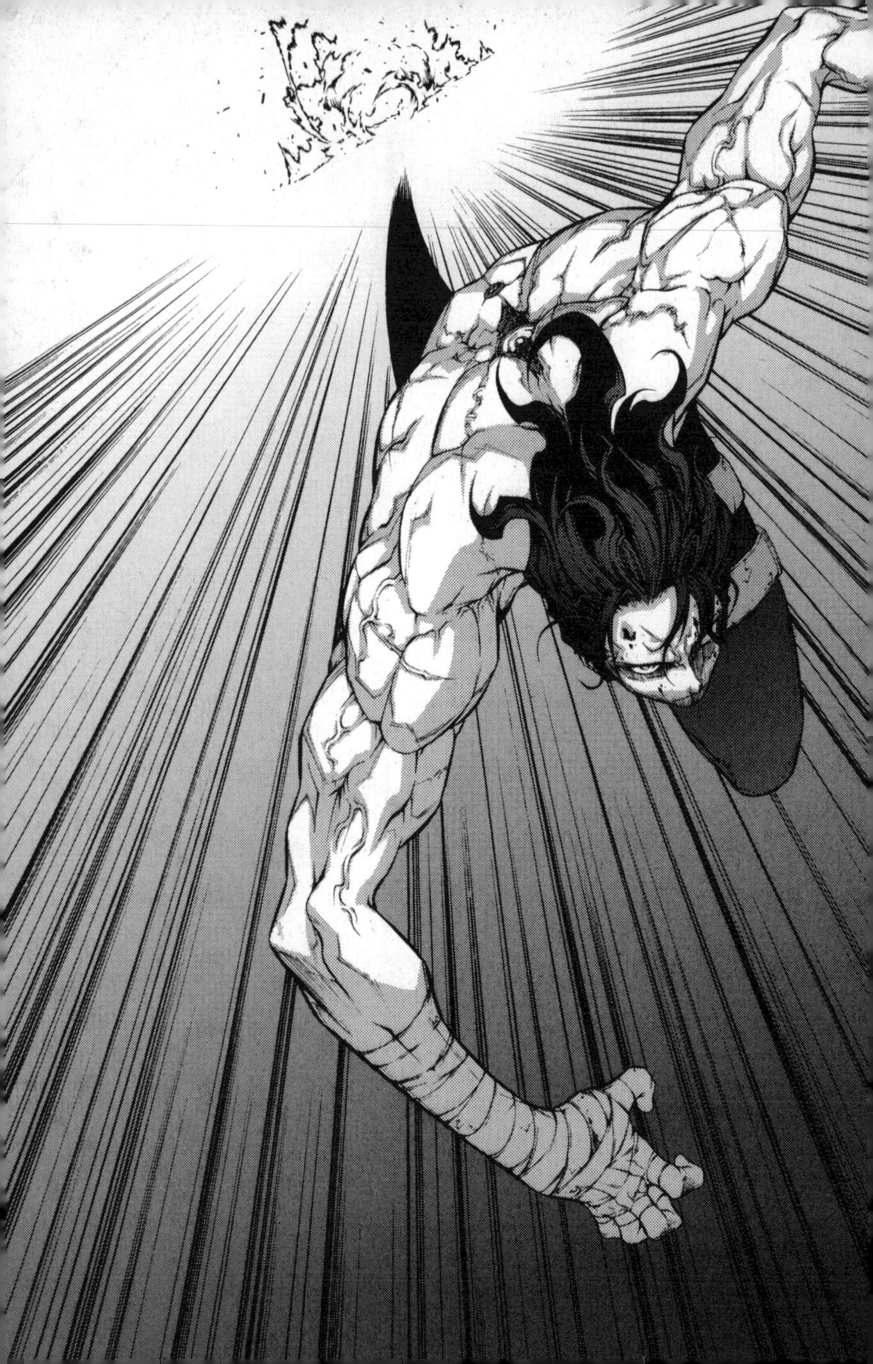

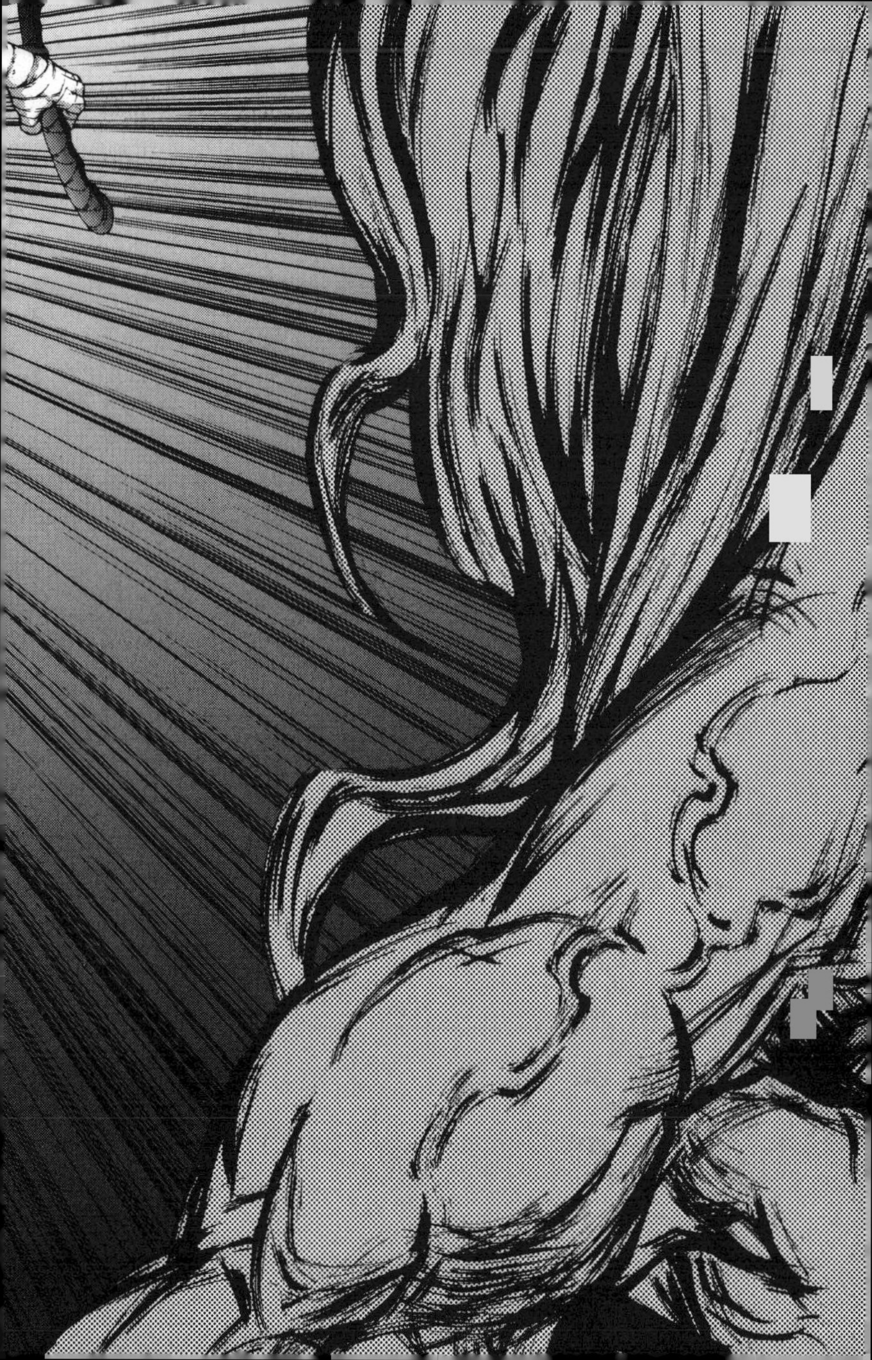

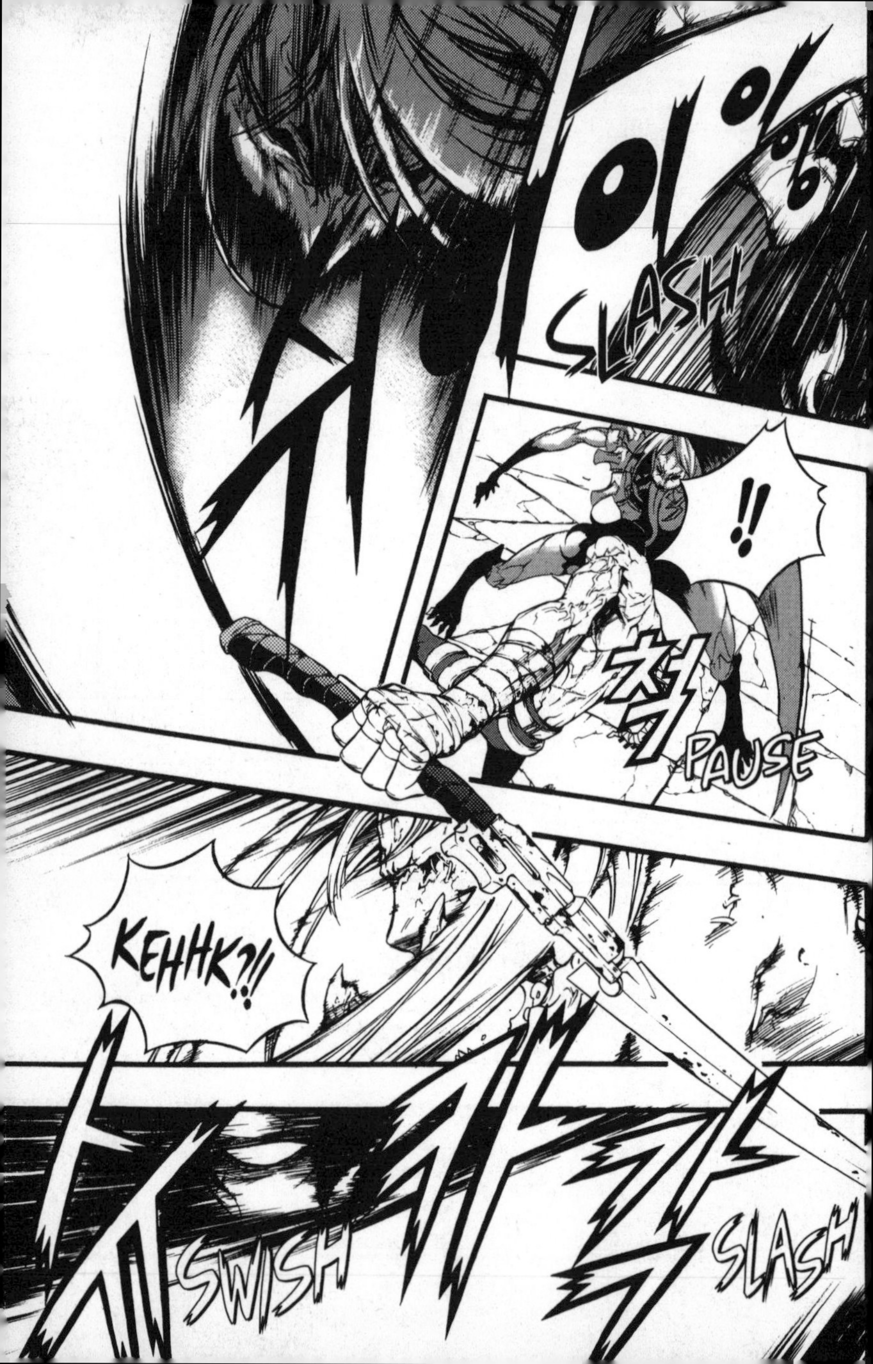

SLASH
!!
척
PAUSE
KEHHK?!!
SWISH
SLASH

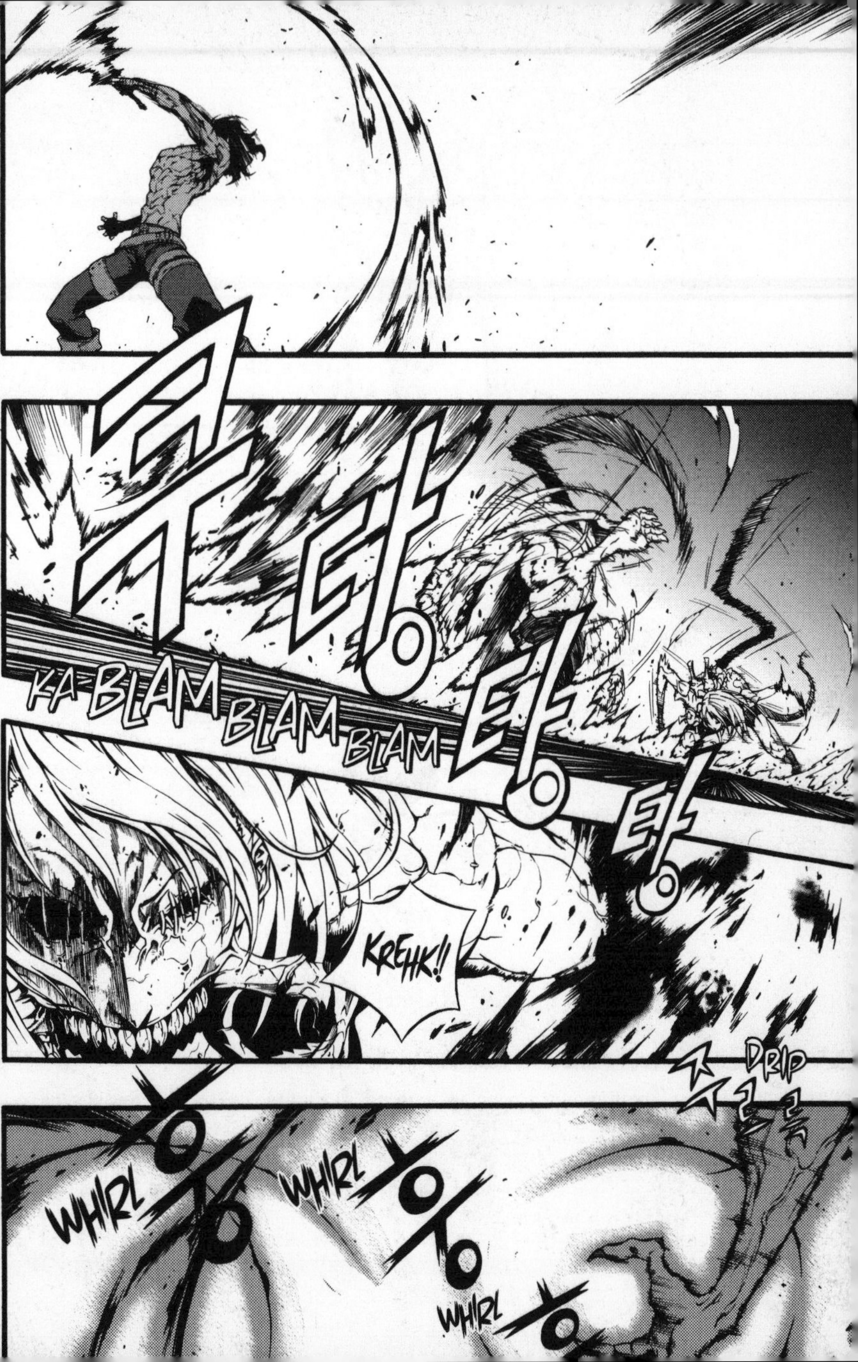
KA BLAM BLAM BLAM
KREHK!!
DRIP
WHIRL
WHIRL
WHIRL

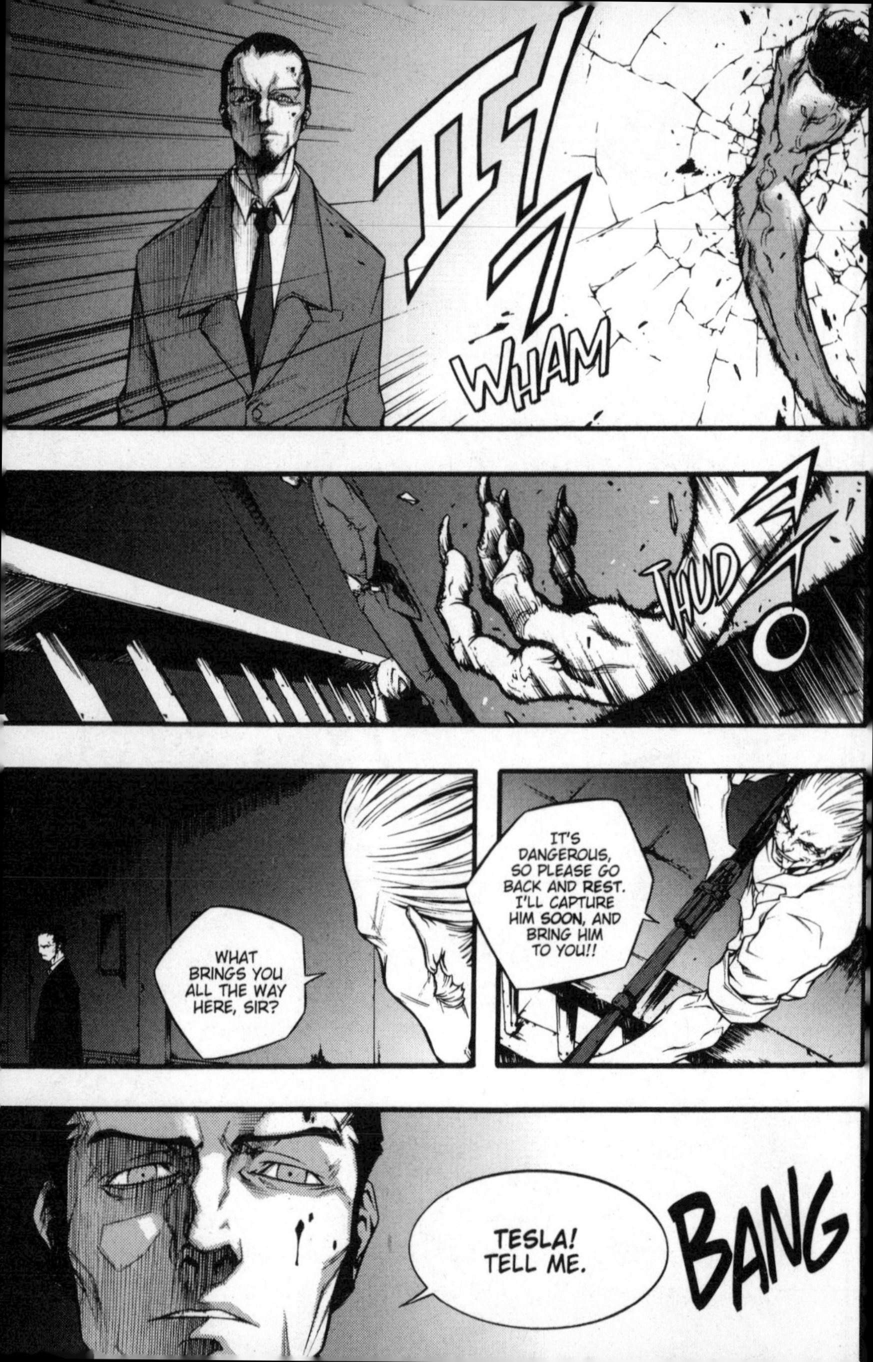
WHAM
THUD
WHAT BRINGS YOU ALL THE WAY HERE, SIR?
IT'S DANGEROUS, SO PLEASE GO BACK AND REST. I'LL CAPTURE HIM SOON, AND BRING HIM TO YOU!!
TESLA! TELL ME.
BANG

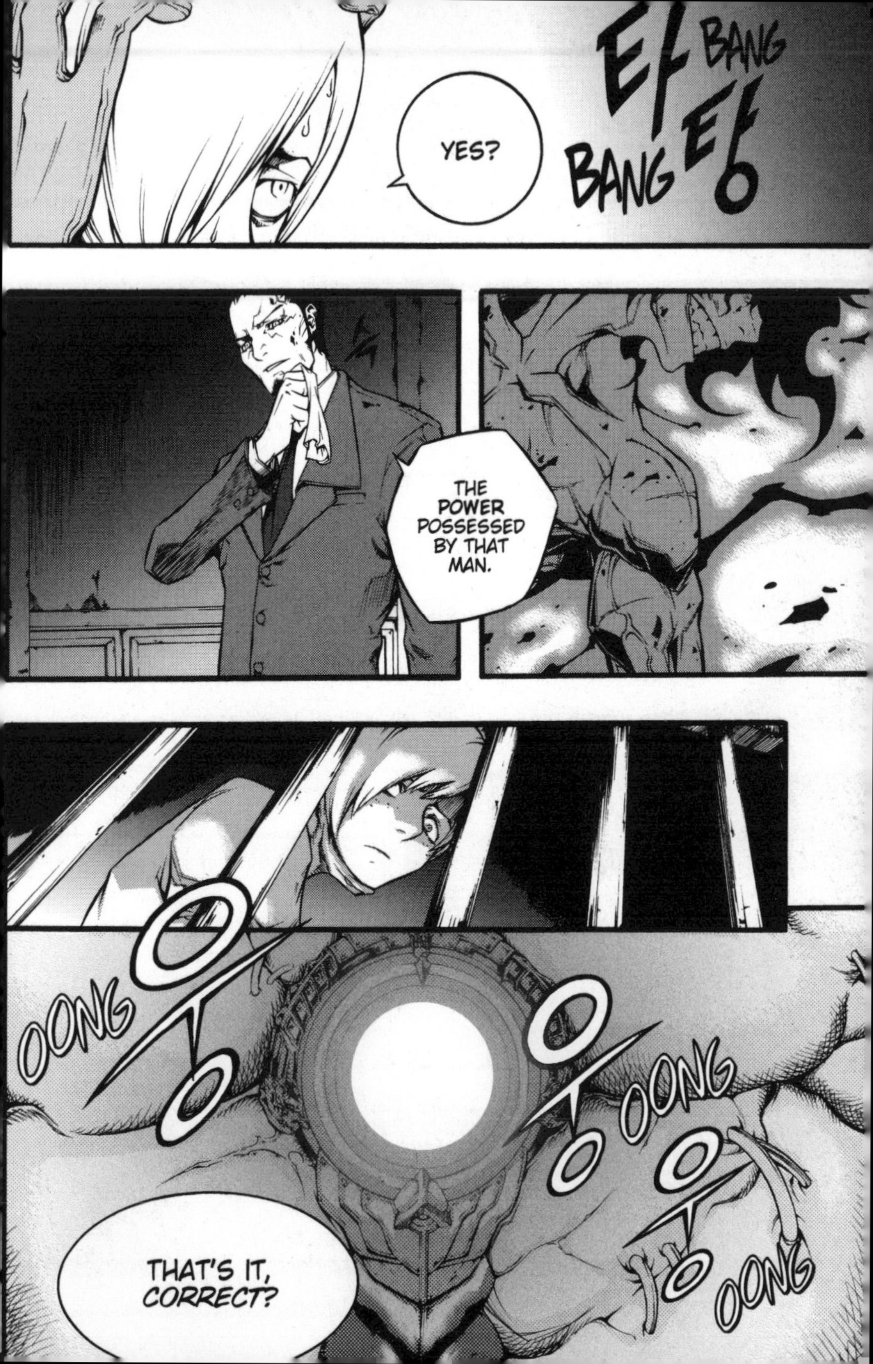

YES?
BANG
BANG
THE POWER POSSESSED BY THAT MAN.
OONG
OONG
OONG
THAT'S IT, CORRECT?

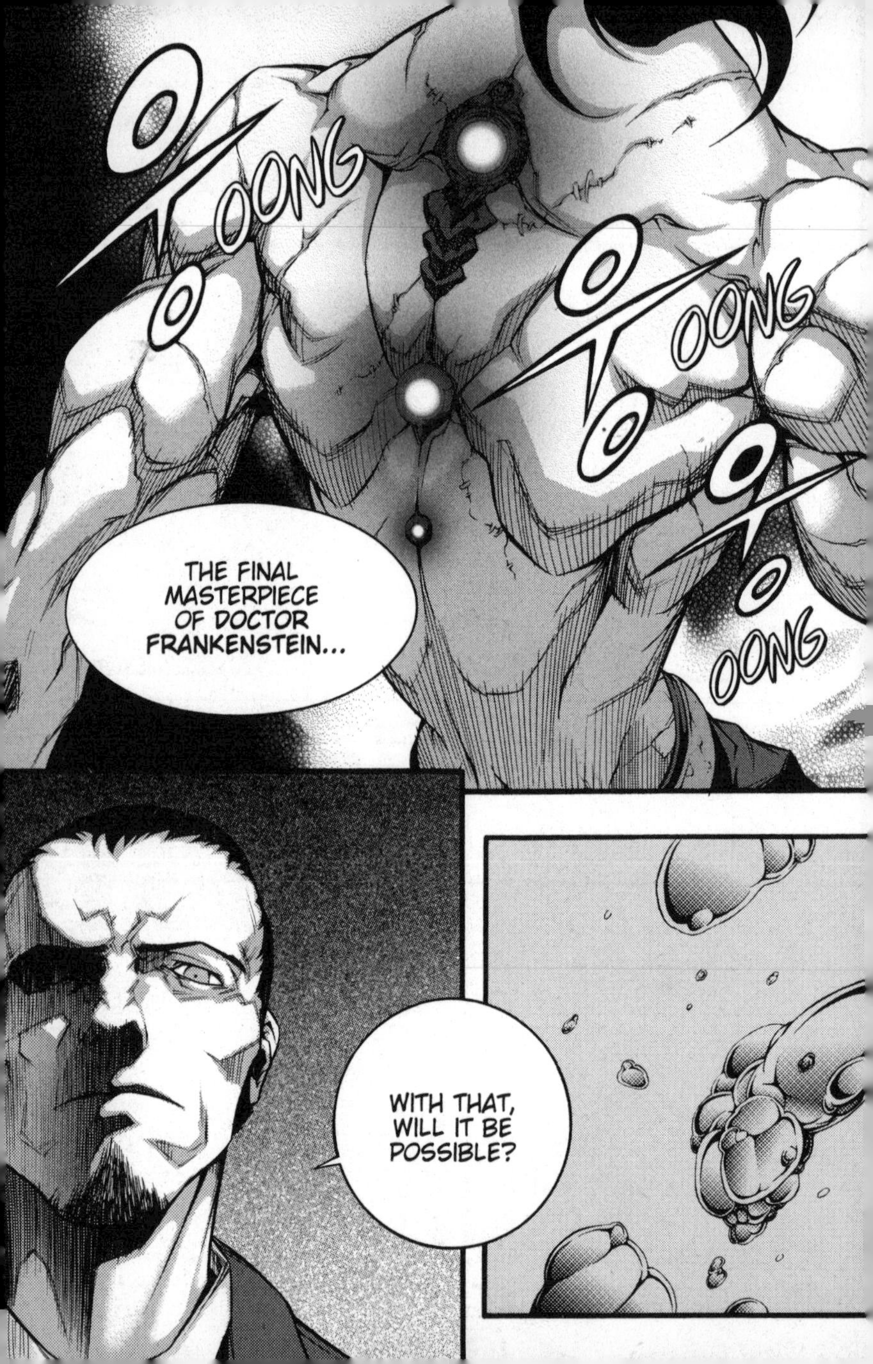
OOONG
OOOONG
THE FINAL MASTERPIECE OF DOCTOR FRANKENSTEIN...
WITH THAT, WILL IT BE POSSIBLE?

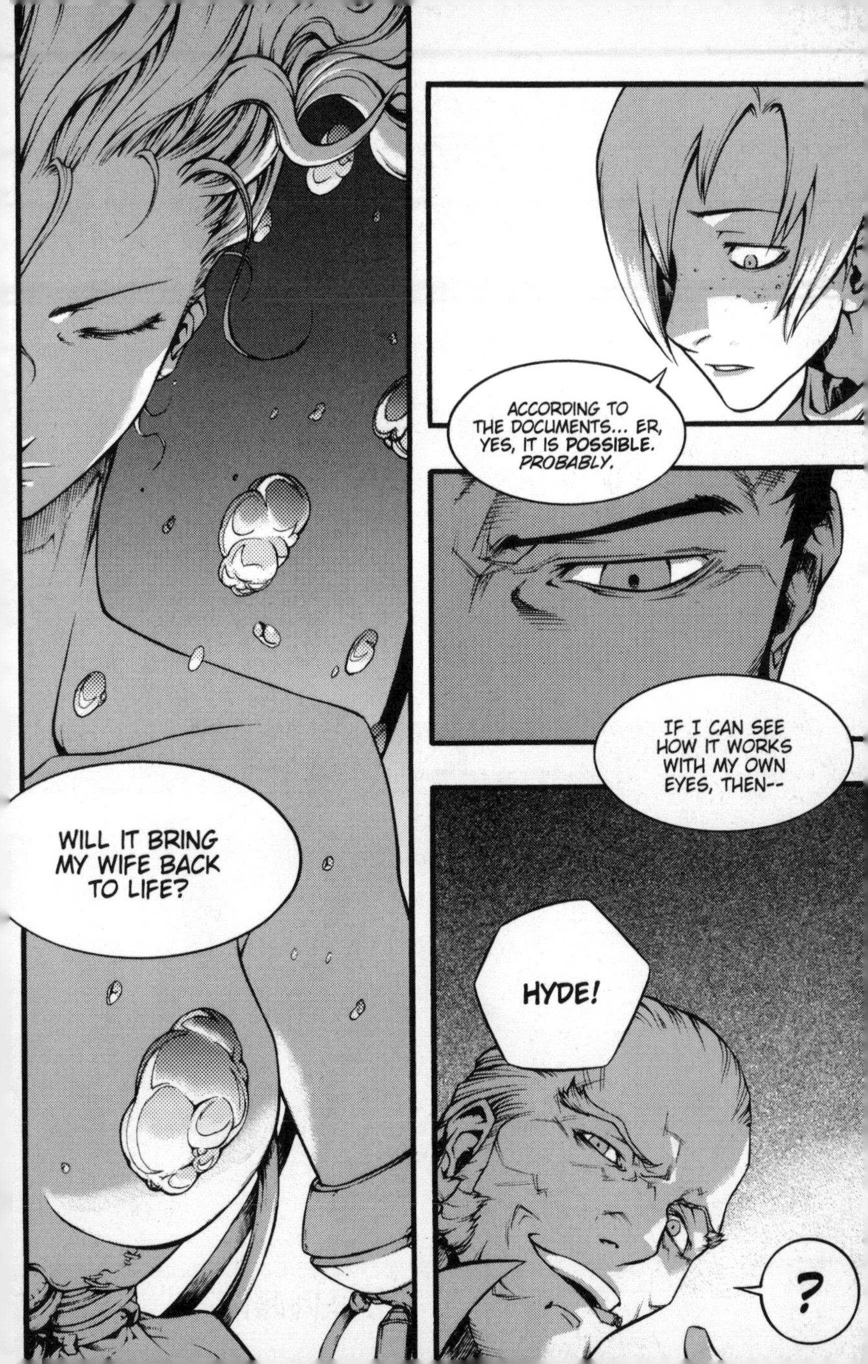
WILL IT BRING MY WIFE BACK TO LIFE?
ACCORDING TO THE DOCUMENTS... ER, YES, IT IS POSSIBLE. *PROBABLY.*
IF I CAN SEE HOW IT WORKS WITH MY OWN EYES, THEN--
HYDE!
?

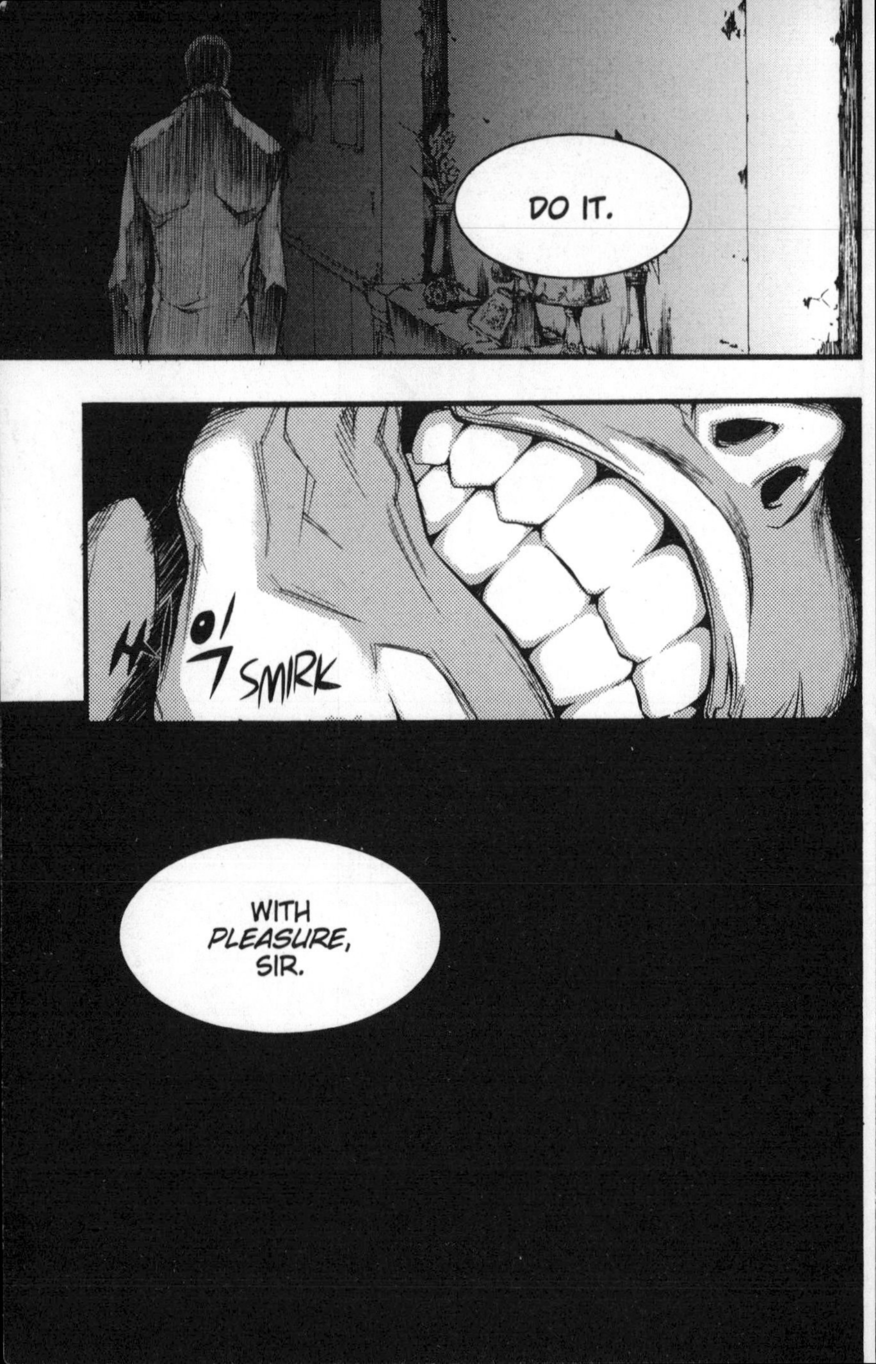
DO IT.
SMIRK
WITH PLEASURE, SIR.

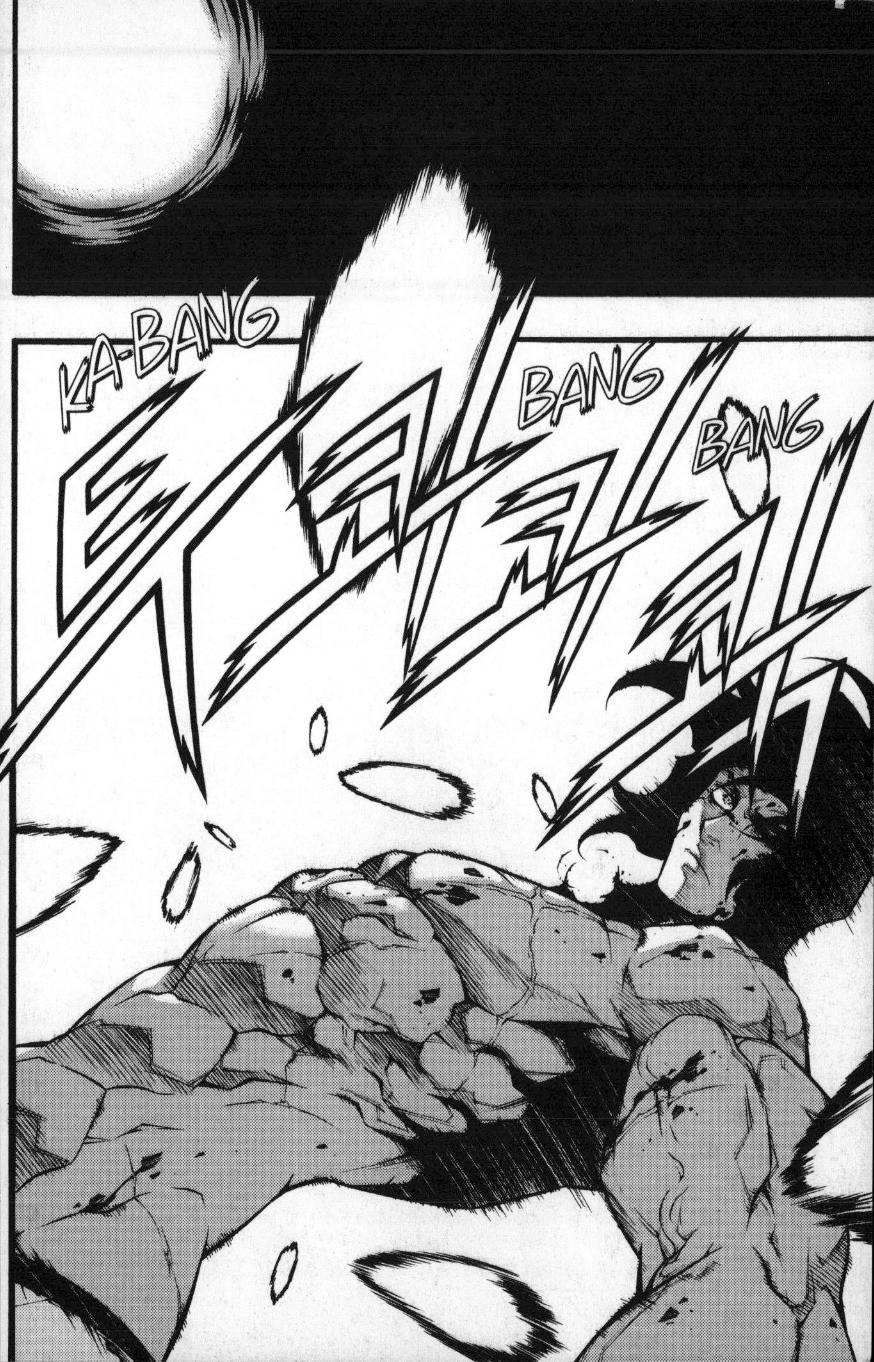
KA-BANG
BANG
BANG

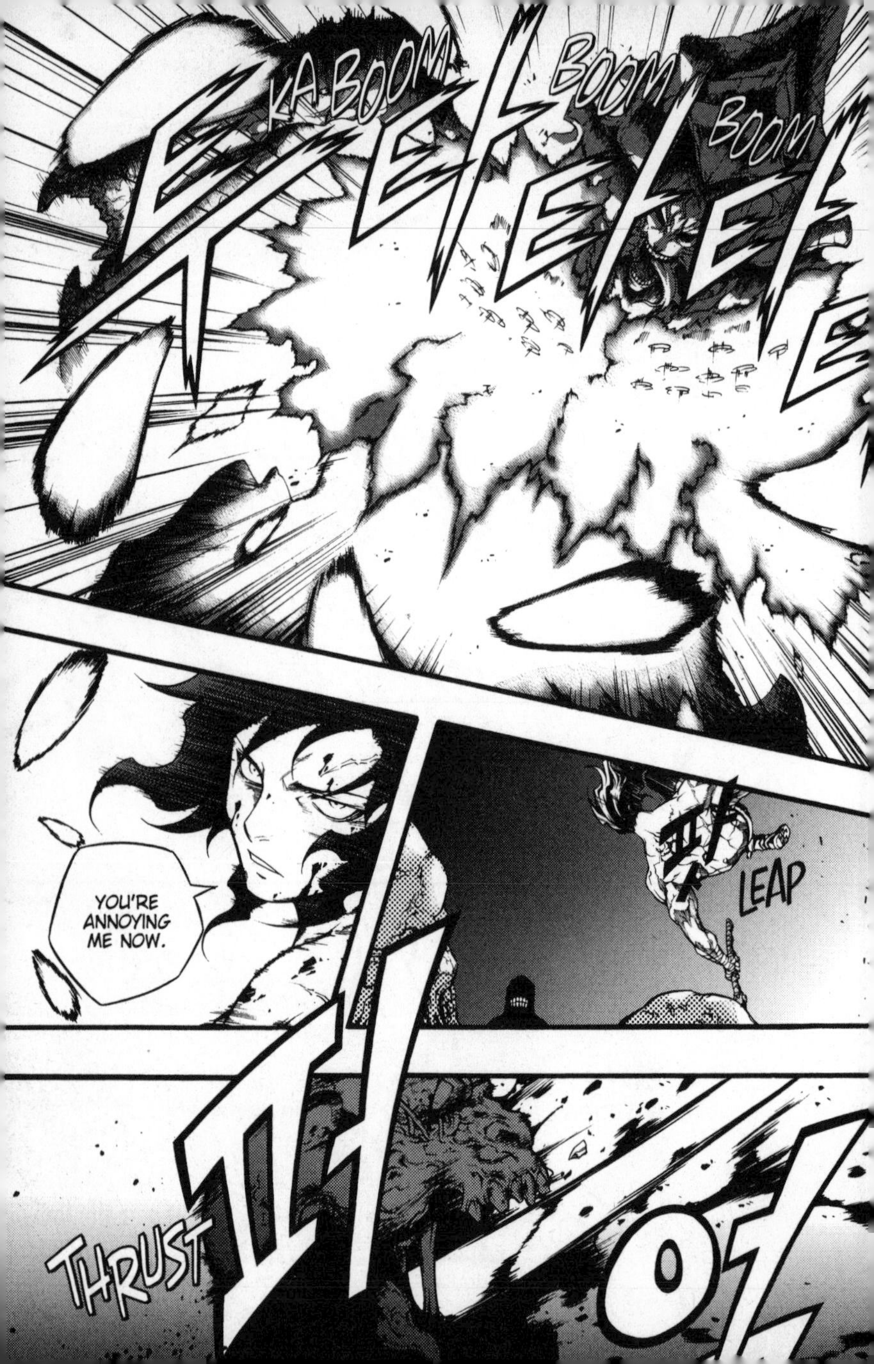
KA-BOOM
BOOM
BOOM
YOU'RE ANNOYING ME NOW.
LEAP
THRUST

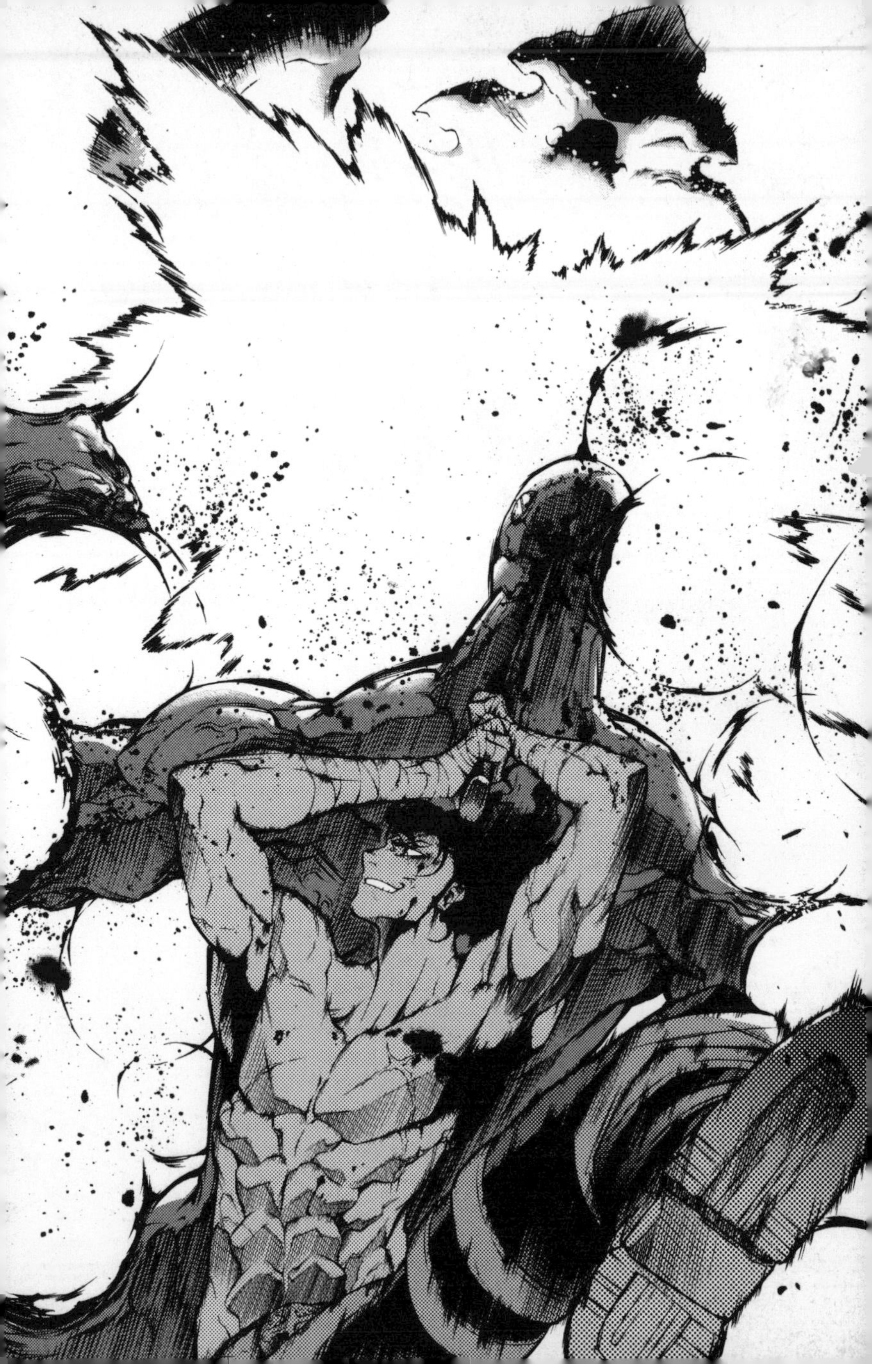

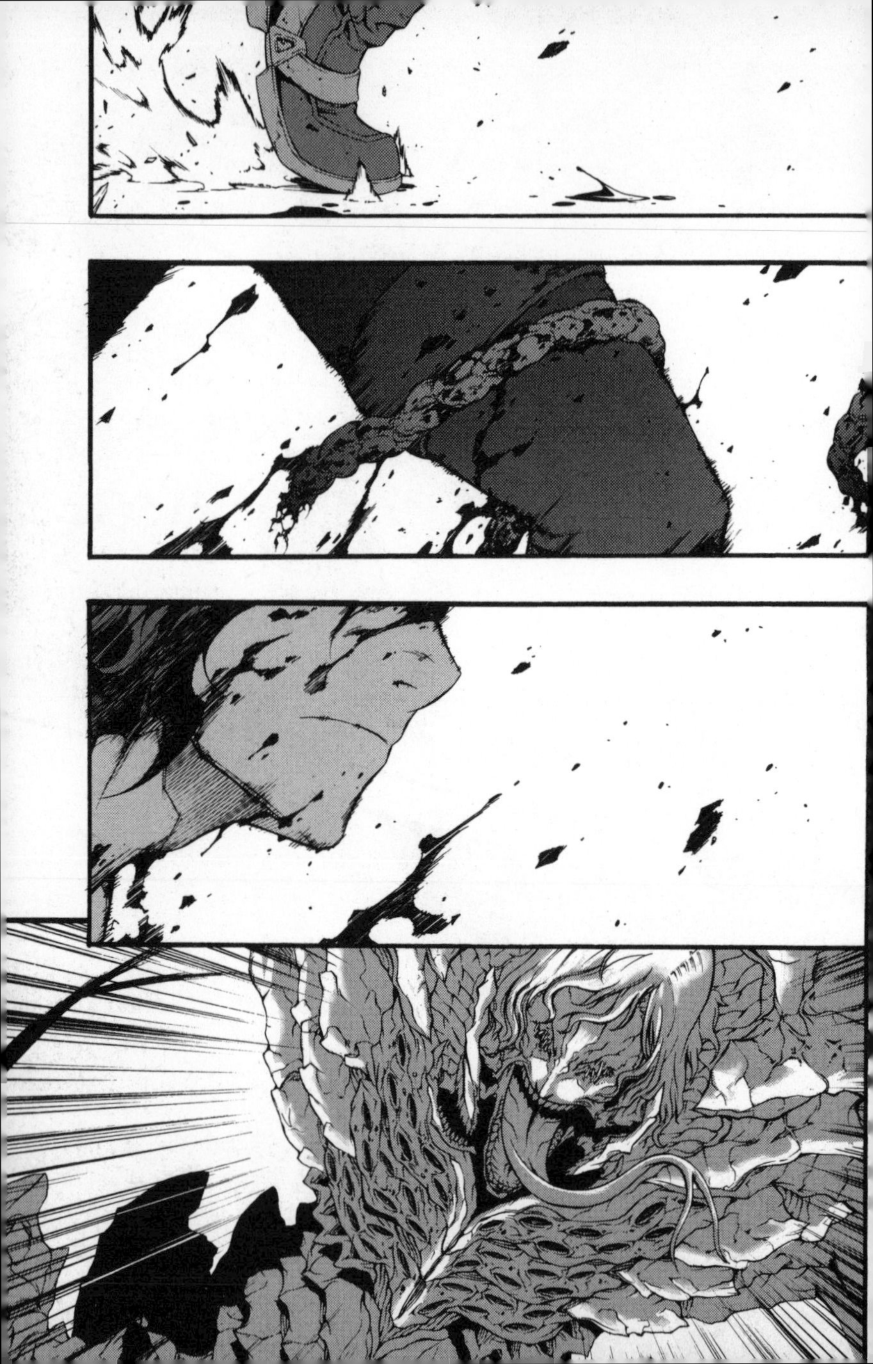

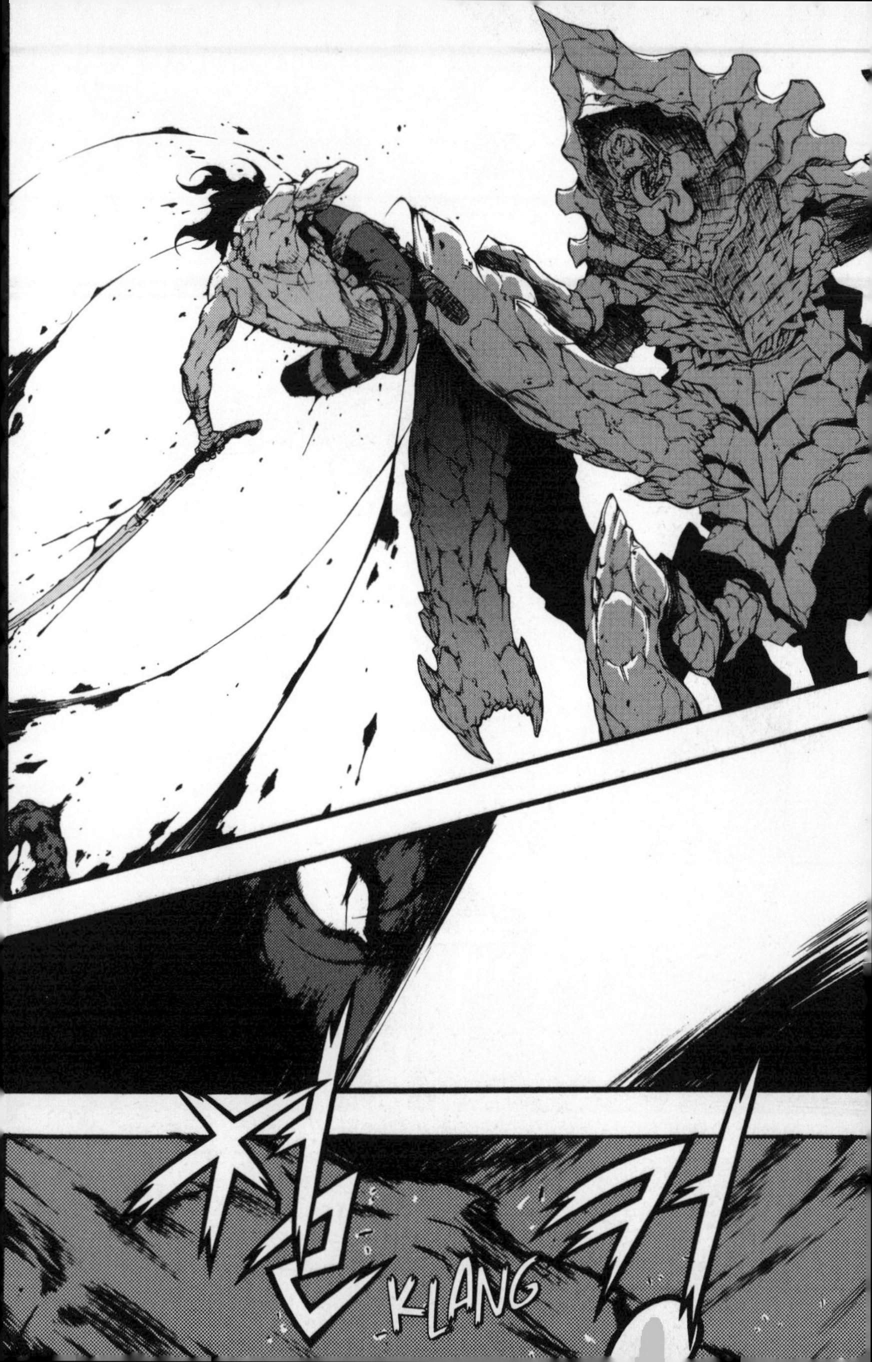
KLANG

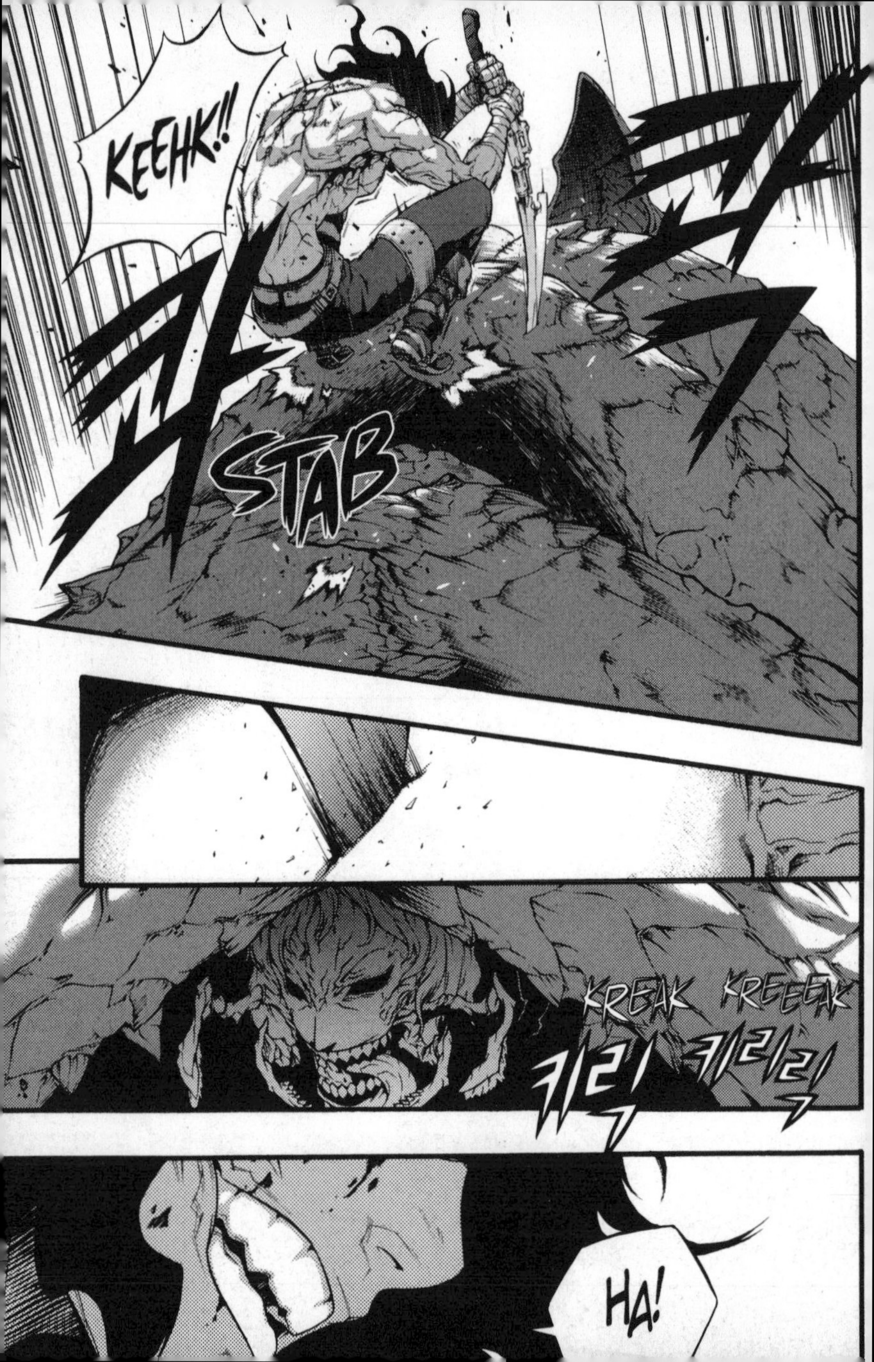
KEEHK!!
STAB
KREAK KREEEAK
HA!

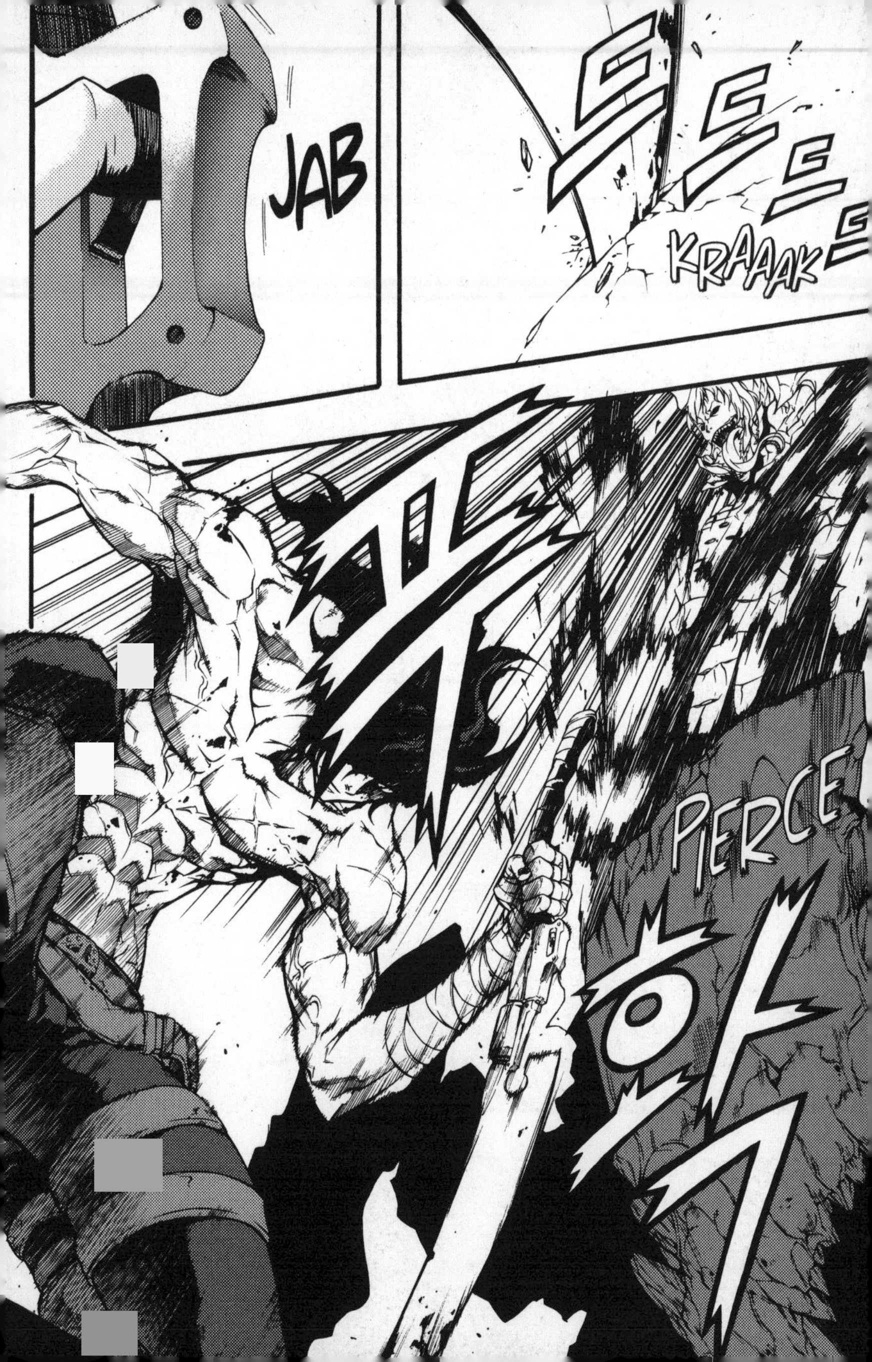
JAB
KRAAAK
PIERCE

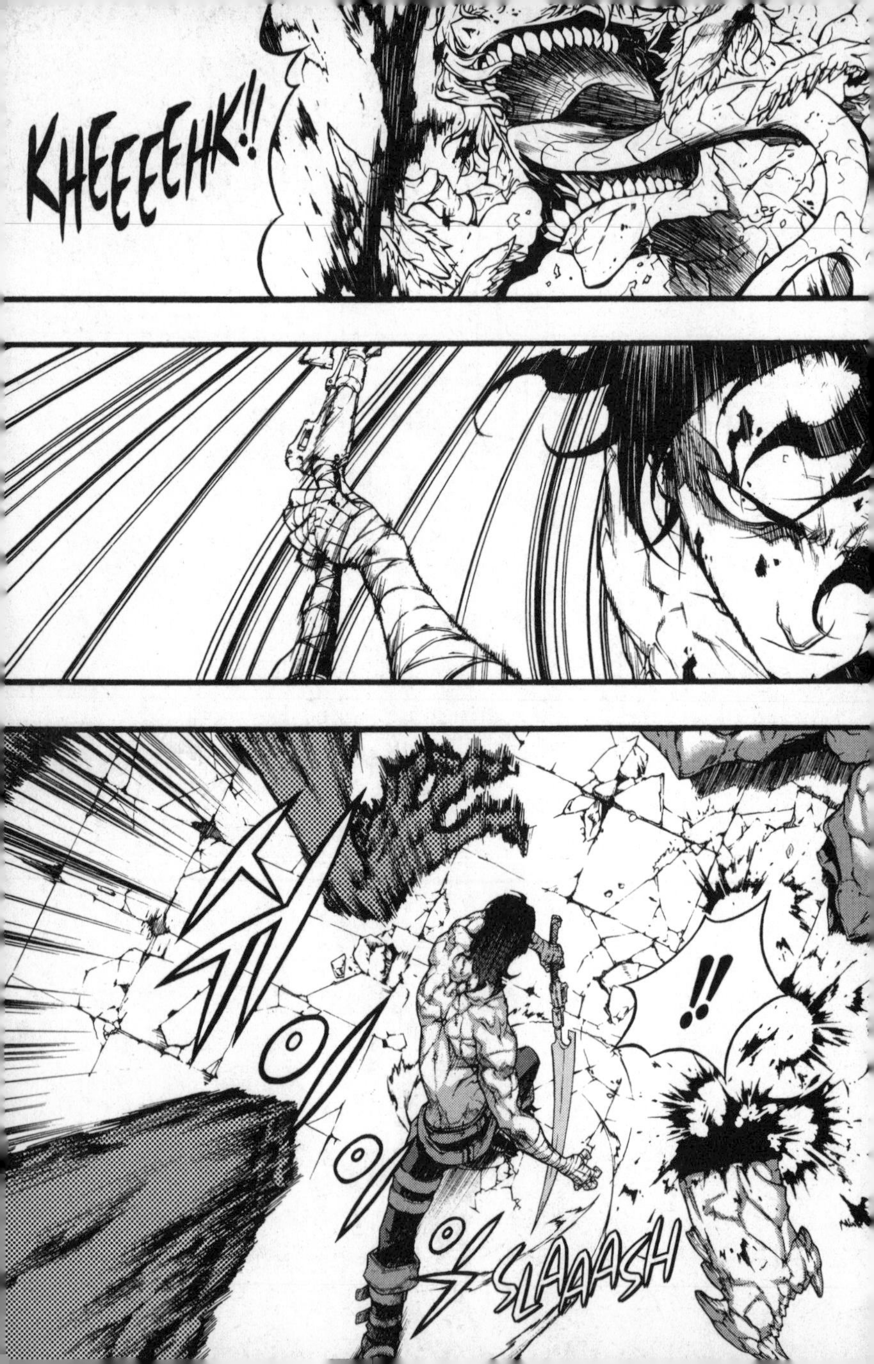
KHEEEEHK!!
!!
SLAAASH

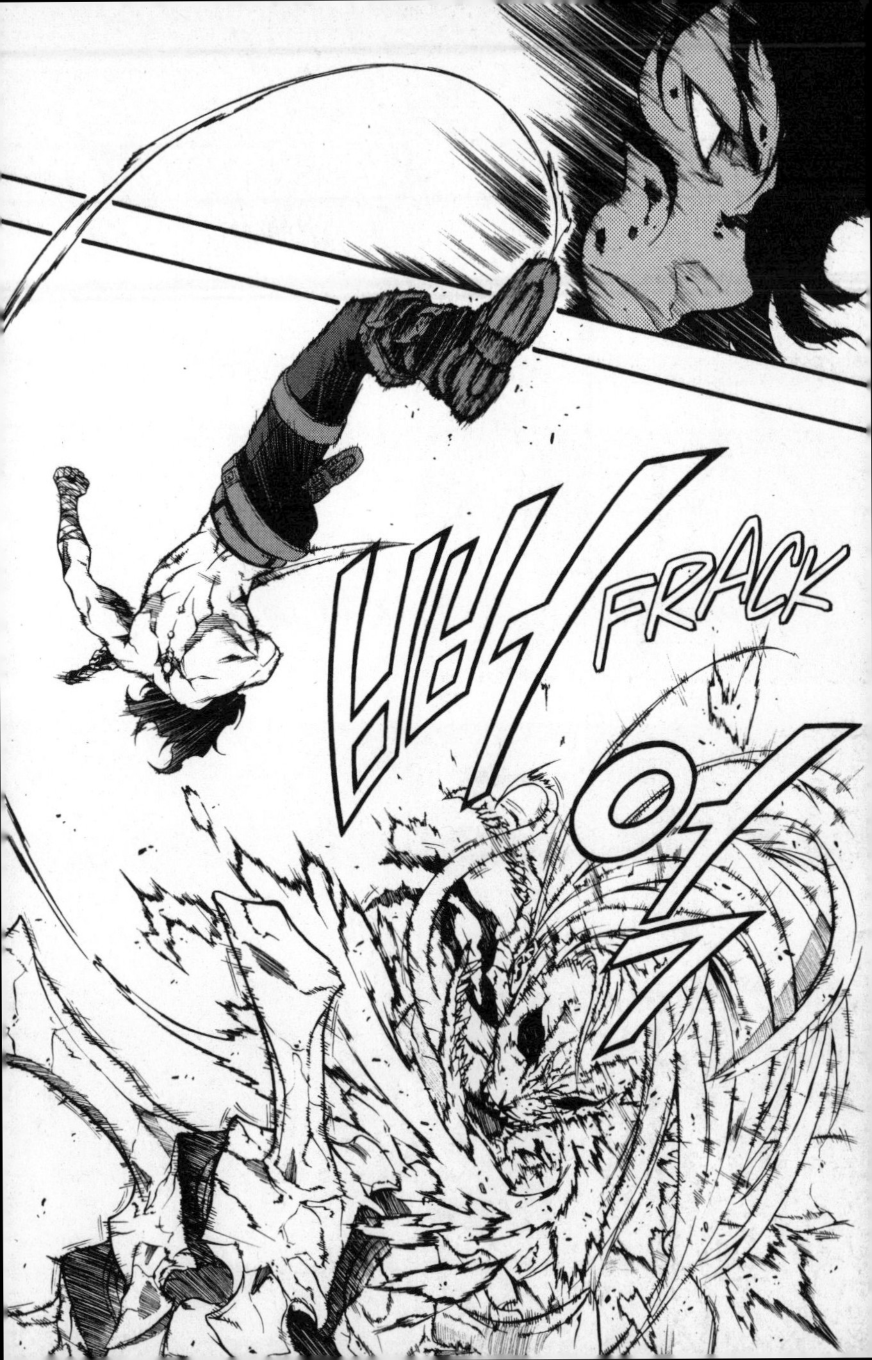
FRACK

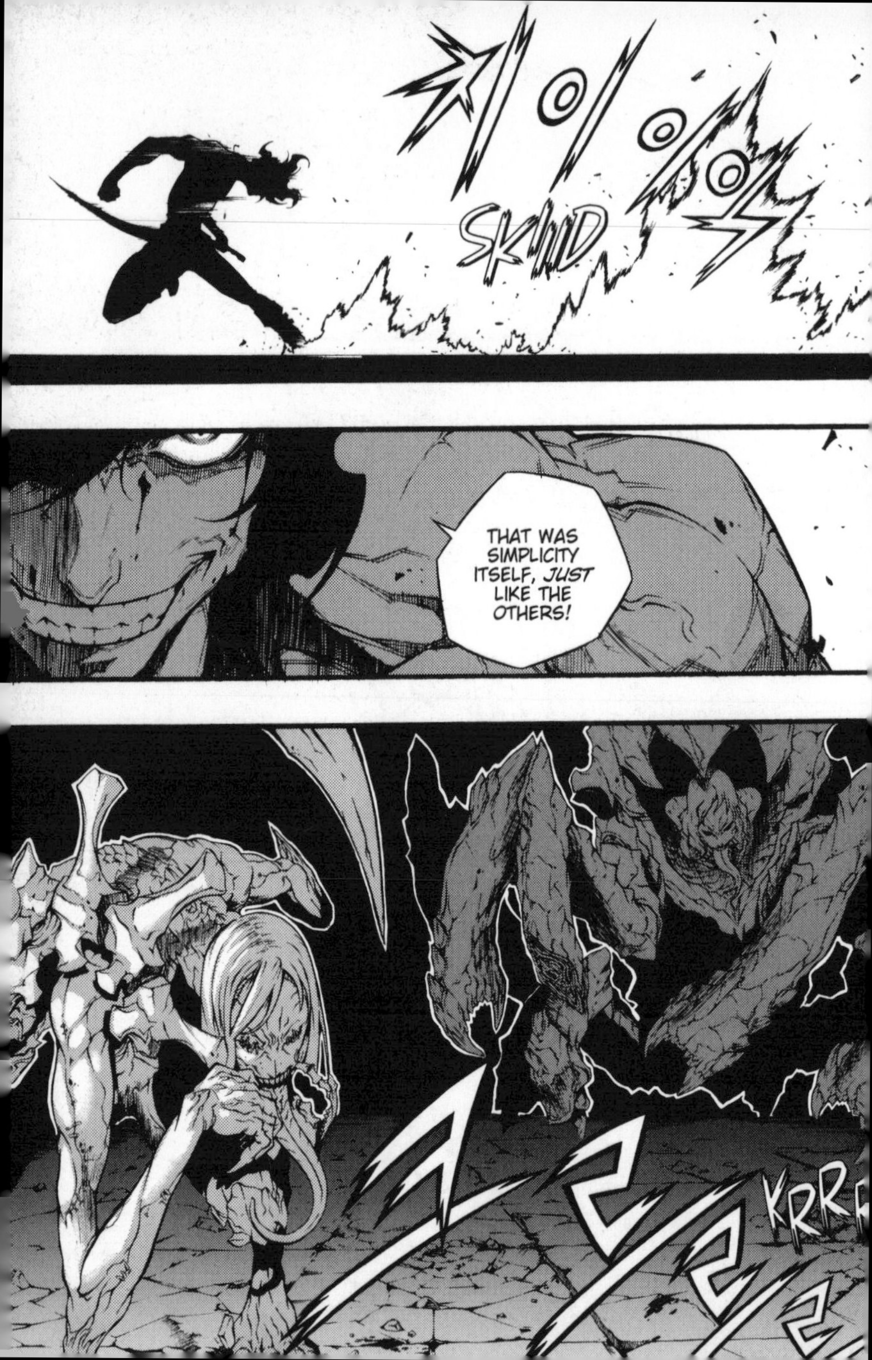
SKID
THAT WAS SIMPLICITY ITSELF, *JUST* LIKE THE OTHERS!
KRR

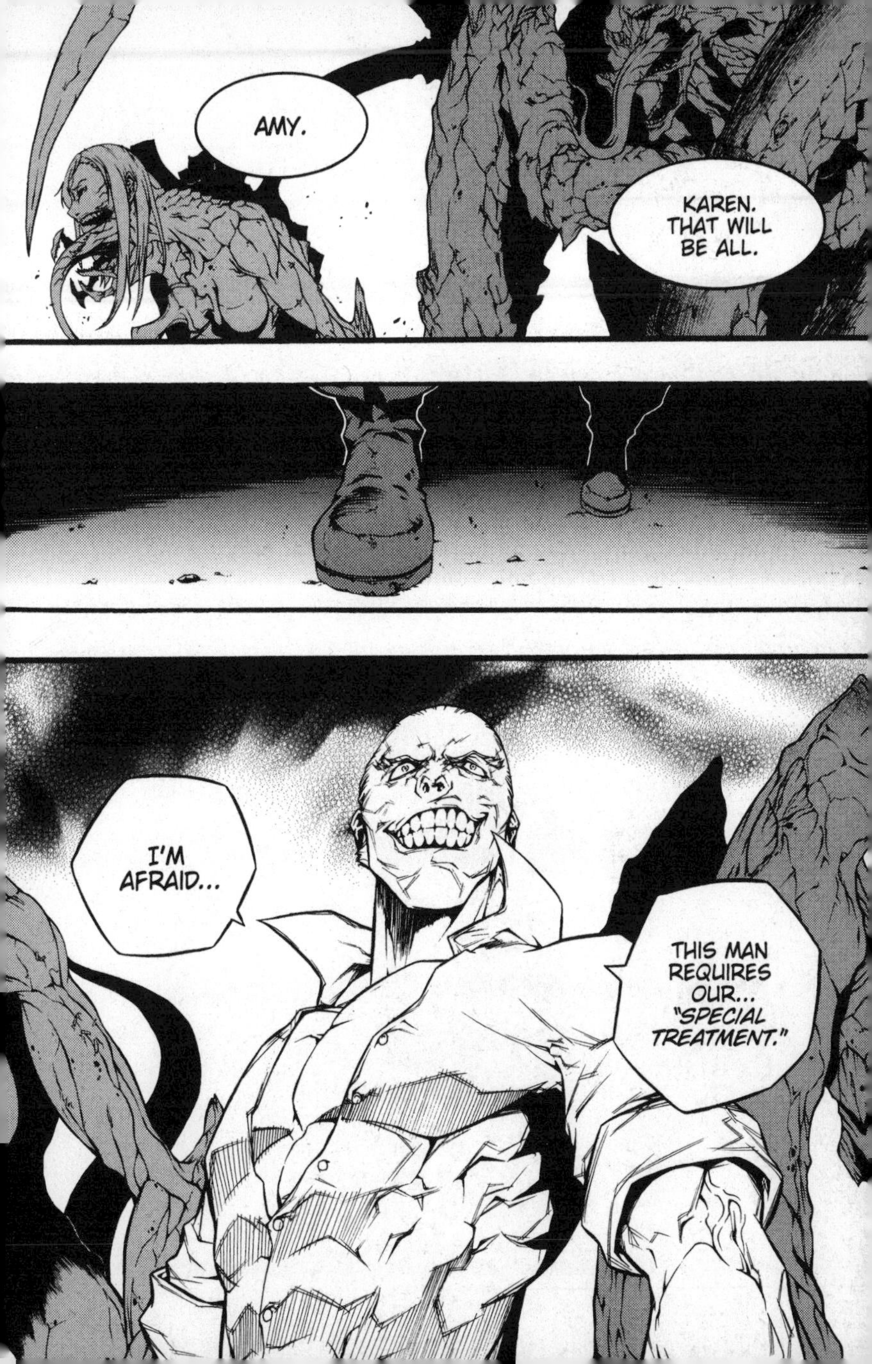
AMY.
KAREN. THAT WILL BE ALL.
I'M AFRAID...
THIS MAN REQUIRES OUR... "SPECIAL TREATMENT."

JACK THE RIPPER
HellBlade

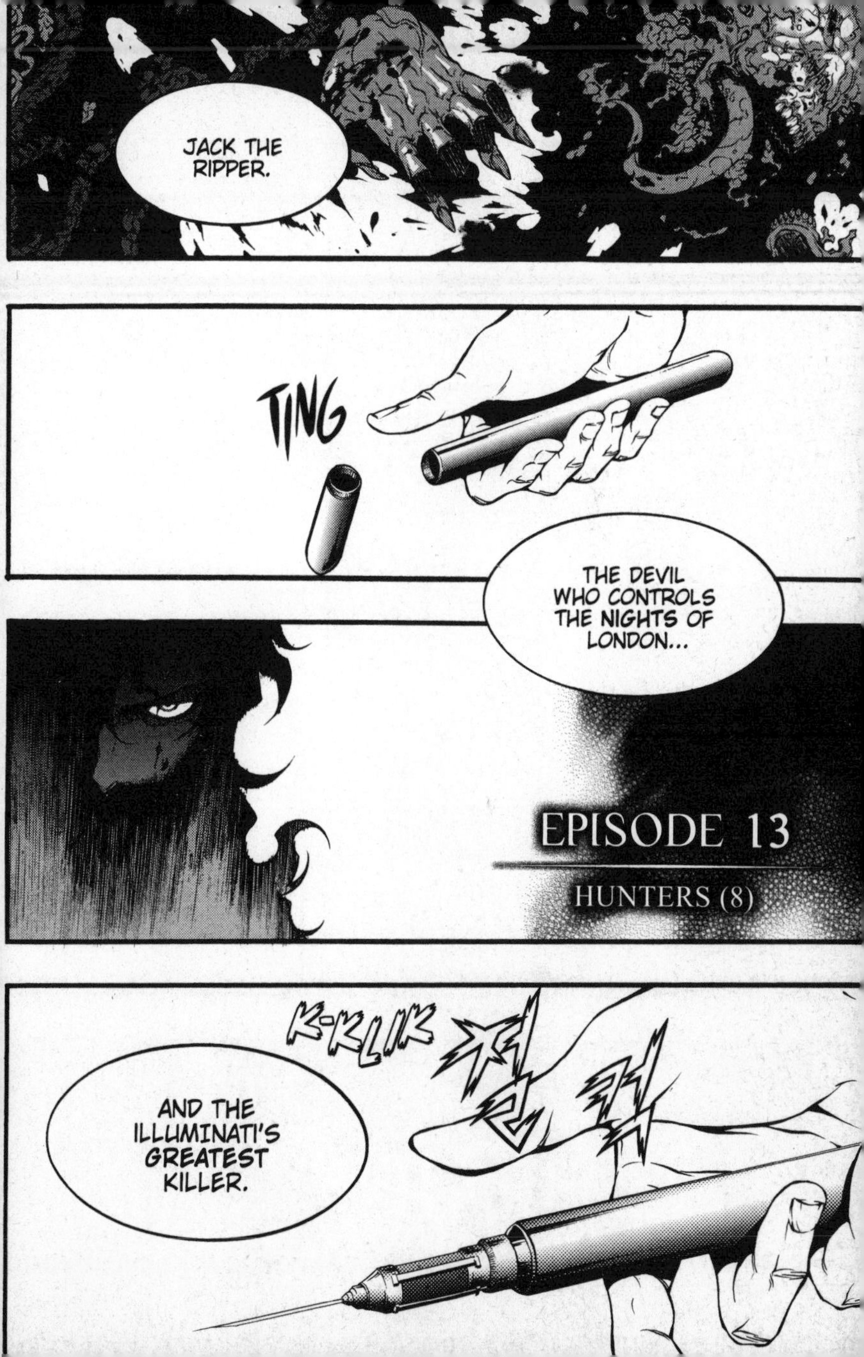
JACK THE RIPPER.
TING
THE DEVIL WHO CONTROLS THE NIGHTS OF LONDON...
EPISODE 13
HUNTERS (8)
K-KLIK
AND THE ILLUMINATI'S GREATEST KILLER.

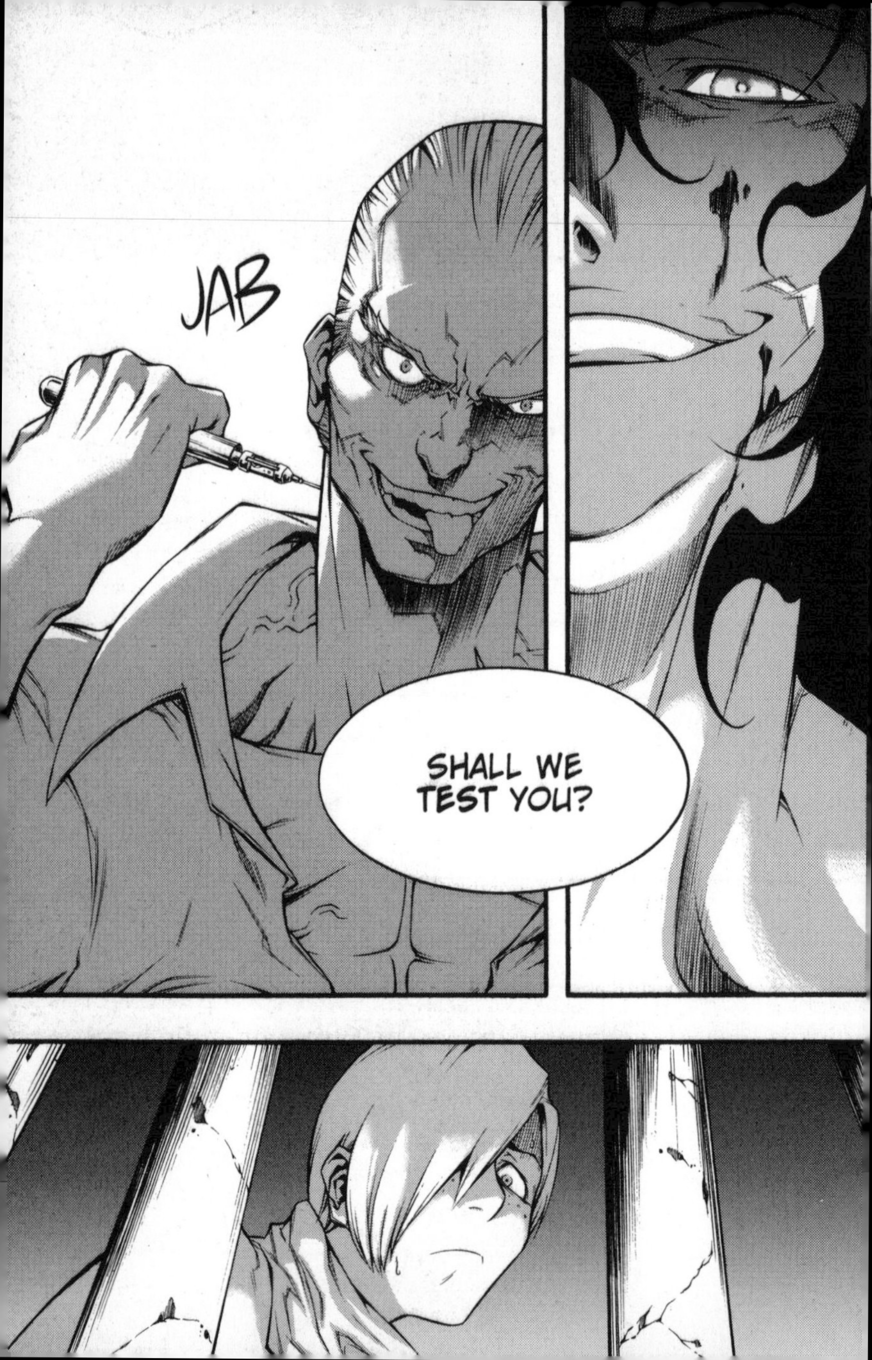
JAB
SHALL WE TEST YOU?

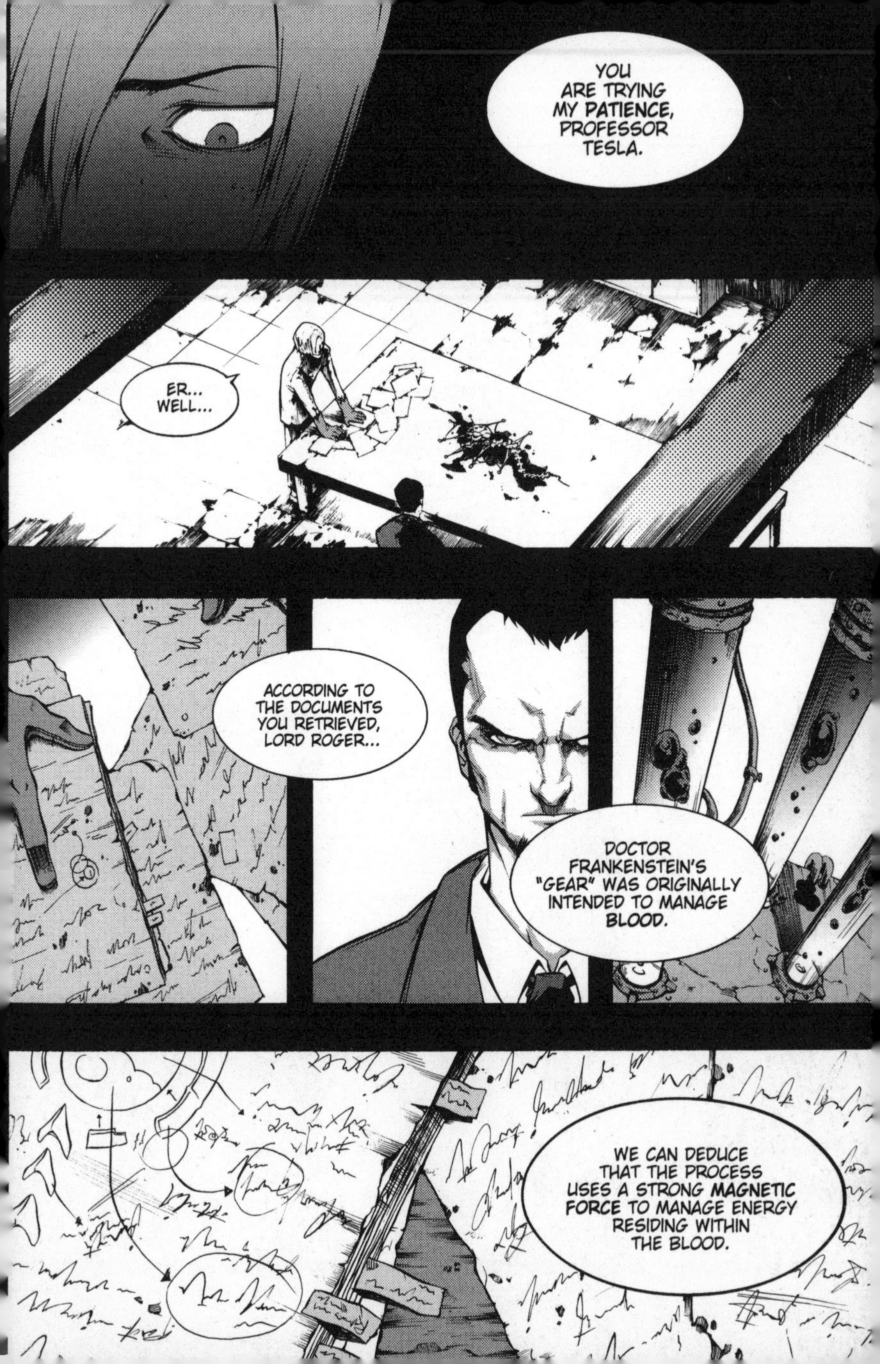
YOU ARE TRYING MY PATIENCE, PROFESSOR TESLA.
ER... WELL...
ACCORDING TO THE DOCUMENTS YOU RETRIEVED, LORD ROGER...
DOCTOR FRANKENSTEIN'S "GEAR" WAS ORIGINALLY INTENDED TO MANAGE BLOOD.
WE CAN DEDUCE THAT THE PROCESS USES A STRONG MAGNETIC FORCE TO MANAGE ENERGY RESIDING WITHIN THE BLOOD.

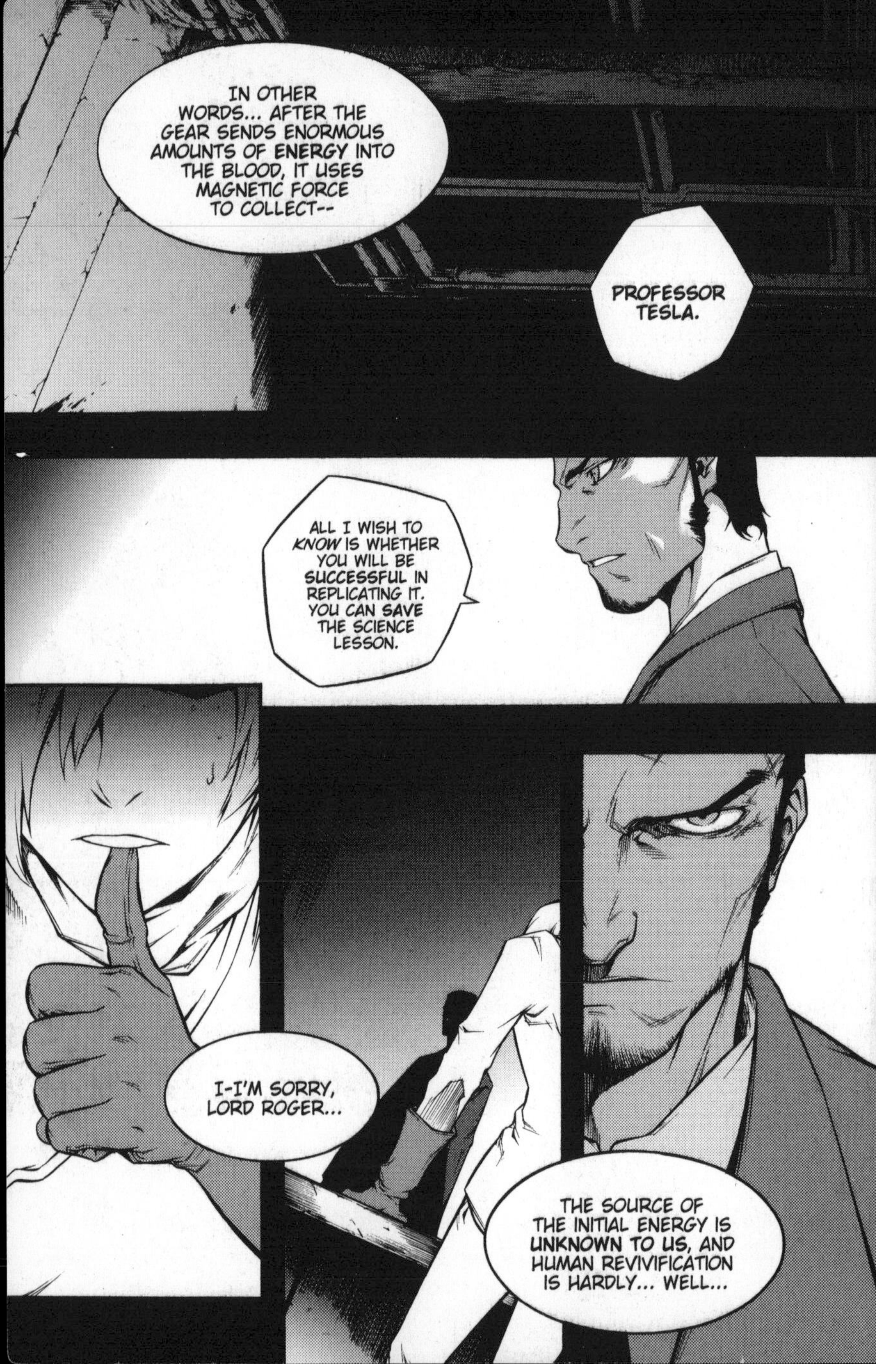
IN OTHER WORDS... AFTER THE GEAR SENDS ENORMOUS AMOUNTS OF ENERGY INTO THE BLOOD, IT USES MAGNETIC FORCE TO COLLECT--
PROFESSOR TESLA.
ALL I WISH TO *KNOW* IS WHETHER YOU WILL BE SUCCESSFUL IN REPLICATING IT. YOU CAN SAVE THE SCIENCE LESSON.
I-I'M SORRY, LORD ROGER...
THE SOURCE OF THE INITIAL ENERGY IS UNKNOWN TO US, AND HUMAN REVIVIFICATION IS HARDLY... WELL...

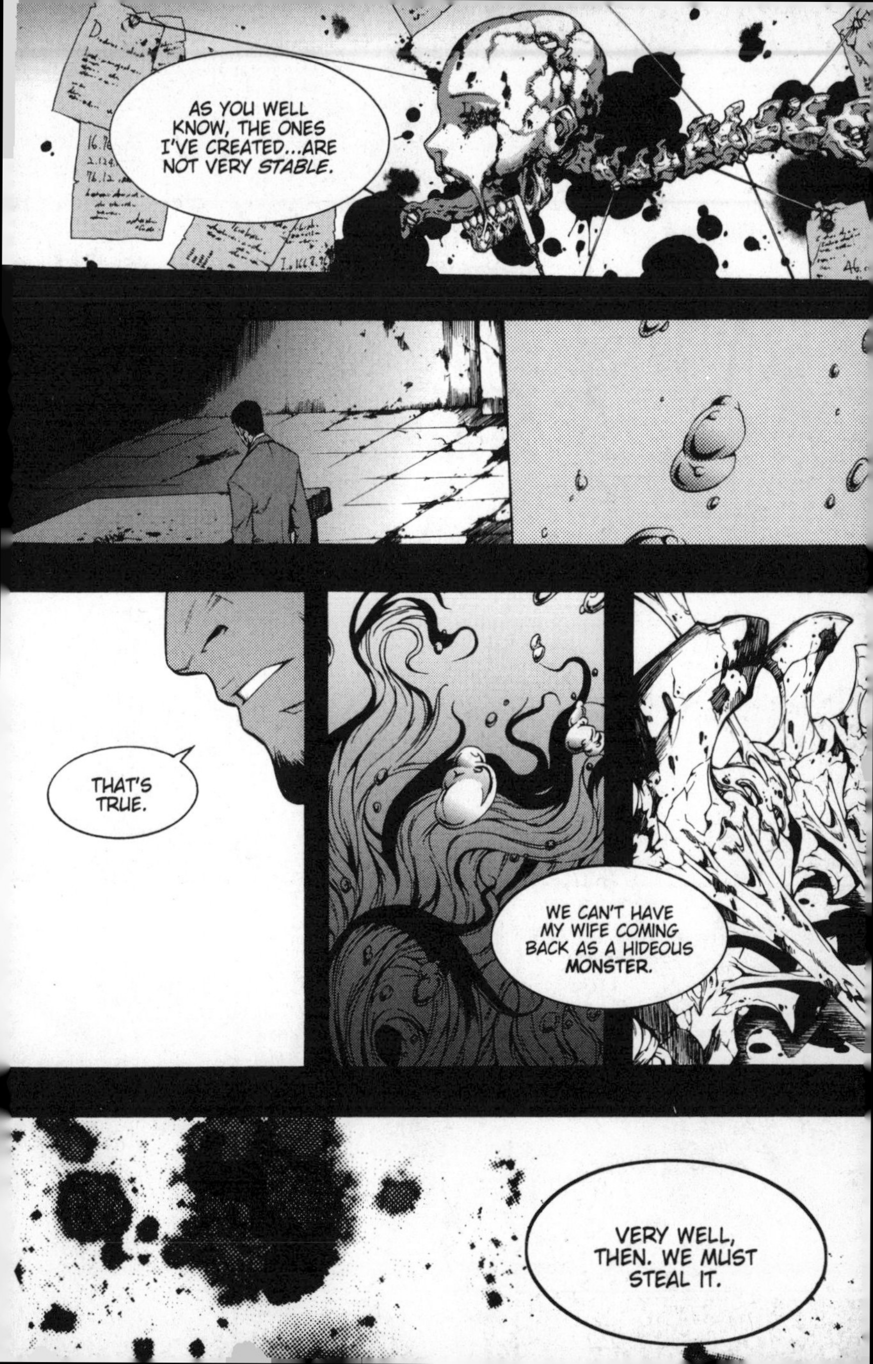
AS YOU WELL KNOW, THE ONES I'VE CREATED...ARE NOT VERY *STABLE*.
THAT'S TRUE.
WE CAN'T HAVE MY WIFE COMING BACK AS A HIDEOUS MONSTER.
VERY WELL, THEN. WE MUST STEAL IT.

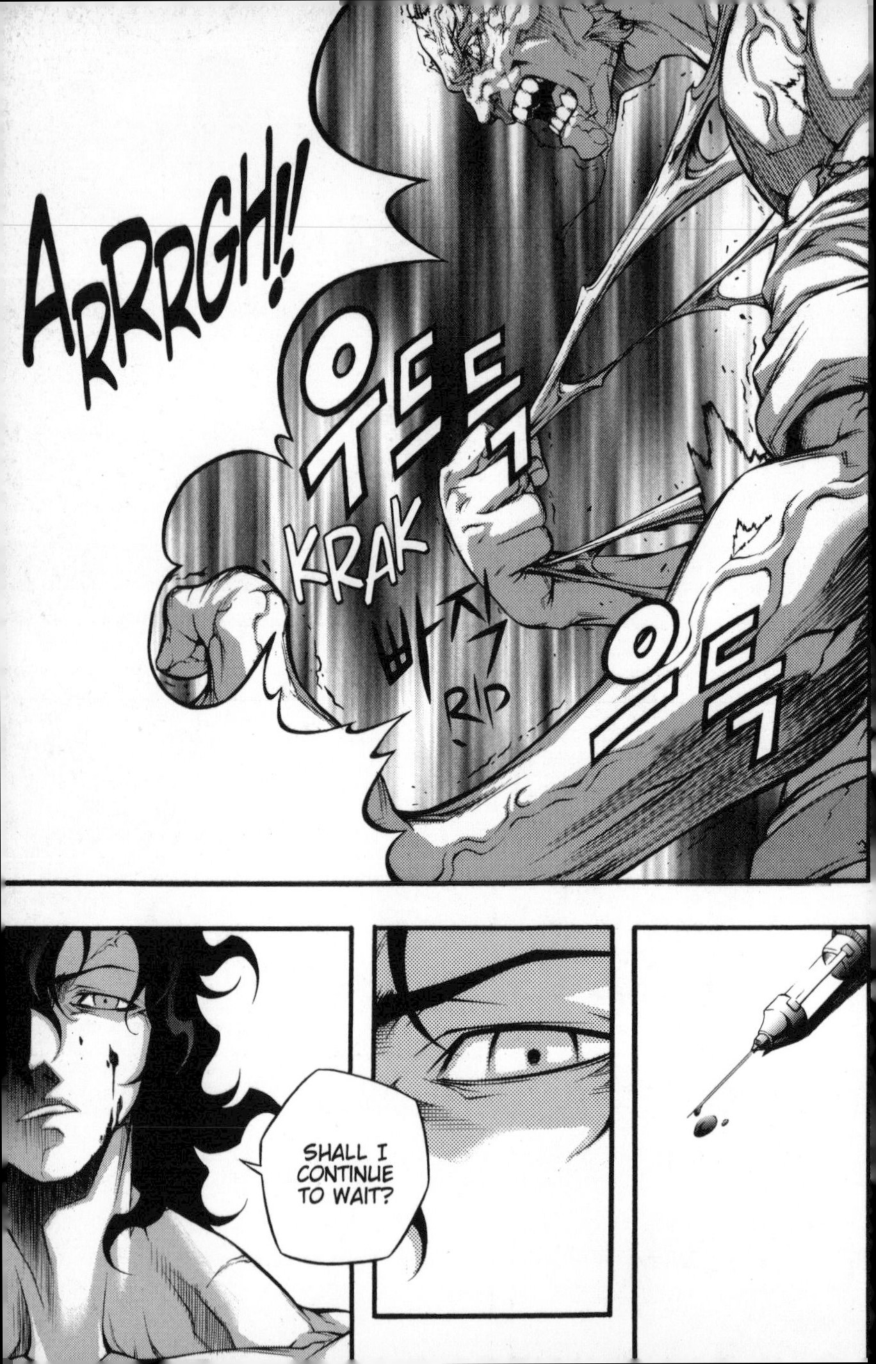
ARRRGH!!
으드득
KRAK
빠직
RIP
으득
SHALL I CONTINUE TO WAIT?

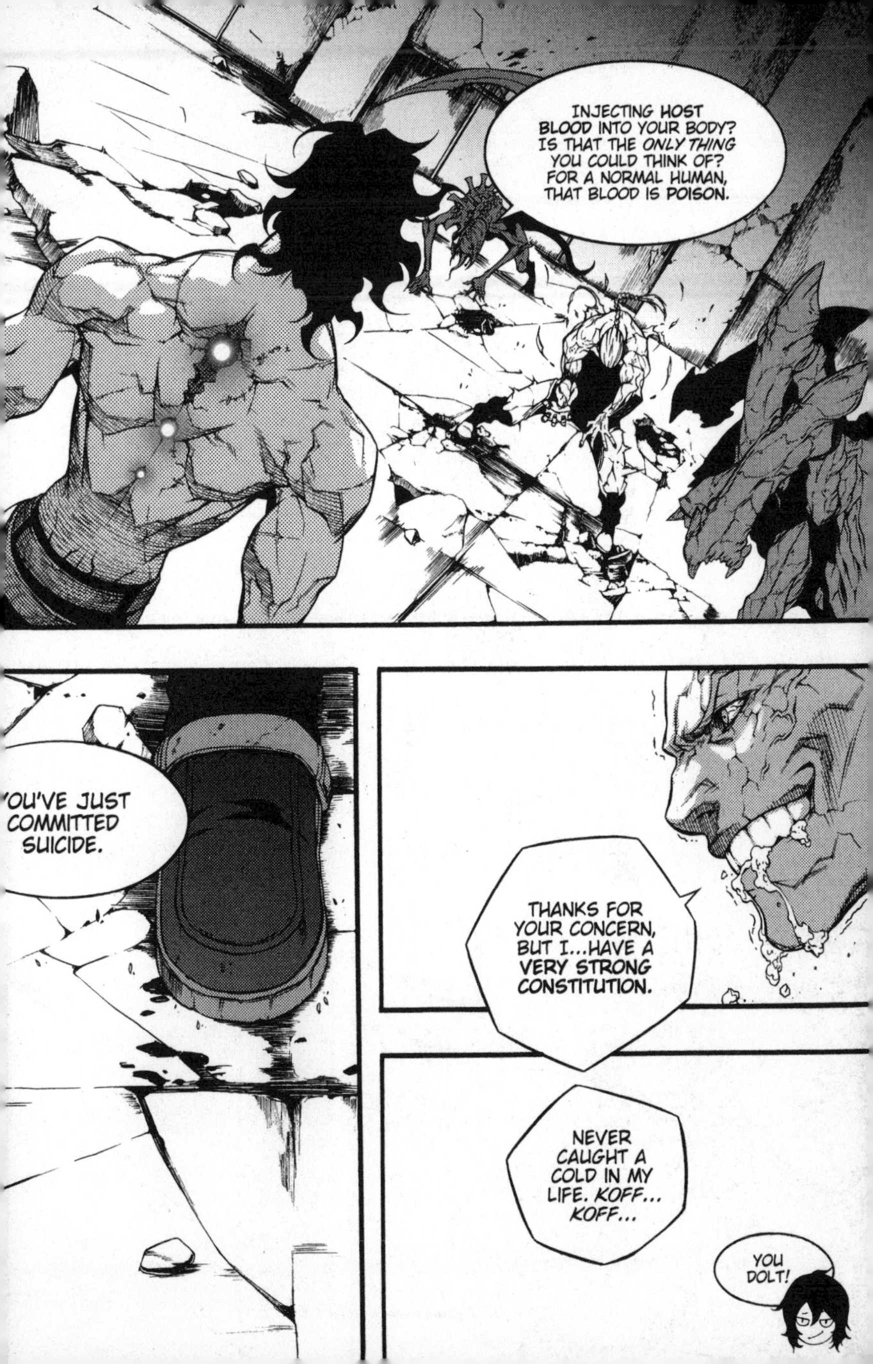
INJECTING HOST BLOOD INTO YOUR BODY? IS THAT THE *ONLY THING* YOU COULD THINK OF? FOR A NORMAL HUMAN, THAT BLOOD IS POISON.
OU'VE JUST COMMITTED SUICIDE.
THANKS FOR YOUR CONCERN, BUT I...HAVE A VERY STRONG CONSTITUTION.
NEVER CAUGHT A COLD IN MY LIFE. *KOFF... KOFF...*
YOU DOLT!

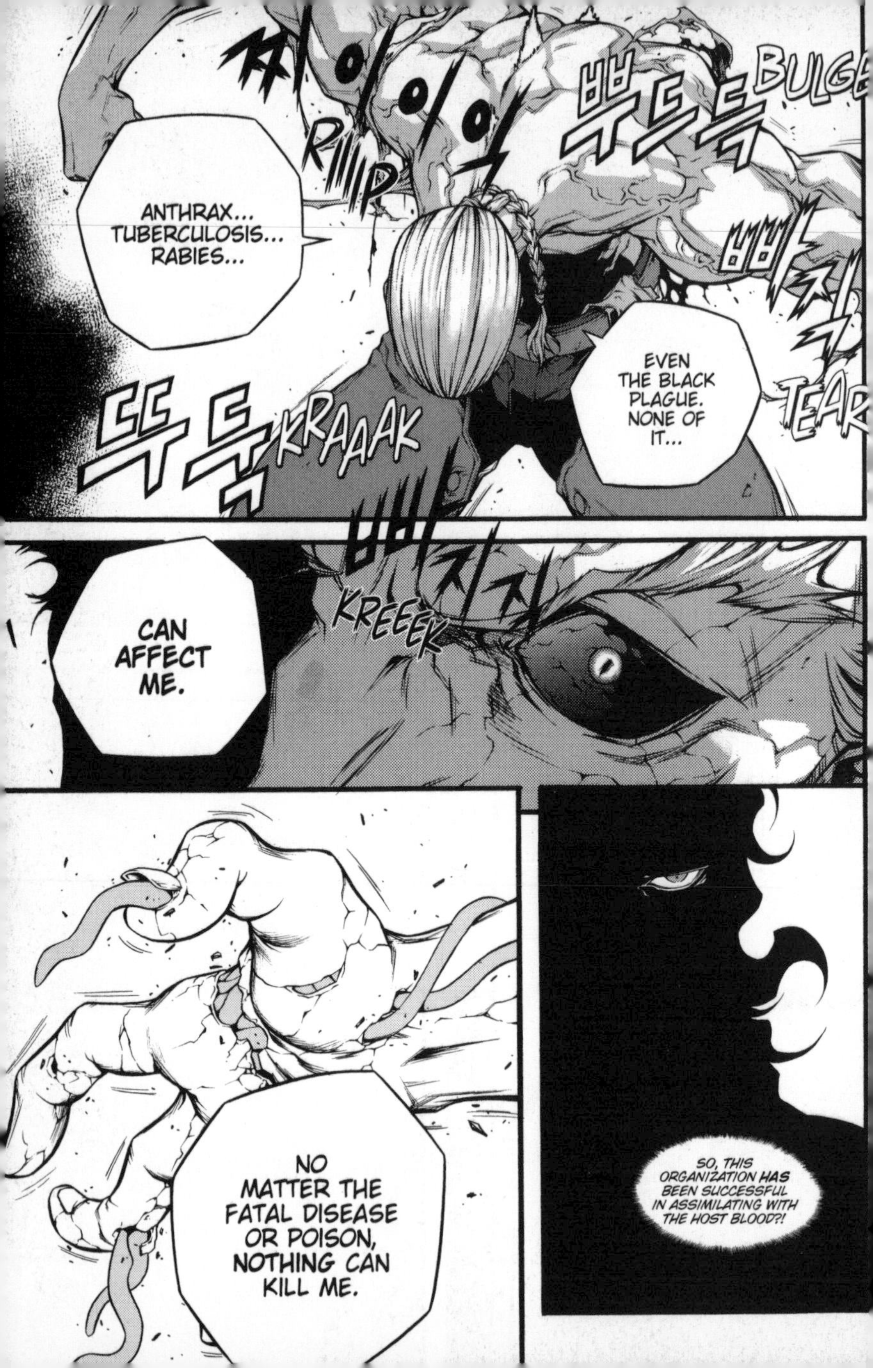

RIIIP
BULGE
ANTHRAX... TUBERCULOSIS... RABIES...
TEAR
EVEN THE BLACK PLAGUE. NONE OF IT...
KRAAAK
KREEEK
CAN AFFECT ME.
NO MATTER THE FATAL DISEASE OR POISON, NOTHING CAN KILL ME.
SO, THIS ORGANIZATION HAS BEEN SUCCESSFUL IN ASSIMILATING WITH THE HOST BLOOD?!

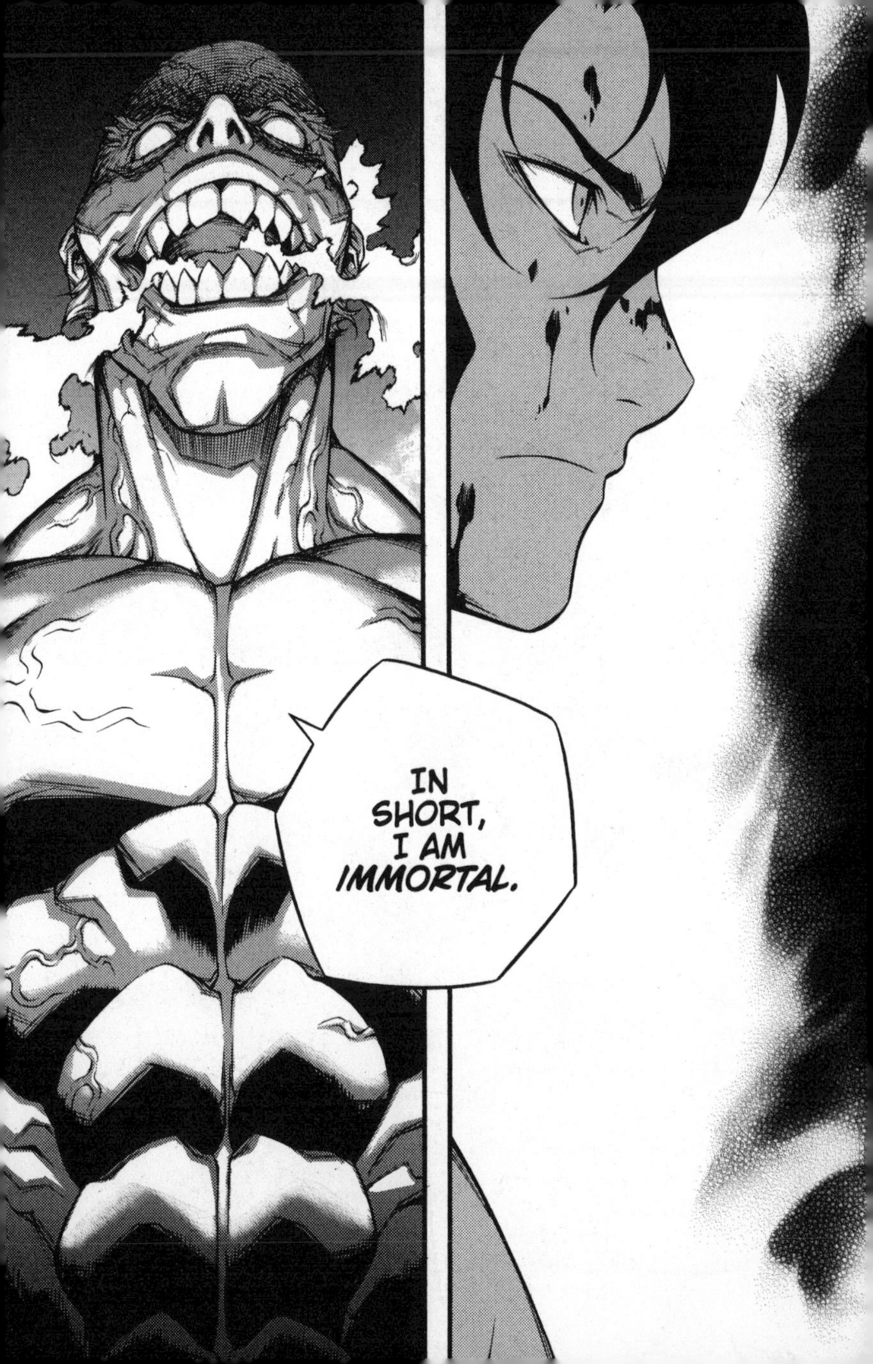
IN SHORT, I AM *IMMORTAL.*

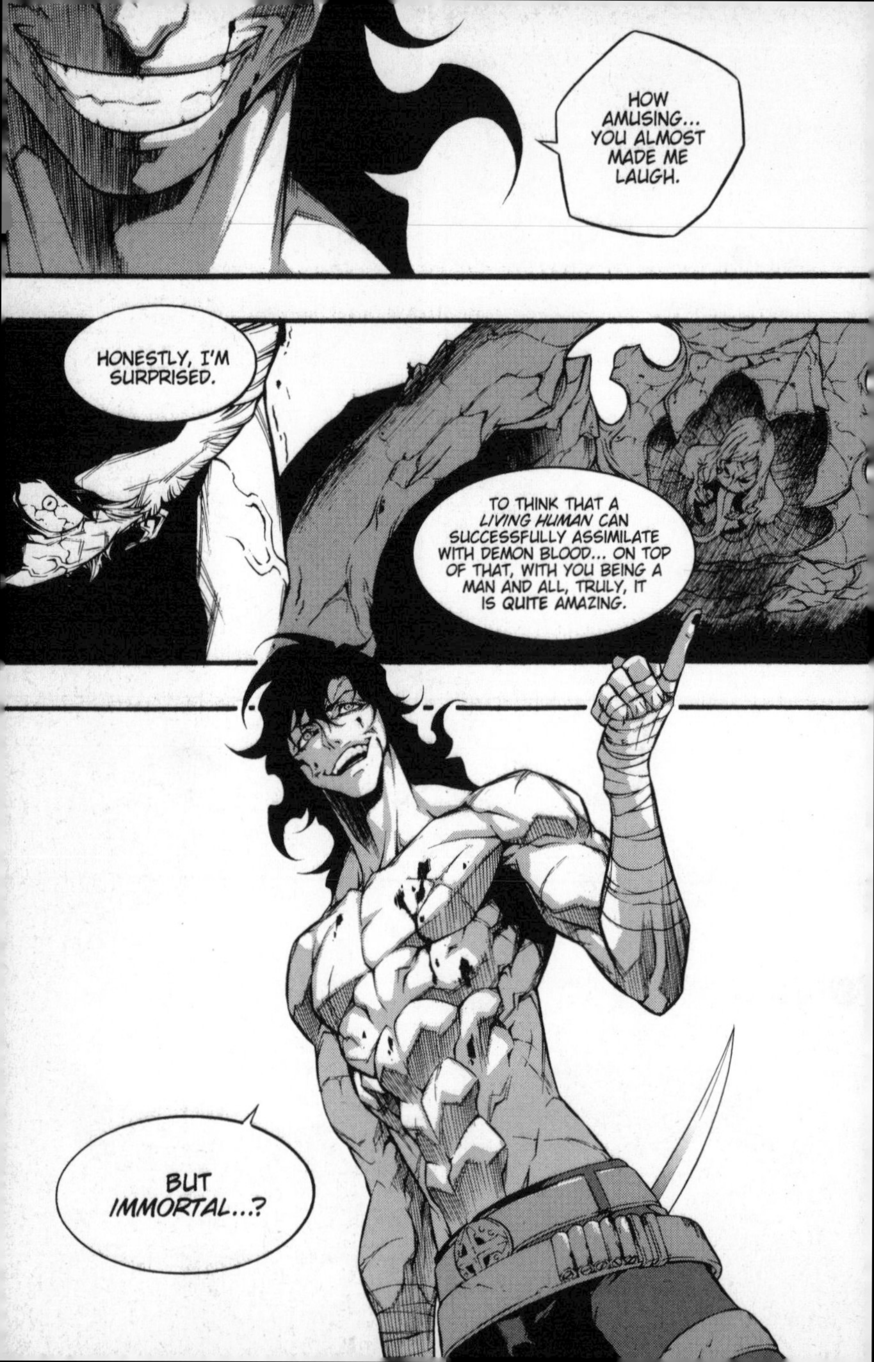
HOW AMUSING... YOU ALMOST MADE ME LAUGH.
HONESTLY, I'M SURPRISED.
TO THINK THAT A *LIVING HUMAN* CAN SUCCESSFULLY ASSIMILATE WITH DEMON BLOOD... ON TOP OF THAT, WITH YOU BEING A MAN AND ALL, TRULY, IT IS QUITE AMAZING.
BUT *IMMORTAL*...?

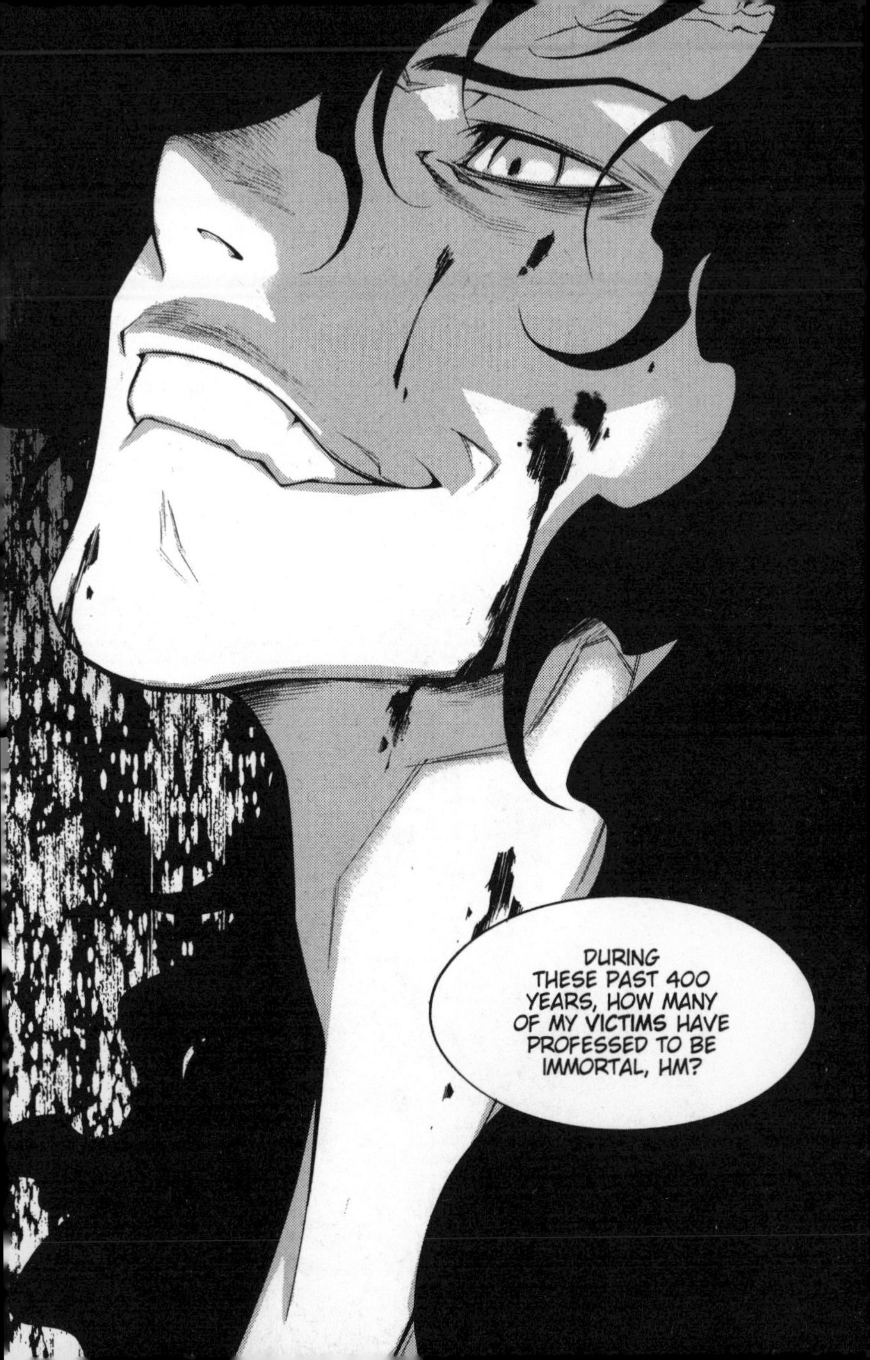
DURING THESE PAST 400 YEARS, HOW MANY OF MY VICTIMS HAVE PROFESSED TO BE IMMORTAL, HM?

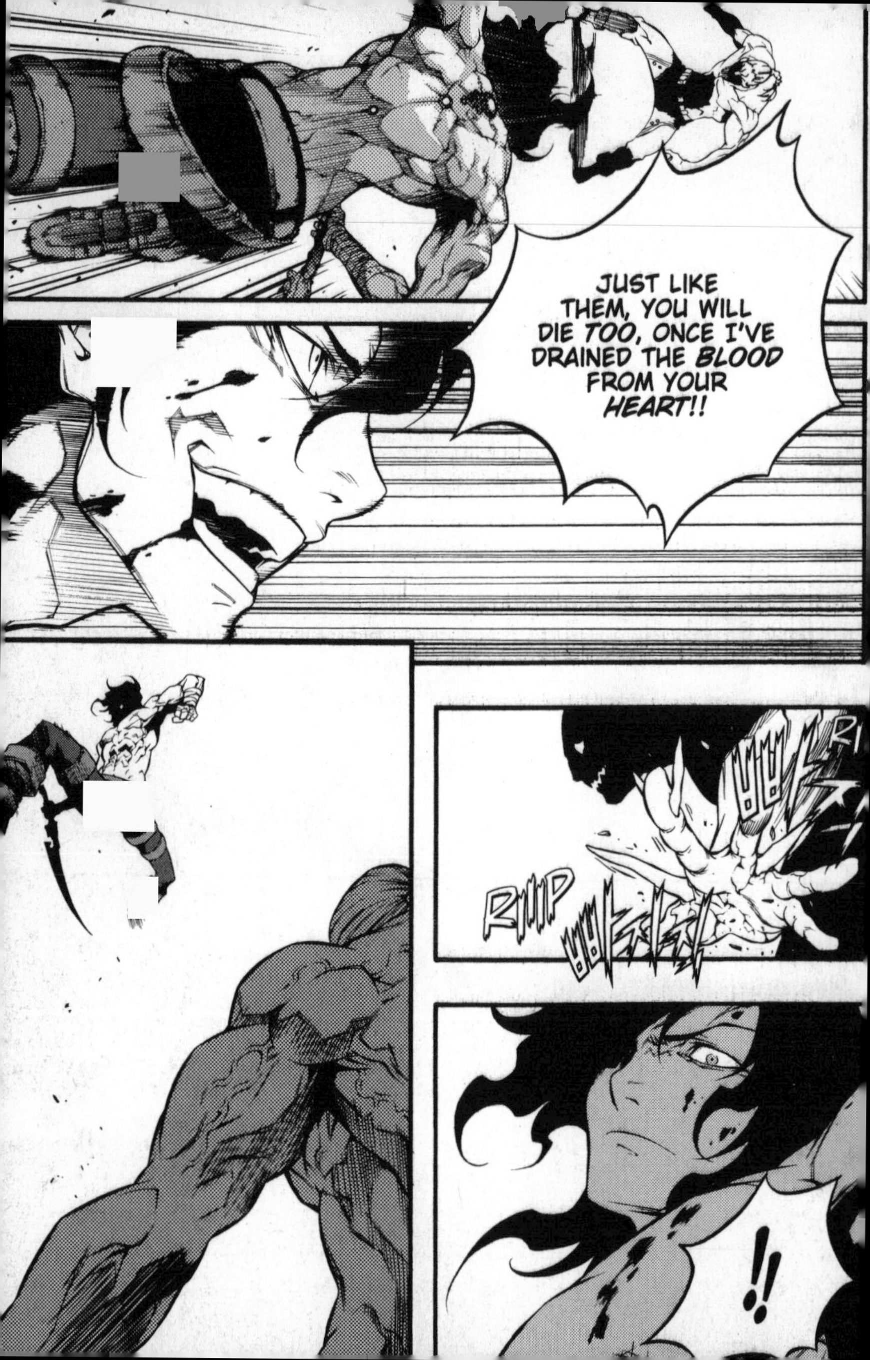

JUST LIKE THEM, YOU WILL DIE TOO, ONCE I'VE DRAINED THE BLOOD FROM YOUR HEART!!
RIP
!!

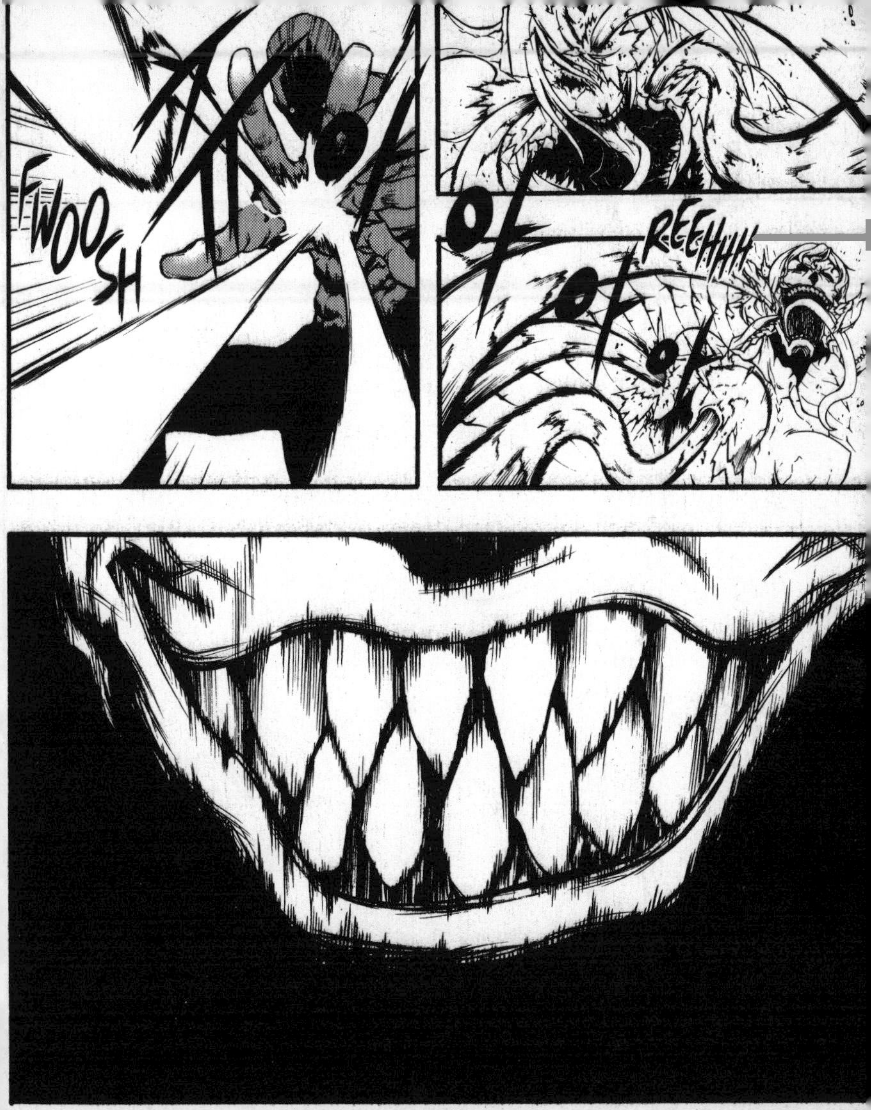
FWOOSH
REEHHH

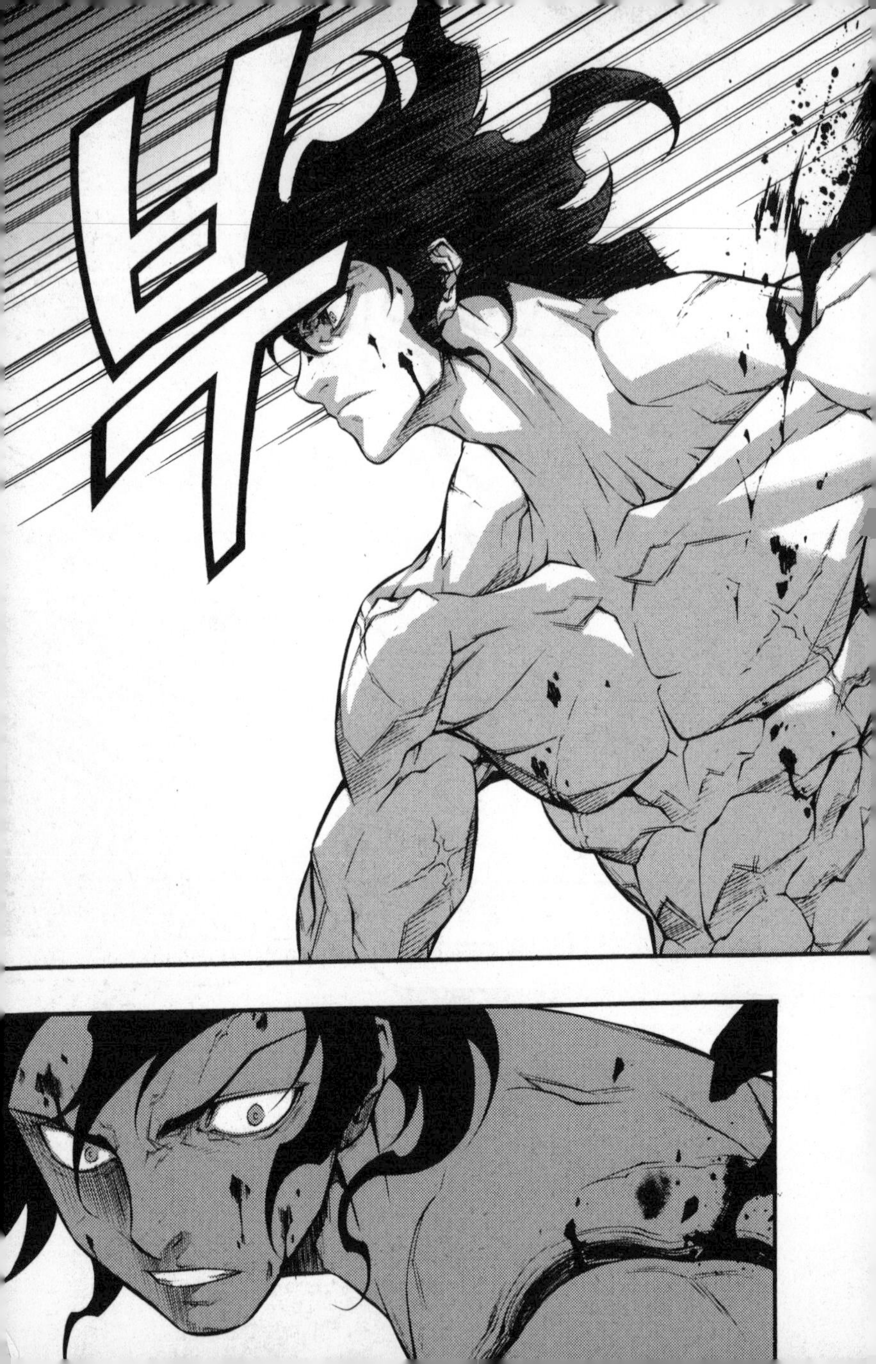
ヒイ

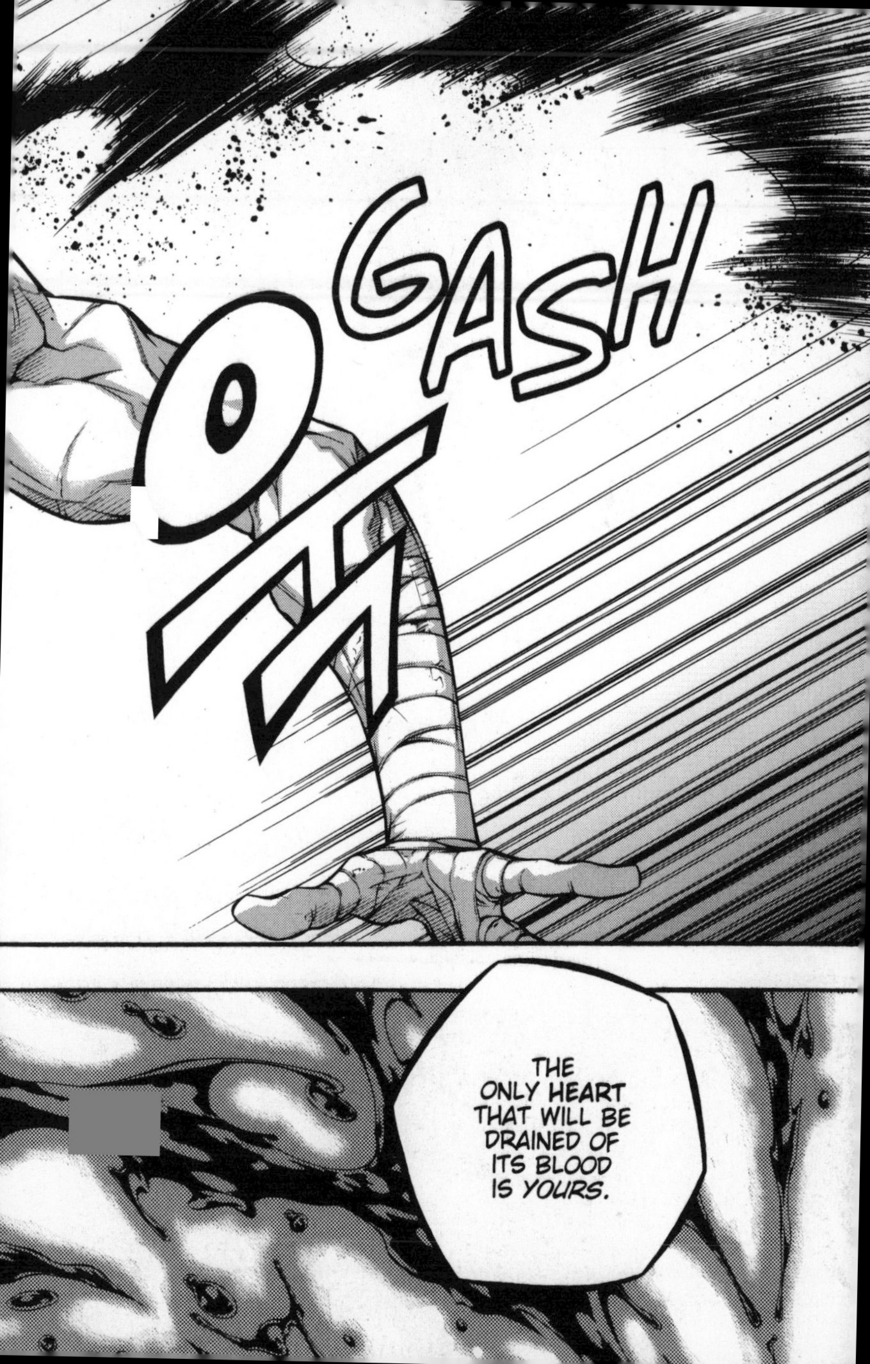
GASH
THE ONLY HEART THAT WILL BE DRAINED OF ITS BLOOD IS YOURS.

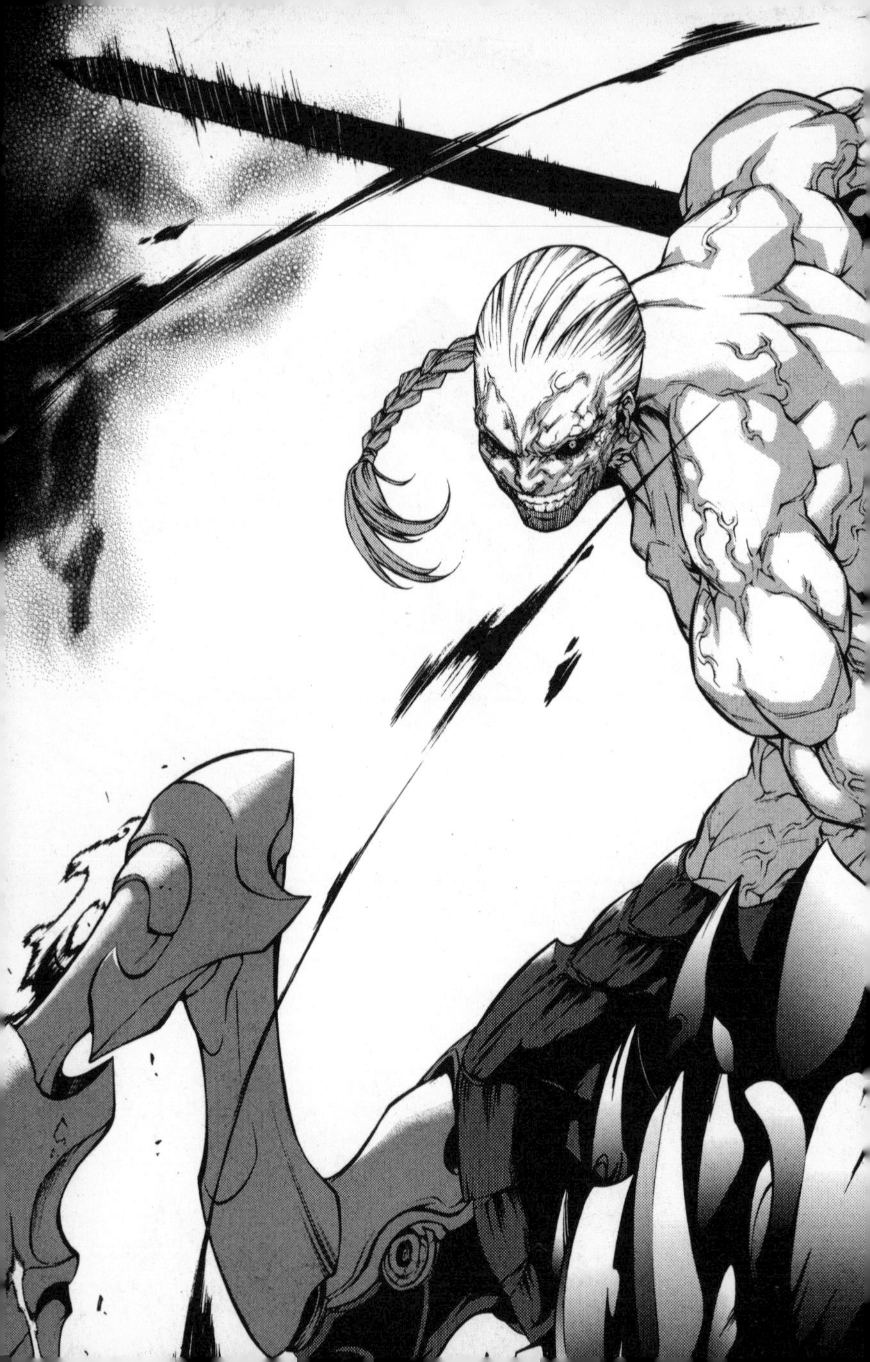

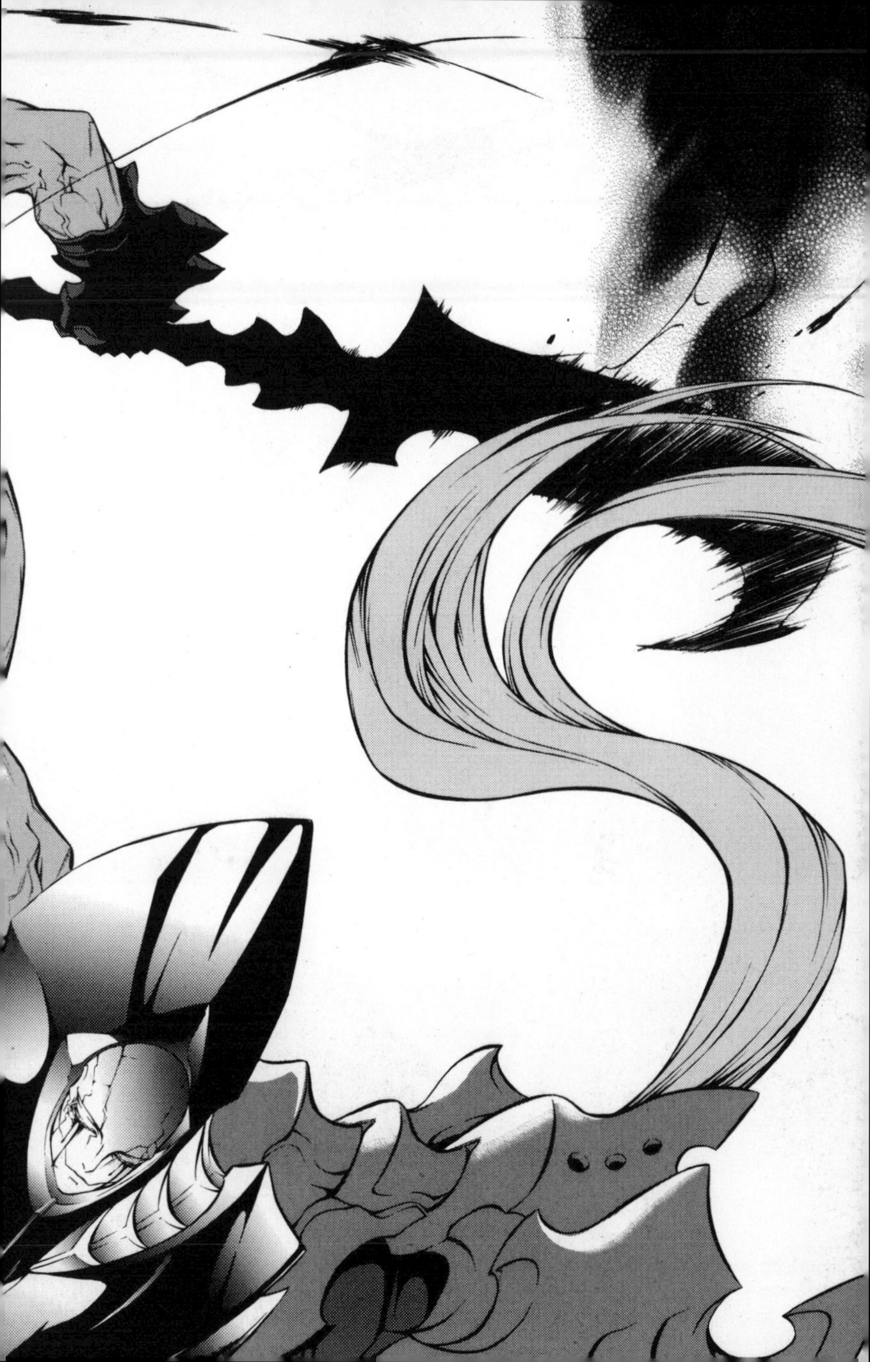

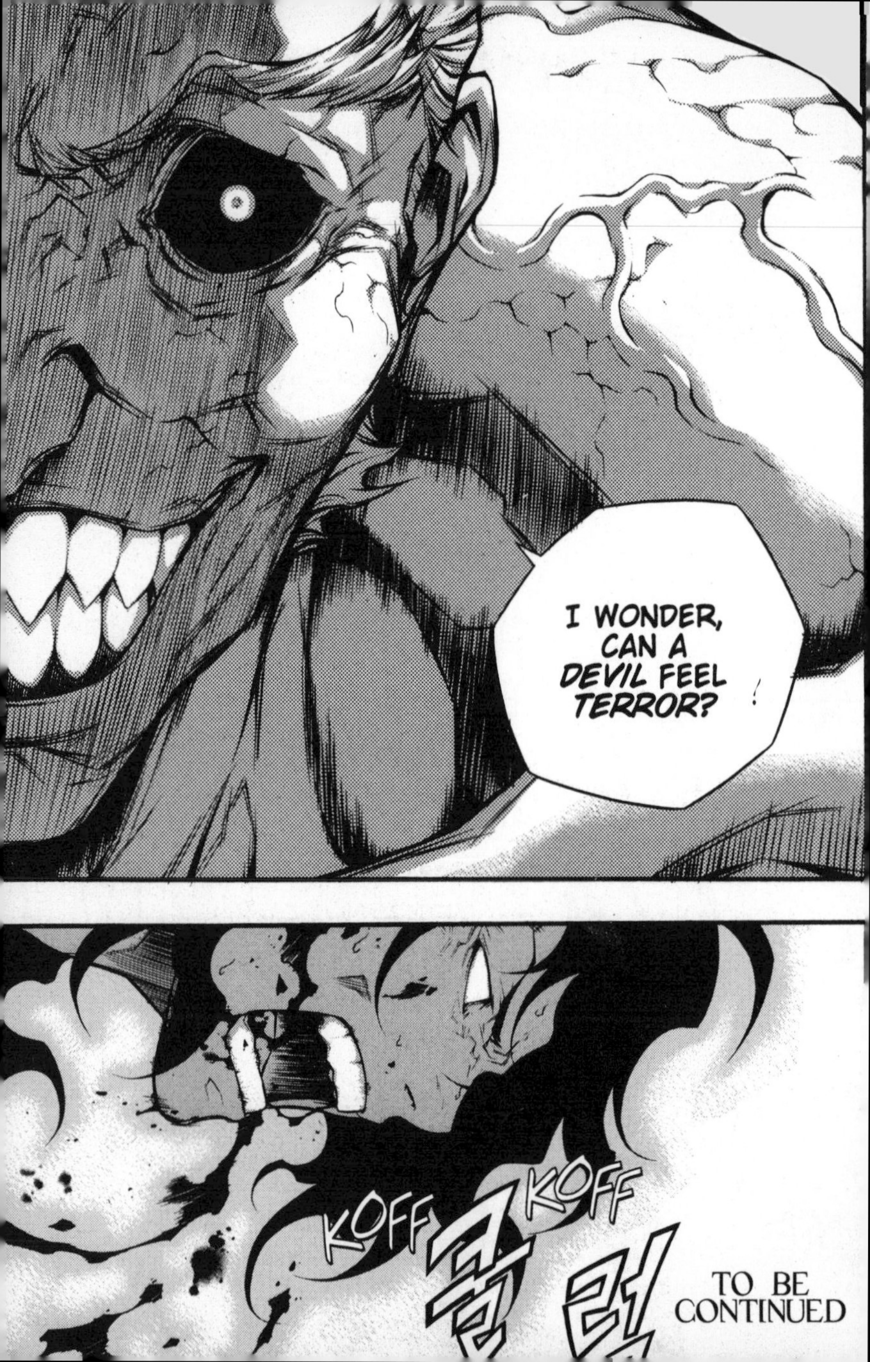
I WONDER, CAN A DEVIL FEEL TERROR?
KOFF KOFF
TO BE CONTINUED

STUDIO DIARY 1

By Sunny

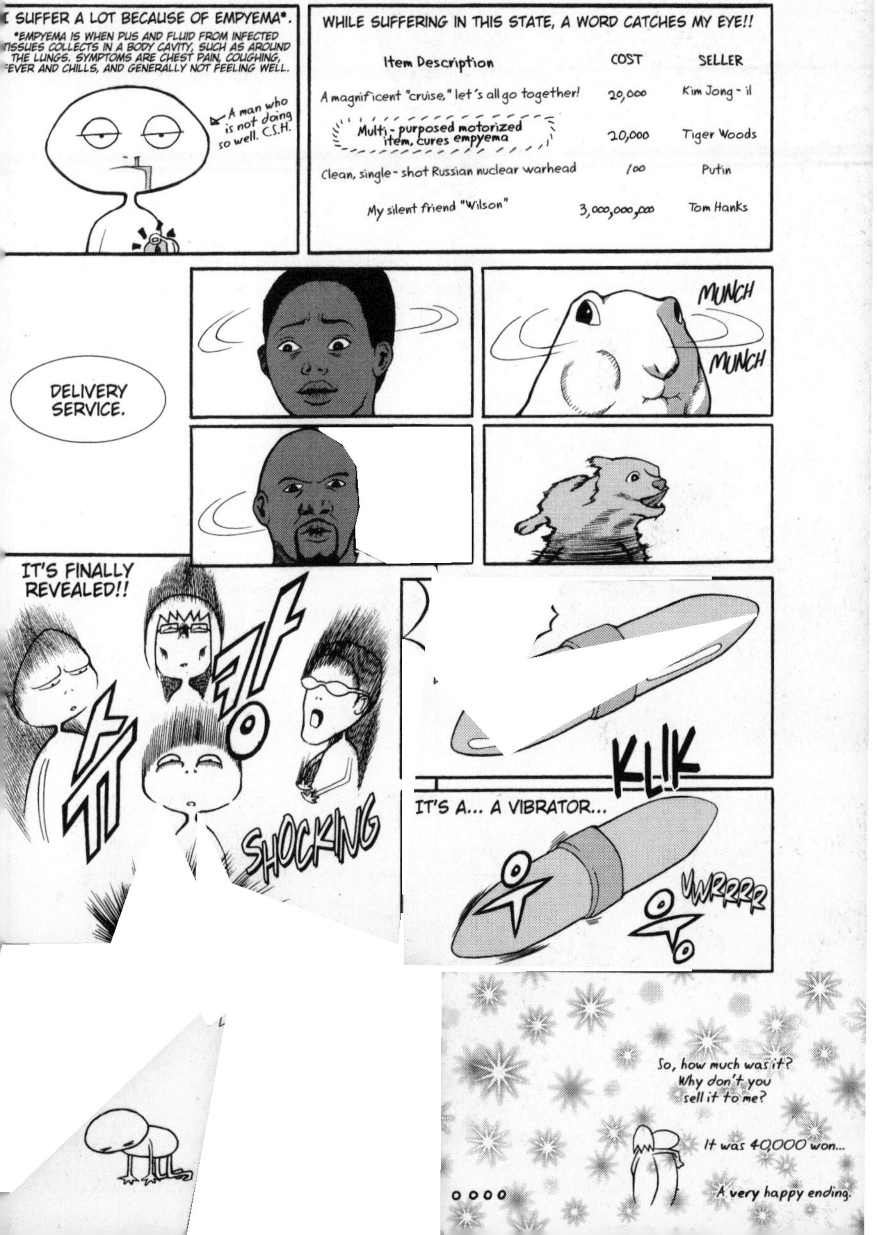
I SUFFER A LOT BECAUSE OF EMPYEMA*.
*EMPYEMA IS WHEN PUS AND FLUID FROM INFECTED TISSUES COLLECTS IN A BODY CAVITY, SUCH AS AROUND THE LUNGS. SYMPTOMS ARE CHEST PAIN, COUGHING, FEVER AND CHILLS, AND GENERALLY NOT FEELING WELL.
A man who is not doing so well. C.S.H.
WHILE SUFFERING IN THIS STATE, A WORD CATCHES MY EYE!!
Item Description / COST / SELLER
A magnificent "cruise," let's all go together! / 20,000 / Kim Jong-il
Multi-purposed motorized item, cures empyema / 20,000 / Tiger Woods
Clean, single-shot Russian nuclear warhead / 100 / Putin
My silent friend "Wilson" / 3,000,000,000 / Tom Hanks
DELIVERY SERVICE.
MUNCH
MUNCH
IT'S FINALLY REVEALED!!
SHOCKING
KLIK
IT'S A... A VIBRATOR...
VWRRRR
So, how much was it? Why don't you sell it to me?
It was 40,000 won...
A very happy ending.

STUDIO DIARY 2

By Rak

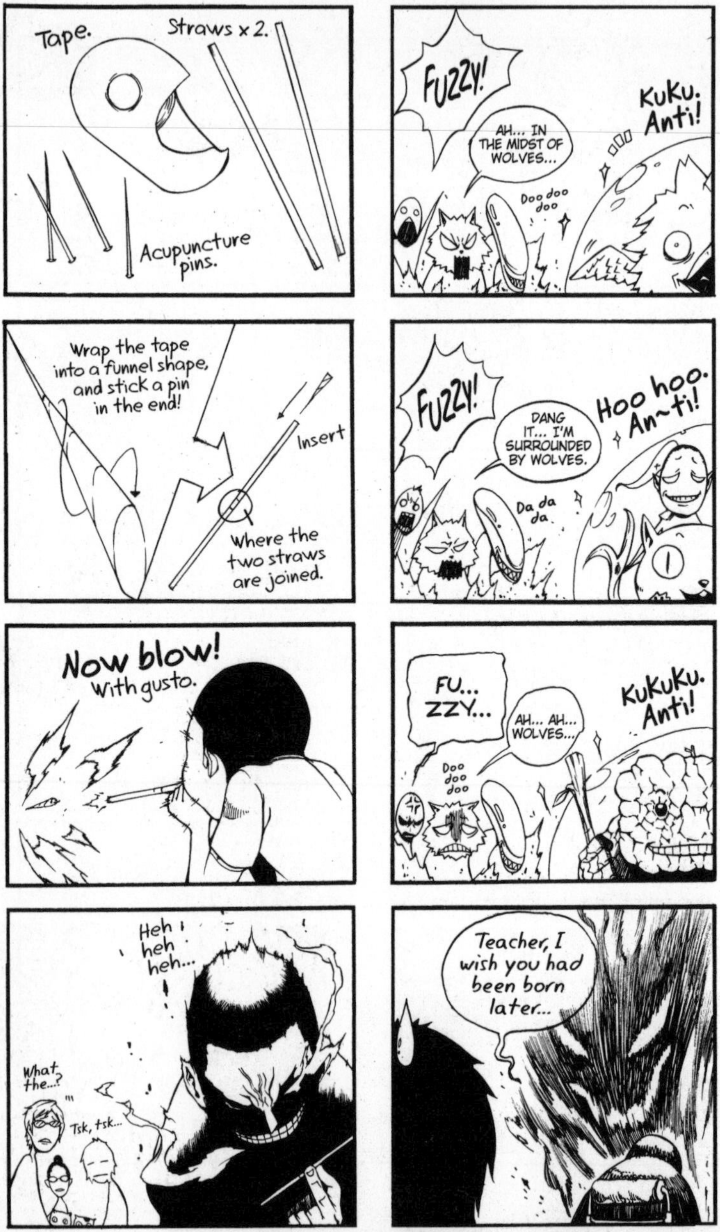
Tape.
Straws x 2.
Acupuncture pins.
Wrap the tape into a funnel shape, and stick a pin in the end!
Insert
Where the two straws are joined.
Now blow! With gusto.
Heh heh heh...
What the...?
Tsk, tsk...
FUZZY!
AH... IN THE MIDST OF WOLVES...
KuKu. Anti!
Doo doo doo
FUZZY!
DANG IT... I'M SURROUNDED BY WOLVES.
Hoo hoo. An~ti!
Da da da
FU... ZZY...
AH... AH... WOLVES...
KuKuKu. Anti!
Doo doo doo
Teacher, I wish you had been born later...

STUDIO DIARY 3

By Thomas

FIRST IMPRESSIONS

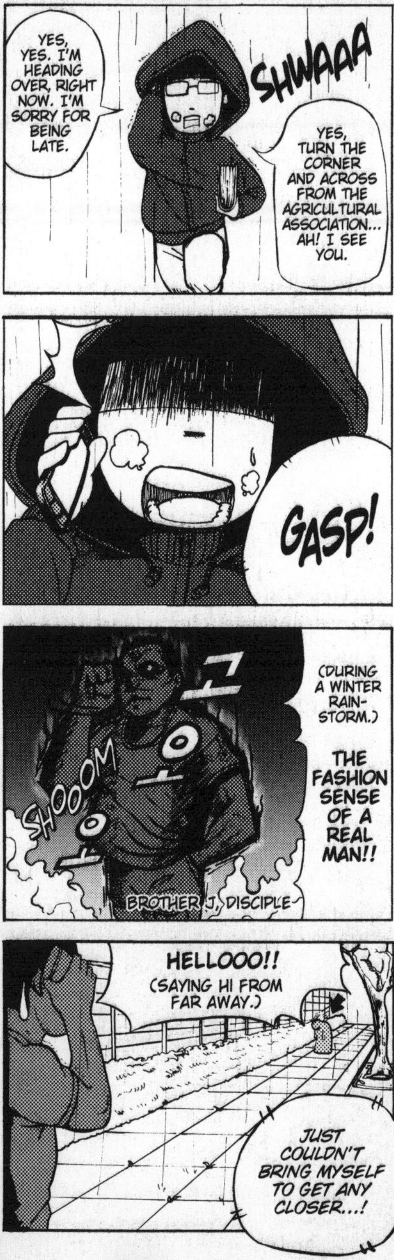

YES, YES. I'M HEADING OVER, RIGHT NOW. I'M SORRY FOR BEING LATE.
SHWAAA
YES, TURN THE CORNER AND ACROSS FROM THE AGRICULTURAL ASSOCIATION... AH! I SEE YOU.
GASP!
SHOOOM
(DURING A WINTER RAIN-STORM.)
THE FASHION SENSE OF A REAL MAN!!
BROTHER J, DISCIPLE
HELLOOO!!
(SAYING HI FROM FAR AWAY.)
JUST COULDN'T BRING MYSELF TO GET ANY CLOSER...!

INTERVIEW

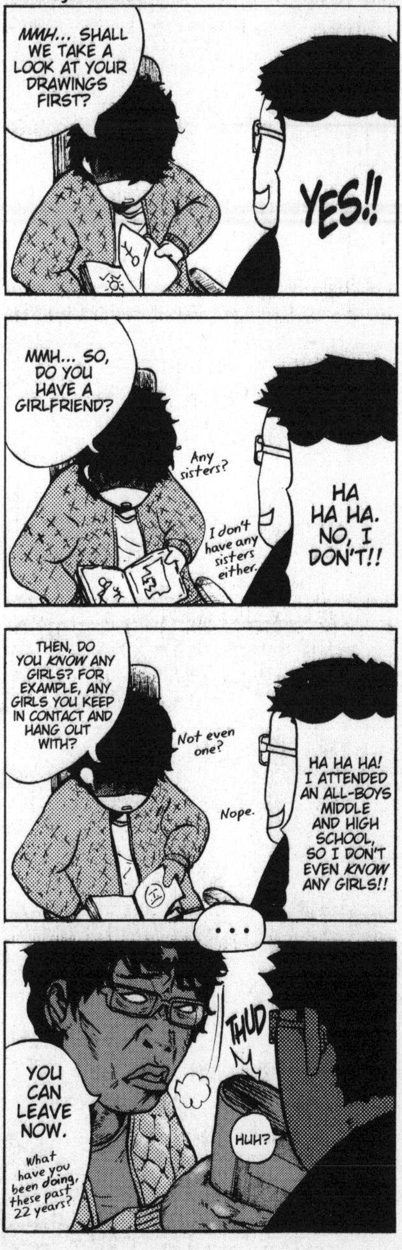

MMH... SHALL WE TAKE A LOOK AT YOUR DRAWINGS FIRST?
YES!!
MMH... SO, DO YOU HAVE A GIRLFRIEND?
Any sisters?
HA HA HA. NO, I DON'T!!
I don't have any sisters either.
THEN, DO YOU KNOW ANY GIRLS? FOR EXAMPLE, ANY GIRLS YOU KEEP IN CONTACT AND HANG OUT WITH?
Not even one?
HA HA HA! I ATTENDED AN ALL-BOYS MIDDLE AND HIGH SCHOOL, SO I DON'T EVEN KNOW ANY GIRLS!!
Nope.
...
THUD
YOU CAN LEAVE NOW.
What have you been doing, these past 22 years?
HUH?

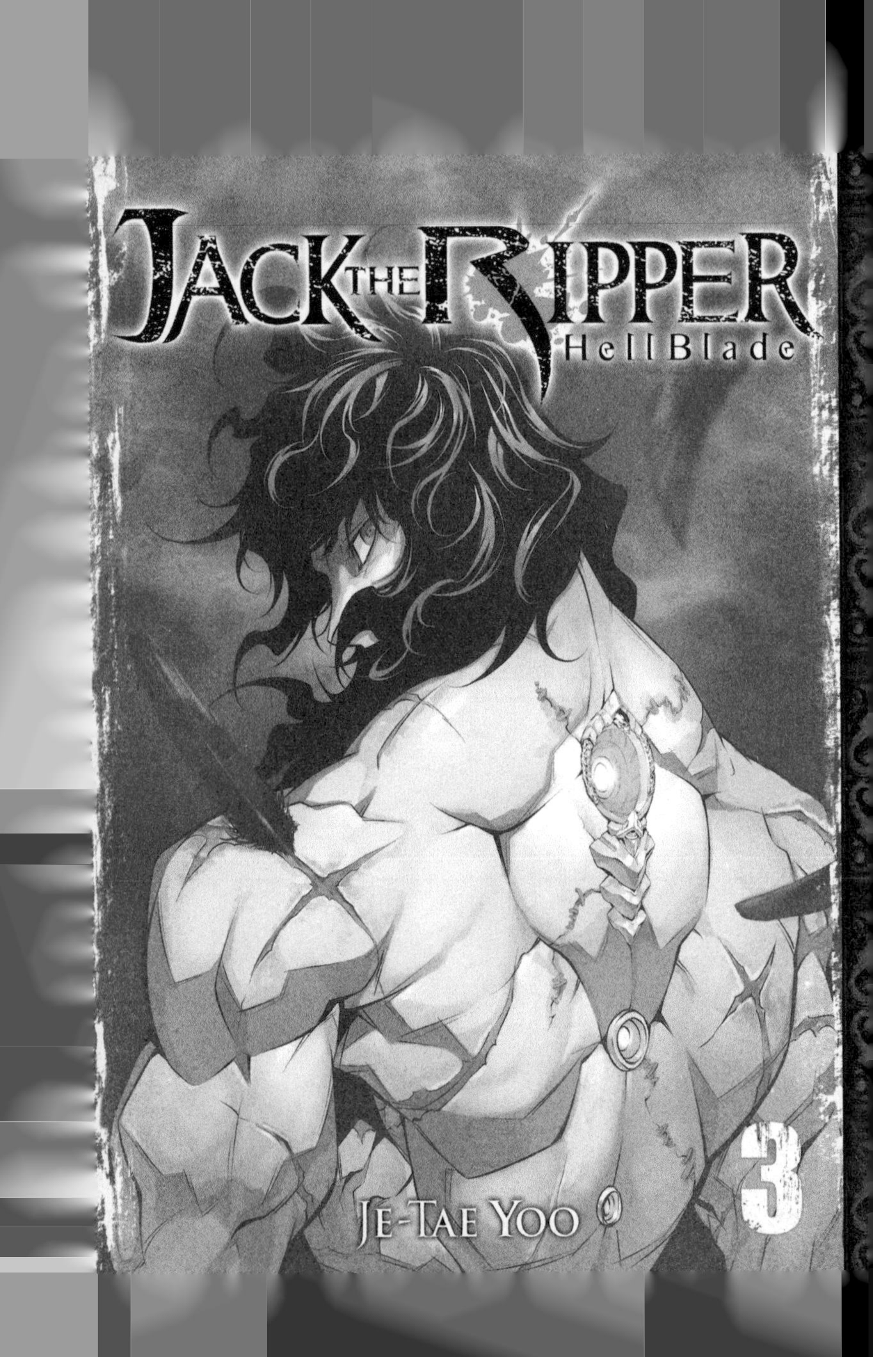
JACK THE RIPPER
Hell Blade
3
JE-TAE YOO

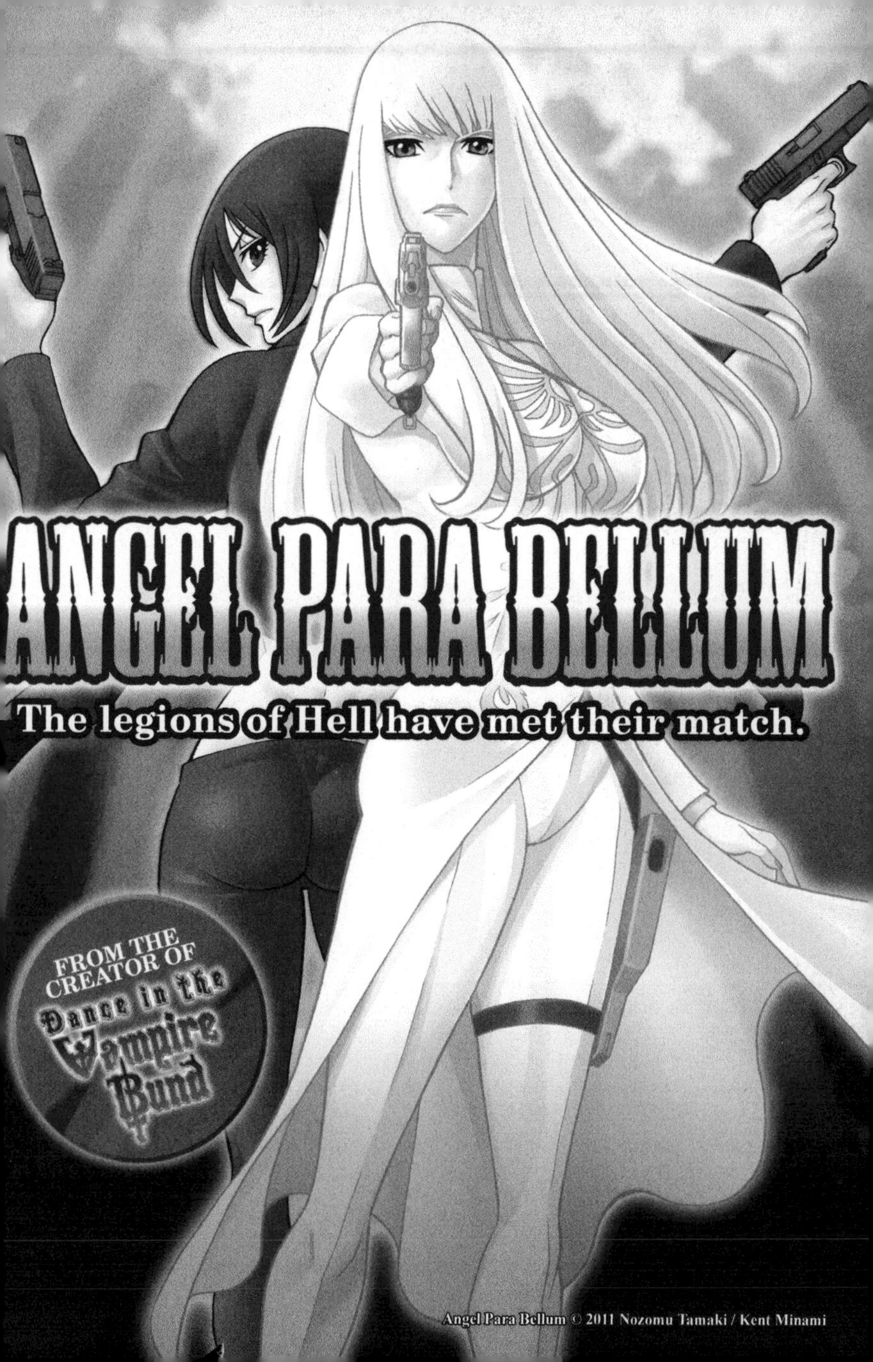
ANGEL PARA BELLUM
The legions of Hell have met their match.
FROM THE CREATOR OF
Dance in the Vampire Bund
Angel Para Bellum © 2011 Nozomu Tamaki / Kent Minami

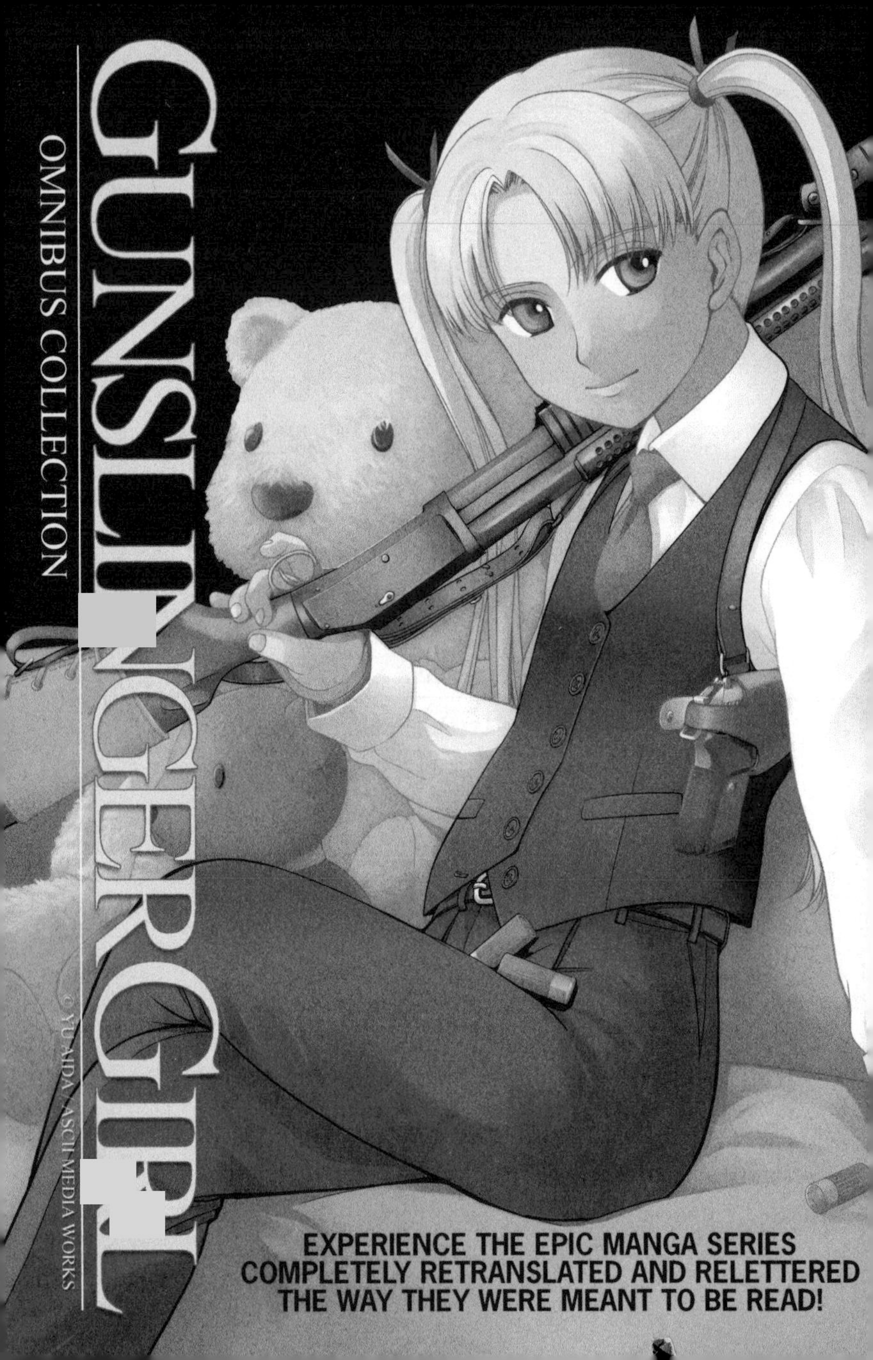
GUNSLINGER GIRL
OMNIBUS COLLECTION
© YU AIDA / ASCII MEDIA WORKS
EXPERIENCE THE EPIC MANGA SERIES
COMPLETELY RETRANSLATED AND RELETTERED
THE WAY THEY WERE MEANT TO BE READ!

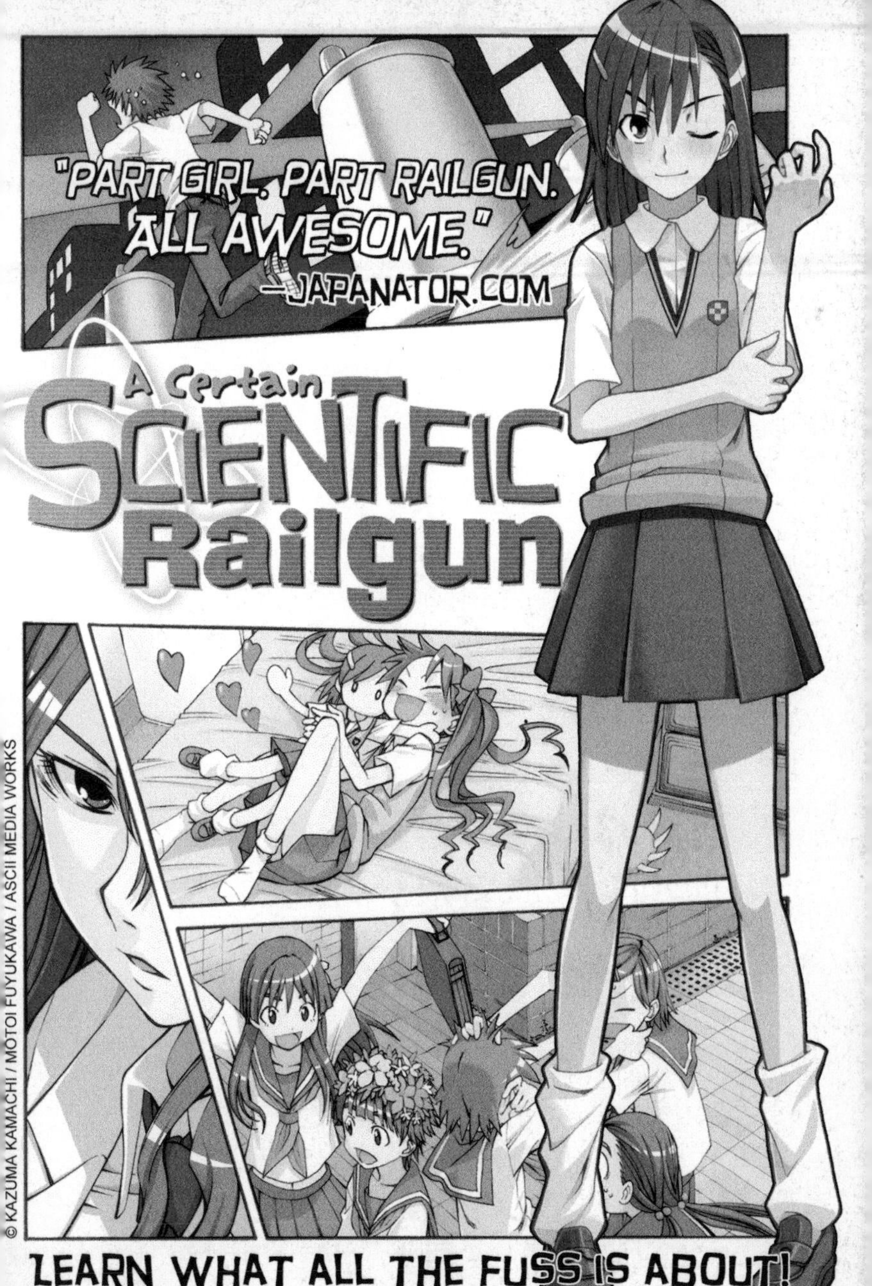
"PART GIRL. PART RAILGUN. ALL AWESOME."
—JAPANATOR.COM
A Certain SCIENTIFIC Railgun
LEARN WHAT ALL THE FUSS IS ABOUT!
© KAZUMA KAMACHI / MOTOI FUYUKAWA / ASCII MEDIA WORKS

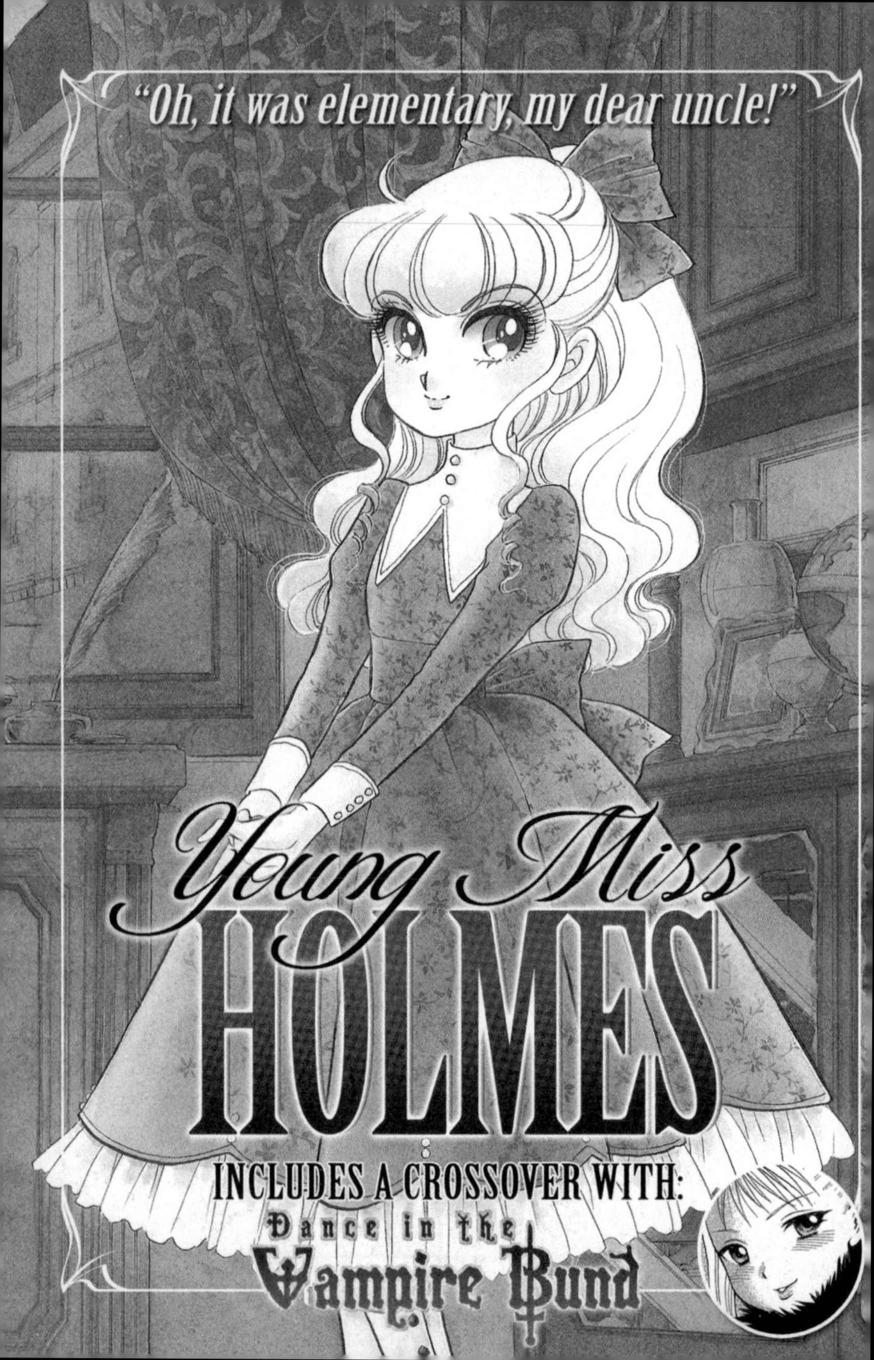
"Oh, it was elementary, my dear uncle!"
Young Miss
HOLMES
INCLUDES A CROSSOVER WITH:
Dance in the
Vampire Bund

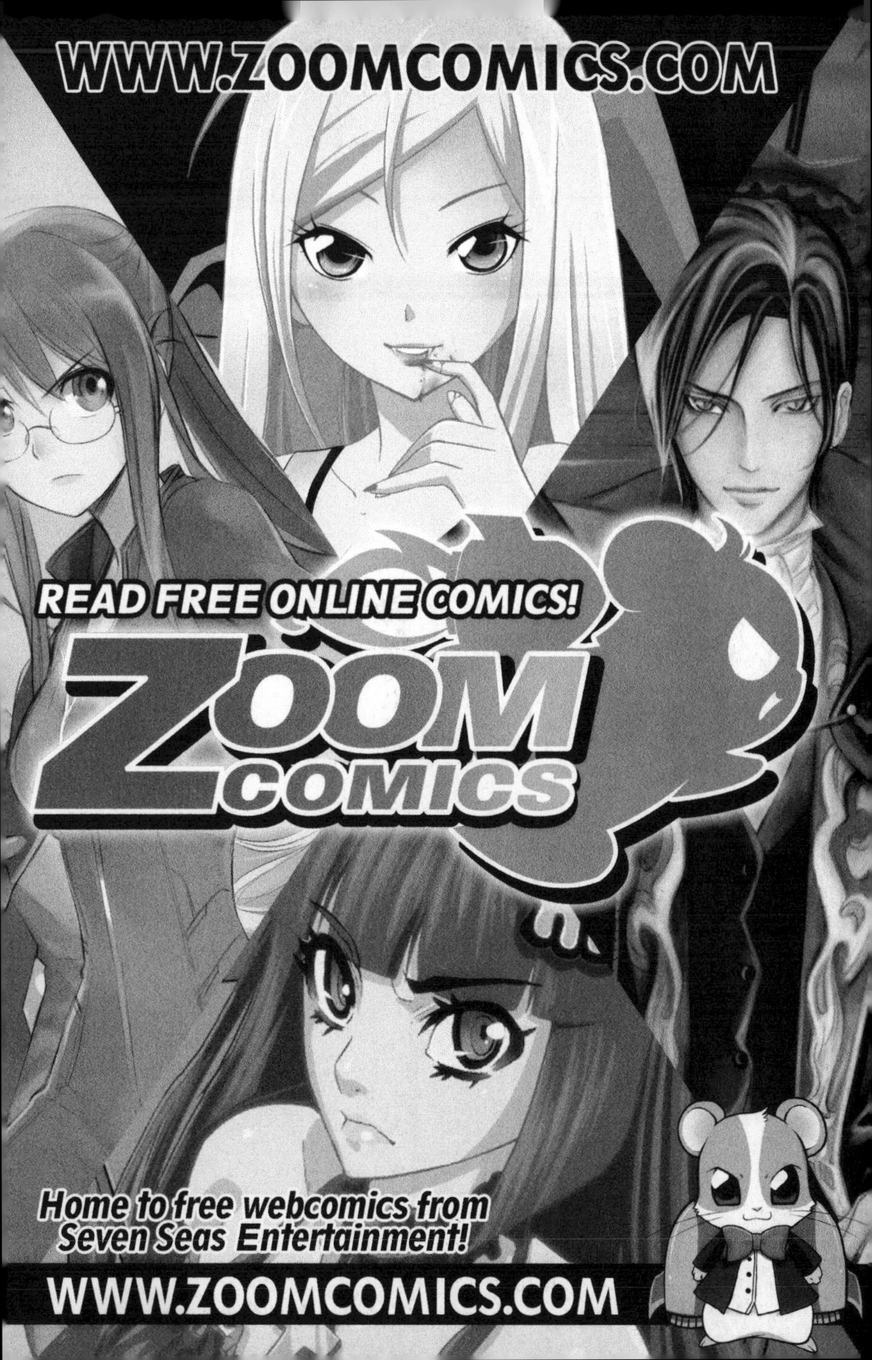
WWW.ZOOMCOMICS.COM
READ FREE ONLINE COMICS!
ZOOM COMICS
Home to free webcomics from Seven Seas Entertainment!
WWW.ZOOMCOMICS.COM

Experience all that SEVEN SEAS has to offer!

Visit us Online and follow us on Twitter!
WWW.GOMANGA.COM
WWW.TWITTER.COM/GOMANGA